The making of a ruling class

The making of a ruling class

ruling class

The Glamorgan gentry
1640 – 1790

PHILIP JENKINS

Assistant Professor, History of Justice
Pennsylvania State University

CAMBRIDGE UNIVERSITY PRESS

Cambridge

London   New York   New Rochelle
Melbourne   Sydney

Published by the Press Syndicate of the University of Cambridge
The Pitt Building, Trumpington Street, Cambridge CB2 1RP
32 East 57th Street, New York, NY 10022, USA
296 Beaconsfield Parade, Middle Park, Melbourne 3206, Australia

©Cambridge University Press 1983

First published 1983

Printed in Great Britain at
the University Press, Cambridge

Library of Congress catalogue card number: 82–14703

British Library Cataloguing in Publication Data

Jenkins, Philip
The making of a ruling class.
1. Glamorgan–Gentry–History
I. Title
305.5′232   HT647

ISBN 0 521 25003 X

MU

Contents

List of maps and tables   *page*   ix
Acknowledgments   xi
List of abbreviations   xiii
General introduction   xv

PART I SOCIAL AND ECONOMIC STRUCTURE

Introduction   3

1 Land and people   5
   1 The two lordships   5
   2 Communications   7
   3 The sea   9
   4 Population and social structure   12
   5 The Vale   13
   6 'An ungovernable people'   15
   7 Radicals and dissenters   17

2 The gentry   20
   1 How many gentry?   20
   2 The elite   22
   3 The lesser gentry   30
   4 Professional and commercial families   35
   5 Destruction and renewal   38

3 Economic development   44
   Introduction   44
   1 Wealth   45
   2 The leviathans   49
   3 An age of improvement   51

4 Stewards   *page* 54
5 Industry 57
6 Modernisation 62
7 The impact of war 65
8 Debt and credit 67

Conclusion to Part I 71

PART II LOCAL AND NATIONAL POLITICS

Introduction 75

4   **Law and order** 78
    Introduction 78
    1 The growth of local independence 79
    2 The militia 81
    3 The JP 83
    4 Other offices 92
    5 'Georgian tranquillity'? 94
    6 Crime and social protest 96

5   **Political history 1640 – 1688: the heroic age** 101
    Introduction 101
    1 Worcester's ultras 104
    2 Pembroke's moderates 105
    3 The royalist coalition 107
    4 The 'ill times' of the gentry 109
    5 Shades of royalism 114
    6 The 'southern flames': the royalist reaction 1660 – 1675 117
    7 Moderates and presbyterians 121
    8 Anti-popery 124
    9 The Popish Plot 128
   10 Towards revolution 1685 – 1688 131
    Conclusion 132

6   **Political history 1688 – 1790: the new order** 134
    Introduction 134
    1 The new whigs 136
    2 King or country? The tories 139

3 The new Church party   *page* 142
4 Party or faction? Family feuds under William and Anne   146
5 A Mansell monarchy?   149
6 Sky-blue incorruptibles: the jacobite interest   152
7 Whig oligarchy   157
8 Tory survival 1720 – 1740   162
9 'Broad-bottom': the tories and the opposition whigs   166
   1730 – 1745
10 Towards stability: the aftermath of 1745   172
11 The crisis of confessional politics 1720 – 1760   177
12 The triumph of patronage   180
13 From jacobite to jacobin   184
14 The great reaction   187

Conclusion to Part II   189

PART III SOCIETY AND CULTURE

Introduction   193

7 **The idea of a gentleman**   196
   Introduction   196
   1 Display   196
   2 Honour   199
   3 Kinship   201
   4 A community of belief   205
   5 Loyalties   208
   6 Religion and hierarchy   211
   7 Justifying gentility   212
   8 English and Welsh   213

8 **Education and culture**   217
   Introduction   217
   1 The grammar schools   218
   2 The 'great schools'   220
   3 Private education   222
   4 The universities   223
   5 Other forms of higher education   225
   6 Foreign travel   227

7 The political element   *page* 228
8 Libraries   230
9 Reading and scholarship   231
10 The antiquaries   234

9 **The spread of metropolitan standards**   239
Introduction   239
1 London   241
2 Provincial cities   244
3 Remodelling the towns 1750 – 1790   246
4 Domestic gentility   250
5 Redefining the family   255
6 Parents and children   260
7 'Foxhunters'   263
8 Horseracing   266
9 The 'country' resistance   268

Conclusion to Part III: 'conspicuous antiquity'   272

Aftermath: towards the Victorian world   274

Conclusion: from Civil War to Industrial Revolution   276

Appendices
1 Parliamentary service by Glamorgan landowners 1640 – 1800   289
2 The 'secondary' gentry families   292
3 The 'tertiary' families   293
4 The Mansell family and their connections with the greater gentry   295
5 The roundhead and puritan family links of the Thomases   296
    of Wenvoe

Notes   297
Index   335

Maps

1 Glamorgan: roads and rivers   *page* 8
2 The great gentry seats c. 1660 – 1700   23
3 The 'secondary' gentry families c. 1660 – 1700 31
4 Blome's 'gentlemen', 1673   33
5 The 'tertiary' gentry   34
6 Continuity: the seats of the landed elite in 1873 43
7 Glamorgan's regions to illustrate the geographical distribution 86
 of JPs

Tables

 1 Titles, houses and income   24
 2 The gentry elite 1670 – 1690 25
 3 A decline in family size   39
 4 The failure to produce male heirs 39
 5 A tendency to remain unmarried 40
 6 Where the gentry found wives 1660 – 1760 40
 7 Estate incomes   46
 8 Incomes of grades of gentry 49
 9 Sources of militia horses 82
10 Justices and deputy-lieutenants 82
11 Numbers of justices   84
12 Geographical origins of JPs 87
13 Origins of categories of gentry 88
14 Clerical justices in Glamorgan 90

15 The 'ultra' leadership   *page* 105
16 The roundheads   110
17 Activity in religious persecution 1660 – 1688   123
18 The political connections of Francis Gwyn   140
19 The connections of the Mackworth family   168
20 The Aubrey and Jephson families   203
21 The Carmarthenshire Mansells   204
22 Glamorgan matriculations at Oxford   224
23 Attendance at university and Inn of Court   226

Dating

Dates before 1752 are old-style, except that the year is taken as beginning on 1 January.

Placenames

The tendency among recent Welsh historians has been to achieve 'pure' Welsh forms – even to the extent of using 'Abertawe' for Swansea, or 'Caerdydd' for Cardiff. I have generally compromised by following the spelling of the Ordnance Survey's one-inch series of maps, which are usually an excellent reflection of local practice.

Acknowledgments

The research on which this book is based was largely undertaken for a Cambridge Ph.D thesis between 1974 and 1978. That work had three supervisors, to all of whom I owe a considerable debt of gratitude: Jack (Sir John) Plumb, Peter D. G. Thomas, and Brian Outhwaite. It was the last of these who manifested astonishing dedication (not to say stamina) by reading my final manuscript in handwritten form. To all, my sincere thanks.

In the last eight or ten years, I have had occasion to discuss matters relating to this work with a wide variety of people, and I feel sure that any list of acknowledgments is likely to be sadly incomplete. However, I would like to mention the help given by the following colleagues and friends: Linda Colley, Roger Schofield, Joanna Martin, Daniel Katkin, John Miller, John Gascoigne, and Derek Beales. I owe much of what historical understanding I possess to my teachers as an undergraduate at Cambridge, among whom I would especially record thanks to Peter Hunter Blair and the late Kathleen Hughes. Sir Leon Radzinowicz has also been a most dependable mentor and friend.

Among those who have helped me in my research on the seventeenth and eighteenth centuries, a particular debt must be recorded to John Morrill. He has done much to provide themes and connections between ideas, of which I have made great use both here and in other publications. Also, he did much to guide the transformation of my original thesis into a book. All in all, his contribution can only be described as invaluable.

I am also indebted to those who helped me locate or consult the manuscript sources on which this book is based. These include Sir John Aubrey-Fletcher, who was so very helpful on the history of his Aubrey ancestors. I am grateful to the Duke of Beaufort for permission to consult the Badminton estate papers in the National Library of Wales; and to the Trustees of the Chatsworth Settlement for materials on the Dukes of Devonshire. Among public record sources, I have been greatly assisted by the friendly and cooperative attitudes of most of the county and local record offices visited. Among these, I would particularly single out the manuscript room of the NLW. On paintings, the National Museum of Wales in Cardiff was kind enough to let me explore the works on reserve which so rarely see the light of day.

I am sure I have omitted some names from these brief acknowledgments of help and guidance; but I must not fail to thank my wife Liz for years of advice, support and encouragement.

Abbreviations

Arch. Camb.	*Archaeologia Cambrensis*
BBCS	*Bulletin of the Board of Celtic Studies*
BIHR	*Bulletin of the Institute of Historical Research*
BM	British Museum
Bodl.	Bodleian Library, Oxford
CCL	Cardiff Central Library
CSPD	*Calendar of State Papers, Domestic*
Cal. Comp.	*Calendar of Compounding*
CUP	Cambridge University Press
DNB	*Dictionary of National Biography*
DWB	*Dictionary of Welsh Biography*
DWT	Diary of William Thomas of Michaelston-super-Ely, in Cardiff Central Library
Ec.HR	*Economic History Review*
EHR	*English Historical Review*
GCH	*Glamorgan County History*, vol. 4 (Cardiff, 1974)
GRO	Glamorgan Record Office, Cardiff
HMC	Historical MSS Commission
KT	Kemys-Tynte MSS in NLW
NLW	National Library of Wales, Aberystwyth
NLWJ	*National Library of Wales Journal*
NMW	National Museum of Wales, Cardiff
OUP	Oxford University Press
P&M	Penrice and Margam MSS in NLW
PRO	Public Record Office, London
RISW	Royal Institution of South Wales, Swansea
TCS	*Transactions of the Honourable Society of Cymmrodorion*
TRHS	*Transactions of the Royal Historical Society*
UCNW	Library of University College of North Wales, Bangor

ULC	University Library, Cambridge
ULS	University Library, Swansea
ULS Mackworth	Mackworth MSS in ULS
WHR	*Welsh History Review*

General introduction

To explain the purpose of this book, a short autobiographical excursus is required. The origins of the book lie at least five years before I began undertaking the research on which it is based: they lie in a summer of the late 1960s when, in the space of a few days, I discovered that Glamorgan possessed two of the finest monuments in Britain from the period we call 'early modern'. The first I encountered was the Mansell series of tombs in Margam Abbey, which dates from between 1560 and 1640. It is the last tomb in the series (that of Sir Lewis Mansell) which is of such quality that it may fairly be set beside any piece of art in Britain from that outstanding century. The second 'find' was the deserted roofless manor house of Beaupre (pronounced *Bewper*), which stands almost forgotten in the rolling meadows south of Cowbridge, the countryside often called 'The Garden of Wales' (less restrained local patriots drew comparison with Arcadia or Eden, but 'Garden' will suffice). The house's best feature was a two-storied columned porch in the 'English Renaissance' style of about 1600, and it was quite magnificent. I have never seen a photograph which succeeded in catching or defining its splendour, and its image remained with me when in later years I was pursuing more serious historical studies.

But these artifacts also raised difficult historical questions. There can be few parts of Britain where the transition from 'the world we have lost' is quite as apparent as in Glamorgan, a county now famous above all for industry, pollution, perhaps for radicalism, and increasingly for industrial decay. Margam itself stands only a mile from the gargantuan Abbey steelworks of Port Talbot. In contrast, these monuments – of the Bassetts of Beaupre and the Mansells of Margam – conjured up the society which lay beneath the Industrial Revolution, a totally different world of thought, belief, superstition and commonplaces, an ancient Celtic world where bards still wandered from mansion to aristocratic house as late as 1720, in the world of Pope and Walpole. It was a strange combination of ideas. At that stage, my interest in the county's history was in writing a social history modelled on some of the ideas of the *Annales* school, reconstructing a lost world of thought and life by asking questions about people's attitudes to their immediate family, to birth and death, to the passage of time, to animals. What were their geographical perspectives, where did they place the boundaries between the normal and the supernatural, or the decent and the deviant, how far were their ideas conditioned by their natural environment and the level of available technology?

Antiquarian as it was, there were interesting points in such a study. For example, even from a romantic perspective, I would be amazed to learn just how remote from modern ways of thought this area was in late Stuart times. In the last years of Charles II, a visitor to South Wales might enter the country by way of Abergavenny, where he would see the holy mountain of Skirrid, cleft at the moment of Christ's crucifixion and still a centre for large-scale catholic pilgrimage.[1] If the traveller entered Glamorgan from the north, he passed at Abercrave a stone circle still believed to represent the guardian spirits of these barren mountains. At Margam, he found a superb natural environment now wholly lost, with great flocks of geese migrating over the highest sand dunes and some of the best coastal scenery in Europe – lands which since the 1940s have been overwhelmed by the steelworks. At Margam House, the squire Sir Edward Mansell (1636 – 1706) patronised bards, and refused to demolish a decrepit gatehouse for fear of an ancient curse.[2] He also recounted (and no doubt believed) stories of the appearance of miraculous salmon in the local river – and the salmon had possessed a sanctity among the Celts long before the coming of Christianity.[3] There were legends surrounding local Dark Age monuments, and still-current tales of a seventh-century Welsh king who had retired to a hermitage only a mile from the great house.

But more remarkable was the juxtaposition of this amazingly primitive thought-world with the material achievements of the family and the area. Sir Edward was as thoroughly in touch with Continental painting and architecture as was any connoisseur of his age, as he showed when the ancient gatehouse was joined among Margam's buildings by a superb and very contemporary Italianate summerhouse. Equally strange was the modernity of the economic life of Sir Edward and his neighbours. They corresponded nervously about the Monmouth rebellion, as much for what it would do for their coal sales in Devon as for any political consequences. They were among the first customers for Newcomen steam engines; and when they engaged in feuds over manorial boundaries or ancient borough charters, it was usually with the 'modern' intent of driving out an industrial competitor. It was squires like these who took the initiative in proposing to Bristol merchants that their particular borough should be the centre of a new coal and copper complex, with a massive expansion of port facilities and shipping.[4] We are facing the problem left unanswered in Macaulay, of *how* the barbarous backwoods squires of 1685 became the cultivated country gentlemen of 1840; for Glamorgan seemed to suggest that aspects of the two types had coexisted in almost shocking proximity.

This raises an interesting problem of historiography, in that it is now easy to find material on the 'Classical Age' of the gentry between about 1560 and 1640, or on the critical years of the mid seventeenth century; but the century after the Restoration is by no means as well covered. For South Wales, there are excellent gentry studies by Professor Williams, and by Drs Jones, Robbins and Lloyd, but all concern the period before 1640.[5] Volume 4 of the *Glamorgan County History* covers gentry life in detail up to 1640 and gives a historical narrative up to 1790, but we are nothing like as well informed on the post-Restoration period as we are on the gentry who became sheriffs under Elizabeth, or who served in Jacobean parliaments. On other areas of Britain, there is some material – Professor Mingay's fine syntheses, Professor Chambers' studies on Nottinghamshire, Dr Moir on Gloucestershire local government. We also have Dr Roebuck's account of Yorkshire baronets and Dr Beckett's description of the economic activities of the Cumbrian squires.[6] Of course, there is also the strictly economic debate on the development of the great estates, with work by Drs Clay, Beckett and Habakkuk.[7] But there is little to set beside a book on the earlier period like Dr Cliffe's on the Yorkshire gentry, or some of the Civil War studies like Dr Morrill's on Cheshire.[8] This is curious: the families who opposed James I or Laud, who have been analysed in minute detail for their reactions to the coming of war in 1642, were still leaders in county society at least until the end of that century. Participants in the Civil Wars often lived on to serve or oppose William III, no doubt strongly influenced by their wartime loyalties and experiences. To study county communities only during the Civil Wars and Interregnum is to miss at least half the story. More local research might even produce evidence that there were other later years like 1642, in which a 'high road to civil war' was blocked at the last moment (1681 and 1715 come to mind here).

Outside the strictly political arena, the neglect of the century after 1660 means that we lack essential components for an account of the background to the Industrial Revolution, and an answer to the question, 'Why was Britain first?' There had been a real modernisation of thought in a relatively short period of the early eighteenth century, so that Sir Edward Mansell's ideas about ghosts, legends and hermits already seemed absurd within thirty years of his death; thirty years later they were ready for revival as an artistic style, sufficiently distant to be a fit subject for exotic fiction. On many major issues, it will be argued that a great gulf separates the life and thought of the generation that was old in 1720 from that of the mid eighteenth century. Moreover, this was a time of rapid political and economic change, and of an enormous increase in Britain's power and prestige in the world. In the 1660s, the country was a pensioner of France; by 1760, it was well on the way to possessing a world empire, with the strongest economic base of any leading power.

Two questions emerge here: given the enormous economic role of the landed classes, how had changes in their outlook, their tastes or assumptions, contributed to this shift; and in turn, how did this reversal alter the character of their domestic life and social relationships? The former question is one of peculiar interest given the archaic manorial framework in which landowners and their stewards operated, and the latter gains relevance from the degree to which patriarchal theory would have to be set aside during rapid industrialisation. There can be no doubt of the zeal with which squires and peers pursued these goals, not least from the evidence of their membership in the many societies for 'improvement' which flourished after 1760. Indeed, 'improvement' became as much a vogue word then as 'development' has been in many countries of the Third World in the last two decades. Another interesting parallel is the role in such 'improvements' – of roads, harbours, towns, agriculture – of a closely defined and homogeneous group of political radicals and progressives, who were usually freemasons and anticlericals. One theme of this work will be a quest for the origins of this 'improving' ideology.

Alongside the question of modernisation, I will study what might be called the growing cosmopolitanism of the local landed elite, so that merchants, gentry and aristocrats came by the end of the eighteenth century to form one ruling class, divided neither by aspirations, educational background, cultural tastes, standards of life and thought, nor economic or political outlook. It will be argued that we can observe a process very much like that described by de Tocqueville for contemporary France, where increasingly cosmopolitan local elites were detached from the assumptions and 'moral economy' of their poorer neighbours. They tended to become a *rentier* class, whose enforcement of archaic rights caused great rural discontent in the years leading up to the Revolution in 1789.[9] In Glamorgan there was no revolution – but new forms of social protest will be increasingly noted from the 1720s.

This book hopes to show the crucial importance of the century after 1660 in creating such a sophisticated ruling class, one so modern in political and economic outlook that the state it governed would dominate the politics of the world for over a century. The value of Glamorgan for such a study is readily explained. First, the county combines two very different geographical areas, each representative of a large part of Britain. The upland north closely resembles the central massif of Wales, and what we find here about social and economic patterns is likely to provide a model for much of pastoral upland or moorland Britain. The lowland south – the territory centred on Beaupre – is more like the fertile and gentrified areas of southern and western England, so the development of the Glamorgan gentry is likely to resemble that in those counties. Moreover, because it is a *Welsh* county, it will be easier to trace and observe the gradual detachment of the upper classes from the culture and sentiments of their social inferiors. Between 1715 and 1750, the class line in this county also became a linguistic frontier, a fact of immeasurable importance for any discussion of the survival of the 'paternalistic' ideology. Finally, Glamorgan was one of the first areas in the world in which we can speak of an 'Industrial Revolution', so the internal social developments leading towards this are of obvious interest.

Once the value of such a study is decided the sources available to the historian are surprisingly rich: there are excellent collections of manuscripts and, notably, of correspondence for several gentry families, particularly the Mansells and Kemys's. There is also one source for which it is difficult to think of an exact parallel, a diary slightly reminiscent of the *History of Myddle*. This was kept from 1762 to 1794 by the schoolmaster William Thomas, and it preserves what was intended to be a complete list of newsworthy events that came to his attention.[10] Most days therefore record a marriage, death or local scandal, in most cases including remarkably extensive biographical material on the participants. For a critical period of Glamorgan's history – the first years of industrialisation – it is possible to form an excellent impression of lower-class life and social attitudes in the county. It therefore becomes possible not only to describe the gentry and their attitudes, but to place these in a wider social context, and to examine the differential rates of change in social and economic outlook.

1. Structure

The book will begin by creating and populating a landscape, providing a society of the past with scale and dimensions. It will then seek to apply a steadily narrowing focus on the landed community. Next, we can examine the role and importance of the gentry in their 'habitat', in guiding the economic, political and administrative life of that society, and can study how patterns of power changed over this critical time. Having done this and provided ourselves with a framework, we can examine in detail how views and attitudes changed between the 1640s and 1780s, and especially in the years between 1715 and the 1740s. From this point, we will be able to trace the growth of the common national culture and standard of material life on which the new ruling class was based, and the effects of these changes on material conditions and economic life in the wider society.

2. Geographical context

Part I of this book tries to recreate the natural environment of this society and the geographical perspectives of the time. It will, for instance, be argued that events at the end of our period 'turned the world upside down' and not merely in the sense of social disorientation or political radicalism. Today the 'real' Glamorgan is found in the urban conglomerations of Cardiff, Swansea and the northern valleys, with the southern Vale a rural hinterland – which is also a growing country suburb for a burgeoning middle class. In 1750, the southern Vale was the thriving heartland of a gentry society little inferior to any in Britain for wealth, power and aspirations, while towns like Swansea and Cardiff based their prosperity on their role as markets for Vale produce. It will be stressed that the towns were vital political arenas in such a society, but as battlegrounds for rival gentry factions, rather than as centres of an autonomous political culture. The hill country was backward, despised, perversely radical in political and religious opinions, and simply outside the county's political mainstream.

The question 'Where is Glamorgan?', at any point before the eighteenth century, evoked a complex response: by sea (the most logical means of travel) it was a virtual suburb of Bristol, and very central for routes to Cork, Cornwall or Bordeaux. While not badly placed for land access to London or the Welsh interior, most of England north and east of a line from Shrewsbury, via Aylesbury, to London did not exist in contemporary Glamorgan perceptions. 'Pre-industrial' Glamorgan looked to south-west England, where there existed the same types of English dialect or customary acres, the same surnames and the same dependence on metropolitan Bristol. 'Modernisation' here came in the later eighteenth century, when the emergence of Swansea as an industrial and commercial town in its own

right was instrumental in creating a new social and economic region of
South Wales. Industrial growth in the hill country likewise turned the area
towards the north and east, towards the new British nation-state. We must
not forget that hitherto, the owner of a house like Beaupre had looked out-
wards, to south and west, into Bristol's zone – to Ireland, the Scillies, and
beyond to the distant colonies.

3. The gentry

Having described the society, the structure of economy and population, we
can then proceed to define the different grades of gentry which dominated
it, and the framework of kinship and clientage which bound together this
ancient and deep-rooted community. Until about 1700, we will observe
the development of the landed classes as a gradual process of organic
growth; but then, in the space of a generation, we encounter a violent caes-
ura (one in fact that overcame landed elites throughout Britain), a demographic catastrophe that thoroughly changed the composition and character of the Welsh gentry.[11] Between the 1720s and 1750s, a resident squire
was a *rara avis* in Glamorgan, and the old patterns of authority and respect
must have been severely shaken. When a new community re-established itself after 1760, it was a very different gentry – more English, more the pro-
duct of government service, closer to families made rich through careers in
commerce or the professions. Throughout the following study, we will
find the same themes and the same chronological structure: the survival of
the ancient dynasties into the eighteenth century, followed by a pattern of
extinction or ruin, and then the creation of a new elite oriented not to the
county, but to England, to London, to the central government.

I have tried to demonstrate elsewhere the number of communities to
which such a dramatic change occurred, and if this hypothesis is correct,
then we might choose this event as the natural conclusion to the numerous
gentry studies which have been written about Elizabethan or early Stuart
times. Certainly it marked a fracture of historical continuity far more useful as a dividing line than 1660. The ramifications of this change extend
throughout whatever aspects of cultural life we consider – tastes in literature or music, education, activity in building or cultural patronage. Much
of the new gentry culture which emerges in the 1760s will be seen in the
context of a deliberate 'invention of tradition', an attempt to disguise the
breach in continuity by the assumption of pseudo-antiquity. To take just
one example, the new public school was a facet of this, and it also provided

the new ruling class with the common form of speech that was the trademark of the break with provincialism. These developments form the subject of Part III of this book, where consideration will also be given to the effects on the wider society by these changes of thought and attitude among this narrow but immensely influential segment.

4. Economic history

One of my purposes in this study is to show the close relationship between political and economic aspects of life. Part I concludes with a history of the steps toward industrial revolution in Glamorgan, stressing the economic role of the gentry throughout in developing their society, but definite political conclusions will also emerge. Firstly, I have attempted to give proper emphasis to the pressing financial needs of landed society in explaining the bitterness of political conflict in the later seventeenth century. It will be suggested that the peculiar commercial and industrial orientation of this area went far towards determining the desperate party hostility under Anne, and in turn the relaxation of partisan hostility by the 1740s. Tory 'blue-water' policies were not the result of ignorance of military developments or of foreign affairs. Quite the contrary, they arose from the squires' sophisticated industrial needs, their links with Bristol's colonial trade, and the need to preserve markets – first in western Europe, later in the western hemisphere. Given also the frequency of industrial activity and innovation by high tories, catholics and jacobites, it sometimes seems as if the classical Weberian or Tawneyan theory of industrial origins could be opposed by a model using a slogan like 'backwoods squires and the rise of capitalism', or even 'the jacobite work-ethic'. It was, for example, a catholic marquis of Worcester who invented a steam engine in the Interregnum, his son who evicted commoners to gain timber for his ironworks, and later jacobite and nonjuring members of the family who built the metallurgical industries of west Glamorgan, in partnership with catholic and nonjuror entrepreneurs and managers. No wonder that a jacobite list of likely supporters in the 1720s found most optimism in the industrial areas of north and west Britain; and it is hoped this may suggest lines of inquiry for explaining the high toryism of other advanced industrial areas of the English Midlands or North-East. It is no longer adequate to explain this in terms of the survival of primitive patriarchal structures of loyalty and obedience.

5. Politics

This was a highly political age because of the direct relevance of partisan success and failure to everyday life and economic prosperity. Furthermore, Chapter 4 will show the almost total control which the landed gentry had over most aspects of life and government in the wider community. There need therefore be no elaborate justification for the decision to include here a chronological political history; especially as the existing *Glamorgan County History* account leaves room for a much fuller analysis of events, particularly one based on a wider range of sources than are there employed. Three main themes will be examined here:

The development of a gentry ideology
The formation of a characteristic body of attitudes will be traced against the events between 1640 and 1688, critical years in which the local power of the gentry, even their existence as a class, were repeatedly challenged. Throughout these events, it will be suggested that three distinct parties can be observed in operaion. Two of these were linked to great peers – extreme royalists to the Marquis of Worcester, moderates to the Earls of Pembroke – but politics were not simply a matter of aristocratic faction. Apart from the extremes of royalists and parliamentarians, there was a third group, here tentatively described as 'moderates', who appear to have been central to political history in these years. They were not exactly the great gentry presbyterians described by Professor Everitt, nor the neutralists of Dr Morrill, yet they resembled both. They were a faction of great gentry who reacted violently against challenges of religious extremism, catholic and absolutist, or puritan and republican.

I have laid such stress on this group for three reasons. First, they help to explain the very advanced state of party development in South Wales by the end of the seventeenth century – in fact, they appear to have been the core of the new whig party that emerged in the late 1670s. Second, it will be suggested that in terms of local politics, 1688 should be considered the real point of transition from the alignments of the Civil War years: 1660 merely changed the balance of forces between competing sides, while 1688 changed fundamentally the composition and purpose of these sides. Finally, the examination of this faction suggests the very constant stress on anti-popery in Welsh politics until about 1690, a local peculiarity of immense consequences. Far from accepting the traditional view of the Welsh

gentry as fanatical royalists, it will here be argued that the fear of catholicism made a large section of the great gentry less sympathetic to Stuart governments than was apparent anywhere else in Britain. 'Moderates' from
this area went on to play a substantial role in national politics – Robert
Harley is the best-known example – so we are not merely dealing with a
squabble of local importance. The forces shaping the ideology of the gentry in South Wales and the Borders were different in vital respects from
those affecting the squires of Norfolk or Kent.

From faction to party
It was in the 1950s and early 1960s that historians began to apply the in-
sights of Namier into the age of George III to earlier periods of 'party' conflict, so that it was often questioned whether 'whig' or 'tory' under Anne
had any more meaning than in the age of Newcastle. This extreme view
was rebutted by Professors Plumb and Holmes,[12] and contemporary perceptions of the 'rage of party' are now treated with more respect. But the
origins of these parties at local level has not been researched as thoroughly as
might be expected, given the undoubted importance of parties in political
conflict from the 1680s – perhaps before. Here, I wish to analyse the parties that crystallised in the 1690s into their distinct elements, and study the
processes by which they were united and acquired their particular
ideologies. Kinship is clearly one element and groups of related families
can be seen to have pursued coherent policies over periods of a century and
more. In one case (the Kemys – Aubrey – Jenkins group) a clique led the
high anglican 'ultra' faction for at least half a century, before being converted *en masse* to Court whiggery in the 1690s. Equally enduring was
clientage to aristocrats like Worcester or Pembroke. This might be through
what we could call the 'ghost interest', a group of families acting together
as a faction in support of a lord, and maintaining this cohesion and tradition of collective action sixty years after that lord's family had ceased to
have any connection with the area. Whiggery arose in Glamorgan from
three main elements: old roundheads and republicans; the Kemys –
Aubrey – Jenkins clique; and part of the 'ghost' interest of the Earls of
Pembroke, after this party finally dissolved in the 1690s. This coalition
was soon strengthened by the force of direct government patronage, especially with the presence in the county of leading government office holders
and magnates. We therefore have a fairly clear example of how the seventeenth-century factions based on kinship and clientage became a remarkably modern party structure with all that implied for the role of managers
and electoral experts.

On the other side, it may well be that this county played an important part in uniting diverse factions into the new toryism of the 1690s, as Robert Harley's closest friends and allies included Glamorgan magnates like Francis Gwyn and Thomas Mansell. Perhaps we shall not understand fully British politics in the generation after 1688 until a first-class biography is produced of Gwyn, that ubiquitous civil servant and go-between. This book makes no attempt to write that biography; but it tries to depict the world in which he moved. We can observe the growth of Glamorgan toryism as well as that of whiggery, and this subject gains added interest from the decades in which the tories were excluded from office and patronage, and needed to maintain their existence by other means. Hence we can study the sudden growth of sophistication in party structure, propaganda and organisation after 1714. Moreover, evidence from this area tends to undermine the idea that jacobitism was entirely a government bogey, as was argued by Dr Fritz.[13] While not agreeing, either, with Dr Cruickshanks that jacobitism was the tory mainstream until well into the 1740s, real conspiracies can be traced at least until the late 1720s, so return to large-scale civil violence could not be discounted.[14]

Towards political stability

Party bitterness declined from the 1720s, and men of property gradually reached an accommodation in which all could claim a general whig viewpoint sufficiently to petition for the charity of the government. This was ably described by Professor Plumb in *The growth of political stability*, and his hypothesis stands up very well when tested against the situation in Glamorgan and other counties of South Wales. But more can be said about how stability came about here, and perhaps how the means of achieving stability sowed the seeds of conflict later in the century. Firstly, demographic changes in the gentry community will be taken into account, as will the economic pressures on the entrepreneurial landed gentlemen. Put crudely, they needed the distinctively tory war policy in Anne's time for the sake of their industrial and commercial interests, just as they were prepared wholeheartedly to support a government which fought for their interests by engaging in the 'blue-water' and colonial struggle usually described as the Seven Years War. Equally, a revival of party conflict after 1775 was likely when the government endangered their vital markets and sources of raw material in America and Ireland. Of course, economic determinism is not an answer in itself: there was also the decline of religious controversy, and the emergence of the masonic movement from the new deist consensus.[15] This in turn would, from the 1760s, do so much to unite gentry, professionals and merchants in progressive campaigns to improve the economic infrastructure, and in political reform campaigns.

By the 1760s, the new alignment of local elites could begin to be described as a national ruling class, and novel patterns of social relationship met opposition from traditionally-minded social inferiors. Between 1730 and 1770, a whole series of new forms of social protest emerged: riots, sabotage and coastal wrecking. Conflicts were very bitter when traditional social values encountered the new property ethos over matters like plundering ships, smuggling, or resisting a militia that took local men outside the county (and de Tocqueville cited the last as a special grievance in contemporary French society). What was national defence or international politics to the humble neighbours of William Thomas – and still more, what did it matter to them that colonial goods could safely travel to Bristol? But such considerations had become an essential part of the squires' life, no matter what the damage to social relations with tenants. Perhaps the new ideas of property and discipline could somehow be instilled into wrongdoers; and from the 1770s, the gentry made vigorous efforts to build a new model prison for deviants. The old world had by no means been a 'one-class society', but there had been a community of attitude, culture and belief which was now irretrievably shattered. A concluding section will assess the importance of the new class alignments for the county's industrialisation, and discuss the contribution of the various social, political and economic factors for the vital 'take-off' of the late eighteenth century.

This introduction began with the very archaic thought-world of Sir Edward Mansell, who died in 1706. In the 1760s, a more representative character might be one Robert Jones of Fonmon, a Wilkite, radical and freemason, a champion of political reform movements throughout South Wales; and a model justice of the peace, who tried to stop coastal plunder, and to moralise the poor by encouraging methodist preachers. He was also, of course, a leading figure in the militia, a champion of national defence in the wars which benefited himself and his friends. Almost certainly he did not speak Welsh, and he spent as much of his life as he could in London. Between 1700 and 1770, we seem to have travelled from one world which looked back to Elizabeth into one which looked forward to Victoria. The world represented by Beaupre and the Mansell tombs died with surprising rapidity – and they were separated by one a very few decades from the new civilisation represented by names like Merthyr, Dowlais and Cyfarthfa.

PART I

Social and economic structure

Introduction

The first chapter describes the *habitat* of the gentry and the geographical perspectives so essential to the development of a sense of community. In Wales, miles are less important than hills: that is, two lowland communities ten or twenty miles apart might be 'closer' than villages separated by only a mile or two of steep hills and dangerous torrents. This meant that southern Glamorgan – the gentry homeland – had close ties with the coastal plain of south Monmouthshire, but very few links at all with the Welsh interior; and sea communications became of disproportionate importance at all levels of society. A study of Glamorgan's common people almost suggests that we are dealing with two distinct communities. Half the county looked to Bristol as its capital, half to Brecon or Carmarthen. In this context, southern Glamorgan was only ambiguously 'Welsh' before 1800, and one theme of this book will be the fusion of the county into new Welsh entities, both cultural and economic.

Links with south-western England were to be of profound importance beyond the economic sphere. Bristol connections also linked the area to Ireland and the colonies, sources of raw materials, and markets; but the western lands were not always so fruitful or rewarding. Until 1689, Ireland meant the catholic threat, which would thus be much more feared in coastal Wales than in more protected areas of the interior. This meant that for much of our period, the presence of catholic peers in Wales would be a source of peculiar concern, and attitudes to them would be the chief political issue for generations. A degree of geographical determinism cannot be avoided against such a background, as Glamorgan's situation largely decided both the political and the economic context in which its factions emerged, and its industries developed.

1. 'Dramatis personae'

Our next priority will be to define some criteria for identifying the gentry. There are no problems in finding the elite families, the 'dynasties' like the

3

Mansells and Aubreys; but delineating the lower levels of the landed community gains some importance when it was to be largely this segment – professional men and petty squires – who would themselves assume the leading role in Glamorgan society by the end of the period. We will therefore describe the geographical and social structure of landed society about 1700, in the last days of 'traditional' organisation, and then show the effects of the demographic transformation by mid-century. Such a change could not be without far-reaching effects for wider society, given the gentry's economic hegemony and power in administration and local government; and the extent of such changes will be described in Part III.

2. Wealth

In studying the economic development of the gentry in Chapter 3, it will first be stressed that the Glamorgan elite were landowners on a scale substantial by both British and European standards. The sources of this wealth will be studied: the concentration of lands, agricultural improvements, better management, and finally industrial activity. It will be emphasised that the economic health of the community demonstrates the falsity of the traditional image of early modern Wales as backward or impoverished, with all this implies for 'patriarchal' relationships between landlord and tenant.

Obviously one aspect of this study will be the process of industrialisation and modernisation in the county, but here there is an unusual problem. The historian has no difficulty in identifying groups within society who were active entrepreneurs and advocates of economic development: the gentry had always filled this role, at least from Tudor times. So what, if anything, was new about the 'modernising elite' of the mid eighteenth century, that presided over the economic 'take-off'? It will be suggested that the new factors were largely political, and were concerned with the role of government, and questions of war and peace.

Part I therefore introduces the central themes of the remainder of this book: the key role of the gentry in society; the transformation of that community, and its detachment from local society; and the economic and geographical background to the county's bitterly divided political history.

1

Land and people

1. The two lordships

The county of Glamorgan was created in the time of Henry VIII by merging two lordships: to Glamorgan proper was added the lordship of Gower and Kilvey, which lay west of the river Tawe. The new county's internal geography ensured that its culture would always be an amalgam of very diverse elements. The pre-Tudor divisions between east and west continued to exist because of the survival of the lordships of Gower and Glamorgan, each with their own lord claiming particular rights and dues. In the seventeenth century, this schism acquired political significance. While Gower was a possession of the catholic Marquis of Worcester, Glamorgan was held by the puritan Earls of Pembroke, and the repercussions of this will be a major theme of our study of Glamorgan's political history.[1]

Of still greater structural importance was the enormous contrast between the barren pastoral area to the north of the county and the prosperous arable landscape of the south, which distinction was not recognised by any formal or legal boundary.[2] The north, or *Blaenau* (uplands), is a plateau cut by deep valleys, an area which at its worst was a wilderness of barren moors and peat-bogs. Large parts of Glamorgan were dismissed by travellers as featuring only 'horrid rocks and precipices', and some of the coal-rich lands on which the country's Victorian prosperity was based were almost unvisited before 1800. However, most of the *Blaenau* were a landscape of hill-farms, based on a pastoral economy which had possessed some industries from the earliest times. In contrast to this very 'Welsh' area was the Vale, or *Bro*, the southern third of the old lordship of Glamorgan, a countryside roughly delineated by a line from Cardiff to Margam. Geologically, no less than socially, the affinities of this area were with south-west England, especially the Vale of Gloucester; and the only areas of Wales which it resembled were Gower and the southern parts of Monmouthshire and Pembrokeshire. The *Bro* was a prosperous agrarian landscape, with many small rivers watering its light, fertile and easily workable soil. In so many ways, life here was essentially that of the arable areas of southern England. Its principal crop in the eighteenth century was wheat, not the 'pastoral' staple of oats. There was excellent fertiliser available locally in the form of lime, and the Vale had good local building stone, so that travellers fresh from the poverty of North and West Wales were delighted at the solid and attractive limewashed cottages which they now saw. Here, they changed the sour tone they normally adopted to portray Welsh 'barbarism' and adopted new adjectives, like 'rich', 'pleasing', 'fertile', 'cultivated'. In a word, it was 'Arcadia'.[3] Of course, one reason for this praise was that Glamorgan *looked* like an English shire: it was a countryside of nucleated villages with their ponds and greens, towered churches and ancient manor houses, a land of squires and parsons.

Historically too, north and south diverged, as the ancient material remains to be found in upland Wales were rugged fortresses intended to garrison unruly natives. By contrast, the south-eastern coastal strip provided a congenial environment successively for Roman villas, Dark Age monasteries, medieval manors and Stuart mansions – all of which had flourished (for example) around the town of Llantwit Major. It was a land capable of supporting a wealthy gentry society; and one which could not but provide them with a sense of long history and continuity, of being rooted in an ancient past.

Of course there were Border territories which fell short of 'Arcadia'. In the Vale proper there was some marginal land, notably near the coast. Sand invasions were a constant peril – as would be apparent to anyone who passed the slowly disappearing remains of the medieval borough of Kenfig. Serious flooding often assailed the Glamorgan coast, the worst catastrophe (in 1607) affected 26 parishes, but there were at least four smaller occurrences between 1720 and 1770.[4] Landlords and stewards faced a permanent battle to ensure that the land improved or reclaimed in one area was not exceeded by that lost to sand or sea in another, and this concern still animated the leaders of the societies for agricultural improvement at the end of the eighteenth century. Indeed, prominent 'improvers' like John Franklen often lived and farmed in such marginal areas, like Candleston or Sker.[5]

A simple division between *Bro* and *Blaenau* would not strictly apply to the whole of Glamorgan, especially as one of the most important regions of the county would not readily fit into either category. Neath and Swansea stand on low coastal lands narrowly placed between hills and sea, with all the difficulties of the *Bro* coastline, but both towns were also close to their

Blaenau hinterland. In the seventeenth century the great forests of the Tawe valley had almost approached the sea between Neath and Swansea, before they had been depleted by the depredations of industry. Further west, the landscape seems to resume the dual structure of *Bro* and *Blaenau*. The lordship of Gower had been divided from medieval times into a pastoral upland 'Welshry' centred on the parish of Llangyfelach, and an arable coastal 'Englishry' divided into twenty small nucleated parishes. Despite its proximity to Swansea, Llangyfelach was culturally as Welsh as any parish in the north or west of Wales. If one travelled a few miles to the south, one found in lowland Gower a countryside that had looked to England for so long that it spoke an ancient dialect related to that of Devon. Gower represented in miniature the cultural divisions which marked the history of the whole of Glamorgan.

2. Communications

The county was also divided roughly into two halves from the point of view of ease of travel. Most Welsh roads were proverbially bad, but the main route through the Vale from east to west was not significantly worse than the southern English norm.[6] This was part of the great road from London to St David's, and the section between Newport and Cowbridge was regularly described as 'good', 'fine', or 'excellent' long before the coming of the turnpikes – astonishing in the context of the normal experiences of tourists in Wales. At least from Caerleon to Loughor, the road generally followed a Roman predecessor which passed through the Roman stations of Cardiff, Cowbridge and Neath. Even off this road, Wesley's journeys show that there were few difficulties in travelling between the towns and villages of the Vale.[7] West of Swansea, 'Welsh' patterns reasserted themselves, so that an unwary traveller might find himself in mortal danger – at least until the late eighteenth century, when the road from Swansea to Pembrokeshire was developed as part of a main route to Ireland.

'English' conditions therefore prevailed as far west as Swansea. To travel north into the Welsh interior meant a very rapid transition from Vale conditions into the different world of the *Blaenau*, which one crossed by means of the old Roman roads which ran through Caerphilly and Merthyr Tydfil, or from Neath to Brecon. To English travellers, this seemed to be a return to the familiar Welsh landscape of impossible roads and wearisome hills – in short, of 'break-neck-shire'. But such hill-roads and tracks as did exist assumed disproportionate importance, and the

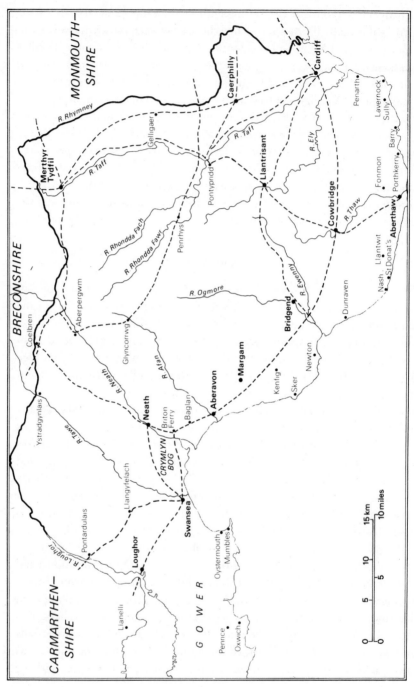

Map 1. Glamorgan: roads and rivers

8

north of Glamorgan possessed road junctions of immense social and political significance. Examples were Merthyr Tydfil, Llangyfelach and Gelligaer, which were all great puritan and radical centres many years before industrialisation.[8] But this vital and active area receives almost no attention in the correspondence of the county's gentry, who generally lived only a few miles to the south, across the critical mountains.

Difficulties of communication made the *Blaenau* hinterland very remote from the rest of the county in terms of language, or patterns of religion and social authority. Problems of access were not really solved until the end of that century, with the large-scale building of turnpike roads, bridges and canals, and the growth of vast centres of population in the uplands. By 1800 tourists were noting the ignorance of national affairs found in southern towns like Cardiff or Chepstow, and contrasting this with outward-looking and politically conscious Merthyr Tydfil.[9] Industry was (in more senses than one) reversing the whole orientation of the county.

3. The sea

Before the improvement of the roads, sea travel was much exploited, so that even travellers from South Wales to London sometimes preferred to go by ship from Swansea or Newport rather than use the relatively fine road. Sea transport was much cheaper and easier for freight and there were regular trade routes from Neath to Cornwall and Lancashire, and from Swansea to Cornwall, France, Ireland, and the Channel Islands.[10] Indeed, in this context, it would be better to consider Glamorgan as almost central to western Britain, rather than to view it with metropolitan eyes as a distant outlying province. Towns like Neath or Swansea looked west and south, their coal and copper industries relying on trade with Ireland, France and the West Country; and they had far more in common with Cork, Plymouth, or even Bordeaux than with great towns of eastern England like York or Norwich. This was the ancient 'Marine Antechamber of Britain', through which ran long-established and much-travelled sea-routes.[11] From an archaeological perspective, only this maritime context can explain the location in south-east Glamorgan of some of the richest and best fortified settlements in the western half of Britain – sites such as Cardiff castle, with its awe-inspiring Roman walls, or the key Dark Age fortress of Dinas Powis.[12] Only in the late eighteenth century did the population of Glamorgan begin to look inland, to north and east, for their main directions of trade and travel. We must always remember the economic importance of this zone if we are to understand the constant concern of Glamorgan society for political life, affairs of war and peace, and relations with maritime powers like Holland and France.

Good sea communications also meant frequent links between Glamorgan and nearby areas of south-west England. Swansea, Neath and Cardiff all had important contacts across the Bristol Channel, but much of the trade was carried on from the numerous creeks (or 'pills') and small ports of the Glamorgan coast, so that few places in the Vale were more than a few miles away from such a route. The greatest of these minor ports were Aberthaw and Newton, which remained in use until Victorian times. Aberthaw had an ancient connection with Minehead, which can be observed from the frequent appearance of north Somerset placenames as Glamorgan Vale surnames. Aberthaw was quite simply 'the seaport of this neighbourhood'.[13] It was on the regular route for travellers from Brecon or Mid Wales to south-west England, and was much used by the coasting traffic between Pembrokeshire and Monmouthshire. Once again, we can see the Vale as a crossroads rather than a backwater. Other major routes between Wales and the West Country were from Swansea, Neath and Newton, from which ships sailed to Bristol, to lesser ports like Barnstaple and Bridgewater, or to one of the countless small creeks of Devon and Somerset.

Regular use of such easy means of communication had wide effects on the social and economic life of south Glamorgan and other coastal regions. Frequent trade gave an extra source of livelihood to the population of the Vale, but it also posed administrative problems of law and order, because of piracy, wrecking, smuggling and gun-running. There were close contacts between suspected and persecuted groups on either side of the 'Severn Sea' – quakers and dissenters in the seventeenth century, catholics and jacobites in the eighteenth.[14] Criminals or refugees could escape easily by taking a ship to Devon or Somerset, a means successively used in the 1640s by puritans, catholics and royalists. Very close trade links existed throughout the period, Welsh exports including coal, cattle and corn, while Bristol was increasingly the source of capital and technological expertise for Glamorgan's growing industries.[15] Bristol was the vital regional centre of services, legal and financial, for South Wales. Many of Glamorgan's common people knew the city through apprenticeship or seasonal employment there; and the economic life of the county relied heavily on Bristol's great fairs for the sale of agricultural produce.

South Glamorgan was part of Bristol's 'metropolitan' area, which also included Monmouthshire and the English counties bordering the Bristol Channel, and which was economically close to Ireland and the counties of the Severn valley. South Glamorgan belonged to this region, rather than to the Welsh shires with which it still shared a common language and culture, and even the 'Welsh' *Blaenau* were linked to Somerset and the South-West by their important clothing industries.[16] In this context, it is often difficult to see Glamorgan as part of a 'Welsh' unity, especially when the counties of North and Mid Wales looked respectively to Chester and Shrewsbury as 'metropolis', and the Council of Wales was based at Ludlow. I know of no case in which a member of a Glamorgan gentry family in this period married anyone from the six northern counties of Wales, while about 10 per cent of all gentry marriages were made with families from south-west England. Moreover, this orientation appears to have been very ancient. Social patterns and folk-cultures on either side of the 'Severn Sea' suggest contacts over millennia. The vernacular house-types of Glamorgan were reminiscent of those of south-west England rather than the rest of Wales, and the English dialect of Gower was very similar to that of Devon or Somerset; while the Devon customary acre was used in south Pembrokeshire.[17] Professor Bowen has shown how studying the medieval cults of early saints like Cadoc of Llancarfan can demonstrate the ancient homogeneity of this culture area in south-east Wales, Devon and Cornwall, southern Ireland, and Brittany.[18] Indeed, by the eighteenth century there were many Glamorgan people who were more comfortable linguistically with Bretons than with Englishmen – or than with some of their landlords.

There were family links across the Bristol Channel in our period, between the landed elites, but also at much lower social levels. We certainly find trading families straddling the Channel, men whose wills describe them as 'of Minehead and Aberthaw', or 'of Swansea and Bideford'. Such people were influential in ensuring that coastal Glamorgan adopted the 'English' form of Wesleyan methodism, rather than its 'Welsh' and calvinistic counterpart. Medieval gentry houses like the Stradlings owned lands in Somerset and Wiltshire, as West Country squires like the Pophams were landlords in Glamorgan, and cadet branches were founded over the centuries. Together with actual migration, this meant that old gentry names were widespread throughout the region. Glamorgan families could claim kin in several counties of western England or southern Ireland.[19] When we look at a list of the Glamorgan gentry, we find many names which could equally well be those of the elites of Dorset, Cornwall or Somerset – the magnates of the Vale were just as likely to bear ancient names like Carne, Bassett, Wyndham or Turberville. Below the gentry, Bristol trading families had kin among the mercantile rulers of Cardiff, and the hatters or tanners of Vale villages were often conscious of Somerset origins. Very close connections between the communities on either side of the Bristol Channel demonstrate that this was for them a highway rather than a moat; and this proximity will be a recurring theme of this study.

4. Population and social structure

From Stuart times, Glamorgan was probably the most populous county of Wales, although precision is difficult, and Carmarthenshire was a close rival until the end of the eighteenth century.[20] The hearth-tax returns of the 1670s suggest that Glamorgan contained about 9,300 households, so that it had a population of about 45,000, with an average density of 56 persons per square mile. As in 1801, the county would therefore have a smaller population than every English shire but three. The figure was also liable to short-term fluctuations,[21] but it grew steadily with the rise of industry from the mid eighteenth century, so that it exceeded 70,000 by 1801. In 1670, about 80 per cent of the county's population lived in small houses of one or two hearths, and this included the quarter of society excluded from assessment because they were 'paupers'.

At the beginning of the period, only about 15 per cent of the people lived in the seven major towns, so that the 'urban' proportion of the population in 1700 was little different from what it had been in 1400.[22] Even the towns that did exist were overshadowed by those of other Welsh counties. The largest town populations in the Wales of 1700 were probably those of Carmarthen, Haverfordwest and Brecon – each with about 3,000 people.[23] Glamorgan had Swansea (with 2,500 people) and Cardiff (with 1,800). Smaller still were Neath and Cowbridge, each with 700 to 1,000 people; and Llantrisant, Llantwit and Loughor may have had 300 or 400 each. By the start of the nineteenth century there had been considerable change: Swansea and Merthyr Tydfil each had over 6,000 people and now represented clearly the greatest urban centres of Wales. But one fact remained constant: town dwellers still represented only some 30 per cent of Glamorgan's population, so it would be well into the process of industrialisation before the county ceased to be predominantly rural.

The hearth-tax returns also provide evidence on the social hierarchy of the county, allowing us to deduce the numbers of families in houses of various sizes. But before this society can be discussed, it is first necessary to stress that social organisation has to be examined in the context of Glamorgan's sharp geographical divisions. As we have already noted, Glamorgan was almost two counties in some respects, one 'English' and gentrified, one 'Welsh' and peasant. Of perhaps 120 parishes, less than 20 comprised the *Blaenau* which made up half the county's area, while the Vale had 80 parishes and south Gower another 20; so the lowland region was much more accessible to the authorities, both civil and ecclesiastical. Firstly, we will consider the social structure of the Vale, an area dominated throughout by squires and clergy. We will then contrast this with the much less controllable uplands, an area where gentry power was a more distant concept.

5. The Vale

Most Vale parishes in the seventeenth and eighteenth centuries had at least one resident squire as well as a parson, and no one in this area lived more than three miles from a justice of the peace. The Vale was controlled socially and economically by the gentry, who were not only the greatest landlords, but also major employers of labour, both agricultural and domestic.[24] This power was reinforced by their domination of the Church: in that part of the county within the diocese of Llandaff, over 60 per cent of ecclesiastical livings were in the gift of the local gentry in 1721, with another 14 per cent in the hands of non-resident peers.[25] Apparently, this control received popular acquiescence, so that the Vale of the late eighteenth century was praised by tourists for the deference shown by its people.[26] It will be argued below that this tranquillity was something of an illusion, but at least what protest there was in the Vale took less explicitly political forms than in the uplands.

By the late eighteenth century, the Vale was an area of 'closed' parishes, with the gentry owning over two-thirds of the land in about 84 per cent of parishes. At least from early Stuart times, land was increasingly concentrated in the hands of the gentry and wealthy yeomen, while smallholders often became paid labourers.[27] By the 1750s, most farms were between 30 and 50 acres, anything over 100 acres being considered very large; but by the 1790s, a 'large' Vale farm was more likely to have been between 400 and 800 acres. The French wars at the end of the century accelerated these developments, and, by 1814, the great majority of Vale farms were probably between 100 and 500 acres.[28] Alongside the newly prosperous were a number of the less efficient families whose wealth and lands had declined, but who often maintained a title like 'gentleman' when it no longer made economic sense.

Of course, not all who lost their smallholdings were reduced to penury, as was demonstrated by the praise of tourists for the good housing and simple but adequate food of Glamorgan's common people.[29] Such writers were naturally seeking an idyllic countryside and idealising what they found, but the Vale was indeed rich in natural resources. Wages were at least as good as those of most of southern England.[30] Income was supplemented by industries like weaving, tanning, and stocking-knitting, and the vigorous trade in wool and dairy produce to south-west England suggests frequent surpluses.[31] It also indicates the demand for Glamorgan's exports: in their day, the cheeses of Llandaff and Cowbridge were as distinctive and as much esteemed as those of Caerphilly. In 1741, Llandaff fair was the source for 'coarse or homemade cloths, flannels, shoes, woollen stockings, pedlary of all sorts, wool, cheese, etc.'.[32] The coastal trade could in itself provide additional employment, and small ports like Aberthaw or Newton had communities of yeomen who were also active in ship-building and small-scale mercantile enterprise. Trade flourished, but it depended on land, and towns like Cowbridge, Llantwit and Cardiff were primarily markets for the produce of their neighbourhood, while Cardiff's exports were overwhelmingly wool and dairy items.

The society of the *Bro* bore a close resemblance to that of south-west England, being centred in gentry-dominated villages,[33] but it was separated from adjacent areas by language. Welsh was spoken until the nineteenth century, so the county possessed linguistic unity, despite wide disparities in other matters. South Gower had long been English-speaking, but it was very unusual in this. The Vale – now as English as Surrey, and equally suburban – was in the eighteenth century a Welsh-speaking area, despite recent theories to the contrary.[34] Such theories place a great deal of emphasis on the remark of a rector of Coychurch, who in 1696 complained that frequent commerce with Devon and Somerset 'spoils our Welsh'. But this is heavily outweighed by other evidence. Other sources describe Coychurch itself as virtually monoglot Welsh throughout our period, and so were towns closely connected with Bristol – like Cardiff or Bridgend.[35] It may be that the rector was only complaining of frequent English loanwords, which a purist would find offensive. The prevalence of the Welsh language in the Vale is confirmed by the records of ecclesiastical courts,[36] which invariably state the language in which an alleged slander was spoken, and in Glamorgan this was most commonly Welsh. From this evidence, we can show that in the eighteenth century, Welsh was still spoken in parishes near the coast or main roads, even those with old links with Bristol or Minehead – places such as Llancarfan, Cowbridge or St Athan, or at Caerwent in neighbouring Monmouthshire. The region was therefore subject to influences from both the Welsh north and the English south.

6. 'An ungovernable people'

Language united *Bro* and *Blaenau*, but there were so many differences between the two societies that it seemed a remarkable accident that they had been combined in one shire, and there is some evidence of mutual hostility. The hills were sparsely populated, settlements usually being straggling hamlets or isolated hill-farms, and the heavily wooded valleys were 'dotted with farmhouses'. But this area supported a surprisingly large population, and in 1670 over a quarter of Glamorgan's people lived in just fifteen sprawling upland parishes. This largely pastoral region had a different way of life from the arable south, with a poorer diet, as the common people lived on oatmeal (not wheaten) bread, coarser cheese and beer. However, there were some tendencies in common, like the ruthless concentration of landed wealth in the hands of a few great gentry and freeholders. The Prices of Penllergaer, or Llewellyns of Ynysgerwn grew in wealth in the same way as the great squires of the Vale,[37] and often used unscrupulous methods 'to encroach the poor people's freehold'.[38] Tenurial arrangements were also broadly similar to the lowlands, but there were important distinctions, such as the higher proportion of freehold land and of Welsh customary tenures, in the uplands. Also, especially west of the Tawe, there were a great many cottagers settled on wasteland or newly cleared forest, where they held land by customary right. As elsewhere in Britain, this was probably in response to a need for casual labour in industry, and the dramatic increase in cottages between 1715 and the 1730s reflected the growth of coal, iron and copper undertakings.[39]

The hill parishes were more 'egalitarian' than the lowlands, containing more people living in one-hearth houses, fewer rich and fewer paupers. This suggests a marginal subsistence economy, but little real want. The concept of 'gentleman' itself preserved an older and very different connotation in the uplands. In 1690, a list of gentry gave only one 'gentleman' for the parish of Llangyfelach, and four for the whole hundred (0.5 per cent of the population), but there were many others in such an area who would have described themselves as 'gentlemen', using the older Welsh criteria of pure birth and an impressive genealogy, recognised in the praises of the bards.[40] Such families often maintained patronymics until the later seventeenth century, and an influential family like the Llewellyns of Cwrt Colman did not adopt a surname until after 1730. The separation of gentlemanly status from wealth was encouraged by the survival of partible inheritance in the hills, so that all the sons of a landowner acquired the title of 'gentleman', but with only a little land to support it.[41] Such reduced Welsh 'gentlemen' were notorious for their pride, although contemporaries were uncertain as to their status. In a parish like Llangyfelach, it is common to find the same family indiscriminately described as yeomen and gentlemen in successive generations, or even the same man variously known by both terms.[42] The area's social ethos, no less than its economic arrangements, made its people hostile to encroachment on their rights and independence, creating a tradition of violence and social unrest. Also significant was the influence of such views in Swansea, which depended on the trade of its hinterland in Llangyfelach and Llansamlet. It is not therefore surprising to find Swansea's religious and political traditions closely aligned to these upland parishes, rather than to the Vale.

Economic rivalries aggravated social tensions in this already fluid situation. Coal reserves had long been known and exploited in the west, and these rich prizes were pursued both by local gentry and by non-resident lords, by means of the stricter enforcement of vague legal rights as well as more dubious encroachments on commons. Established freeholders fought against enclosures and newly settled squatters, as at Aberdare and Rhondda in the late eighteenth century.[43] These disputes focussed such diverse issues as communal grazing rights and the danger posed to cottagers by enclosure, the rivalry between neighbouring coal-owning squires, and even matters of religion and national politics. The Lords of Gower were Earls of Worcester (from 1682, Dukes of Beaufort) and resistance to their power over mineral or grazing rights could lead to the adoption of political views diametrically opposed to theirs: puritanism against their catholicism, whiggery against their jacobitism.[44] In 1688, the Revolution provided the opportunity for a widespread attack on enclosures in Gower, and there were similar incidents in later years.[45]

The most prolonged and bitter struggle in the Glamorgan *Blaenau* arose in the 1740s, when a group of powerful gentry families sought to acquire mineral and, especially, coal rights under Beaufort's lordships, on the commons of Llangiwg and Llangyfelach.[46] This was to be done by denying the Duke's seignorial rights, by cutting trees, quarrying stone and fishing the rivers; when these privileges were established, mineral exploitation would fall open to the most vigorous local families. Chiefly, this was a dispute between factions of the gentry and aristocracy, but the group opposing the duke attempted to obtain widespread support by claiming the coal for all freeholders, and asserting that many below that rank had only lost their status through the machinations of attorneys.[47] The opposition were appealing to the great potential for resistance among the small independent yeomen and freeholders of the hills.

7. Radicals and dissenters

Disputes like those of the 1740s illustrate the near impossibility of imposing in the hills the relatively stable social hierarchy of the south, but weakness in parochial organisation – no less than poor communications – meant there could be no firm religious supervision. There were accusations that such areas were rife with atheism, indifference, or active popery.[48] Radically puritan ideas began to spread during the Interregnum, when the greatest prizes fell to those religious groups congenial to this decentralised and individualistic society, especially the anabaptists. Glamorgan's roundhead leaders were drawn from the petty gentry of the north and west, united in the baptist congregations of Ilston (Gower) and Gelligaer.[49] These developments were carried still further by some 'shattered baptists' who adopted ranter or quaker ideas. Parishes like Merthyr Tydfil long kept alive the military and millenarian traditions of the 1650s, and old Merthyr roundheads were said to be active in puritan or republican plots at least until the 1680s.[50]

The history of dissent in Glamorgan illustrates much about the county's geographical polarity.[51] By 1760, dissent was strong in Glamorgan, but it had largely vanished from the southern parishes which had once been its strongholds. Almost half of Glamorgan's parishes reported no dissenters, while many of the others mentioned only one family or one individual.[52] By contrast, visitation returns from the huge hill-parishes of Gelligaer or Merthyr Tydfil suggest that nonconformists were heavily in the majority, and still comprised extreme presbyterians or 'obstinate and rigid anabaptists'. They also remained very strong in Swansea. Elsewhere in Britain, these years were regarded as a dark period of indifference for the sects – but in upland Glamorgan, rural evangelism actually continued under the first two Georges.[53] Nor did dissent ever lose its lower-class character, for it drew its ministers from colliers, weavers, tailors and hill-farmers.[54]

It also developed a strong rationalistic streak, manifested after 1720 in the growth of arminian and arian ideas. Many congregations were deeply split by the 1730s, and it was the unitarian groups which best preserved the old radicalism. We can observe this in some detail by studying the books read by a circle of dissenting ministers and schoolmasters in the hinterland of Neath and Swansea about 1790. One minister, John Davies of Llansamlet, recorded the books he purchased and lent: apart from mainstream protestant theology and latitudinarian works, the list also included mystical writers like Ruysbroeck, Julian of Norwich, Ignatius Loyola, Augustine Baker – and they even read Gerrard Winstanely, who was unknown even to metropolitan radicals of this time. When it is considered that traditions of political activism were probably *weaker* here than in the eastern uplands, it will become apparent that radicalism was a distinct native growth. Also, Davies' friend Richard Price did not emerge from a politically sterile or 'backward' Wales to shine in London.[55]

Similar radical traditions existed in other pastoral and industrial areas like west Yorkshire and the north Midlands, and it was these once remote and barren parts which were the centers of economic growth after 1760. Populations swelled, and wholly new settlements arose. The uplands of eastern Glamorgan and west Monmouthshire grew in population by some 30 per cent in the first decade of the nineteenth century, and in the west, it was feared in the 1790s that the new industrial village of Morriston would dwarf Swansea itself.[56] Industry and the nascent working classes contributed to the development of the radical and egalitarian ideas long prevalent in these areas, but did not create them. The alleged failure of the anglican Church to meet the challenge of industrialisation is not entirely fair, as it is doubtful whether the Church had ever been strong in such areas.[57] However, these older traditions now merged with class ideologies to create one of the most politically conscious areas of Britain.

Since the 1720s, there had been a series of strikes and riots by the industrial workers of Neath, Swansea and Llanelli,[58] and now industry was attracting thousands from backward rural areas into this radical ambience. Only in Swansea did Glamorgan's dearth of 1766 lead to active protests by the 'poor and distressed'. These involved anonymous threats of revenge against the town's magistrates, and rumours of great gatherings by 'tradesmen, colliers and distressed labourers'.[59] In the widespread Welsh riots of the 1790s, only at Swansea and Merthyr did wage demands accompany the destruction and the clamour for bread, and the Swansea 'patriots' issued a powerful manifesto attacking corn dealers and warning of the revolutionary example recently set by France.[60] The crowd included a large contingent of colliers and copperworkers from the old roundhead parish of Llangyfelach. A very similar pattern can be traced in Merthyr Tydfil, where the radicals read Paine and Voltaire, and accepted the most advanced ideologies of the day.[61] The chartism and industrial radicalism of South Wales were built on foundations centuries old.

When attempting to place the gentry in their social context, it must be emphasised that we are almost invariably dealing with only one of Glamorgan's two societies – that of the south. For the squires, the world of John Davies and the radicals of Merthyr or Llangyfelach belonged to an alien periphery which rarely impinged on their consciousness. Their 'Arcadia' had its boundaries where the hills began. 'Glamorgan' for them meant the peaceful arable Vale country, a rich and long-settled countryside populated by (apparently) docile tenants. Within this narrower geographic context, their authority had been challenged – most clearly at the beginning of our period, more indirectly at its end – but the landed community was normally secure, stable and independent.

At the end of the seventeenth century, the gentry appeared to be at the height of their power. Overt political challenges had been defeated, the economy was expanding rapidly, and the great houses were still inhabited by an ancient and remarkably homogeneous group of families. The next chapter will describe the structure of gentry society at what seemed to be the beginning of such a great age. It will then describe the remarkable rapidity with which the community crumbled from about 1720.

Generally, the period falls into three board segments. There was an age of growing power and independence and self-confidence, from 1660 to 1720; a time of rapid transformation, perhaps even of disaster for some houses, from 1720 to 1760; and finally the construction of a new and very different county community with a renewed aristocracy, from 1760 to 1800. These changes will form the essential framework for the later discussions of economic, political and cultural development.

2

The gentry

1. How many gentry?

Glamorgan's society was dominated by a gentry community very wealthy by Welsh standards, and little inferior to their English counterparts. In the century after 1660, they were also free of the need to compete for social and political power with local aristocrats – the constant problem of their relatives in the counties of Carmarthen and Monmouth. Before the Civil War, Glamorgan had been ruled by the Earls of Pembroke, but this interest was declining by the 1630s. In the 1660s, Glamorgan was again represented in parliament by the last of many MPs from the Pembroke family, but this was the end of a long tradition; and land sales in 1666 and 1668 virtually ended the direct 'Pembroke interest'. It was never fully replaced either by Pembroke's successor (Lord Windsor) or by the Dukes of Beaufort.[1] About 1700, there were still several lords in the county with considerable estates which gave them patronage and electoral influence. Pembroke and Beaufort each dominated the electoral affairs of two of the seven boroughs which combined to elect Glamorgan's borough MP, while major landowners included Lords Ashburnham, Brooke and Abergavenny, and the Earl of Leicester.[2]

However, none of these peers was resident. The Dukes of Beaufort technically had a seat at Swansea Castle, but by the mid eighteenth century this was so dilapidated that it became first a workhouse, and later a debtors' prison. The dukes were therefore distant figures, seen usually on their rare progresses. In the first quarter of the eighteenth century, the only lords who spent any long periods in the county were Lord Windsor (on sporadic visits to Cardiff), and Jocelyn Sydney, a younger son of the Leicester family who had settled at Coity near Bridgend. Nor did the gentry have to concern themselves with episcopal power. Extensive plunder at the Reformation had left the diocese of Llandaff one of the poorest in the Church of England. Even in the village of Llandaff itself, the deteriorating fabric of the cathedral was overshadowed by its neighbour, the mansion of the gentry family of Matthews. Aristocratic power over the gentry was not great by 1700, and it declined still further with their land sales over the next thirty years. By the 1780s, there had been something of an aristocratic revival, with enormous power enjoyed by several resident peers, but it must be emphasised that this was a development from the mid-century.

In the century after the Restoration, Glamorgan was very much a gentry county, and although the greatest family (the Mansells) were raised to the peerage in 1711, this did not have a great effect on the social balance. Nor should it remove them from the scope of the study, for they were still the traditional leaders of the gentry, to whom they remained closely linked by marriage and kinship. However, other problems arise as to the precise definition of the gentry, because contemporary estimates differed so widely as to who constituted the gentry community, or 'gentlemen' at all. Blome[3] in 1673 named 90 Glamorgan 'gentry' below the rank of peer, while Adams[4] in 1690 gave the total as 219, so these two estimates alone differ as to whether the gentry comprised 0.9 or 2.4 per cent of the county's families. We can begin to resolve this problem by applying economic criteria, based on the evidence of the hearth-tax. Firstly, it is very difficult to imagine anyone recognised by contemporaries as a 'gentleman' living in a house of less than 4 hearths, which (in 1670) immediately removes about 92 per cent of households from consideration.[5] In practice, gentry were rather to be found in households of 6 or more hearths, of which there were about 180 in the 1670s, perhaps 2 per cent of the total population. Even a house of 6 hearths did not represent great wealth or state when set against the 18 hearths of the Herberts of Cardiff, or the 30 of the Stradlings of St Donat's. At least, it provides a minimum figure.

The hearth-tax also shows the prosperity of Glamorgan in relation to other Welsh counties of similar area and population. Glamorgan had eight houses with more than 20 hearths, compared to the two of Carmarthenshire or the one of Pembrokeshire. This had important social implications: in Glamorgan the owners of very large houses each represented a very powerful interest, so no one family could long exercise dominant power. By contrast, other Welsh counties were more polarised in wealth, and more prone to magnate domination. In Pembrokeshire, there were thirteen houses with more than 10 hearths (in contrast to Glamorgan's forty-nine), but three of these belonged to one squire. In Carmarthenshire, the Earl of Carbery's house of 50 hearths found its nearest rivals in three mansions with only 18 hearths apiece.

I certainly do not wish to claim that we can use the hearth-tax figures as the basis for any kind of political determinism, but they can be used to suggest the rough balance of power among the elite. They also confirm the theory that Glamorgan's gentry structure was heavily anglicised. Professors Lawrence and Jeanne Stone suggested that some 'index of gentrification' could be produced from calculating the number of very large houses (20 or more hearths) in a county and dividing that into the county's acreage.[6] Surrey would therefore be among the most gentrified, with one great house for every 5,000 acres, followed closely by Hertfordshire with one for every 7,000. These would give 'index numbers' of respectively 5 and 7.

If we extended this, then we would find index numbers between 10 and 20 for counties like Cambridge, Oxford, Suffolk, Warwick or Bedford. Stafford and Dorset would lie between 21 and 30, Shropshire at 60, and the Isle of Ely at 120. Welsh counties would be very much non-gentry areas: Carmarthen's index would be 294, Pembroke's 393. Glamorgan's index (65) would place it close to English border shires like Shropshire or Hereford – but of course, its houses were heavily concentrated in only a quarter of the shire's area. At worst, Glamorgan was as gentrified as a poorer English shire; at best, the Vale was as gentrified as the English Home Counties.

2. The elite

There are many criteria which may be applied to deduce the number of the elite group at the head of the community at any given period. Contemporaries found the leading gentry among those bearing the titles of knight, baronet and esquire – and ten Glamorgan estates were occupied by knights or baronets at some time between 1660 and 1760. In 1673, Blome's *Britannia* listed about 90 leading gentry in the county, including 7 knights and baronets, 37 esquires and 46 gentlemen, and the figure for esquires was roughly confirmed by a list of the 1640s which gave 33 men bearing this title.[7] The division by title is apparently reflected in the distribution of wealth. 'Esquire' and 'gentleman' had not yet become synonyms for mere respectability. There was still a real division between the two, in status and wealth, and in the material possessions which characterised the elite. For instance, 'esquires' in the later seventeenth century were still much more likely than 'gentlemen' to have a house with ten or more hearths, or an income exceeding £500 a year.[8]

This was an intensely hierarchical society, a fact reflected in the care

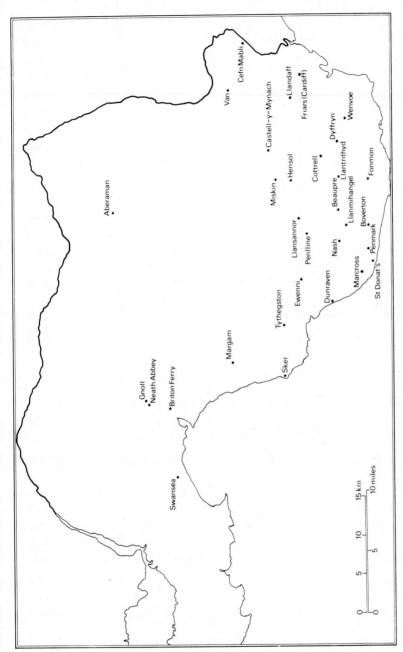

Map 2. The great gentry seats c. 1660 – 1700

Aberaman
Van
Cefn Mabli
Castell-y-Mynach
Llandaff
Friars (Cardiff)
Wenvoe
Dyffryn
Miskin
Hensol
Cottrell
Llantrithyd
Fonmon
Beaupre
Llanmihangel
Boverton
Llansannor
Penlline
Nash
Penmark
Marcross
St Donat's
Ewenni
Dunraven
Tythegston
Margam
Sker
Gnoll
Neath Abbey
Briton Ferry
Swansea

15 km
10 miles

23

Table 1: *Titles, houses and income*

| | Number of families in each social group (Blome) | Owned house of ten or more hearths (1670) | Annual income | | | |
| | | | 1645 | | 1677[a] | |
			£500 – £999	£1,000 or over	£500 – £999	£1,000 or over
Knight/Baronet	7	7 (owned 11 such houses)	0	6	2	5
Esquire	37	22 (owned 26 such houses)	7	4	9	9
Gentlemen	46	2 (owned 2 such houses)	1	0	2	0
Other	0	10 (owned 10 such houses)	2	0	0	0
TOTAL	90	41 owning 47 houses	10	10	13	14

Source: [a] PRO SP 29/398, fos. 257 – 8.

Table 2: The gentry elite 1670 – 1690

Family	Estate	Title c. 1680	Income 1677	Hearths 1670	Deputy-lieutenant	Militia horse[a]	Estate produced MPs 1660–1790
Aubrey	Llantrithyd	Bart	1,300	20(5)†	x	2	x
Bassett*	Beaupre	Knight	500	10(6)	x		
Bassett*	Miskin	Knight	–	10	x		x
Button*	Cottrell	Esq.	500	10	x		
Button*	Dyffryn	Esq.	600	12	x	1	
Carne*	Ewenni	Esq.	500	17(7)			x
Carne*	Nash	Esq.	300	9		1	
Evans	Gnoll	Knight	600	10	x	1	x
Gwyn	Llansannor	Esq.	–	11			x
Herbert*	Friars	Esq.	1,000	18(18)	x		x
Hoby	Neath Abbey	Gent.	800	17	x	1	x
Jenkins	Hensol	Esq.	1,300	18		2	x
Jones	Fonmon	Esq.	1,200	15(7)		2	x
Kemys*	Cefn Mabli	Bart.	1,200	20	x	1	x
Lewis*	Penmark	Knight	500	21	x	1	
Lewis*	Van	Esq.	1,400	20(13)	x	3	x
Lougher	Tythegston	Esq.	300	10	x		
Mansell*	Briton Ferry	Esq.	1,000	22	x	3	x
Mansell*	Margam	Bart.	–	32	x	4	x
Matthews*	Aberaman	Esq.	500	6	x		
Matthews*	Castell-y-Mynach	Esq.	700	10	x		
Matthews*	Llandaff	Esq.	400	13		2	x
Seys	Boverton	Esq.	900	15	x	1	x
Stradling	St Donat's	Bart.	1,500	30(13)	x	1	x

25

Table 2: (*continued*)

Family	Estate	Title c. 1680	Income 1677	Hearths 1670	Deputy-lieutenant	Militia horse[a]	Estate produced MPs 1660–1790
Thomas	Llanmihangel	Knight	1,700	15(9)	x	2	x
Thomas	Swansea	Esq.	800	10(10)			
Thomas	Wenvoe	Esq.	2,000	24(19)	x	2	x
Turberville*	Penlline	Gent.	500	11		1	
Turberville*	Sker	Gent.	300	–			
Van	Marcross	Esq.	–	9(8)			
Wyndham	Dunraven	Esq.	1,000	11(10)		1	x

Note: * Denotes a family whose members served as Glamorgan JPs between 1540 and 1580.
† Figures in parentheses denote the number of hearths recorded in the 1670 tax list.
Source: [a] P&M 3467.

taken to note precedence in lists of gentry, whether these were taken for private or administrative purposes, and these record the 'pecking order' of county society. In 1661, for example, the county's magnates contributed to the royal subsidy separately from the rest of the population, and the list began with Glamorgan's two baronets, followed by two knights and ten esquires.[9] These were part of a widely recognised county elite, whose position was signified by the offices they held, notably as deputy-lieutenants, and of course as members of parliament. Glamorgan had only two seats, but the gentry were sufficiently wealthy and well-connected to obtain seats elsewhere in England or Wales. Between 1660 and 1790, there were 43 MPs whose main interests lay in Glamorgan, representing eighteen estates, and parliamentary representation was widely shared among the elite of the county community: four estates were each represented by 4 members (Margam, Briton Ferry, Gnoll, Llantrithyd); five more were represented by 3 members each (Cefn Mabli, Hensol, Dunraven, Llanmihangel, Llansannor). There were also three estates each with 2 members, and a further six with one each.

There were many other miscellaneous symbols of status which mark this group, like the contribution of a horse to the militia, or widespread ecclesiastical patronage. In 1720, the ability to appoint to three or more livings was held by Lords Mansell and Windsor, and another eight of the great families.[10] Generally, one can discern an elite group of about 25 to 30 families, including all the knights and baronets, and a majority of the esquires. This was a very consistent pattern: of 21 families among the leading gentry in 1600, at least 16 were still among the ruling group in 1700. The families had changed by the nineteenth century, but still in 1873 there was an elite of some 30 great landowners, usually at the seats of their Stuart predecessors.[11]

The geographical distribution of the seats of major families was also remarkably consistent. About 1700, none of the twenty-five greatest houses was in the *Blaenau*, or west of the river Neath. The great house of Margam lay on the western fringe of the Vale, and once a traveller went further west he was leaving the gentry heartland. Only Gnoll and Briton Ferry remained to be seen – and once the river Neath were crossed, Blome only recorded six gentry of any quality whatever. Seventeen of the great houses were in the Vale, all but five being south of the ancient Roman road or 'portway', and it was the Vale that Blome described as 'thick beset with towns, and houses of the gentry'. In the 1870s, it was still said that 'perhaps no part of Wales or England abounds more in spots of distinction and good families than does the district between the river Rhymney below Caerphilly, and Aberavon'.[12] This concentration in the extreme south of the county did not of course mean that their influence was confined here, for they owned land in all parts of the county. Each of the old families had branches scattered throughout Glamorgan, as well as in neighbouring counties. In Blome's list of 90 gentry, no less than 35 derive from just eleven great and long-established houses.

Table 2 lists the families comprising the gentry elite under Charles II, together with the symbols which marked them as leaders of the county community. Such leaders usually came from families who had held county office for at least a century. They were at least esquires, lived in houses of ten or more hearths, and their income often exceeded £1,000 a year. They were members of parliament, deputy-lieutenants and JPs, and they contributed horses to the cavalry of the county militia (this elite segment contributed two-thirds of the militia's horses in the 1670s). Socially they were regarded as worthy companions of the aristocracy, with whom they frequently made marriage alliances.

Most of the great families in 1700 had been established for at least two generations, and some for three centuries or more. At the head of the gentry community in 1700 were the Mansells, who had numerous branches in the west of the county, and those established at Margam and Briton Ferry were among the richest squires in Glamorgan. In 1705, the head of Margam was one of the 'overgrown commoners of vast estates',[13] on a par with West Country magnates like the Seymours and Courtnays. In the next year, this wealth was augmented by the inheritance of Briton Ferry. The Mansells were a medieval family with many offshoots in Ireland and south-west Wales, while the Margam line was much intermarried with most of the other great houses of Glamorgan, like the Carnes and Bassetts.[14] After so many centuries of power and standing, such families had spread their influence and their family connections over a wide area, so that most of the ancient lines were by 1700 established in four or five estates. They might have their rivalries – there might be catholic Matthews at Radyr and extreme whigs at Llandaff – but these 'clan'-like connections were of political substance. A branch of the Carnes or Matthews might so fall on evil days that members of the house might be forced to enter domestic service; but an upstart merchant or parson would soon learn that insulting or abusing such a fallen house meant retaliation from one of the 'Leviathans', the squires of Ewenni or Llandaff.[15]

The history of the gentry community from the fifteenth century to the seventeenth had been one of remarkably steady organic growth. A roll-call of local partisans in the Wars of the Roses would have been remarkably similar to that of the royalists in the Civil War: both would have begun with Mansells, Herberts, Carnes, Matthews and Bassetts. Of course, some families had risen while others had failed, but to a remarkable extent, the winners from political conflicts between 1450 and 1640 had been the old Norman houses. These were the beneficiaries of Tudor policies – not least of the Reformation. Neither Carnes nor Mansells allowed papist sympathies in dogma to overcome the desire for monastic land, and both acquired new seats – respectively at the monasteries of Ewenni and Margam.[16] The Herberts were still more successful, and apart from the main branch at Wilton and Cardiff Castle (the Earls of Pembroke), there were four Glamorgan offshoots. Three of these estates were combined by one branch of the Herberts after the Civil War, which left the Herberts of Friars as one of the wealthiest families in Glamorgan. By 1700, they owned two of the county's largest houses, but they were 'of very ordinary parts'[17] and made little political impact after the Restoration.

Other families rose in Tudor times by a fortunate marriage, a legal career, or success in the general scramble for land. These included the Seys's of Boverton and Gwyns of Llansannor, and Aubreys of Llantrithyd, all as prominent in Georgian times as they had been under Elizabeth, and all represented in many parliaments. Among other families founded on the profits of law and land speculation before the Civil War should be included the Jenkins's of Hensol and Wyndhams of Dunraven, both central to the county's political life at the end of the century.

This community survived the Civil War very well indeed. The leading families in 1700 were almost exactly those who had been sheriffs, JPs or MPs under the Tudors, but there were some newer families – new to Wales, or else new to social power within the county – and the Civil War had been a catalyst for their emergence. Roundheads like Evan Seys or Philip Jones benefited from the temporary eclipse of the power of the Church and the Marquis of Worcester, and from the collapse of the Bolingbroke estate.[18] They were able to create major new Vale estates, Seys at Boverton, Jones at Fonmon. Seys had some inheritance on which to build, as a result of his family's endeavours under Elizabeth, but Jones represented a different breed. He was a military adventurer, said to have increased his annual income from £20 in 1640 to between £1,000 and £2,000 by 1660, and his descendants represented the county in parliament. His ally Edmund Thomas of Wenvoe was a fellow 'Lord' in

Cromwell's 'Upper House', and his heir was another of Glamorgan's five baronets at the end of the century. Other great beneficiaries of the Civil War were the Mackworths of Shropshire, who had also been faithful Cromwellians in a mainly royalist county, and they had been rewarded accordingly. In 1687, they acquired by marriage the Glamorgan estate of Gnoll.

Political adventurism could, however, have its dangers, as is shown by the Thomases of Llanmihangel, who had become one of the county's richest families by 1642, in which year they received a baronetcy. The second baronet, Sir Robert, sought influence and prestige far beyond his means and was ruined by the 1680s. In 1700, Llanmihangel was occupied by Sir Humphrey Edwin, a dissenting London merchant who established his descendants as squires. Apart from these major lines, other landowners had interests which straddled county boundaries. An example was Sir Charles Kemys, who united the two great Glamorgan estates of Ruperra and Cefn Mabli until his death in 1702. The family was widely connected, with four lesser Glamorgan branches, which all looked to Sir Charles as head of the line, with appropriate responsibilities to his 'clan'.[19] Social and economic links between Glamorgan and its eastern neighbour Carmarthenshire were extensive, while west Glamorgan families like the Mansells had junior branches in that county.

3. The lesser gentry

Another group of varying size was also counted as gentry, although not placed among the chief families, and Blome enumerated about sixty from this category. In the late seventeenth century, there was a 'secondary' group of about thirty families who had at least one feature in common with the leading houses, like the title 'esquire', the office of justice, contribution of a horse to the militia, or ownership of a house with more than ten hearths – but their possession of 'elite' offices and titles was sporadic. Below these again, Blome listed 36 'gentlemen' who would never themselves become either a justice or a deputy-lieutenant, and whose houses usually contained between five and eight hearths. Further still down the hierarchy were other families not mentioned at all by Blome, but who would certainly be regarded as 'gentlemen' by themselves and their neighbours. In late Stuart times the lesser gentry were usually constables and sometimes sheriffs, but from about 1710 they were increasingly likely to become justices of the peace as the social group from which the com-

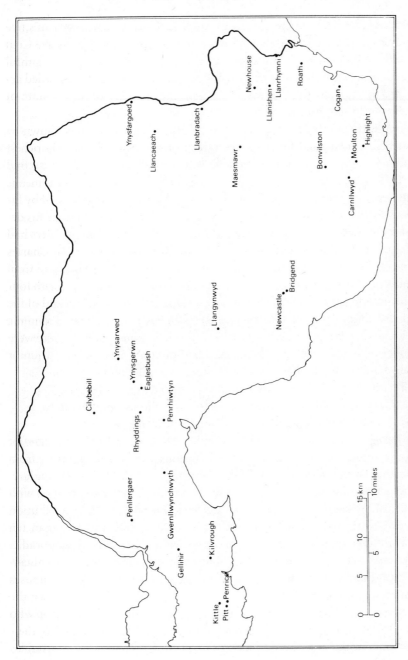

Map 3. The 'secondary' gentry families c. 1660 – 1700

missions were drawn was greatly expanded. About seventy lesser gentry families were added to the Bench for the first time between 1710 and 1763, and this dignity helped to raise their status to 'esquires'.[20] Many of Blome's 'gentlemen' were 'esquires' by the 1730s, and most of these families had attained this level by the 1760s.

I would therefore conclude that at any one time there were normally about thirty families in the gentry elite, another thirty 'secondary' families just below them, and finally some thirty to forty lesser 'tertiary' houses, making a total of ninety to a hundred gentry families.

There was a striking geographical division between the elite group and the remaining gentry, as the lesser squires often lived in areas of the north and west where great seats were not found. There were over a dozen lesser gentry houses west of the river Neath, and a similar number in the *Blaenau* east of it. In the western uplands, for instance, there were important families like the Llewellyns of Ynysgerwn, the Popkins's of Forest, or the Prices of Penllergaer, all of whom were sufficiently powerful to present significant opposition to the Duke of Beaufort in the 1750s. Their geographical distribution meant that these lesser families had a rather different economic basis from the greater estates, and placed most emphasis on coal, timber or sheep farming. Of course, this should not be exaggerated: the great families did not ignore the resources of the hill-country, for the Mansells and Mackworths both exploited the coal and timber of the neighbouring *Blaenau*. Such families owned lands over a wide area of the county, and so inevitably had property of many types. The Van estates owned land in 26 parishes, Margam in 20, Cefn Mabli in 16 (besides 13 more in Monmouthshire). Some families even had mansions in both *Bro* and *Blaenau*, like the Turbervilles (Ewenni and Cilybebill) and the Franklens (Llangyfelach and Clemenston). Moreover, many of the *lesser* gentry lived in the Vale, in the same areas as their greater compatriots. The distribution of justices' seats in the more 'democratic' 1760s did not therefore form a radically different pattern from that of a century earlier. New families added to the Bench in the 1730s and 1740s included old Vale lines like the Deeres or Nicholls, so the geographical division between greater and lesser gentry was by no means absolute.

Nor is there evidence that the two groups saw themselves as distinct bodies, much less as hostile to each other. Many lesser families were offshoots of the great houses and conscious of the fact, while marriages took place between the groups. In the mid seventeenth century, the 'tertiary' Williams's of Aberpergwm were related by marriage to great houses

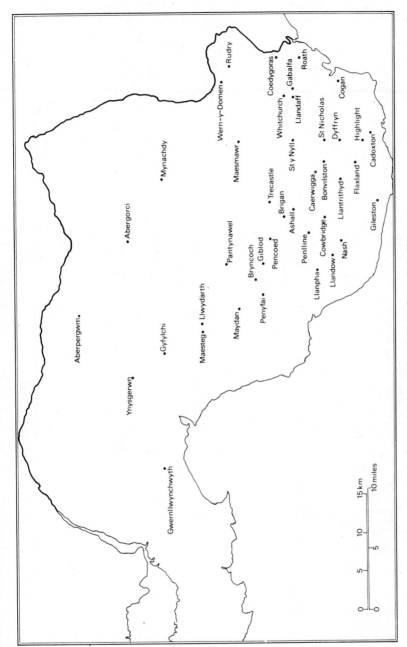

Map 4. Blome's 'gentlemen', 1673

Gwernllwynchwyth

Ynysgerwn

Aberpergwm

Gyfylchi

Maesteg • Llwydarth

Maydan

Penyfai

Abergorci

Mynachdy

Pantynawel

Bryncoch
Giblod
Pencoed

Llanpha
Llandow
Nash

Penlline
Cowbridge
Llantrithyd

Caerwigga
Bonvilston

Gileston

Trecastle
Brigan
Ashall

St y Nyll

Flaxland
Cadoxton

Wern-y-Domen

Maesmawr

Coedygoras
Whitchurch
Llandaff

St Nicholas
Dyffryn
Highlight

Rudry

Gabalfa
Roath

Cogan

15 km

10 miles

33

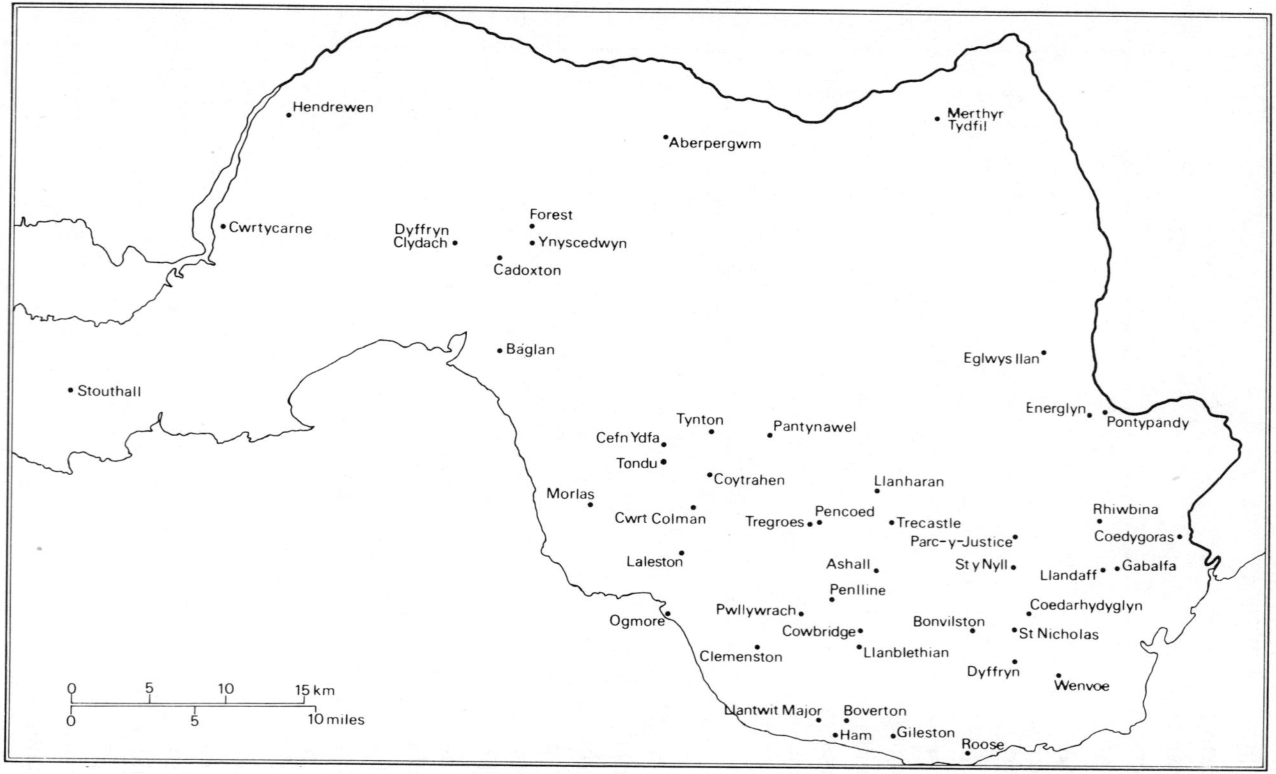

Map 5. The 'tertiary' gentry

34

like those of Beaupre, Miskin, Gnoll, and Briton Ferry. There is little evidence that political or religious conflicts disguised deeper rivalries between the two groups. On the one hand, the minor gentry did predominate in the leadership of the roundhead cause in the 1640s, and in the support of dissent after 1660. Junior branches of families like the Stradlings and Herberts were especially active radicals, and early quakers tended with striking consistency to live in houses of between three and six hearths – the 'rank next JP' as it was aptly described. However, parliament's supporters also included some of the greatest gentry, like the Lewises of Van and Mansells of Briton Ferry. The greater and lesser gentry formed one broad community intimately connected by kinship. It is very difficult to mark definite points of division in the social continuum which extended from the fringes of the aristocracy in one direction to the upper ranks of the yeomanry in the other.

4. Professional and commercial families

Below the gentry proper, there were also 'middle-class' groups which was in itself a fact of some rarity in Wales. In Cardiff, Swansea, Neath and Cowbridge, about 4 or 5 per cent of the population bore some title like 'Mr' or 'gentleman' and lived in a house with six or more hearths. These were town merchants – some as wealthy as considerable squires – or they might be lawyers, doctors, stewards or clergy. All these categories represented means of social advancement for the able and ambitious of quite humble origins, and were ways in which the declining fortunes of petty gentry lines could be restored.[21] Doctors could achieve spectacular success, as did Sir Noah Thomas of Neath who became physician to George III.[22] Others rose through legal careers to achieve the leisure, landed income and official positions which characterised a gentleman, and new estates were created in the eighteenth century by the attorneys Thomas Edwards, Thomas Edmondes, and Anthony Maddocks. The last was said in 1740 to be 'so very proud and rich' that only the personal request of Lord Mansell could win him over in an election.[23] Several others achieved substantial prosperity, often through their participation in vigorous political activity, usually in the whig cause. Two such political barristers became knights – although both George Howell and Thomas Jones were the sons of yeomen.

An example of such a new family taking advantage of political turmoil to clamber up the social hierarchy was the Gibbs' of Neath.[24] In the 1630s,

David Gibbs was a burgess dabbling in the mining and export of coal. He sent his sons to the Inns of Court, and a combination of legal acumen and political adventurism raised the family to the fringe of the gentry elite in the 1690s. David's grandson Marmaduke was a deputy-lieutenant, a whig party organiser received in the greatest houses, and he even married the daughter of a baronet. In Stuart society, politics, law and land speculation were capable of transferring a family from the ranks of the 'pseudo-gentry' in a provincial town to the elite of a wealthy county society.

Success in trade accounted for the prosperity of other 'middle-class' lines, and one could illustrate the rise of mercantile wealth at Cardiff by the history of families like the Purcells, Priests, Richards or Shiers, who were closely intermarried both with each other and with neighbouring doctors and lawyers. At Swansea, there were the families of Padley, Shewen and Rogers, all close to Bristol and the West Indies trade; and such 'dynasties' can be found in all the boroughs. A characteristic figure was the Neath lawyer Elias Jenkins, whose brother was a doctor and JP of nonconformist sympathies, and whose sister married the steward and attorney Hopkin Llewellyn. Such families benefited from the development of industrial and colonial wealth, which set a new premium on professional and commercial expertise. Another major factor was the distribution of government patronage in a county where the tory gentry were largely excluded from office after 1714. In the great election contest of 1745, most of the great gentry were tory, but the whig victory was made possible by the local power of the 'middling' men who were creditors to many local freeholders. These were lawyers like Maddocks and Nathaniel Taynton, or a doctor like Richard Bates, or a vigorous improving landlord and petty squire like Matthew Deere.[25] They were linked to central government by patronage, but they were also close to the whig gentry of the Vale. The wealth and pretensions of these groups grew accordingly, but one rarely hears expressions of 'middle-class' solidarity against the gentry, because the two communities depended so closely on each other. Also, lawyers and merchants were often intermarried with petty gentry, and both groups shared the same aspirations, for the 'middle class' wished to emulate the leisured existence of the squires, together with their more 'honourable' income from land. Of many examples, one could take the Wells family of Cardiff, aldermen at the beginning of the eighteenth century, West Indies merchants and 'squarsons' at its end. The son of the lawyer Thomas Edwards likewise became a 'squarson', with a great house at Llandaff.

The acceptance of this new blood was not difficult for the older gentry, as some of the latter had themselves risen within living memory through trade or the law, and they were still engaged in considerable mining and metallurgical enterprises. The squires were eager to marry the daughters of rich merchant families in London or Bristol, and sons of the gentry were established in trade at Bristol or Swansea. Hostility between provincial towns and the neighbouring gentry was most unlikely when the leading families of even Cardiff and Swansea were Mansells and Herberts, and when local gentry regularly held urban offices like Mayor and Constable of the Castle.

The greater urban families retained a remarkably deferential attitude to local squires at least until the end of the eighteenth century, while each gentry family had its following of influential men in the towns.[26] Commercial and industrial activity brought the gentry into contact with merchants as business partners. Early iron partnerships like the Dowlais venture of 1759 included local gentlemen, and social contacts naturally followed between squires and entrepreneurs. The close interdependence of gentry and professional groups is demonstrated by studying the powerful stewards and estate agents employed by the greater squires. Some were professionals and 'new men', but they were often derived from one's neighbours and relatives among the lesser gentry.

A study of the clergy also suggests the homogeneity of county society, as these were often drawn from the gentry and their relatives.[27] Families with members ordained in the diocese in this period included Carne, Bassett, Gamage, Turberville and all the leading names. As with stewardship, clerical office was an opportunity to rise in the ranks of county society, perhaps by clientage to a great man – even to a royal chaplaincy. There was the remarkable example of John Deere of Penlline, the son of a petty squire, who became a naval chaplain and allegedly left £10,000 at his death in 1764. A *ben trovato* story told by his contemporaries was that he had served Sir Clowdisley Shovell, but had escaped from the wreck which killed his master in 1707; Deere had then swum ashore in the Scillies, carrying a large quantity of the ship's treasure.[28] Wherever the fortune came from, it secured the Deeres in county society thereafter. There was a considerable overlap between gentry, clergy and stewards, and the last two groups were often drawn from the same minor families for generations; and there were cases where clergymen also served as stewards. Ultimately, they could hope to become squires themselves, a success shared by the Portreys, Savours' and Hancornes, as well as the Deeres. Merchants and the rural 'middle class' formed part of one broad county community, of which the landed gentry were the core, and in which the outer limits of gentility are extremely hard to define.

5. Destruction and renewal

The Glamorgan gentry community was close-knit and long-established, but it had dissolved with remarkable rapidity by the mid eighteenth century. It was destroyed by demographic changes similar to those described for the English peerage by Professor Hollingsworth and recently discussed by Dr Bonfield, but in Glamorgan the changes were on a still worse scale.[29] Only four great houses were occupied by the same families in 1770 as in 1650, and the transformation was concentrated in the first half of the eighteenth century. Of thirty-one great estates, only ten were occupied in 1750 by an heir in the male line of the head of the estate in 1700; and two of these ten had only recently arrived in the county in 1700. Hensol was lost by its previous owners when the family failed in the male line in 1721; the same occurred at Dunraven (1725), Cefn Mabli (1735), Van (1736), St Donat's and Friars (both 1738) and Margam (1750), and the rapidity of the changes in the 1730s naturally caused contemporary comment. Some of the estates were divided among heiresses or sold piecemeal, like those of Beaupre and Marcross, while others passed intact to relatives within the county. For example, Richard Carne of Ewenni was the last of his line, and his estate passed in 1713 to his brother-in-law Edward Turberville. Turberville's son later acquired the Cilybebill estate by similar means on the failure of a branch of the Herberts. Such changes affected the balance of wealth and power in county society, and contributed to the reduction of the number of estates by the 1760s – a phenomenon recently described by Dr Martin.[30] Still worse for traditional society was the number of properties passing to families from outside the county, usually of English origin. Of the 25 greatest Glamorgan gentlemen in the 1760s, 12 came from families which had no discernible Welsh links before 1680, and 7 of those had owned no Welsh lands before 1735. By passing through daughters, the line of descent to such estates was maintained, but inheritance by English or out-of-county families implied major social and political changes.

　　The 'strange fatality' of Welsh families from the late seventeenth century was partly attributable to financial problems, and debt caused the loss of the Llanmihangel estate in the 1680s, of Dyffryn in the 1740s, and of Wenvoe in 1769. But more serious was the tendency of families to die out in the male line, which accounted for the change of ownership in nineteen of the

Table 3: *A decline in family size*

Average number of children to father born:	Pre-1640	1641 – 80	1681 – 1739
Group I (greater gentry)	5.0	2.26	2.58
Group II (lesser gentry)	3.85	3.1	3.6

Table 4: *The failure to produce male heirs*

Head of estate	Died unmarried	Married but no children	Married but no surviving male offspring	Total
Group I	12	11	10	33 (34%)
Group II	15	8	23	46 (25.4%)
TOTAL	27	19	33	79 (28.4%)

thirty-one great estates between 1670 and 1770. I have recently studied this phenomenon elsewhere, and attribute the demographic crisis to several factors:

Firstly, there was a sharp decline in the number of children born to fathers who had themselves been born between 1641 and 1680. The decrease was much sharper among the greater gentry (see Table 3). (In the tables which follow, group I represents 97 men from twenty-seven families, who were heads of greater Glamorgan estates between 1660 and 1760; group II represents 181 men from fifty-one families, who headed a secondary or tertiary estate in the same period.)

It can also be shown that it was strikingly common for squires to fail to produce heirs (see Table 4). A third of greater squires and a quarter of lesser squires failed to produce heirs, and particular interest attaches to those who appear to have deliberately created this situation by failing to marry. In a case like the second Lord Mansell (died 1744), his death at the early age of 25 may have tragically prevented his marriage. But there were many cases in which squires reached old age unmarried, although they were well aware that this would mean the end of their lines. In several other cases, great squires left marriage until perilously advanced ages – like their late 40s – and narrowly escaped the loss of family continuity.

Thirdly, a tendency to remain unmarried contributed to the crisis, especially among the greater gentry. The head of a greater gentry estate born

Table 5: *A tendency to remain unmarried*

Head of estate born:	Pre-1640	1641 – 80	1681 – 1739
Group I	–	2 (6.1%)	10 (29.4%)
Group II	2 (3.8%)	2 (3.8%)	11 (14.5%)

Table 6: *Where the gentry found wives 1660 – 1760*

Head of estate married in:	Glamorgan	Rest of Wales	England	Other	Total
Group I	49 (55.1%)	3 (3.4%)	33 (37.1%)	4 (4.5%)	89
Group II	118 (78%)	27 (17.9%)	4 (2.7%)	2 (1.3%)	151

after 1681 was twice as likely to die unmarried as his counterpart from one of the lesser families (see Table 5).

Marrying outside the county community was a fourth factor. The estates of the greater gentry were likely to pass from the older families, but were also more likely to fall to new owners from outside the county altogether (see Table 6). Heads of greater estates were often sufficiently wealthy by 1700 to make their marriages with the daughters of aristocrats or London merchants, or with 'the multitude of great estates and great fortunes in the west of England'.[31]

Finally, the early eighteenth century was an age of heiresses. From roughly 30 great gentry estates, there were no less than eleven occasions between 1721 and 1750 when a great squire died leaving his property to an heiress. Also, these were just the worst years: there were six such occasions between 1681 and 1720, and five more between 1751 and 1780. The opportunities that now presented themselves will be apparent from the career of Thomas Wyndham (1686 – 1752) of Norfolk.[32] He acquired the Dunraven estate by marrying the cousin and heiress of John Wyndham, who died unmarried in 1725. Thomas's second wife was Ann Edwin, whose brother Charles was tory MP for the shire and owner of the Llanmihangel estate. Charles Edwin died in 1756, married but without children – and so Thomas's family now acquired another great estate. Dunraven and Llanmihangel were thus combined into one estate of immense wealth and influence.

But the men who were able to take advantage of this situation were usually English. Daughters of greater gentry were much more likely to marry in England than were the girls of lesser families. Under 4 per cent of lesser gentry daughters married Englishmen, as opposed to 27 per cent of greater gentry daughters. Great estates were therefore likely to pass to English families. For example, the estates of Margam, Briton Ferry and St Donat's were united during the eighteenth century in the hands of one Mansell branch, but after 1750 they each passed to a new English family, respectively from Wiltshire, Derbyshire and Buckinghamshire. Tythegston went to a Bristol family and Cottrell to a Gloucestershire line.

The county's ruling elite became more English – and at the same time, increasingly aristocratic. Already in the 1730s, Lord Talbot owned Hensol and Castell-y-Mynach, while Van and St Fagan's were held by the Earl of Plymouth. By 1770, Glamorgan had ceased to be the pure gentry society it had been in 1700, as the elite now included a group of very rich peers – Talbot, Plymouth, Bute, Vernon and Llandaff. The first four of these all acquired their Glamorgan properties (between 1721 and 1766) by marrying heiresses. By the beginning of the next century, this aristocratic revival was pushed still further when the marriage of heiresses permitted the establishment in the county of the Earls of Dunraven and Dynevor.

The process of change did not work solely to the disadvantage of Glamorgan families, and some English gentry who similarly failed in the male line sometimes left their estates to their Glamorgan heirs. These latter often preferred their new homes as a permanent residence, and so they became absentees in their original county, thus weakening still further the traditional community. From the 1630s, the Lewises of Van were as likely to live in Wiltshire, Buckinghamshire or Hampshire as in Glamorgan, and the line failed altogether in 1736. In the eighteenth and nineteenth centuries, the Aubreys preferred their Buckinghamshire estate of Boarstall to such an extent that Victorian writers compared them to the worst Irish absentees. Francis Gwyn of Llansannor was born at the Somerset home of his mother's family, and he obtained by marriage the Dorset estate of Forde Abbey, so the Gwyns spent little time in Glamorgan after about 1720. The last of the Matthews's of Llandaff died in Bath, where he had spent many years, and the last Herbert of Friars lived and died at Windsor. Absenteeism among the few surviving ancient families was reflected in the lack of significant building activity in the county in the first half of the eighteenth century, and a decline in those forms of art and literature traditionally patronised by the gentry. A community which had experienced few radical changes since before the days of Elizabeth was thus transformed in a generation.

A spate of new building from about 1760 marked the establishment of a new county community on the ruins of the old, and these new families were by the 1780s the main elements of Glamorgan's political society. They were of very diverse origins, with a few families representing industrial and commercial wealth already becoming justices or deputy-lieutenants, but these were few considering the enormous economic changes under way in much of the county. There were some old families from the gentry elite, like the Joneses, Gwyns and Mackworths, and others were the English heirs of great families of Stuart times, like the Tyntes, Hursts or Jenners. However, the new gentry elite was largely composed of families long-established in the county, who can often be traced from the Middle Ages, but who had been of little account before 1700. Some were petty offshoots of the Carnes, Bassetts and Mansells, others were less prestigious, but the common factor was that they had risen through professional careers, as clergy, stewards, or lawyers, like the Nicholls, Deeres, or Powells of Llanharan. About twelve of the 42 deputy-lieutenants of 1790 were from the minor families gradually added to the Bench of justices from mid-century,[33] and others had succeeded through law or commerce, for there were five 'urban' gentry who gave their addresses only as Neath, Swansea or Cardiff. This new county community is clearly apparent from the 1760s when it was responsible for the new building activity: about eighteen new gentry houses were built in Glamorgan between 1760 and 1810, as compared with only nine between 1640 and 1760. Moreover, these families often survived into the twentieth century. They maintained a long dominance over the county's political life, and resumed to some degree the patronage of its culture which had characterised Glamorgan's ancient Norman families.[34]

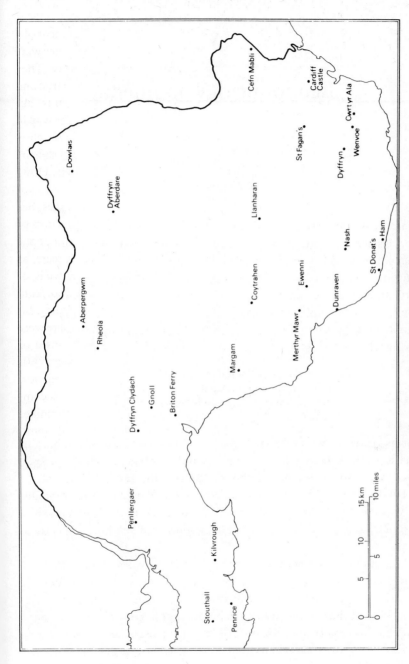

Map 6. Continuity: the seats of the landed elite in 1873

3

Economic development

Introduction

I have referred to the elite families as 'great gentry' in the context of Glamorgan, but this does not suggest their status relative to landowners from elsewhere in Britain. Wales was proverbial for poor but proud gentlemen who would have been dwarfed by even the yeomen of Kent or Norfolk. In Caernarvonshire or Merionethshire in the early eighteenth century, an annual income of only £800 was very rare, at a time when this would not have put most English squires in the first rank of their communities. A typically Welsh pattern was that of Radnorshire, where the saying went:

> 'Alas alas poor Radnorshire
> Never a park, not even a deer,
> Never a squire of five hundred a year
> Save Richard Fowler of Abbey Cwm-hir.'

But as so often, we find that Glamorgan followed English rather than Welsh patterns. If we take the English criterion of 'great gentry' as those possessing annual incomes of about £1,000 in the 1670s (£2,000 about 1710) then about fifteen Glamorgan estates would qualify. This community was not dissimilar in wealth from Dr Roebuck's sample of Yorkshire baronets; and (it will be argued) at least equal to many European aristocrats.

This chapter examines the means by which the wealth of the gentry rose dramatically during the eighteenth century, and stresses both demographic factors and improved estate administration. In the light of Dr Martin's recent study of the landed estate in Glamorgan, I have not made a detailed study of this county in the context of the debate over the 'rise of the great estates'. Professors Habakkuk and Mingay suggested that small estates were swallowed up by their richer neighbours, but Dr Martin shows that the Glamorgan pattern was more complex. Estates did grow, and there was a concentration of landed wealth, but it was by no means all to the advantage of the great gentry. Indeed, she shows that the lesser estates stood a good chance of surviving intact the century after 1660: 70 per cent of these remained in 1760, while only 50 per cent of the great estates were so fortunate. I would differ from her findings in only one major matter, which is to place more emphasis on demographic change. This made the fate of landed estates into much more of a lottery in which great or small landowners could win or lose all.

But if soaring wealth cannot be attributed to the greater acreage of estates, how is it to be explained? A major theme of this chapter is the process of intensive development and general 'improvement' which prevailed in the county during the long depression of agricultural prices between about 1660 and 1750. Two main phases can be noted in economic development (both agricultural and industrial – the two were closely related). In the first, between about 1680 and 1710, Glamorgan acquired a large industrial base through the activity of the greater gentry. In the second, between 1760 and 1790, a group of new gentry embarked on a far-reaching campaign to make Glamorgan fit for the new industrial world, with adequate agriculture, roads, harbours and towns. In studying the origins of this second movement, I will examine the concept of a 'modernising ideology', and concentrate on the role of certain professions in society. Stewards seem to have been particularly important in the personnel of the 'improving' movements and these will be considered in detail. Finally, economic development will be examined in its political context, with especial regard to the importance of war and government office for economic survival.

1. Wealth

Glamorgan seems from the tax assessments of the late seventeenth century to have been poorer than all but a handful of English counties, but this is misleading, as such assessments were notorious in underestimating wealth in the north and west.[1] In fact, the gentry had access to a large variety of sources of income in a county rich in minerals and fertile land, while a great estate could normally raise three or four thousand pounds from timber sales in time of crisis.[2] Tithes were a major element in most estates, and most of the larger families owned properties in at least one other county;[3] while government office provided incidental income for the great houses.[4] However, the most important single item throughout the period was the income from agriculture, the rental and the miscellaneous dues surviving

Table 7: Estate incomes

Family	Estate	1645	1660	1677	Rentals	Estimates
Aubrey	Llantrithyd	1,000				
Bassett	Beaupre	1,000		1,300		1,000 (1696)[l]
Bassett	Miskin	600	800	500		
Button	Cottrell	400			1,100 (1685)[a]	
Button	Dyffryn	400		600	800 (1731)[b]	
Carne	Ewenni	1,000		500		
Carne	Nash			300		
Evans	Gnoll		1,500	600	2,000 (1729)[c]	
Gwyn	Llansannor	600				
Herbert	Friars	1,000	1,000	1,000		
Hoby	Neath Abbey			800		
Jenkins	Hensol		1,500	1,300		1,500 (1660s)[m]
Jones	Fonmon			1,200		1,500 – 2,000 (1670)[n]
Kemys	Cefn Mabli	1,800		1,200	1,500 (1670s)[d] 2,500 (1720)[e]	1,800 (1650s)[o]
Lewis	Penmark	800		500		
Lewis	Van	5,000		1,400		5,000 (1670)[p]
Lougher	Tythegston	400		300		
Mansell	Briton Ferry			1,000		2,000 (1700)[q]
Mansell	Margam	4,000			2,700 (1650s) 2,700 – 3,000 (1700 – 10)[f]	
Matthews	Aberaman	800		500		
Matthews	Castell-y-Mynach	800	1,100	700		1,000 (1662)[r]
Matthews	Llandaff		1,000	400		1,200 (1662)[s]
Morgan	Ruperra	1,000				
Seys	Boverton			900		

Table 7: (cont.)

Family	Estate	1645	1660	1677	Rentals	Estimates
Stradling	St Donat's		2,000	1,500	1,883 (1710)[g]	
Thomas	Llanmihangel	1,600		1,700	1,800 (1670s)[h]	
					900 (1681)[i]	
Thomas	Swansea	600		800		3,500 (1680s)[t]
Thomas	Wenvoe	2,500		2,000		
Turberville	Penlline			500	700 (1680s)[j]	
Turberville	Sker	600		300	200 (1680)[k]	
Van	Marcross	500				
Wyndham	Dunraven			1,000		

Source: [a] P&M 1027, 1031, 1035.
[b] CCL MS 4.722.
[c] ULS Mackworth MSS 163, 1454.
[d] Newport Public Library M 466.7, 5961.
[e] CCL MS 2.1261.
[f] GRO D/DMa/1-4; D/DP/877; P&M 2479, 2265, 6778. For the 1650s, P&M 2265.
[g] Merthyr Mawr House, Glamorgan, unnumbered rental.
[h] NLW Add. MS 1102E, fo. 22.
[i] CCL MS 3.722.
[j] L. J. Hopkin-James, Old Cowbridge (Cardiff, 1922), p. 198.
[k] Ibid.
[l] E. Lhuyd, 'Parochalia', Arch. Camb., 6th ser., 11 (1911), supplement, 'Miskin'.
[m] John Aubrey, Brief lives, ed. O. L. Dick (London, 1972), p. 334.
[n] Veysey, 'Philip Jones', pp. 283 – 6.
[o] Country Life, 24 (1908), p. 742.
[p] W. J. Smith (ed.), Calendar of Salusbury correspondence (Cardiff, Board of Celtic Studies, 1954), pp. 192 – 3.
[q] P&M L13373.
[r] G. T. Clark, Limbus patrum Morganniae et genealogiae (London, 1886), Matthews genealogies.
[s] Ibid.
[t] HMC 78 Hastings MSS, vol. 2, pp. 234 – 7.

from feudal titles. Any survey of the economic position of the gentry must therefore begin with the lands.

Unfortunately, not all the gentry left as many records as the Mansells of Margam, so knowledge of a family's income often depends on chance references and estimates, though these may be very inaccurate. It was a friend and contemporary who described the head of Margam in 1706 as 'Tom of ten thousand',[5] even though this may have involved trebling his income. Nor can the ownership of manors prove the precise wealth of a house. All that can be said is that, generally, the leading owners of manors were also the wealthiest gentry – the Mansells, Stradlings, Aubreys, Bassetts, and Lewises.[6] On the other hand, we are fortunate in having a list written by Sir Edward Mansell of Margam in 1677,[7] where he tries to give exact figures for the incomes of the various squires. Both he and his stewards were widely connected with the county families, and the figures set out in Table 7 agree broadly with those given by Richard Symonds in 1645[8] and a government estimate of 1660,[9] so they provide a fairly reliable basis for the economic structure of the community.

Glamorgan's greater estates were usually worth over £500 a year, and at least eighteen of them were credited with an income of £1,000 or more at some time between 1640 and 1710. This omits the aristocratic estates of Pembroke, Leicester and Worcester, each drawing between one and two thousand pounds a year from Glamorgan in the 1670s.[10] By about 1710, gentry families with over £2,000 per annum included all the five baronets, two knights and two esquires, so the highest gentry titles continued to correspond to real wealth and power. It is striking to find that the Glamorgan community was therefore not inferior to the income levels of English gentry families at this time as analysed by Professor Mingay.[11] Of course, by Welsh standards it was a very wealthy community indeed. The Morgans of Tredegar[12] (Monmouthshire) and the Mostyns of Flintshire[13] may have had three or four thousand pounds a year in the later seventeenth century, but normally it was very difficult to find a Welsh or Border squire worth over £1,000 a year. Great landowners like the Harleys[14] or the Vaughans[15] were remarkable in their respective counties (Herefordshire and Cardiganshire) with incomes of about £1,500, which would only have put them on terms of equality with ten or more Glamorgan houses.[16]

Below the Glamorgan magnates, there is not nearly so much evidence for the thirty-six 'secondary' families of lesser 'esquires' and more substantial 'gentlemen'. Sir Edward Mansell listed four of this group because of their contemporary political significance, and placed all at between £250

Table 8: *Incomes of grades of gentry*

Type of gentry	Number of families	Range of income c. 1700 (£)
Elite	25 – 30	400 – 5,000
Secondary	30 – 40	150 – 400
Tertiary	30 – 40	50 – 200

and £350 a year. Tentatively, we may place most of this group at between £150 and £350 a year, a typical example being David Evans of Gwernllwynchwyth, 'gentleman', with a house of six hearths in 1670, and an annual income of £250. Below these again were the 'gentlemen' mentioned by Blome, of families not added to the Bench until the mid eighteenth century. Their income is largely a matter of speculation, and of extrapolation from the wealth of their heirs. In the 1670s this group probably had incomes of between £50 and £200 a year, although some might have had as little as £30. There would have been no hard-and-fast divisions between these lesser families and the yeomen below them, or the greater families above. Again, most of the county's clergy were on a level with these tertiary gentlemen.[17] Only nine livings had over £100 a year, including only one over £150; and this relative poverty explains the slowness of the Glamorgan gentry to accept clerical justices in the eighteenth century.[18] I would suggest a structure like that shown in Table 8.

2. The leviathans

General economic fluctuations could have a dramatic effect on the wealth of Glamorgan estates. The thirty years after the Restoration were by general agreement parlous for rents, and many causes and nostrums were suggested by pamphleteers, but the economic effects of the lack of demand were indisputable.[19] In the 1670s, minor markets like that of Aberafan ceased to function, while the great livestock marts of Cardiff and Newport produced few sales. Low rents gave an advantage to tenants, and money was short for landlords, 'land being a very drug, and no tenants that will pay honestly are to be had in the country'.[20] In the 1690s, John Wyndham of Dunraven urged his son not to evict tenants, 'which God forbid', and this may have owed less to social paternalism than to his awareness of the difficulty of finding replacements.[21] Monmouth's rebellion aggravated the situation,[22] while landowners complained ceaselessly of the land tax of the next decade.[23] Agriculture enjoyed better times in the eighteenth century, despite a depression in the 1730s and 1740s, 'bad for corn and horn', when a period of low demand and prices alternated with a brief time of terrible weather and food shortages.[24] Dr Martin has recently suggested that this depression was much milder in Glamorgan than in some English counties, but my findings tend to support Professor Mingay's original suggestion that we are dealing with a widespread crisis.[25] Neighbouring Monmouth-shire experienced it badly, and the diary of William Thomas shows what a frightful memory these years still left in popular memory a generation later. There were also widespread food riots in West and North Wales.[26] But despite these problems, it was in these years that the advantage passed to the landlords, for whom there began a long age of prosperity. Landed income rose steadily and the greater families who had had an annual rental of £1,000 a year in the 1670s had often trebled this by the 1790s, while an income of £1,000 came to mark the 'tertiary' estates.[27]

This was one symptom of a concentration of landed estates, caused less by any inherent advantages of the largest properties (or any new legal processes)[28] than by the same genealogical trends which helped to eliminate the old county families.[29] Failures in the male line often caused the combination of already substantial properties, so that in the 1740s Lords Mansell and Talbot each owned at least two estates which had once supported a member of the county elite.[30] (The Mansells had Briton Ferry and St Donat's, and Talbot had Castell-y-Mynach as well as Hensol.) Sir Charles Kemys-Tynte gained Penmark and Highlight in addition to Cefn Mabli and his original properties in Somerset. By contrast, some families were forced to sell their estates because they were unable to cope with social obligations and new tastes, or with economic fluctuations, and so sank into debt. Some properties passed intact to new owners, but others like Marcross were divided among great landlords. This increased still further the power of the 'Leviathan of law and lands'[31] which was threatening the unfortunate and inefficient. Another element was the tendency of families whose chief interests lay outside the county to dispose of their Glamorgan estates to solve temporary difficulties, for the purchasers were often established gentry. The Earls of Leicester gradually disposed of their lands for such reasons in the 1730s, and Lord Windsor's sale of his western lordships in 1715 greatly benefited the Mackworths. Not until the very end of the century was the Marquis of Bute (heir of Windsor) able to halt encroachment on his land by local squires.[32] By the late eighteenth century, the nineteen leading families of the Vale owned two-thirds of the area's land, and very similar concentrations took place about this time in the counties of Pembroke and Monmouth.[33]

This scale of wealth established the Glamorgan gentry as worthy counterparts of the English squires, and not merely as 'Welch ragamuffins', but
it should be emphasised that it made them substantial figures by European
standards. It is often surprising to a British economic historian to find just
how small 'great' estates were on the European Continent in comparison
with those of the English or even Welsh gentry. In the area of Brie, south-
west of Paris, 'large estates' about 1730 might only be of 500 acres, on a
par with the properties of some yeomen in the Vale. The Venetian 'great estate' of Anguillara covered only 1,000 acres in the 1760s, a period in which
Glamorgan perhaps had fifty estates exceeding this size.[34]

Of particular interest here is Dr Forster's study of the diocese of
Toulouse in the eighteenth century,[35] for this was an area of roughly the
same size and rural population as contemporary Glamorgan. There were
226 nobles here, as compared with about 90 gentry in Glamorgan. In
Toulouse, the noble families owned 44.4 per cent of the diocese's land
about 1750; by contrast, in the Glamorgan of 1780, Mr Brian James's
study of landownership patterns has shown that forty-seven families
owned 80 per cent of the land.[36] In Toulouse, the seven greatest noble
houses each owned over 1,000 acres and the richest in 1750 had 1,621
acres. In 1780, the Vale alone had nineteen estates of over 1,000 acres, and
this included Robert Jones of Fonmon with nearly 9,000 acres, Sir Thomas
Aubrey with 6,000, and another four with about 4,000 acres. The richest
marquis in Toulouse owned the same amount of land as, say, the Reverend
John Carne of Nash or the *nouveau riche* Thomas Edmondes of Cowbridge. Clearly, 'esquire' in eighteenth-century Glamorgan implied an
economic status at least equivalent to the highest Continental titles of nobility.[37]

3. An age of improvement

However, the rise in landed incomes is not merely a matter of increased acreage: even after his land sales, the Glamorgan income of Lord Windsor
rose by some 66 per cent between 1670 and 1745. Similarly, the Margam
estate was in the 1750s divided from its recent acquisitions at Briton Ferry
and St Donat's, but this did not prevent its income rising during the course
of the century from three to eight thousand pounds.[38] Mineral exploitation
can account for only part of the remaining increase, and the answer must
partly be sought in improvements in agricultural techniques, which allowed more profitable land-use.

It was widely recognised that land in Glamorgan was often yielding only

a part of its true potential. Documents often mention lands where improved techniques could raise the value by 200 per cent or more in a primitive area like Llangyfelach, and also in the heart of the Vale, and such estimates are found at least as early as the 1650s.[39] Opinions varied as to the
zeal of the landowners in meeting this challenge. In 1768 Arthur Young
found the husbandry of the western Vale 'the most imperfect I ever met
with',[40] while others would later attack Glamorgan practices like 'paring
and burning' which impaired the long-term fertility of the land.[41] However, Young admitted that he had not carried out an exhaustive survey of
the county's economy, and he was prepared to admit that the methods he
was advocating might be less suited to a county with such a strong element
of dairy agriculture. There was considerable awareness of new techniques,
which at least some squires were prepared to put into practice. There is no
evidence in Glamorgan to support Professor Mingay's suggestion that the
low level of prices 'had much to do with the larger owners' loss of interest
in commercial farming', which resulted from their preference for other
forms of investment.[42] Agricultural improvement continued apace, and
was actually stimulated by improvements in other areas of activity such as
industry.

Already in the 1670s, Sir Edward Mansell mentioned three greater gentlemen 'wholly addicted to husbandry' like Martin Button of Dyffryn, 'improving his estate being his greatest study'.[43] The Kemys family of Cefn
Mabli were close to the improver Yarranton – perhaps through mutual
friendship with Lord Wharton.[44] The efforts of such men were obvious
long before Young's visit: Glamorgan actually influenced other counties
by its use of lime as a fertiliser, and the Vale was so little affected by enclosures in the eighteenth century because the process had gone so far in the
previous two centuries.[45]

Another index of improvement was the introduction of clover, which
was known in Gower from at least the 1680s. With trefoil, evir and ryegrass, clover was commonplace in the county in the 1740s and 1750s,
when it was mentioned at Margam, Nash, Gnoll, Cottrell and Merthyr
Mawr.[46] Young believed that the use of turnips was unknown in the
county, and that an Englishman who introduced them was at first thought
mad by his Welsh neighbours; but turnips were known at Gileston in
1740, and the county may even have exported them a century earlier.[47]
These crops permitted the improvement of livestock, for there was less
need to slaughter beasts at the commencement of winter (the Welsh word
for November is *Tachwedd*, 'Slaughter'). More scientific interest could

develop in stockbreeding, by squires like Richard Turberville or Herbert Mackworth.[48] Yet another aspect of agrarian improvement before 1700 was the interest taken by Sir Charles Kemys in recently developed types of apple from Herefordshire and Monmouthshire, for these could improve the manufacture of cider.[49] It is a striking tribute to the work of such men that most of the enthusiastic improvers of the late eighteenth century found little but praise for some aspects of Glamorgan's agriculture, including its rotations, fertilisers, enclosures and farmhouses, although they were normally prepared to criticise bitterly anything which fell short of their ideal.[50] Young might have found Glamorgan agriculture at a low ebb; but seventy years earlier, it had been extremely progressive.

Ultimately, the greatest stimulus for 'improvement' probably came from the growth of industry, firstly around Neath and Swansea from the 1690s, and later on a much larger scale at Merthyr Tydfil. By the end of the eighteenth century, demand had risen to such an extent that Glamorgan became a net importer of corn, and Malkin in 1803 said that land there could fetch a rate as high as if it were within five miles of London.[51] But there were other incentives to improvement, not least from books and journals.[52] For new methods were propagated by books and journals, like the *Mistery of husbandry* and the numerous works on fruit trees found in the Margam library of the 1740s. In 1765, Herbert Mackworth's purchases included Randall's *Seedplough*, Duhamel's *Agriculture* and the *Museum*. Undoubtedly the close economic relationship with the South-West helped the spread of new ideas: Devon's agriculture had been regarded as among the best in Britain in the 1650s, and clover and ryegrass seeds were shipped across the Bristol Channel to Aberthaw in the 1690s.[53] Several Glamorgan landlords also held properties in other progressive areas, like Thomas Wyndham of Dunraven who had estates in Norfolk as well as Glamorgan and Gloucestershire. The Duke of Beaufort was one of the greatest magnates in Wiltshire and Gloucestershire as well as in South Wales, and in 1741 he helped his friend Herbert Mackworth hire a Wiltshire shepherd to teach the latest methods of penning sheep – a process which Young later described as unheard of in Glamorgan.[54]

There were powerful forces resisting innovation, such as the tithes denounced as a 'tax' on improvement by several progressive writers, or the heriots in kind which discouraged better stockbreeding.[55] There was also the conservatism of tenants, although we must remember that Thomas Wyndham was fresh from Norfolk when he wrote of Cowbridge in 1745, 'the meadows, pastures of a pound an acre ancient rent, are ruined for want of a day's labour to clear the ditches, open the drains, cut the fen, etc., which no Welsh tenant will do'.[56] In 1750, the steward of St Donat's commented that 'there is no changing tenants in this country, the country is so universally poor and changing is generally for the worse'.[57] But the chronology of such comments may only reflect a temporary loss of the initiative to tenants in time of depression.[58] However, new processes would clearly need vigorous policies from the landlord and his agents before they would be accepted, and this appears to have been the decisive element in raising the income of the great estates. Better administration can be detected in the widespread replacement of leases for years for terms of lives, a change well under way by 1750. Casual charges like heriots and entry fines were exploited more efficiently, and these accounted for nearly half of the 17 per cent increase of the Margam rental between 1724 and 1729.[59] As the agricultural environment recovered, the landowners were taking every opportunity to defend and extend their rights.

4. Stewards

Such policies put a very high responsibility on the estate stewards, the importance of which office for agricultural development has been stressed by Professors Mingay and Hughes, and more recently in Dr Martin's study of Glamorgan estates.[60] Stewards were employed by virtually all the gentry elite by the late seventeenth century, although there were occasional cases where relations might administer a property during a minority. Stewards were essential where lands were widespread – perhaps over several counties – and they might employ a small hierarchy of officials. By the eighteenth century, the administration of the great estates was increasingly imitated by rising families like those of Forest and Llanharan, and no doubt many others who now acquired professional agents. Stewards were responsible for the collection of rents and for everyday supervision of the great estates; they drew leases and served as the master's legal representative in frequent legal disputes, while elections required their services in gathering votes. Their functions were numerous, but were perhaps best epitomised as constant vigilance. They had, for instance, to preserve coastal lands, to take immediate action when a casual charge fell due (as when a tenant died) – and even to undertake historical research, in the form of transcribing ancient deeds and charters.[61] An enormous variety of functions is described in the diary of John Bird, the Bute steward at Cardiff in the 1790s. He was responsible for distraints and evictions, attending trials at Hereford, purchasing lands, maintaining the sea-wall, improving roads and lighthouses, and transcribing charters.[62] At Cardiff, the Bute stewards held civic offices, so Bird was often Constable of the Castle, or Mayor.[63]

A special burden fell on the steward during a minority in his lord's family. Dr Roebuck's study of Yorkshire estates regards a minority as a golden opportunity for a family to retrench and control expenditure, but it was also a time of danger.[64] Encroachments were doubly likely, and many of Beaufort's disputes in the 1750s stemmed from policies in the third Duke's minority from 1714 to 1728.[65] There were normally minorities in two or three of the great estates at any one time, as in the mid-1720s when Fonmon, Wenvoe and Margam were all affected. When a steward had so many diverse functions, it could justly be remarked that rent-collection was the least important aspect of his responsibilities, and the wide range of skills he required was recognised by a good salary. In the 1660s, the Margam steward was earning £40 a year, in addition to board and lodging, so he was on terms of equality with petty gentlemen. In 1765, Hopkin Llewellyn was engaged at Margam at a salary of £100, with £20 more for a 'writing clerk', and this rose to £230 by 1798, making him well-paid by the standards of English stewards.[66] During this period, there appeared a number of excellent manuals for the growing profession of stewards, but the best index of their increased skill and diligence is the greater wealth of the landed estates by the end of the eighteenth century.

A steward could either simply collect rents and supervise the estate, or else seek to improve its value by a more advanced leasing policy, new farming methods and more intensive mineral exploitation: but whether he was to maintain or to improve depended on the outlook of his master no less than on his own ability. For example, although the execution of improvements was in the hands of subordinates, it was essential to give full support to an efficient steward who would inevitably arouse fierce opposition – as did all the Gabriel Powells, Hopkin Llewellyn of Margam, and Thomas Edwards of Cardiff. Squires had to control and supervise the powerful stewards who handled large sums of money on their behalf, and had to exercise care in choosing men like the Margam agent who in 1661 could be trusted to carry £300 to Bristol.[67] Other stewards founded landed estates by their exploitation of dubious titles to land properly belonging to their employers: Philip Williams of Dyffryn was able to do this from the 1690s when the Neath Abbey property he administered passed to absentees.[68] Stewards were often attorneys who worked for several gentlemen apart from their employers, and it was necessary to ensure that lawyers did not betray the interests of their lords. For example, the first Gabriel Powell (died 1736) worked for half a dozen local gentry houses in addition to the Duke of Beaufort whom he theoretically served. Stewards were frequently accused of petty offences like grazing their own livestock in the deer park, taking the estate's lime or building stone for personal use, or using the lord's workmen, as well as of minor peculation and neglect of duty.[69]

Therefore, the squires themselves were chiefly responsible for economic success or decline. Both Herbert Mackworths were deeply interested in improvement, by means of which the value of the Gnoll estate increased in the eighteenth century from two to five thousand pounds a year. The first Herbert Mackworth appointed efficient agents whom he could trust and regard as friends, and who undertook the exploitation of the estate's resources, both in Glamorgan and Shropshire. Like so many other squires, Mackworth tended to use English stewards, who did not have local relatives to benefit at the expense of the estate. There were long lists of English names among the stewards of the Mackworths, Morgans of Tredegar, and Earls of Pembroke. One could also seek security through the employment of men of similar religious and political sympathies, as in the 1670s when the recently catholic Marquis of Worcester employed as steward the Glamorgan catholic, Charles Price. Philip Jones the roundhead used his radical puritan ally and kinsman Evan Lewis in this capacity, but these links did not prevent Lewis from embezzling five or six hundred pounds from his master.[70]

The Mackworths were well served; but at the opposite extreme were the Aubreys of Llantrithyd, who owned over 6,000 acres in the Vale, but who were notorious absentees. Perhaps predictably, their stewards rose from being petty tradesmen and attorneys to the position of great gentry in their own right, so the new house of Edmondes entered the county community. They acquired the Beaupre estate in 1755, and it was soon said that they were richer than their masters. It may be an adverse comment on the level of supervision exercised by some gentry that so many fortunes were made by the families of stewards. During the eighteenth century, the Windsor estate was served as stewards by members of the local families of Traherne, Lloyd, and Llewellyn. The persistent rumours about their corruption seem to be well confirmed by the fact that all rapidly managed to raise their families from the mere fringes of gentle status to the highest ranks of the county community. It may in fact be that the long absence of resident landlords permitted through such means the creation of a new gentry drawn from the ranks of the professional classes.

So despite the county's potential wealth, the improvement of the great estates during the eighteenth century must have owed much to the diligence no less than the entrepreneurial ethos of the gentry. Only within this framework of supervision and support could estate administration have become so profitable.

5. Industry

We will also observe this pattern in examining industrial development, where the traditional gentry were clearly active and progressive improvers highly conscious of the need for financial survival. It is sometimes tempting to relate the increased efficiency of administration to the influence of new families – perhaps puritans – who were not constrained by traditional social obligations, and who felt that a higher rental outweighed the advantages of a numerous, loyal, but poor tenantry. Sir Humphrey Edwin was such a 'new man', whose rigid enforcement of his rights at Llanmihangel in the 1690s evoked a series of protests and lawsuits from tenants.[71] But the economic backwardness of the older families should certainly not be exaggerated, for they had no prejudices against commerce or industrial exploitation. In the 1670s, the estates of Tredegar, Fonmon and Briton Ferry had all owned and traded with ships, and the main lesson that emerges from studying gentry economic activities is their total opportunism.[72] If a squire lived in coal country, he owned mines; if near the sea, he traded; if neither of these, he prospected for what minerals there might be. Finally, if all these resources failed, he loaned money at interest. When new industrial opportunities appeared after the Restoration, the gentry became the most fervent of entrepreneurs.[73]

Glamorgan's industrial development began in medieval times, with monastic exploitation of the coal reserve near Neath and Margam.[74] By our period, there were still piecemeal coalworkings for the domestic needs of local farmers, as at Cilybebill where squire Richard Herbert had in the 1690s 'good coal works for his own use and his tenants'.[75] There were, however, serious obstacles to the growth of large-scale industry, which make still more impressive the achievement of the gentry. They could not yet overcome the geographical isolation which prevented the use of rich areas like the Rhondda valley until Victorian times. They also had to face social factors in those areas where exploitation was technically possible, as in the west where there was widespread hostility to commercial mining among small farmers, who feared the depletion of reserves. Moreover, traditional society disliked industrial workers whose mores and social organisation they could neither tolerate nor understand. Great hostility was expressed to such groups by the burgesses of Neath and Cowbridge, who also feared an increased burden on the poor rate.[76] Industrial pollution was already a grave problem around Neath and Swansea in the eighteenth century, while even those who supported industrial development often saw it as a form of charity to poor workmen, or at best a useful but limited supplement to the agricultural income of an estate.

But however many may have been appalled by mines and factories, there is abundant evidence of the commercial orientation of the Glamorgan gentry, at least from Tudor times. Throughout the seventeenth century many gentlemen were prospecting for coal, and were anxious to expand their production and secure a wharf at Neath or Swansea. Before 1660, there are records of such activity by most of the gentry from the Neath and Swansea valleys, both elite and lesser families; and they had many counterparts on the county's eastern border, around Caerphilly.[77] Moreover, participation in industry bore no relation to political affiliations, as it included the parliamentarian Mansells and Bowens, and the royalist Thomases of Swansea and Evans's of Eaglesbush. There is no evidence here of a struggle between industrially progressive puritans and backward royalists, as members of all factions were equally prepared to exploit their opportunities to the full.

The coal trade suffered in the general economic depression of the 1670s and both Neath and Swansea were hard hit. Trade revived at the end of the century, when landowners with coal mines acquired a substantial source of income – worth perhaps one-third of the total for great houses like Gnoll and Briton Ferry.[78] Also in the late seventeenth century, the gentry were active in various industries which used timber or coal as a fuel for smelting, and which would therefore increase demand. Sussex ironmasters had worked in Glamorgan in Elizabethan times, and the iron industry revived after the Restoration with strong gentry participation, especially around Caerphilly. Forges were established in this area in 1662 by the Lewises of Van and their kinsmen, and Sir Charles Kemys was considering taking up their lease when it expired in the 1670s.[79] Others active in the trade about 1680 were the Thomases of Wenvoe, the Morgans of Tredegar, and the latter's kinsmen, the Mansells of Margam. Both at Caerphilly and in the west, this was the start of a long tradition. The commercial outlook of the Glamorgan gentry was unmistakable:[80] when Francis Gwyn of Llansannor acquired his Dorset estate in 1690, he was soon sending samples of ore for assay in Bristol, obviously hoping to develop enterprises comparable to those of his home county.[81]

The general revival at the end of the century was dwarfed both in scale and the degree of innovation by Sir Humphrey Mackworth's efforts at Neath.[82] His mining enterprises were remarkable technologically, as innovations included the use of steam engines, deeper mineshafts, canals and tramways – and the last were powered by horses or sails. He travelled widely in north-east England and the Midlands, and so was aware of the latest technology, while skilled men were brought both from Germany and these advanced areas of Britain. However, the central importance of his activities was that they were not solely directed towards the sale of coal, but that they created a large industrial complex which in turn increased the local market for coal. The Neath works smelted copper, with by-products including silver and litharge, and Mackworth's interests were broadened by his partnership with John Hanbury in the Ynysgerwn ironworks of 1697. His company of 'Mine Adventurers' also had substantial interests in the ore-producing areas like Cornwall and Cardiganshire, and the works at Neath were therefore integrated into a widespread and interdependent economic region. Increased trade benefited the borough of Neath, while greater demand helped other coalmasters, but Mackworth's success caused rivalry, which was exacerbated by the domination he had secured over the borough machinery through his office as Constable of the Castle.

To the economic threat posed to his neighbours was added the prospect of a political 'Universal Monarchy' and his challenge in the electoral boroughs caused a major assault on his position by the local gentry – the Mansells of both Margam and Briton Ferry, and the Popkins's of Forest.[83] This culminated in major riots at Neath in 1705, and contributed to the bitterly contested Glamorgan election of 1708. The tactics employed here illustrate the breadth of the issues at stake, no less than their real importance to the parties, as the rival factions freely made and unmade burgesses and sought to place supporters in key offices in the Customs and on the Bench. Workmen of rival employers were threatened with violence and imprisonment, or were conscripted for service in the European wars. In retaliation, Mackworth referred these activities to the committee on parliamentary privilege, and became the moving force in a group of major gentry dissatisfied with Margam's dominance of the county's politics. Ultimately, he was defeated less through these local battles than by the collapse of his company by 1710 amidst grave charges of peculation. His work was much more enduring, for his family maintained their interests in coal, iron and

copper throughout the century. Of wider significance was the re-establish-
ment of a major coal trade, and the precedent of a thriving copper industry
in Glamorgan. Both were to be vital for the neighbouring gentry who had
opposed him so bitterly.

After 1700, coal exploitation took place broadly in the same areas as
hitherto, but on a much larger scale and at many more workings, involving
more secondary families. A familiar cliché for describing the produce of
Glamorgan estates now came to be 'corn, coal and cattle'.[84] Coal was
chiefly exported to the South-West, especially Minehead and Bridgwater,
but also to Ireland and the Channel Islands. Further afield, the 'great market' for Welsh coal in 1706 was described as 'Brittany, Normandy and
downwards as far as and beyond Bordeaux'.[85] The gentry were the most
important coal producers throughout the period, at least until after 1750
when some squires began to lease their estates to entrepreneurs; but the
owners of Penllergaer and Eaglesbush mined coal until the end of the century. Gentry coalmasters were responsible for many innovations in the industry, including the early use of steam engines by both Mansells and
Mackworths, and new techniques such as wagonways or canals.[86]

In economic terms, the main significance of Glamorgan's coal production was that it served as an attraction for the copper industry at a time
when the Bristol capitalists who dominated Cornish ore supplies were trying to find areas of cheap labour and coal.[87] Ore could then be taken there
for smelting, rather than importing fuel to Cornwall. Glamorgan fulfilled
these requirements, and had good port facilities; while after the work of
the 'Adventurers', it had some skilled labour that could be supplemented
from Cornwall. In the 1720s, it was estimated that the cost of smelting
copper in Swansea was nearly 40 per cent less than in Cornwall, and that
20 per cent profit could be relied on in Glamorgan.[88] Works were established at Landore in 1717 and White Rock in 1737, both representing
alliances between local gentry and Bristol capital; while the firm of
Lockwood and Morris was founded on London money in the 1720s. These
firms contracted to take as much coal as local gentry could produce, so the
squires benefited from this new investment. The second Lord Mansell
appears to have had some such interdependent complex in mind with his
grandiose proposals to Bristol merchants for working copper at Aberafan,
with an expansion of coalmining and port facilities.[89]

Copperworks required large supplies of timber and especially water,
and this set a premium on the full exploitation of (often archaic) manorial
rights, which stewards now had to supervise still more diligently. The con-

centration of these works west of the river Neath, and particularly west of the Tawe, meant that such rights and responsibilities fell chiefly on the Beaufort estate, and above all on its stewards. As early as 1723, a dispute over common rights at Swansea was really motivated by the possibility of mineral discoveries, rather than the alleged issue of pasturage.[90] Coal rights were the crucial issue in Beaufort's disputes in the 1750s, whatever rights of cutting trees or sinking stone quarries were ostensibly at stake. Similarly in 1756, the conflict between Gabriel Powell and neighbouring stewards over the lordship of Cadoxton was discussed in terms of medieval law and manorial custom, but the main concern for both sides was control of the water supply for a copperworks owned by the London entrepreneur, Chauncy Townsend.[91]

Developing industries tended to stimulate one another, especially when a need for raw materials attracted large investment. Chauncy Townsend's son acquired a local estate, and spent £30,000 (and thirty years) prospecting for coal east of Swansea; and the copper industry soon gave rise to further offshoots, with works for the exploitation of alum, vitriol and copperas.[92] This pattern of diversification may also be discerned in the iron industry, which was chiefly in the hands of the same families who produced the coal, and likewise depended on the South-West for capital and export markets. The Mansells sold their iron at Plymouth, while the Machen forge found its markets in Bristol, and Bristol capital was essential for the iron and tinplate works of south Carmarthenshire in the 1750s.[93] The Ynyscedwyn forge of 1729 was founded by a consortium of men already deeply involved in coal and allied to the coppermakers – men like Robert Popkins and John Llewellyn of Ynysgerwn. English merchants and entrepreneurs generally took a more active role from the 1740s; but gentry like Thomas Price of Watford were vital in the foundation of the great Dowlais works in 1759. The gentry family of Wilkins were equally significant in founding the Hirwaun works. The number of iron furnaces in this area grew from two in the 1750s to thirteen in 1796, in which year south-east Wales was producing one-quarter of British iron.[94] Once again, new families tended to expand their interests from iron into new industrial undertakings, which increased the demand for coal still further – so, for example, the ironmaster William Coles founded the Swansea pottery in 1764.[95]

These staple industries did not exhaust the economic activities of the Glamorgan gentry. They took an interest in the mining and smelting of lead, for which Neath was a port, and in the 1730s the Cottrell estate was being prospected for lead, tin and copper.[96] Mansells and Hanburys founded the Welsh tinplate trade,[97] while the occasional privateering ventures in wartime were run on a joint-stock basis.[98] There were also a host of abortive schemes, for instance to establish the manufacture of linen or glass in the county,[99] but the most remarkable success was by the last Sir Herbert Mackworth. In 1787 he was described as 'one of the most extraordinary geniuses of this kingdom', who was responsible for banks, glasshouses, saltworks, collieries and thriving agricultural improvements; and on his death in 1791 he was described as a 'great banker' rather than a squire.[100] The Wilkins's of Llanblethian were equally striking. Originally, they were minor gentry and squires who made a fortune in law and colonial commerce during the eighteenth century. They invested the profits in the 'Brecon Old Bank', a highly successful venture which provided much of the capital on which the Industrial Revolution of South Wales was built. Once again, success in one field aided development in others, a pattern well exemplified by quaker families like the Lloyds or Gibbins's, active in iron, copper and banking; or by the great agricultural improver Samuel Richardson of Hensol, who founded a bank at Cardiff in the 1790s.[101]

6. Modernisation

Professor Mingay has emphasised that many gentry were gravely disappointed in their quest for an industrial 'El Dorado'; but he also points out that when squires were successful, this had major consequences for their fortunes. Moreover, 'improvement' in one area tended to spill over into others, so that industrial development promoted agricultural or urban growth, and general modernisation: Mingay cites as an example of this the work of the Curwens and Lowthers in north-west England.[102] In Glamorgan, this can be observed with particular clarity from the mid eighteenth century, when there seems to have developed an 'ideology' of improvement – and I will examine this in the light of more recent theories of how societies modernise.

From the 1750s, numerous societies were formed for the promotion of agriculture, manufactures, towns and communications. Breconshire led the way with its Agricultural Society of 1754, whose members included Glamorgan men like Gabriel Powell of Swansea; and similar bodies existed in all the counties of South Wales by the 1780s. The same names frequently recur in the leadership of these movements throughout the region: there were some great families (and not merely as figureheads), but also many lesser gentry and professionals. Nonconformists and particularly methodists were active, including Thomas Price of Watford, but there were many others like Herbert Mackworth or Thomas Mansell-Talbot who were strongly orthodox anglicans. Often, the improvers were of new families, who had perhaps been successful only from the early eighteenth century, and who were therefore aware of the potential of innovation and enterprise. In west Glamorgan, the Collins's, Lucases and Morrises were all active in the promotion of new roads, bridges and agricultural techniques, and these families had all risen since 1720 through (respectively) medicine, agriculture, and industry. They were associated with radicalism and freemasonry (further discussed in Chapter 6) and in the 1780s they joined the industrialist Sir Watkin Lewes in a political campaign for the improvement of Swansea's paving and harbours.[103]

Another prominent example was John Franklen, described by contemporaries as Glamorgan's best agriculturist; and whose half-century career as a steward began in 1770. He was the founder and treasurer of the county's Agricultural Society in 1772, and he corresponded with progressive farmers in Breconshire and Buckinghamshire, urging the use of turnips and new fertilisers. He reclaimed waste land at the mouth of the Ogwr, became the first Glamorgan man to use a threshing machine, and was commemorated by a new 'Franklen's Fair' which he established at Cowbridge. Apart from agricultural development, he was active in the societies for the promotion of new turnpike roads.[104] Other new men, often of professional origins, were nearly as ubiquitous as Franklen in encouraging the 'spirit of improvement' after 1760, including the lawyer John Wilkins, the steward Thomas Edmondes, and the industrialist Richard Crawshay.

Naturally, such men were in part simply following the traditional opportunism of the county community, 'improving' to meet the needs of industrial advance. Industry required a superior network of communications and an increased food supply. It was both a promise and a threat: the presence of manufactures gave the opportunity of a much-expanded market for industrial produce, and made land values soar. If, however, the challenge was not met, there was the possibility of food riots, endemic throughout South Wales' industrial areas from the 1750s, and reaching a critical point in the revolutionary 1790s.

Improvement was therefore a pragmatic response to practical need; but can we explain how a generation of modernisers so readily arose to meet the new circumstances? I have emphasised the family background of such leaders, and particularly the way in which these houses had established themselves through innovative professions. Parallels may be sought here in the literature on the modernisation of the contemporary Third World – although as Dr Wrigley has reminded us, industrialisation was not the inevitable consequence of 'modernised' attitudes.[105] One useful theory is that of Professor Apter, who has emphasised the importance of a modernising elite associated with innovative professions.[106] 'Modern' careers emerged alongside the more hidebound professions, and shared common elements of skill, technology, rationality, functionality. Holders of such positions were particularly associated with the 'aura of modernity' which was so important as an incentive to growth and competition. They were often linked to government office, probably to the governing party – which was in turn an agent of modernisation and 'nationalisation', through widespread dissemination of techniques of management and media use. When the new elite had secured its hold on the nation, modernisation had to be disguised by the 'invention of tradition', to provide a false continuity from antiquity. In its most advanced political manifestation, the new order adopted a 'secular – libertarian' ideology, opposed to both 'sacred' and collective social norms.

This modern theory – evolved to describe contemporary Africa and Asia – has strong points of similarity with eighteenth-century Glamorgan. The new gentry which emerged after about 1750 included families who had risen through service to the ruling whig party, like the Matthews's (Navy) or Talbots (law). There were certainly representatives of the new careers, like 'improving' stewards (Franklen, Edmondes, Gabriel Powell), and industrialists (Morris, Crawshay). All therefore shared the 'aura of modernity' in their awareness and frequent use of the latest technology and methods of administration and management. In this context, it is especially interesting to find among the chief freemasons, reformers, and improvers so many representatives from the Navy – at once servants of the government and the ruling party, and men constantly on the frontiers of available technology. These naval 'improvers' included Thomas Matthews, Christopher Bassett, and Richard Knight – and here we should recall the strength of freemasonry in the armed forces throughout their history. By the 1780s, the masons were in the vanguard of secular (anticlerical), populist and libertarian electoral campaigns throughout South Wales.

How far can this theory be applied to the county's industrialisation as a whole? One problem is that so much of an 'aura of modernity' emanated from some very traditional figures, like the Mansells or Mackworths at the end of the previous century – and they were nothing to do with either innovative professions or the armed forces. However, such men only began the process of economic growth, which did not reach take-off point until much later – in the 1750s and 1760s. It might therefore be appropriate to place great stress on the links between the professional middling classes and the whig establishment, through office and patronage. The theory is very suggestive, but there was another element apparently vital in stimulating development throughout, which is linked indirectly with Apter's thesis; and that was war. War provided demand, and the armed services provided many of the personnel for modernisation; and it will be suggested that both Glamorgan's prosperity and its industrial progress became directly dependent on continuing war.

7. The impact of war

During the eighteenth century, matters of war and peace were central to Glamorgan's economic growth, which also brought economic survival into the political arena. But was war something the squires should seek or avoid? There were strong cases to be made on both sides, but on balance industry needed war, *if* it was fought on tory 'blue-water' terms.

At first sight, it is strange to suggest that a vulnerable coastal county should view war with anything other than despair. Imports of ore and exports of agricultural and industrial products made sea communications of central importance to the county's economy, and any disruption of these could be a major disaster. Every major war posed the threat of privateers and commerce raiders in the Bristol Channel and off the Cornish coast. Economic disruption was aggravated by the threat of impressment for naval service, which could cause a panic in Swansea or Cardiff until well into the nineteenth century, and Herbert Mackworth in 1740 complained of the 'press and privateers'.[107] The coal trade was damaged by the closure of its 'great market' in France; commerce suffered through increased rates for freight and insurance, and the danger to imported raw materials, as in 1718 when the danger of a Swedish war caused disquiet to the western ironmasters.[108] Even the gentry not concerned with industry suffered from the land tax, and imports like wine became 'extravagant dear' in the scarcity caused by war.[109] There could moreover be potential physical danger to everyone in the county, as there was a constant threat of armed incursions from the sea – from the French, the Dutch, even from the Barbary pirates. A work of the 1690s attributed the large number of castles in Glamorgan to its great vulnerability to invasion, which was believed to be

imminent in 1690, 1708, 1746, 1779 and 1797.[110] It is not surprising that
the prospect of peace in 1667 or 1714 was received with great joy – nor
that Swansea in particular (a coal-port) should dread the long continuance
of a war.[111] As was remarked in 1748, peace would bring 'a mountain of
gold'.[112]

But war was not necessarily an unrelieved disaster, and could actually
benefit the county if fought with a strong fleet and sound naval strategy.
For example, Herbert Mackworth could view with equanimity the approach of war in 1740, because the Navy was capable of defending the
Bristol Channel and the coal market in south-west England, while rivals
from Newcastle would find the longer journey to Plymouth much more
hazardous.[113] Commerce was endangered less after the evolution of the
convoy system, and local gentry and merchants had interests in their own
privateers, which could be very profitable. Christopher Bassett of Bonvilston was believed to have made a profit of £10,000 from such a venture
in 1760, thus restoring an almost ruined family.[114] Great estates like Margam and Gnoll were rich in iron and timber, the two main war materials in
an age of wooden navies, and large sales to the Navy Office appear to have
helped the Mansells avoid financial disaster in the 1740s. The main expansion of the iron industry coincided with the wars beginning in 1756 and
1775, and the annual rent specified in ironworks' leases rose eleven-fold
between 1756 and 1764; while both the copper and tinplate industries
benefited from a shipping boom.[115]

The wars at the end of the century were particularly useful from the
point of view of war contracts and industrial growth, and therefore for
prices and agricultural demand. The towns grew – the tonnage of shipping
using the port of Swansea rose five-fold between 1768 and 1800 – and
land values soared. Between 1780 and 1796, Glamorgan acquired at Morriston a new town of 600 people, besides the growth around Merthyr, and
so it is not surprising that the county started to import corn. War also provided abundant patronage for the disposal of those fortunate gentlemen
who had the ear of the ministry of the day. The correspondence of leading
squires during major wars often appears to become little more than a series
of appeals for commissions or promotions. By the 1790s, most landed
families also had at least one son in the armed services.

The Glamorgan gentry might therefore be expected to favour tory views
on a 'blue-water' war, before 1714 as in the 1740s, for this would bring the
advantages of war with few of its dangers. The county's economy was so
closely tied to that of Bristol that a war to seize colonies and expand the
slave trade was a sensible political objective. This would enrich the Bristol

merchants who supplied capital, a particularly important goal given the unique dependence of South Wales industry on mercantile capital, a point recently stressed by Professor Daunton.[116]Colonial issues had still more direct relevance for Glamorgan at this time. By the 1760s, the copper-works of White Rock and Swansea were chiefly engaged in producing copper rods as slavers' currency in Africa, and all the produce of the Penclawdd works went for this purpose in the 1780s.[117] Welsh cloth was much used on slave plantations; and trading expeditions to West Africa attracted interest from Cardiff merchants like the Priests. There were also close commercial links with America and the West Indies.[118] If the gentry were to be heavily taxed as landed squires, this might at least be for a type of war which protected and expanded their commercial interests. When in the 1750s a successful war was waged on these lines, victories were greeted with remarkable unanimity not only by whigs like Sir Edmund Thomas of Wenvoe but by high tories like Beaufort and Herbert Mackworth.[119] In this context it seems unwise to talk of the rival views on war and peace in this period in terms of a struggle between landed and moneyed interests, for at least in Glamorgan the issue was more likely to lie between varying commercial factions.

8. Debt and credit

Questions of war and peace gave a profoundly political colour to the economic interests of the gentry; and the importance of party politics was reinforced by issues of patronage. The squires needed government office – or at least government sympathy – to save their fortunes, as even such a powerful community as Glamorgan needed this supplement to rescue it from debt. At first sight this may appear paradoxical, but debt was a continuing problem for most of the great estates. Building, electioneering, gambling, all contributed to the accumulation of vast debts. Sir Charles Kemys owed £35,000 at his death in 1735. In the 1760s, Robert Jones burdened the Fonmon estate with debts of £50,000;[120] and in the same years, the £20,000 owed by Sir Edmund Thomas led to the loss of the Wenvoe estate.[121] Nor did such disasters happen only to the very imprudent. In 1739, the wife of the sober Herbert Mackworth complained of their 'plenty of children and scarcity of pence... Such poor people as we are... can hardly get money for necessaries.'[122] This concerned a family deeply involved in industrial development, with a rental income of £2,000 in Glamorgan and large estates in Shropshire.[123]

Debts could arise through hard economic times, so that the 1670s and

1730s were both difficult; but political crises also left their mark. The Civil
War caused 'a real and deep crisis across broad sections of landed society'
to quote the conclusions of Dr Broad's research on the Verneys of Buckinghamshire.[124] Moreover, not all Glamorgan families were as fortunate as
the Verneys in restoring their fortunes under Charles II. Only the Earls of
Bolingbroke actually lost their Glamorgan estate through war and compounding, but other families may have suffered blows, the full effects of
which did not become apparent until much later. Losses in the Civil War
probably caused Sir Edward Stradling's debts of £21,000, which led him to
default on a huge bond. This, in turn, ruined the Bassetts of Beaupre and
Vans of Marcross, as well as members of his own family, who had gone
surety for him; and this completed the damage wrought by the roundheads.[125] The largest sum paid in compounding by a Glamorgan family was
£3,500 from the Kemys's, which family accumulated vast debts by the end
of the century, and the £2,195 paid by Sir Edward Thomas of Llanmihangel may have begun the ruin of that family.[126] The latter process was
completed by the political ambition of Sir Edward's son, 'Sir Robert the
ass', from the 1660s.[127] By 1683, Sir Robert was literally begging his creditors to allow food and clothing for his wife and 'three destitute children',
and he owed over £15,000, despite attempts at salvage dating back over
ten years.[128] The defeat of the whig cause merely added the final blow to
the estate.

So indebtedness could be a life-and-death matter, and it often seemed a
very narrow margin that made the difference between survival and ruin.
Perhaps the closest-run case was that of the Mansells of Margam, an estate
which could reckon on at least £2,000 a year clear profit in 1740, from a
rental of about £5,000; but by 1750 the family had debts of £40,000 and
mortgages not fully settled until the next century.[129] The estate had passed
to two younger sons of the first Lord Mansell between 1744 and 1750.
Both of these had earlier received separate establishments (Bussy at Briton
Ferry, Christopher at Newick in Sussex) and both already had heavy debts,
Christopher's largely through neglecting his estate. Bussy's long decline
had begun with heavy debts at Oxford, which were then aggravated by the
attempt to maintain the family's electoral interest during a twenty-year
minority of the Margam heir. The final years under Bussy Mansell, who
united the various family properties, saw a slide to near disaster which was
halted only by retrenchment by the Talbot heir after Bussy's death.

Political involvement could damage an estate, but it could also be useful.
From the later seventeenth century, we frequently find political allies

working together to support their weaker friends. For instance, wealthy metropolitan whigs like Sir Robert Clayton loaned extensively to whigs and old roundheads like the Thomases of Llanmihangel, Joneses of Fonmon and Arnolds. In Bristol – the main source of credit and capital for Glamorgan – the tory MP Edward Colston similarly served as banker and money-lender for tories like Lord Mansell.[130] The health of an estate could also be helped by securing political office, although some were ruined by the expense of electioneering. The prospect of Sir Charles Kemys and Herbert Mackworth seeking to enter parliament caused their respective wives to write them long, sarcastic and pleading letters urging them not to ruin their families by such an insane adventure.[131] However, these fears were not wholly justified, as politics was a lottery in which a fortune could be either won or lost. At the simplest level, being an MP prevented one from being arrested for debt. More significant were the spoils of office, for oneself or one's relations, bringing an additional income and at the same time solving the problems of clamorous relatives. Powerful connections could be made, useful in lawsuits, and which increased one's chance of making a wealthy marriage. Lord Mansell's time in office was particularly successful both in presenting new financial opportunities, and in confirming his role as head of the county by the grant of favours to tenants and relatives, like the Carnes, Bassetts and Gamages. He participated in the tory government's African venture of 1710 – 14, was influential in appointments to the Newfoundland Company, and he had an early interest in the South Sea Company.[132] He could also campaign for Glamorgan county interests, as when he attempted to ban imports of Irish wool, which competed with Welsh products.[133]

'Office' in this period not only referred to administrative posts in central government, for the spoils of a successful faction included jobs in the armed services as well as useful local positions in the customs or post office.[134] However, this was an age of great colonial expansion, when dramatic success was possible for an able man who could secure a post in companies trading to the East or West Indies, and these were jobs obtained through political influence. Other fields of enterprise included army and navy contracts, while even a naval chaplaincy proved the basis of John Deere's prosperity.[135] However, all such offices were in the gift of politicians and the government of which they were part, so political activity was necessary to win these regards. Of course, political success would not inevitably stave off ruin. Sir Rowland Gwynne of Miskin died in poverty in 1726, although he had been Treasurer to William III; while the Wenvoe

estate was lost soon after Sir Edmund Thomas had gained office at the
Board of Trade. But economic considerations aggravated the already bitter
ideological issues dividing political society from the late seventeenth century, and for some it was a matter of simple survival to be on the winning
side. To take an extreme case, Llanmihangel's finances were in such a parlous state by 1680 that Sir Robert Thomas could have been saved by little
other than a successful role in a renewed civil war, so he had nothing to lose
by extremism. His whig allies like Edward Turberville of Sker and Edward
Matthews of Llandaff also came from families whose income had declined
steeply after the Civil War. Financial survival was often closely linked to
political and factional success, and this was a very dangerous equation for
the peace of the state.

Conclusion to Part I

Part I has given an account of the social structure and economic development of one Welsh shire in the century before industrialisation and has attempted to show that this society was distinctly unlike many traditional
images of Wales, both contemporary and more recent. The mythical Wales
was, above all, a poor and remote land. Its landowners were either exceed-
ingly rich, or they were equal to English yeomen, but with absurd pretensions. The famous text for this view was the remark by a despairing Cromwellian Major-General that it was easier to find ten Welsh squires of £50 a
year rather than one of £500.[1] This meant that offices like that of justice
were hard to fill, so presumably party purges were more difficult to carry
out. Such gentry as there were could be viewed as the ultimate
backwoodsmen – simple, rough-hewn country tories, like the caricatures
that Georgian dramatists like Gwinnett or Jerningham put on the stage.[2]
As a critic wrote of the royalist Judge Jenkins of Hensol, he was 'bred in the
mountains... [his] understandings were never burdened with weight of an
argument'.[3]

In this picture, this barbarous squirearchy ruled a countryside too poor
to sustain a middle class, and populated by a tenant body as willing to serve
their landlords as were Highland clansmen – and 'clan' terms are actually
used of Glamorgan by Victorian writers.[4] This myth has major implications for both Welsh and British history. First, there is no question here
about the essential unity of Wales. It was one fairly uniformly reactionary
'dark corner of the land'.[5] Second, royalism and toryism were successively
the natural creeds of the Welsh gentry, presumably because they remained
happily unaware of more sophisticated debate – and even the industries
they established did not lead them to more economically sophisticated
views of puritanism and whiggery. Again, the ill-educated common people
were easily led in the Stuart cause. As Dr Manning wrote, generally, 'the
gentry carried the people of Wales into the King's camp'. In Wales and
other remote areas, during the 1640s 'the ruling classes were mostly

royalists'.[6] This in essence supports Christopher Hill's thesis about the Civil War being a conflict between the advanced South-East, and the economically backward highland zone.

This myth developed because it served the interests of dissenters, whigs and liberals throughout Welsh history: of course the common people favoured the anglicans – they were forced to do so by the landlords. If the gentry persecuted dissenters, then they had singularly hardened hearts and closed minds against the Gospel. If they were tory, how much easier it was to assume this was through ignorance. In the last three decades, Welsh historians have undermined some parts of the myth, under the influence of David Williams. For instance, Dr Howell has shown that nineteenth-century Welsh landlords were not the primitive ogres of popular legend;[7] Professors Dodd and Thomas have shown the existence of much subtler political divisions in Stuart and Georgian politics than had hitherto been assumed – and Professor Thomas has also discussed the 'middling' class in eighteenth-century Wales.[8]

Glamorgan diverged enormously from the traditional picture, and this will become apparent in subsequent chapters. It had a numerous and affluent squirearchy, who were highly enterprising in economic affairs. Some were whigs, but many were tory partly because their estates were so industrialised, and so dependent on mercantile capital. The county was prosperous, with a progressive agriculture whose techniques influenced those of English counties. Wales was scarcely a unit, for this southern coastal fringe bore strong resemblances to the society of advanced southern England. Finally, the common people were not docile 'clansmen'. If they followed the gentry into war, they might well have had their own motives for so doing. Large parts of the county were as politically troublesome as the English areas which scholars like Dr Thirsk have made famous for radicalism in the Stuart period – the East Anglian Fens or the Staffordshire moorlands.

We would therefore expect that the political history of the county would be much more complex than might be expected of a simple 'backwoods' region. The leading activists had much to fight for – and so much more to lose than the mere £50 a year of legend.

PART II

Local and national politics

Introduction

I have frequently had cause to stress the lack of continuity between the history of the gentry community before and after about 1720, so that for once a rough division of a period into centuries is not merely a matter of convenience. Glamorgan was a very different society in the seventeenth century from what it was to become in the eighteenth. It was ruled by a differently composed political elite, and traditional aristocratic power declined greatly by the early Georgian period. After 1700 too, industry became a much greater concern of the landed families, so that we enter a world of more economic and commercial sophistication. This might be symbolised by the transformation of the markets and sources of raw materials on which local industry depended, from a western European to an Atlantic scale.

In political affairs also, a major change took place in the nature and intensity of issues and the composition of factions. This too occurred between the 1690s and 1720s, and it will be suggested how closely this change reflected the social background – particularly demographic changes and the decline of aristocratic dominance. The scale of the change was immense. The political rhetoric of 1740 was very similar to that of 1640 or 1680, but this apparent continuity was an illusion. Glamorgan gentlemen in the seventeenth century faced very immediate threats to their power, even their survival – threats from government, from aristocrats, from radicals and dissenters – and there was a very substantial ideological and religious content in each of these challenges. By the 1730s, gentry society was more secure in its wealth and independence, and less immediately afraid of tyranny or religious extremism. A sort of stability had been achieved, based on new political structures and the decline of bitterly divisive religious issues.

The aim of this section is to describe the contrasting political worlds of Stuart and Georgian Glamorgan, and to explain the reasons for this trans-

formation. First, changes will be described in the structure of administration, law enforcement and local power, that is to say, the substance of
political conflict in the localities. A chronological account will then describe the development of political parties and ideologies from 1640 to
1790.

There are several reasons why the political history of the Glamorgan
gentry was of wider national importance at the time, and is of more than
merely local interest today. Firstly, the county could never be simply the
possession of one great lord in the way that neighbouring Carmarthenshire
was the toy of the owners of Golden Grove. The Glamorgan community
was too rich and independent to be bullied: they had to be wooed, by peers,
or by leaders of national parties and factions. And they were emphatically
worth the wooing, because of their wealth and their remarkable parliamentary strength. At issue was not merely political control of one normal Welsh county, with one MP representing the shire, and one for the
borough. If the Glamorgan gentry had been confined to this, then cut-
throat competition would have resulted at every election to obtain this
miserly prize. But in fact the Glamorgan community often won seats
elsewhere, either in Wales or in the wider south-western area with which
they were connected by kinship or friendship. For example, between 1700
and 1750, the House of Commons had twenty-eight members whose main
interests lay in Glamorgan. Only thirteen of these ever held one of Glamorgan's own seats: others were MPs for Westminster, for south Welsh constituencies (Brecon, Cardigan or Carmarthen boroughs) or for south-western seats. Wells and Minehead each had two Glamorgan members in this
period, and other squires held prestigious seats like Hampshire, Southampton or Chippenham (see Appendix 1). In most parliaments of this
period, there were at least five or six members of the Commons who had
major Glamorgan estates, in addition to two or three peers; and in some
parliaments the number might be higher. The gentry elite contributed eight
members of the Commons in the exclusion parliament of 1679, while peers
like Worcester, Leicester and Pembroke all had strong Glamorgan connections.

This parliamentary 'imperialism' strongly suggests the power and
wealth of the gentry community, and helps us to understand why they were
able to produce so many figures of national stature. These include Philip
Jones, 'dictator' of Cromwellian Wales; Judge David Jenkins in the Civil
Wars; Evan Seys in Shaftesbury's whig party; Sir Leoline Jenkins in the
governments of Charles II; Francis Gwyn in the core of every tory move-

ment for fifty years; Lord Mansell in the Harleyite ministries; Sir Edmund Thomas in the opposition whiggery of Prince Frederick's court, and a number of others. The community produced more controversial political leaders who made a national impact. There were a number of important martyrs, like the presbyterian Christopher Love, the royalist Nicholas Kemys, the whig Edward Matthews, or the jacobite David Morgan. This was a powerful community usually close to national affairs.

The county's politics also gain interest from their complexity, their juxtaposition of older patterns of clientage and loyalty with new economic forces. Loyalty to a lord like the Earl of Pembroke could lead squires in one direction, while the need to obtain office and income could lead in another; traditional obligations to the family of the Dukes of Beaufort could lead one way, the need to preserve markets for coal or sources for raw material could pull another. Moreover, by the mid eighteenth century, the factors to be taken into account had expanded to a world scale, so that once disaffected tories were reconciled to a government that so helped them by expanding a commercial empire based on slavery. Glamorgan was as near to a 'pure' gentry-ruled society as was possible; and we have here an opportunity to study the history of that vital class against a background of rare economic complexity and sophistication, of new patterns of political parties and organisation – in which, indeed, the county may actually have taken a lead – and the emergence of regional and national political communities. Finally, we can consider the impact of the thoroughgoing demographic change on patterns of political behaviour and loyalties. This local study strongly suggests that the quest for stability was an extremely complex affair.

4

Law and order

Introduction

As in the economic sphere, the landed gentry normally exercised thorough control of everyday life in the county through the machinery of administration and law enforcement. By the late seventeenth century, the gentry had removed rivals to their power both from above (government supervision) and below (radical municipal corporations). They secured their independence, and a near hereditary right to offices like JP or deputy-lieutenant. The only issues in local government seemed to be the problem of making these men work at enforcing the law, or else extending the commission of the peace to include enough lesser squires who would take on the burden of governing – both very serious problems.

But we find a basic paradox here, one that is important for understanding the nature of gentry power after 1700. With the consolidation and advancement of gentry power, it might seem as if the countryside was as peaceful as any time before or since, and that this would be particularly true of the Vale. But social relationships were subject to serious strains. New families entered the county community, new social groups took over the Bench – and the basic standards and values of those enforcing the law changed from about the 1720s. Any semblance of 'paternalism' now broke down, as the common people found themselves facing the justice of the lawyers, clergy and stewards whom they hated or despised as greedy tyrants. Of course these gentry were not necessarily any worse than the old Stradlings or Herberts – but these latter had been distant figures whom it was possible to idealise, and they had been united to the local community by their language and beliefs.

In the new 'tranquillity' after 1720, we will therefore observe a series of conflicts over rights and obligations in the form of crime and disorder, like wrecking and poaching. A series of such crimes begin to be recorded in precisely those years when the old families were finally vanishing – the 'period of transformation' between 1720 and 1760. So, the political history of the whole period will be seen in the context of the replacement of the old community and the fragmentation of communal standards which that implied.

1. The growth of local independence

The Glamorgan gentry was, by the late seventeenth century, to secure a large measure of independence either from central government or from greater landed magnates. For much of the Tudor and Stuart period, the main organ of central-government control over the Welsh counties was the Council of Wales, with supervisory powers over the local administration of justice.[1] The presidents of the council were often Welsh magnates in their own right, with a considerable local following, and this gave the office its real effectiveness though there were also dangers in so great a concentration of power. This influence was particularly felt in south-eastern Wales after 1660, when the administration was moved from distant Ludlow to the seat of the current president, either Carbery at Golden Grove or the Marquis of Worcester on the Border. Gentry families like the Glamorgan Herberts or Mansells had held office in the lower echelons of the Council, so patronage helped bind the local community to the government.

However, during the seventeenth century, the powers of central authority were repeatedly associated with religious extremism and arbitrary authority, so a continuing theme in the history of the gentry was the bitter struggle to preserve their local power and independence, which movement culminated in 1688. In that year, the presidency passed to the whig Earl of Macclesfield, who had some Welsh connections, but was not a territorial magnate there in his own right, and the Council itself was abolished in 1694.[2] Later, governments tried to maintain supervision through the lord-lieutenants, but these were often placed over groups of Welsh counties, and their direct influence was rarely great. In the 1690s, the Earl of Pembroke served briefly as lord-lieutenant for Glamorgan, but this was very exceptional. Much more typical of the eighteenth-century norm was the Duke of Bolton, a magnate with interests in Carmarthenshire, who was of little use as a government representative in Glamorgan. In 1753, he was not able to recommend justices in one of his counties because he was 'very little acquainted with any gentlemen of the county of Glamorgan', and he left the responsibility to the Lord Chancellor personally.[3] From 1688,

Glamorgan county society was as free of central control as were its English counterparts, and this tradition, too, was well established when local peers began to be appointed in the 1750s. Plymouth was the first such lord-lieutenant and he served from 1754 to 1771. He was succeeded by members of the still more powerful Bute family, who showed considerable energy in times of crisis like the 1790s, but who were normally absentees.[4]

Judges on circuit acted as one channel between central government and localities, for they addressed the county community at the great ceremonial occasion of the Assizes.[5] The Great Sessions are key events in the diaries of John Bird of Cardiff in the 1790s, and he often mentions their state and 'magisterial order' as well as carefully noting the judges' pronouncements on county affairs.[6] The political influence of the judges was apparent from the role of Richard Carter in securing local appointments; and a vacancy on a Welsh circuit about 1714 was the occasion for petitions by the Glamorgan gentry stressing 'the great interest the men of property have in this and every such promotion'.[7] Dependent on government favour, judges could be relied on to support the interests of a ministry against local magnates, while their influence made them worthwhile allies for an aspiring statesman like Thomas Mansell of Margam.[8] Often of humble origins, many acquired estates, and some of the greatest Welsh gentry traced their successes to such a progenitor in the seventeenth or early eighteenth centuries. In Glamorgan, there were the Jenkins's of Hensol, but one might also cite the Powells and Vaughans of Cardiganshire, Romseys of Monmouthshire and Trevors of Denbighshire.

The government could also be kept informed of local affairs through personal contacts and friendships. While the Council of Wales was still in existence, the presidents should have been the main channel of patronage and influence, but personal or partisan links with friends at Court were important throughout. For Glamorgan gentlemen, this type of influence was particularly useful during the presence in Charles II's governments of loyalists and old friends like Sheldon, Leoline Jenkins and Francis Gwyn — but old parliamentarians might find equal success in application to presbyterian lords like Wharton, Manchester and Holles.[9] With the rise of whig power in the eighteenth century, the greatest advantage passed to the Morgans of Tredegar, who came to hold a position reminiscent of the old presidents of the Council because of their weighty contacts in successive ministries. After 1714 they controlled appointments to the Bench and shrievalty in Glamorgan and at least two other Welsh counties in which they held the post of *custos rotulorum*, although their power was often exercised with the consultation of other leading whigs.[10] In Glamorgan, however, there were too many great tory gentry to permit the appointment of a wholly satisfactory Bench, so justices were rarely removed except for flagrant illegality – and not always then. After 1688, local administration was rarely hampered by central interference, so the government generally had to tolerate both county independence and political unorthodoxy.

2. The militia

The government's chief concern in local affairs was defence and internal security. At least after the Restoration, the critical need to re-establish the old order made the gentry accept the integration of Glamorgan's defence arrangements into a provincial system, based on a well-trained and well-equipped militia.[11] For a few years the militia was an efficient, even over-zealous force, whose effectiveness was enhanced by the presence of many ex-cavaliers as officers. However, once the immediate danger had faded, traditions of county independence formed an obstacle to efficient administration, and little is heard after 1670 of the earlier readiness to cooperate with other shires under central direction. The militia continued to meet regularly at well-established places of assembly like Pyle or Caerphilly, but the gentry rejected any change or reform which might interfere with this expression of county pride and loyalty.[12] It was the preserve of the gentry, and therefore a shibboleth of 'country' politics throughout the period, with which the government interfered at its peril.[13] The active militia officers were normally drawn from the gentry elite: in Elizabethan times, the Herberts, Mansells and Bassetts; in the 1670s and 1680s, the Mansells, Stradlings, Kemys's, Herberts, Carnes, Mackworths, Gwyns, Seys's, Loughers and Bassetts.[14]

Contributions to the forces were proportional to social status, thereby reflecting the social hierarchy. In 1690, the company of 50 cavalry found its horses from the greater gentry estates, as shown in Table 9.[15] The ten leading families therefore supplied 23 horses, almost half the total. This dominance by the leading gentry is also apparent from the changing composition of the county's deputy-lieutenants. Their numbers increased in the period, from about 10 in the 1660s to 40 or more in the late eighteenth century, but the lieutenancy remained a much more select body than the Bench,[16] as suggested by Table 10.

The military effectiveness of the body was never tested, but Professor Western has shown how far it lagged behind contemporary methods of

Table 9: *Sources of militia horses*

Number of horses	Number of families supplying
4	1 (Mansell of Margam)
3	1 (Mansell of Briton Ferry)
2	8
1	23
½ share	4
⅓ share	6

Table 10: *Justices and deputy-lieutenants*

Date	Justices	Deputy-lieutenants	Percentage of justices also included in the lieutenancy
1663	40	10	25
1685	24	7	30
1700	32	16	50
1762	115	38	33

war, notably after Marlborough's campaigns.[17] Frequent parliamentary debates on the subject also show the reluctance of the 'country' – that is, the gentry – to take a realistic view of the militia's capabilities. Reforms only took place in the 1750s and 1760s under the threat of war and foreign invasion; and a new militia was created for garrison duties, or the guarding of prisoners to relieve regular troops.[18] Naturally, it was still dominated by the magnates – the Earl of Plymouth, squires like Sir Edmund Thomas, Herbert Mackworth, Robert Jones of Fonmon, and a rising man like Gabriel Powell. Despite some success (such as preventing a riot in Lancaster in 1780) the forces of Glamorgan or Monmouthshire were heard of chiefly when they were criticised for insolence and indiscipline, or rebelled against service in England because of the foreign language and customs.[19] Even the gentry, who advocated a strong militia as a defence of liberty, were not all prepared to devote much effort to this new body, which would serve outside the county. Traditions of private violence and self-defence were by no means dead, and when invasion threatened in 1797 the militia was deserted by the county's greatest squire, Thomas Mansell-Talbot. He took refuge in his Gower castle and promised to raise his own army of a thousand men. The rest of the force was split on matters of tactics and precedence between Colonel Aubrey's cavalry and the infantry under John Llewellyn of Penllergaer.[20] It was fortunate that the Glamorgan militia was so rarely called upon to perform important duties, for the reformed body of the later eighteenth century seems to have been as deficient in county loyalty as in military skill. After the 1660s, the central government never again possessed an effective organisation for provincial defence.

3. The JP

The militia was chiefly needed in time of crisis, but the many and varied duties of the justices made them the essential element in the everyday affairs of local government.[21] Singly or in pairs, they had responsibility for wages, apprenticeships and poor relief, and had general police duties in that they could take sureties from offenders against the peace. Assembled at Quarter Sessions, they could try felonies as serious as murder, assault, theft and burglary, and they supervised the county's roads, gaols and bridges. They could license dissenting meeting houses, alehouses, theatres and printing presses. The system had to be flexible to cope with specific problems which might arise suddenly, like the supply of soldiers for Marlborough's wars, and there might be immediate local issues which could be dealt with long before parliament could act nationally. Such powers were especially valuable in a time of economic growth. The gentry were the leading force in economic development, and their administrative powers as justices were freely used to promote their industrial ventures. The Poor Law could be manipulated to permit the settlement of communities of miners and industrial workers on one's own enterprises, while removing those of an opponent as idle vagrants; or cottages could be licensed to accommodate casual labour. Industry could be promoted by the regulation of labour supply, wages and food prices.[22]

In a sense the Sessions were the 'parliament' of the county community, an oligarchical assembly to which leading men of local influence could contribute; and the justices were simply the official manifestation of the gentry class. The Sessions met at inns like the 'Bear' at Cowbridge, at which the squires also held their lesser social gatherings, and the social aspects of the affair were always stressed. The approach of Sessions meant the necessity to purchase large quantities of beer and wine rather than a revision of legal books. In 1678, Richard Seys transported his brewhouse to Cowbridge for the approaching Sessions.[23] These local 'parliaments' illustrate the independence of the county community throughout the eighteenth century, and the ending of the Council of Wales meant that the only form of central control was the possibility of appeal to the King's Bench; and that right was rarely exercised. The county solidarity apparent in local government easily manifested itself in forms of political organisa-

Local and national politics

Table 11: *Numbers of justices*

1650	20	1695	32	1740	40
1655	22	1700	33	1745	61
1660	44	1705	32	1750	53
1665	42	1710	38	1755	75
1670	45	1715	36	1760	63
1675	36	1720	33	(Thereafter:	
1680	25	1725	42	1762	115
1685	24	1730	38	1774	116
1690	30	1735	45	1793	187
				1836	231)

tion such as the 'Loyal Associations' in times of crisis, or in petitions to the government when the clamour began for parliamentary reform. It could also be seen in 'county' organisations like agricultural societies, masonic lodges and hunts; or in support for 'county' projects like local histories or the repair of public buildings. The strength of the traditional system of local administration lay in the depth and extent of these feelings of county loyalty, and that strength was considerable.[24]

During the period, the composition of the Glamorgan Bench changed considerably, so that it came to represent a much wider section of the landed community. Table 11 estimates the number of Glamorgan justices at five-year intervals.[25] The Welsh counties did not share in the national trend towards a dramatic increase in the size of commissions between the 1670s and 1720s that Dr Glassey has discussed, but these patterns did affect Wales in the next decades.[26] Each commission reached new heights, from 43 in 1722 to 46 in 1734, 65 in 1743, 82 in 1753 and 115 in 1762.

More important in the growth of the Bench were new political considerations, after a long period of factional purges and proscriptions. Every attempt to 'remodel' the Bench involved a conflict between the desire for the political correctness and the obvious belief of the leading gentry that they were entitled by right to hold the position of justice, by virtue of their social status. As a corollary to this, lesser families might occasionally be justices, but any attempt to supplant the greater families on the Bench by the lesser was as much an infringement of gentry rights as actual expropriation. The gentry were appalled when James II added men of low origins, who were also dissenters, but the Revolution confirmed the older view of the Bench as a representative body of the county community, despite the exclusion of the jacobite Carnes.[27] At this stage, only a handful of lesser gentlemen were added solely for their political correctness. One was the Cardiff whig mer-chant William Richards, who in 1689 was abused as 'a pitiful fellow, and it is a scandal that the king should have such a fellow as thee for a JP.'[28]

In the 1680s, changes in the Glamorgan Bench were as violent as any de-scribed in Dr Glassey's study of the commission of the peace.[29] However, with the departure of Beaufort, peace returned to the Bench. With minor exceptions, nothing resembling a purge recurred until about 1710, at which point commenced several years of bloodletting. Six whigs were ejected in 1712 to make way for ten tories, who included five clergymen; and seven tories fell between 1714 and 1717 to be replaced by ten whigs.[30] However, many sound tories remained after 1714: the Glamorgan Bench continued throughout to retain men of high tory or even jacobite inclina-tions, like Francis Gwyn, Robert Jones and Sir Edward Stradling. Indeed, Robert Mansell first appears on a commission in March 1717, at which time he was visiting Bolingbroke and the Stuart Court.[31] It is not surprising that local whigs criticised the half-hearted policies of proscription, or that in 1724, the jacobites were said to believe that no justice in Wales or Shrop-shire would arrest any of them.[32] This was optimistic, for although most tories remained, they were first balanced and then outnumbered by an in-creasing number of whig JPs, who were of necessity drawn from outside the traditional county elite. As Dr Glassey remarks, the trend in Welsh counties was towards inclusion rather than dismissal.[33] Once this prece-dent was established, magnates were able to appoint their dependents from among the lower gentry. This gave rise to some protests, as in 1780 when Bute was attacked for 'stuffing the Commission of the Peace with low characters';[34] but the general trend was never checked. In 1742, Lord Hardwicke simply accepted Lord Mansell's list of nominations for the Bench, and the latter regarded any omission as a 'neglect' or a 'slight'.[35]

This expansion implied a broadening of the section of the community from which the JPs were drawn. From the days of Henry VIII until about 1710, the justices were drawn from the county elite, with the addition of two or three lawyers or lesser gentlemen at any one time. For most of the seventeenth and eighteenth centuries, this core of greater gentry families numbered about twenty-five, and they often had several members serving at once: in 1630, 11 of 26 JPs (42 per cent) were from the three great families of Mansell, Lewis and Carne, and the Herberts often supplied 3 or 4 members of any given commission.[36] On the commission of 42 justices in 1660, 16 (38 per cent) were from the families of Bassett, Lewis, Matthews and Stradling. Thereafter, a few new families were gradually added to the Bench, but the rapid expansion did not occur until mid-century.

The whole community can be roughly divided into five categories, depending on the point at which a family began to be admitted regularly to the Bench. The first category, the permanent elite, presents no problems of identification, and represents some twenty-six families. Before 1710, they had occasionally shared the position of JP with twelve or more houses, who now began to appear consistently on commissions of the peace. A third category included twenty-nine families added between 1710 and 1742. Nineteen more appeared on the next two commissions (1743 and 1753) and finally, twenty were added in 1762. In Table 13 these five groups will be categorised thus:

Group
A – greater gentry elite (26 families)
B – occasional JPs before 1710, regular thereafter (12)
C – newly added between 1710 and 1742 (29)
D – newly added, 1743 or 1753 (19)
E – newly added in 1762 (20)

One effect of the extension of the office of justice was a slight devaluation of gentry status. In 1735, a list of the Glamorgan gentry names a large number of families, some of whom are described as 'esquires' and some 'gentlemen', and these titles appear to have been given arbitrarily; until it is realised that the 'esquires' were all justices, some only appointed in the previous year.[37] This implies that the fact of being a justice made one an

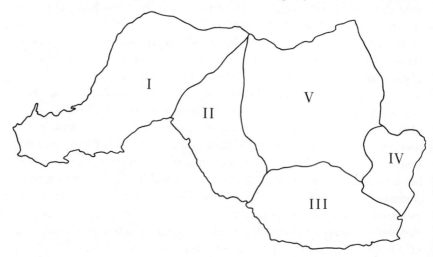

Map 7. Glamorgan's regions to illustrate the geographical distribution of JPs

Table 12: *Geographical origins of JPs* (percentages in brackets)

Region (see Map 7)	Bench of:					
	1689	1710	1726	1741	1747	1762
I West	4(12.5)	4(14)	3(8.6)	7(17)	10(19)	18(19)
II Neath – Bridgend	5(16)	5(18)	3(14)	5(12)	9(17)	17(18)
III Vale	15(47)	15(51)	15(42)	16(39)	17(33)	33(34)
IV East	7(22)	3(11)	10(29)	9(22)	13(25)	13(13)
V Eastern uplands	1	1	2	1	1	3
Uncertain	0	1	0	3	2	13
TOTAL	32	29	35	41	52	97

'esquire', and so this title was spread down the social scale. By 1762, the Bench (and therefore 'esquires') included lawyers, stewards and industrialists, so the concept of gentry status was widened considerably.

The expansion meant that Glamorgan should in theory have been better served by justices. In 1700, for example, there was about one JP for every 1,450 people in the county; but the ratio changed to one to 520 by the 1760s, and one to 374 by 1800. Of course, this assumes that all JPs would be active, which was not the case. The justices also came to be less concentrated in the Vale of Glamorgan, as Table 12 shows. The Vale came to provide about 34 per cent of the Bench by 1762, rather than the 50 per cent common before 1710. This change may have been connected with a deliberate policy of adding justices to under-represented areas, but it was also related to the distribution of social groups within the county. The addition of lesser gentry to the Bench meant an increase in justices from outlying areas. Table 13 shows the geographical origins of the various classes of justice. Some problems, however, were not overcome in this period, notably in the area here labelled 'V', the 'Eastern uplands', which included the huge mountain parishes of Merthyr Tydfil, Gelligaer and Llandyfodwg. Gentry seats were very scarce here, and in the seventeenth century the only possible seats for a justice were at Llancaeach, and at Llanbradach, on the extreme edge of the area. The Church was also very weak here, as suggested by the large number of baptists. One possible solution might be to appoint clergy to police the area, but this did not succeed. The Rev. Thomas Price of Merthyr Tydfil became a justice in 1714, but he was ejected for jacobitism shortly afterwards; and a successor as both rector and JP was

Table 13: *Origins of categories of gentry*

Seats in geographical region	A	B	C	D	E	Total families in each region
I	0	8	9	6	1	24
II	4	1	7	2	4	18
III	17	0	8	9	6	40
IV	5	1	3	1	4	14
V	0	2	1	0	0	3
Uncertain	0	0	1	1	5	7
TOTAL	26	12	29	19	20	106

Gervase Powell, an absentee in Bath. It was in this near-vacuum of civil and ecclesiastical authority that a hugh growth of population and industry took place after 1760. By 1801, the parish of Merthyr Tydfil alone had 9 per cent of Glamorgan's population, and its policing was regarded as a matter of critical urgency. At Cardiff in 1791, the Assize judge spoke of 'the dangerous situation in which that opulent and populous place called Merthyr Tydfil stood in, for want of the due administration of justice', and he urged the Chancellor that here, 'all party recommendations of justices ought to be entirely out of the question, and those only admitted who were likely to be of service in the administration of it'.[38] In the next decade a number of leading Merthyr industrialists like Crawshay and Homfray were indeed added to the commission and they were very active during the social disturbances of the 1790s. At least the traditional system was aware of its responsibilities to such an area, but the massive growth of industry raised the question of whether largely amateur justice could cope, even with the best of intentions.[39]

Glamorgan was well covered by justices but often individuals did not serve. Dr Glassey has shown how often this trend sabotaged the government's effort to direct the political tendency of the Bench: what good did it do to add 20 new whig justices if only a handful appeared at Sessions?[40] We frequently find that only half the gentry on a given commission would swear out the *dedimus* which entitled them to act;[41] and only a fraction of the qualified acted regularly and conscientiously. In the commissions of 1712, 1755, and 1763, the total number of Glamorgan justices who swore out a *dedimus* rose from 15 to 35 and then to 56; but in each year this number was steady at between 45 and 55 per cent of the total Bench. Assuming that about half the justices bothered to qualify themselves to act, how many were actually available to enforce the law? Between 1741 and 1770, a total of 64 justices qualified themselves to act in Glamorgan, perhaps one to every 860 of the population. However, there were difficulties in making these men act. Some justices spent long periods outside the county and served as active JPs in other counties where they held lands, as the Aubreys did in Buckinghamshire or the Kemys's in Monmouthshire. Other gentry from Carmarthenshire or Monmouthshire were on the Glamorgan commission as a matter of prestige, but seldom visited their estates there, so the numbers given in the commission are not a reliable guide to the 'activists'.

Resident Glamorgan families were tempted away by the London season or simply failed to act or attend Sessions through laziness; but the new gentry from lesser families were more likely to be free from such pleasures and responsibilities, and to spend time in fulfilling their duties. If we study the commission of 1722, we find that 22 (half the names) were from social group A (the elite), while the remaining 21 came from categories B or C. Only 20 of the commission swore a *dedimus*, and 14 of these (70 per cent) were from these latter groups. Some of the 'active' justices were only represented by signatures on one to two documents, and by far the most active JPs in 1722 were from lesser families very new to the Bench, like the Powells of Energlyn, Williams's of Dyffryn, or Popkins's and Prices of Gower. These represented new geographical areas, and their Welsh surnames indicate different social origins. From about 1720, the most active JPs were likely to be stewards or merchants, or else new gentry whose fathers had obtained gentle status through such careers.

Another solution to the problem of absenteeism was the appointment of clerical justices, who had been a novelty in Glamorgan in 1710, and who had vanished between 1717 and 1743 because of their associations with jacobitism – and perhaps with a revived Laudianism. The numbers then increased steadily as shown in Table 14. By 1832, Glamorgan had one of the largest proportions of any county in England or Wales, although it was not of course unique in having clerical JPs.[42] As Professor Mingay has shown, in the late eighteenth century other Welsh counties had acquired a similar element, of some 15 to 20 per cent of the total.[43]

Initially, the government had been slow to impose this clerical solution because of the continuing tory threat, but also because of gentry opposition. In 1753, the Duke of Bolton wrote of the Glamorgan commission that he had been reluctant to propose the 'inferior clergy' because he 'had frequent complaints made to me of their being preferred into the

Table 14: *Clerical justices in Glamorgan* (percentages in brackets)

1714	5 (15)
1743	6 (9)
1754	11 (13)
1762	18 (16)
1774	21 (22)
1793	37 (20)

Commission. I know that the reason why the Sessions are not better attended is because gentlemen of estates don't care to be put on a level with those people.'[44] The eventual success of the system was aided by the growing number of clergy drawn from the greatest gentry, and this may reflect a demographic phenomenon. Before the mid eighteenth century it had been common to put younger sons into ecclesiastical careers, in which they were likely to remain as there was little likelihood of them inheriting the estate. I know of no case where a cleric became the head of a Glamorgan estate before this time. However, in the early eighteenth century, families were more likely to consist of only one or two sons. The heir might well die young, or fail to leave issue. He would then be succeeded by his clerical brother – and in the 1750s and 1760s, clerics inherited a series of major Glamorgan estates: Margam, Nash, Dyffryn Aberdare, Boverton, Llanharan and Ynyscedwyn. By the 1790s, a list of 109 leading Glamorgan land-owners would include ten clergy. No commission could reasonably exclude clergymen like Thomas Talbot of Margam, John Carne of Nash, or Thomas Bruce of Dyffryn Aberdare, and thus the precedent was established. In the 1760s, the diary of the schoolmaster William Thomas shows that the five most active JPs in the hundred of Dinas Powis were Sir Edmund Thomas of Wenvoe, squire Richards of Cardiff – and three clerics, Wells, Hopkins and Bassett.

Clerical influence could not entirely solve the problem of a shortage of magistrates. Matters did generally improve, and the number swearing out a *dedimus* rose from 17 in the 1740s to 34 in the 1790s; but there were still Quarter Sessions with only two or three justices in attendance.[45] The Bench was subject to much criticism throughout the period, and not only on the justifiable charge of apathy. 'Justices' justice' in Wales was proverbially unfair, and there were other complaints about the drunkenness and boorish ignorance of the squires who did serve. Under Charles II, there was William Herbert who 'in law matters is scanty'.[46] When Richard Seys destroyed a warrant of Philip Hoby, he admitted the act but in defence claimed that 'whoever lives in the neighbourhood will frequently find occasion from that gentleman, out of kindness, to do so'.[47] The quantities of wine consumed at Sessions lend credence to the partisan claim that the JPs who tried Vavasor Powell in 1669 were very drunk; and such magistrates found suitably bibulous successors in the 1760s with alcoholics like Morgan Williams of Parc.[48]

By contrast, the clerks of the peace provided a nucleus of skilled and experienced men. They were derived from closely interrelated families like the Edwards's of Llandaff and Richards's of Cardiff, who had long traditions of service to the justices. In 1704, Sir Edward Mansell illustrated the importance of the office when he wrote that it would 'be too late to repent' if a 'rotten reed' were chosen; and the professional element increased as the century progressed.[49] Glamorgan's first full-time treasurer was Henry Llewellyn, appointed in 1730, and there was usually a surveyor, although the office might be held jointly with that of clerk of the peace. In mid-century, incumbents were Michael Richards and Thomas Edwards. Nor were the JPs necessarily the slaves of their clerks and other legal advisers, as was suggested by some critics: there is ample evidence that the gentry bought and read the legal manuals published for magistrates, like those of Dalton, Burn and Giles Jacob – and about 1710, Jacob himself visited his patron Sir Charles Kemys, at Cefn Mabli.[50]

More serious a criticism was that the gentry often flouted the law for their own ends, and prevention was difficult if these men were also supposed to be the pillars of local justice. Magistrates were widely accused of tolerating the activities of seditious groups, whether dissenters in the 1660s or jacobites in the next century, and of punishing only those zealots who attempted to interfere with such protected groups.[51] Gentlemen readily resorted to violence for their own political and economic interests; they used mobs for their own purposes, like the prevention of methodist sermons, or (in one case in 1724) the recapture of an errant wife.[52] In another case about 1770, a justice hired murderers to dispose of a personal enemy,[53] and, beside such an incident, it seems trivial that magistrates were constantly involved in poaching or smuggling. The best Macaulay could find to say of such men was that their 'rude, patriarchal justice' was 'in spite of innumerable blunders and occasional acts of tyranny... yet better than no justice at all'.[54]

4. Other offices

The other 'county' office besides justice was that of sheriff; and this also ceased to be the prerogative of the gentry elite, but for very different reasons. The position of sheriff was much more onerous than that of JP, but such prestige attached to the office that sheriffs were still seen as leaders of the community during the risings of the 1640s. Afterwards, the office's burdens so outweighed the honour and status it conveyed that it became deeply unpopular. The sheriff's functions included the receipt of writs and executing the orders of the Westminster courts, so a certain amount of legal skill was required and manuals of instructions and formulae were passed down in Glamorgan over several decades.[55] Where this was inadequate, the under-sheriff provided professional expertise in the law. Fees on entry and departure were heavy, while there were many miscellaneous expenses involved during the ceremonial of Sessions. Professor Mingay has also remarked that even the most vigorous reformer could achieve little in so short a time, with so many corrupt underlings.[56] One's appointment to the shrievalty was therefore an occasion for grief, and a time for vigorous petitions to try and reverse the decision. Between 1660 and 1780, at least fifteen sheriffs were excused after appointment, and this figure does not take into account the influence exercised to avoid the office in the first place. Others tried to avoid the burdens by accepting the post but living outside the county, as at least six did between 1660 and 1700. The dangers of appointment were of course greatly increased if one held land in other counties, and Glamorgan men served repeatedly in neighbouring Welsh counties. Great influence was needed to avoid service altogether, and this was the prerogative of the greatest gentlemen, who had monopolised the office in the time before 1640, when it had been an honour. The proportion of sheriffs from the gentry elite declined from about 50 per cent between 1661 and 1710 to roughly 10 per cent between 1741 and 1790.

Sheriffs had an important political role in elections because they declared the election results, and this role was crucial in two of the most bitterly contested Glamorgan county elections of the period (1734 and 1745), when biassed sheriffs gave false returns. The final decision about an appointment was in the hands of the Lord Chancellor, but from the early eighteenth century it was the Morgans of Tredegar who prepared lists of candidates. They apparently exercised this power humanely, taking into account such extenuating circumstances as dissent, poverty, illness, or a

large family before making a final choice. At times candidates might include a 'common freeholder' or 'an industrious plain farmer who lives in
that low way', men of thirty or forty pounds a year; but such men were exceptional.[57] The men chosen were generally from the broad community of
the gentry, albeit from its lower ranks.

The gentry thoroughly dominated the machinery of administration and
law enforcement at the county level, but their influence also permeated the
lower ranks of society. Below the justices were the high constables, of
whom there were two in each hundred, and who were sometimes drawn
from lesser branches of gentry lines like the Deeres, Aubreys, or Bassetts.
More commonly they were parish notabilities whose yeoman origins are
demonstrated by their Welsh patronymics: in 1733, 17 of the 20 high constables had patronymics, and only the name of William Lucas suggests
even a vague connection with the gentry.[58] Their administrative role was,
however, to carry out the orders of the justices and to keep them informed
of local affairs. They had to keep militia lists and enforce the Game Laws,
which latter involved the search of farmers' houses for guns or traps. This
created a paradox, as they had to enforce these unpopular laws even
though their sympathies were often more with their neighbours than with
their social superiors. Constables were occasionally punished for refusing
to serve, or to obey instructions to seize prisoners or enforce the vagrancy
laws. They were often criticised for weakness, and were easily intimi-
dated – particularly in a well-armed society when constables could be
threatened with guns. What could they do at times like the riot in 1759
when two ships' crews met in Cardiff, and began to fight with 'pikes,
swords, cutlasses, pistols and muskets'? Even if they were prepared to help,
their sympathies might lie elsewhere than in risking their lives for the
squires. In the 1790s, they sympathised with – or even led – riots in support of wage increases, or to demand food.[59]

Below the hundred was the ecclesiastical framework of the parish, with
its many powers and responsibilities; indeed, it was probably the parish
which was the main focus of loyalty and ceremony for the great majority of
Glamorgan's people. This was expressed through rites and ceremonies
which dated back in many cases to pagan or medieval times, like the 'map-
sant' or wake. Officers on this level, like the overseers, were drawn from
the upper levels of village society, and they dealt with matters of local administration like the Poor Law.

The Church's role in administration and as a reinforcement to the
magistrates' power can be seen from the records of the Church courts,

which dealt with legal affairs concerned with marriage or probate. There
was also a great miscellany on matters of behaviour and morality, like the
preservation of good relationships between neighbours, breaches of the
sabbath, and the suppression of clerical immorality. The gentry's influence
over ecclesiastical affairs was partly exercised through powers of ecclesiastical patronage, but they also dominated the vestry, and affairs of parochial importance could involve the exercise of great influence. A faction
feud in the Llantrisant vestry in the 1780s involved some of the greatest
county families,[60] and the vicar's role in this was as one major force among
many powerful lay elements. Indeed, it often seems as if the Restoration
church settlement had established a kind of *de facto* presbyterianism at
parish level – although of the most erastian kind. The different ranks of
clergy were thoroughly integrated into the social hierarchy, and in their
upper levels were the clerical justices of the late eighteenth century. If a
cleric and justice was also a great landowner in his own right, as at Margam or Llanharan, then his local power was very nearly absolute, and there
were an increasing number of such men by the 1750s. Even if this were not
the case, it would be a rare parson who would quarrel with the lay patron,
and thus virtually all the organs of government favoured the gentry.

Glamorgan possessed a number of substantial towns, but these were not
exempt from domination by surrounding landowners. Their corporations
often had an elaborate framework, as at Swansea, whose hierarchy of government included a court baron, a portreeve and a common hall. Town
courts, with their medieval names and forms of operation, continued to
meet into the nineteenth century, and preserved older rights of manorial
jurisdiction.[61] The borough courts of Cardiff or Cowbridge dealt with offences like theft, assault and fortune-telling, besides supervising alehouses,
the quality of bread and apprenticeships.[62] Despite the apparent strength
of municipal traditions, the towns had little real independence, for they
were both administered by the lords and their stewards, and socially dominated by the neighbouring gentry. The complex electoral structure of
Welsh boroughs also meant a constant interplay of factions and a shifting
of allegiances, while burgesses were freely created or dismissed by gentry
or peers in time of political conflict. With this political interest at stake,
municipal independence was not really possible.

5. 'Georgian tranquillity'?

The gentry used their administrative powers as justices of the peace to rein-
force their social and economic power as landlords, so that a gentleman

might exercise power over his locality in either an official or a private capacity. A squire who was also a justice had immense power: he could commit a man as a lunatic, license a drover, or permit a family ruined by some disaster to restore their fortunes by begging far-and-wide. Local control could be exercised by the distribution of official jobs or licences for alehouses: in 1762, the JPs of Dinas Powis hundred renewed the licences of 31 victuallers, though this was only one of ten hundreds in Glamorgan. Squires had great personal prestige, so they were sometimes asked to intervene in local squabbles.[63] Sir Edward Mansell arbitrated between Sir Herbert Evans and Marmaduke Gibbs the lawyer, and kept the papers in the dispute; and later he kept Llandaff's muniments during a minority.[64] At a village level, great landlords like Robert Jones might be drawn into a dispute about granting alehouse licences; and Sir Edmund Thomas and Nathaniel Wells were invoked by a petty schoolmaster to drive out a parish rival. Some gave certificates of personal and political reliability.[65] In 1753, a farmer petitioned the Bench to discipline his unruly sub-tenant, as he was sure there must be some law to this effect.[66]

For the lower classes, the power of the gentry was all-pervasive, and the chief function of this class in their eyes is suggested by the popular name of the Price estate of Parc, known as 'Parc-y-Justice' – the seat of a JP rather than a landlord. We are often impressed by the ease with which gentry power was accepted, the strength of informal means of social control such as patronage and the cult of benevolence. However, as Professor Hay has argued, this 'gentle yoke' was deceptive. Benevolence was 'the obverse of coercion, terror's conspiracy of silence'.[67] As the authors of works like *Albion's fatal tree* have done so much to remind us, 'Georgian' tranquillity was deceptive, and this point can be made just as strongly for South Wales as for England. The years from 1660 to 1688 had been a period of overtly political unrest, of plots and conspiracies; it was, no doubt, memories of this time that made the landlords so anxious to avert a contested election in 1708, with the rioting that might well ensue. One hardly thinks of the Vale of Glamorgan in 1700 as a society obsessed with threats of disorder, yet here is part of a letter written in that year about a gentry feud over the maintenance of Cardiff's bridge and weirs: 'Many plots and contrivances I find are daily hatching by frequent correspondency twixt the weir-nonconformists and the St. Nicholas Mutineers.' They had held a 'great congress... [and] concluded mob-like, one and all, to stand sullen like they are'. Even if this is parody, it shows a remarkable memory of the language of the 1640s.[68]

Resentment of gentry rule might be open (as before 1688) or it might perhaps take the form of rejecting the established Church; but during the eighteenth century, there was a dramatic growth of semi-political forms of protest. These resulted from changes in the composition of the gentry community, in their ideology of gentility (to be discussed in Part III below) and because of economic growth. In both, the first quarter of the century marked a watershed: first, the old families were dying out rapidly; and second, industrial growth was aggravating relationships between landlords and farmers, who resented the new populations. There had always been points of disagreement between landlords and tenants, but peace was more readily restored when the squire was as clearly part of the local community of beliefs and tradition as Sir Edward Mansell. By the 1720s, all the old issues remained – notably the Game Laws – and now rents and dues were to be paid to a new and alien class of landlords. Finally, increased trade was creating a wealthier society with more luxury goods and so more opportunities for theft and smuggling.

6. Crime and social protest

From about 1720, the JPs found themselves facing a wide range of new forms of criminal behaviour in the Vale no less than the uplands, and these appear to reflect a decline in the acceptance of traditional sanctions for power. Perhaps because the Vale was so advanced economically, it appears to have accepted the new fashions in crime. For instance, when Dr Thompson studied the 'Crime of anonymity', he quoted only one eighteenth-century example from Wales, and that was the threat of a food riot at Swansea in 1766.[69] But in the 1720s, both Glamorgan and Monmouthshire had had a wave of attempted blackmail based on anonymous threats of arson, and Pembrokeshire followed in 1738.[70] Stewards were the customary targets – the faces of power and wealth with whom the common people came into most direct contact. Such anonymous threats had spread rapidly throughout England after the burning of the Bristol house of a Mr Packer – and a Monmouthshire letter actually cited this example by name, again reminding us of the influence of Bristol on its localities.

In the same years, there were protests against government officials, and against squires themselves. Customs men and excisemen were challenged with riot and sabotage, in some cases by the popular movement of the 'Corry men'.[71] The horses of excisemen were maimed, and similar motives of social protest may have inspired the poisoning of Lord Talbot's hounds in 1733,[72] and the firing of game heaths in the 1750s.[73] Poaching on the Mackworth estate was said to have reached unparalleled heights in the 1720s.[74] Such a popular undercurrent – directed against government agents and new squires – must have seemed extremely promising to jacobite agents seeking to organise resistance against the new Hanoverian order.

Such opposition never found concrete political expression, but we will often find major differences of emphasis between the new gentry and their tenants, differences which led to crises of law and social order. For instance, landlords' encroachments on common lands had often led to militant resistance and the destruction of enclosures – in south Monmouthshire in 1677, in Gower in 1688, in south Carmarthenshire in 1712.[75] However, the 1740s and 1750s were a time in which campaigns against such encroachments reached unparalleled scale and geographical extent. Indeed, the events of these years belie any suggestion that Wales was peculiarly docile before the coming of industry. Discontent over attacks on common rights (usually for mineral exploitation) was manifested in every county of South Wales.[76] This coincided with food riots by colliers over much of the principality, with terrifying election rioting in Carmarthen, and attacks on Crown agents in west Wales.[77] From the 1750s to the 1790s, there are increasingly common remarks about the ungovernability of certain towns – such as Bridgend and Carmarthen – and certain populations, especially in the industrial areas.

Something of a balance of terror existed: the common people were not roundheads, but they expected certain rights. If the gentry were so inconsiderate as to agree on an electoral candidate without a contest, this did not remove the obligation to treat – or riot might result in as tranquil a town as tory Cardiff.[78] Law and order took their course, with the proviso that the authorities did not arrest highly popular characters like the prostitute Moll Goch.[79] If they did, riot followed. Once the old gentry abandoned traditional standards, then these ways had to be enforced by riot; and that this popular sanction did work is proven by the desperate efforts of the JPs to find corn supplies for the people in 1766 and 1795 rather than face armed riot.[80]

Dr Money's study of the west Midlands suggested the provision riots of the 1760s as the real turning point in social relationships, but I would point instead to the 1720s, suggesting that they mark the beginning of a drastic revision of the terms on which popular acquiescence was secured for gentry rule. In these same years, anti-clericalism reached new heights,

as shown by satirical poems directed against the ecclesiastical courts, and
protests against tithes.[81] In the 1740s, the coming of the clerical justice presumably fostered antipathy. We therefore have abundant evidence to justify describing this period as one of the most turbulent since the years of
conspiracy after the Restoration; and this was precisely the period in
which methodism began to establish itself in Glamorgan. Respect for the
anglican order was at a new low, which might explain why the Calvinistic
methodists of this area were such pioneers in wishing to break away from
the established Church – in Glamorgan, as early as 1745. The elements of
radical continuity in methodism will be examined in a later chapter, but at
this point it should be observed that the favourable environment for
methodist successes was created by the growth of popular unrest under the
first two Georges.

Matters did not improve. Another fruitful source of conflict – this time
in the Vale – was the prevalence of wrecking and coastal plunder, and here
too we can observe a deterioration of order from about the 1730s. Struggles between looters and justices or customs men became more violent
from this decade, though it was not until 1752 that the plunder of a wreck
led to a major riot.[82] There were then six large battles between that year
and 1795, the greatest violence occurring at Sker in 1782, but the 1770s
and 1780s were generally bad.[83] Partly, this was because one would expect
a much greater volume of shipping in the Bristol Channel at that time,
more wrecks, and more ships carrying valuable colonial cargoes. But an
important change had taken place in social relationships: there was a
popular idea that wrecks were communal property, and some petty gentry
retained this view until a late date. In 1782, the steward of Margam[84] believed that 'if the people would let the men belonging to the ship have their
victuals and clothes, they might take the rest'. But gentry opinion was
changing, and this is the background to the new wave of riots. They had
new and conflicting ideas on social duty and law enforcement. Vigorous
action was demanded against wreckers and looters, by those with investments in shipping or the coal trade, but also by squires like Robert Jones of
Fonmon and Pryce of Dyffryn, or by clerical JPs like John Carne of Nash.
In 1775, Glamorgan became one of the few counties to try and prevent
plunder by exemplary executions.[85]

The situation on the coast deteriorated, and to understand this it is
necessary to comment on the assumptions of Dr Rule's essay on 'Wrecking
and coastal plunder'.[86] This suffers from a failure adequately to distinguish
between plundering a wreck – popularly viewed as a *mala prohibita*

offence – and actually causing a wreck through false beacons, which partook of murder. As the two types of crime are seen as closely overlapping, it
is not noticed here that true 'wrecking' was in Glamorgan a very new crime
of the 1760s. Romantic legend suggests otherwise, but the first concrete
references we have to the deliberate luring ashore of a ship are very closely
concentrated between 1769 and 1775.[87] Perhaps once the gentry decided
to enforce the laws against plunder, this broke down inhibitions against
graver crimes – and the Bristol Channel became much less safe. Once
wrecking became acceptable, the people of the Glamorgan coast were sufficiently friendly with those of Cornwall to learn the new skills rapidly, and
Dr Rule shows that wrecking continued in Glamorgan until Victorian
times. There may also have been a growing professionalism in crime: not
until the 1780s does one find a fully fledged professional smuggler and
pirate on the Glamorgan coast, with Knight entrenched in his strongholds
at Barry and Lundy Island. The government had believed and hoped that
this type of menace had ended under Elizabeth – but now such a figure had
a great deal of popular support on which he could count for help.[88]

Yet another divisive issue which arose from the 1750s was that of the
militia. In the patriotic atmosphere of the 1750s and 1760s the Glamorgan
gentry strongly supported a war which seemed to be in their economic interests, and some attempted to establish the new militia organisation of the
county. In 1759, Sir Edmund Thomas of Wenvoe remarked that the gentry
were all zealous, but the 'country people are alarmed at first', and popular
opposition long endured.[89] The lower classes opposed war as an excuse for
heavy taxes, and violently objected to leaving the county, particularly to go
to England. The diary of William Thomas commences in 1762 with
lengthy accounts of the riotous behaviour of the Glamorgan militia in Bristol, and of violent conflicts with citizens, which resulted in some deaths.
There were still Glamorgan men in flight from the legal consequences of
such acts decades later. Others were punished for freeing French prisoners – allegedly as a result of bribery, though perhaps in sympathy for Bretons who spoke a tongue so like Welsh that the two nations were still
mutually intelligible.[90] This may help to explain the common belief that
the county's experienced smugglers had French sympathies.[91] As on so
many issues, the gentry found themselves alienated from the older ways of
life and thought in the county, and having to impose laws which were a
manifestation of newer standards – and of their own essential interests.

In the early nineteenth century, rioting townspeople and industrial workers in Wales tried to appeal to squires and rural justices, because here, they thought, was where real power lay. The squires and justices would also uphold the traditional ideas of popular rights, against the 'market' values of their employers. Their anachronistic views received little sympathy, but it is remarkable that they survived so late: the gentry had long since come to share the market values of the moneyed men, despite the contradictions this involved in their traditional ideology.[92]

5

Political history 1640 – 1688: the heroic age

Introduction

When we examine the political history of Glamorgan, we find a strong gentry class confronting serious potential threats. The great landowners ruled the county – but if their dominance ever faltered they could not but be aware of the presence of a 'disloyal opposition', the natural dissidents of the hills and hinterland who could readily find leadership among the petty gentry of old Welsh lineage. In the prosperous Vale too, any radical challenge would find allies among the lesser gentry and professional families, so challenge from below was to be borne in mind alongside the economic pressures. This had important implications in forming the distinctive ideology of the gentry. Firstly, the community was especially sensitive to threats to its dominance, and in the context of the age, these threats were usually more likely to come from central government than from local revolutionary organisation. A government which was determined to overturn local rulers actually had here a base on which it could work, and on which it could reconstruct a rival consensus. Regimes did this with remarkably thorough success in the 1640s and 1650s, and threatened to do so again in 1688. So, the gentry would at almost any cost defend local independence against central interference or strong government. Such interference was usually associated with religious extremism, so local autonomy tended to be linked to 'moderation' in religion – a moderation best assured by lay control of ecclesiastical appointments. Thirdly, the threat to local power and independence was not just a challenge to the gentry's powers of administration – it could be turned against basic property rights. Arbitrary catholic government might resume ecclesiastical wealth gained at the Reformation, while puritans might attack tithes; and if tithes could be resisted, why not rents? The gentry ideology so aptly summarised as 'religion, liberty, property' arose from very basic needs of self-defence and self-preservation, and the quest for a security that was never really assured between the time of Laud and the fall of James II.

Tracing the development of the gentry's ideology and the story of their fight for security and autonomy naturally focusses on the events of the mid seventeenth century, and the puritan threat. In England, it was common after the Restoration for this powerful mythology of radical and levelling misdeeds to supplant the fear of catholics, who were often fellow-'sufferers' for the Stuart line. But in South Wales, we shall find a peculiar configuration of political loyalties, and of perceptions as to where the greater threat came from. Catholicism was especially strong in lands adjacent to Glamorgan: the recusant heartland of Monmouthshire was very close to the east, while Ireland was a short journey to the west. Still more perilous was the presence of the extraordinarily rich and powerful catholic family of Somerset in the border counties – first as Earls and Marquises of Worcester, from 1682 Dukes of Beaufort. They were also lords of Gower, so that although Glamorgan recusants were pitifully few, local protestants could never sleep easy. The protestant gentry of Glamorgan and Monmouthshire looked instead to the Herberts, Earls of Pembroke as their protectors, and here they found a protestantism so solid that they still looked with nostalgia on the days of the Pembroke dominance decades after it had come to an end. More to the point, the 'Pembroke party' retained an amazing cohesion long after the earls had ceased to interest themselves in Welsh affairs – something which has only been adequately stressed by one of the greatest of Welsh historians, the late Professor Dodd. Aristocratic loyalties arose from and reinforced direct and immediate concerns for life, wealth and security, and these issues pervaded the politics of most of the century.

Gentry politics were often decided by reacting against what was apparently the greatest danger of the day: in the late 1630s, it seemed absurd to fear puritans rather than Laudians; in the early 1660s it took a true protestant zealot to be much concerned with the papist threat while any day, the roundheads could return with Dutch help. But South Wales was different. Protestantism was perceived as much more vulnerable throughout, and great gentry families were supporting very extreme protestant ministers throughout the century – ministers who were among the first Independents and Seekers at a time when most English squires would have regarded these on a par with jesuits. The gentry also remained loyal to these clients when most of their English counterparts were only too willing to persecute dissenters. Gentry royalism took on very strange forms here: unqualified support for the Stuarts meant joining Worcester's catholic faction, so how could the gentry pursue the English pattern of 'Church and King' loyalism? Only after 1688 could the bulk of gentry unreservedly sup-

port king and protestant establishment, which is a major reason for arguing that this was at least some sort of 'revolution'. Equally, only now were
Irish threats removed, while Worcester was finally seen by the central government as the kind of papist and traitor he had always been regarded as
locally.

Before 1688, the politics of South Wales were very different from those
of most of England. However, they resembled those of Scotland and Ireland, where the choice lay between catholic royalist and puritan whig.
These configurations were also more European, in that the central issues at
stake lay between protestant and catholic, and concerned the very existence of protestantism. 1688 changed all this, and the politics of South
Wales became more like the English norm. Until this date too, political divisions had been extremly bitter – perhaps explaining the number of political martyrs from the county, and the violence of the Popish Plot years; and
the central importance of aristocratic faction, based on religious loyalty. It
would be very misleading to study political history only up to 1660, as the
story of the 'revolutionary decades' was then only half-told. After the
watershed of 1688, the political parties and contacts which had been
evolved for this local life-and-death conflict could be turned to the more
familiar struggle for power and patronage between whig and tory.

In this factional history, particular attention will be paid to the development of political sympathies in a few great families over generations – in
the Mansells of Margam, Kemys's or Joneses of Fonmon. While wishing to
avoid merely antiquarian family history, such studies are valuable because
(as will be argued below) the shifts in party loyalty in a family like the Mansells were representative of much wider trends. Only by such individual
studies can we deduce the relative importance of ideology and of family interests in their political behaviour.

Any attempt to understand the changing factions and ideologies of the
Glamorgan gentry community must therefore begin with the Civil Wars;
and the political history of these decades may best be introduced in terms
of three parties, which survived in essence well beyond the Restoration. In
England as a whole, we might discern a pattern of two groups of zealots –
for king or for parliament – together with a third body of neutralists. In
South Wales this was also true, but with some important distinctions.
Apart from the parliamentarian caucus – small before 1645 – there were
two distinct royalist cliques, who deserve to be discussed separately. I have
tentatively called these 'ultras' and 'moderates'.

1. Worcester's ultras

There was clearly a group of royalist ultras centred on the Earl of Worcester and his family and clients. Worcester's main seat at Raglan was a puritan's nightmare, a strategic fortress of immense strength populated by catholic poets, scholars and divines. In the atmosphere of panic prevailing between 1640 and 1642, it is hardly surprising that there were numerous exposés of plots based on Raglan and its occupants. While MPs debated about preventing a concentration of armed strength in the hands of Strafford, Monmouthshire protestants were making desperate efforts to remove the county magazine from Worcester's town of Monmouth to areas like Newport and Caerleon, where the Reformation had at least made some progress.[1] When war came, Raglan was vital to the king's efforts to raise an army, and in the next two decades Worcester's family claimed to have lost some £900,000 in the royal service.[2]

This was 'high' royalism with a vengeance, the sort of attitude which long made Wales proverbial for extreme loyalism. Worcester owned great lands in Glamorgan, where his friends and clients remained loyal to his cause over several generations. Glamorgan's ultra-loyalists included some close to Raglan as clients, servants or 'out-officers', like the Kemys's of Cefn Mabli;[3] and these were central to an extremist clique that held to the Stuart cause until 1688. These leading families were intermarried as is shown in Table 15. Glamorgan had its share of extreme cavaliers who would feature greatly in parliamentarian demonology and later tory hagiography – men like Judge Jenkins who at the outset of the war saw a quick and easy solution to treason by hanging the king's Welsh opponents, gentlemen or not;[4] or his relative Sir Nicholas Kemys, who now adopted a coat of arms with a mailed fist clutching a sword and the motto 'If this hold, woe to the roundhead!' Six Stradling brothers served the king in arms, despite all pressures and incentives to desert, and the Bassetts had similar records of military service. Catholics like the Turbervilles were as royalist as romantic legend would have us believe, for the recusants of the South Wales Border were not so prone to the catholic neutralism which has recently been identified in some English shires by historians like Dr Lindley.[5] Men like Judge Jenkins did much to form the image of the Welshman as a pro-Stuart zealot, and the picture is true in that there were people who saw the war as an attempt to suppress an unholy alliance of aristocratic rebels and a renewed Peasants' Revolt.[6] Wales was the king's main recruiting ground, and the Welsh gentry suffered frightful losses in the early campaigns.

Table 15: *The 'ultra' leadership*

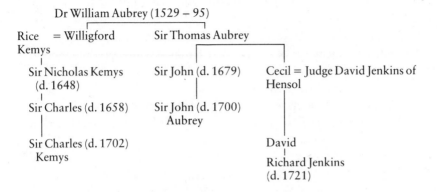

2. Pembroke's moderates

But matters were more complex: we can identify a middle party of very considerable strength, which was certainly not simply a neutralist 'third force'. This was a powerful group associated with the Earl of Pembroke, a great landowner with many tenants and dependents in both Glamorgan and Monmouthshire. Some local gentry had held parliamentary seats as his clients, including the Mansells, Morgans of Ruperra, or Prices of Briton Ferry, while others had benefited from his patronage.[7] The county's royalism in 1642 was not therefore a foregone conclusion. Pembroke's power was greatest in Cardiff, which was (with Swansea and Llangyfelach) one of the few areas in Wales to have a definite puritan element before 1640. The ministers here in the 1630s were William Erbery and Walter Cradock, two of the earliest and most influential Welsh puritans, whose congregation produced many later Independents and quakers; and there would long be a radical tradition in the nearby parish of Roath[8] – where Erbery was born. This had been the home of a Marian martyr, and in the 1630s the living was held by a puritan preacher appointed by the squire, John Herbert, a 'pure precise gentleman' related to Pembroke. Cardiff was apparently the base for missionary activity throughout the *Blaenau* of east Glamorgan and west Monmouthshire before the Civil War. These leaders were in close touch with the better known Independent congregation at Llanfaches near Chepstow, founded about 1639 by William Wroth – an immensely influential figure vital in the early history of dissent even in a great city like Bristol.[9]

The early history of Welsh nonconformity has naturally received a great deal of historical attention, in view of the later influence of dissent in

Wales. Overwhelmingly, the first few decades of this tradition were dominated by the three great names from the south-east, of Wroth, Erbery, and
Cradock.[10] What has not been so well recorded is the remarkable degree of
support these radicals received from some of the greatest lords and gentry,
and not only members of the Herbert family. Glamorgan had a curious
strain of great gentry puritanism which was only paralleled in Wales by the
activity of the Harleys on the Herefordshire borders. Apart from the Herberts, a notable example was the Lewises of Van, probably the richest non-
aristocratic house in Wales. At Oxford about 1602, Wroth had been a ser-
vitor to Sir Edward Lewis, and he would later become Sir Edward's chaplain, and the tutor to his heir. Sir Edward had three brothers: from Sir William of Gelligaer, Wroth received a church living; Sir Thomas of Penmark
appointed William Erbery to the church of St Mary's, Cardiff; and
Nicholas Lewis owned lands at Moulton and Llancarfan, which might
explain the otherwise mysterious flurry of puritan and quaker activity here
after 1640.[11] It was also the Lewises who shared with the Herberts the
three manors into which the parish of Roath was divided.

At the other end of the county, we find similar inclinations in Glamorgan's other great baronet, Sir Lewis Mansell of Margam. He had been a
contemporary of Wroth and Sir Edward Lewis at Jesus College, Oxford
(about 1602), and he married a sister of Sir Edward's. In the 1630s, he
crossed the county in his coach to hear Wroth preach,[12] so he was clearly
sympathetic to aspects of puritanism. He corresponded with Rhys
Prichard, a Pembroke client who wrote very popular Welsh poetry intended to spread religion and morality among the poor.[13] This may indicate the basis for Mansell's interest in the progressive ministers. Many gentry would long favour this sort of popular evangelistic activity as insurance
against catholic revival – a particular danger with the proximity of Worcester's lordship across the Tawe. Moreover, they were not too concerned
as to whether it came from authors or divines approved by the bishops.

So Glamorgan certainly had representatives of the 'puritan squire'. Sir
Lewis Mansell made marriage alliances with opposition peers like Leicester and Manchester, which connected the Mansells with political radicals
like Algernon Sydney. An observer in the 1630s might well have felt that
puritan opposition to the Court stood an excellent chance of winning support in Glamorgan. In fact, this would have been deceptive. Most of the
Lewises fought for Charles I, as did the family of Margam (Sir Lewis himself had died in 1638). Such men represented an important strand of gentry
politics: they agreed with moderate puritans in the need for moral reform,

and they opposed Laud's apparent romanising; but with a very few exceptions, they fought for the King in 1642.

This discussion of royalist factions is relevant in the context of recent discussions of Civil War politics in Wales. Dr Johnson has followed Christopher Hill in asserting that Wales was the darkest of the 'dark corners of the land'[14] in the 1640s, and this is certainly an accurate portrayal of contemporary puritan perceptions. But in such a view, royalism becomes much more homogeneous than it was in reality, and the battle of these decades became a contest between royalist diehard and puritan fanatic. If squires veer between the two schools, they must be seen as trimmers or – in Dr Johnson's phrase – elusive 'survivalists'.[15] In fact affairs were more complex: King Charles's Welsh supporters were a tenuous coalition, likely to fall apart over religious issues – and one part of that alignment was by no means uniformly hostile to moderate puritanism. Perhaps south-eastern Wales was no darker a corner than many an English shire; and only by understanding this can we give sufficient credit to the political sophistication of the gentry in the revolutionary decades. The distinction between the Worcester and Pembroke parties was vital in deciding attitudes to the Civil War, and it would endure in essentials long after 1660.

3. The royalist coalition

In the early years of the war, these royalist divisions were not apparent, and were submerged in the common cause. The handful of vigorous puritans fled to Bristol or Devon in 1642, and Glamorgan's forces made great contributions to the king's cause at the sieges of Gloucester and Bristol. However, this solid loyalty gradually fragmented, especially when there emerged the prospect of defeat and of fighting on the gentry's home territory. Also there was growing opposition to the presence of royalist garrisons, which plundered widely, and whose depredations had caused sporadic violent outbreaks by the common people since the outbreak of war. The gentry shared this hostility to garrisons, financial impositions and plunder, and bitterly resented the loss of county independence at the hands of outsiders, although an extremist like Judge Jenkins fully accepted the need for the English officers.[16] He was supported by ultras like Francis Mansell, who tried to make Glamorgan a refuge for English royalist gentry.[17] Sincere opposition to bloodshed and to war as such became connected to the issue of local independence, and the belief that the county could live at peace if it were not troubled by outsiders. Discontent also resulted from the apparent domination of the royalist cause by catholic interests; and Worcester's son was that Earl of Glamorgan whose Irish negotiations so terrified parliament. The parliamentary blockade of the coast damaged the county's trade, and the fall of Bristol in 1645 threatened ruin, so the 'madness of the multitude' for parliament requires little further explanation.[18]

By the summer of 1645, Glamorgan had a clubman army dubiously credited with 10,000 men, and led by moderate gentlemen whose slogans called for peace, county independence, no excessive taxes, and the security of protestantism.[19] The garrisons were a special grievance, and at least some sections of the movement demanded the removal of all English soldiers from the county. A 'peaceable army' demonstrated before the King, who made some concessions but could not prevent the defection of the South Wales counties during 1645 under 'weathercocks' like Sir Trevor Williams of Monmouthshire. In Glamorgan the Earls of Pembroke and Leicester were believed to have agreed to lead this movement;[20] while in south-west Wales, a similar drift was led by the Earl of Essex and Lord Carbery. The royalist coalition had collapsed. Charles's support in South Wales was soon almost confined to the catholic house of Raglan, with its fanatical protestant allies like Sir Nicholas Kemys. At the end, Worcester himself appealed to the popular neutralism of county society, promising to live in peace as a 'quiet neighbour' and a 'father of his country', but this was to no avail, and the fortress fell in 1646.[21]

This was a triumph for the moderate gentry, who had been greatly strengthened by the popular sentiment represented by the clubmen. However, it was soon apparent that the new parliamentary garrisons were a still greater menace than those of the King, as they imposed an efficient system of financial exactions, and required aid for the equipment of an army to suppress the Irish revolt. Also, the threat to the Church no longer came from Worcester's papists but from the systematic interference with the use of the Prayer Book following the return of the puritan exiles. When radical soldiers introduced idiosyncratic and heterodox practices in Wales, they were widely believed to represent parliament's official policy.[22] New 'Peaceable Armies' appeared in 1646 and 1647 to protest against these developments, and claimed the same rights and privileges they had sought in 1645, although they now expressed support for the imprisoned King. The documents they produced strongly support Dr Morrill's view of the natural localism and conservatism of such communities, although one qualification should be made. The expression of such protests was easily exploited by much more extreme royalists, who would otherwise find it difficult to conduct propaganda for their real views. So, we find 'neutralist', 'moderate' demonstrations after 1646 being orchestrated by royalist diehards like Judge Jenkins, and led by equally dedicated local gentry. In 1647, for example, the main activists in the revolt were all extreme royalists – Sir Edward Thomas, six Bassetts, four Stradlings and fourteen other irreconcilables.[23]

These protests culminated in an alliance of royalists, presbyterians and disgruntled parliamentarians, which led to a rising in 1648; and the New Model Army crushed extremists and moderates alike in battles at St Fagan's and Pembroke. The royalist cause in Wales died with Sir Nicholas Kemys at Chepstow. This campaign ended for over a decade the dominance of the traditional county community with its ideas of local independence, a limited monarchy, and sound anglican teaching; and these battles were also the last efforts by Glamorgan's clubmen. The general atmosphere of royalist conspiracy helped to drive parliamentarian supporters to radical extremes. The extremist Evan Lewis obtained a pro-regicide petition from the county in 1648, while locally, gentry houses were raided and their chapels desecrated. Thereafter the county was ruled by exponents of the nation rather than the region, and of new religious and political ideologies even above the nation.[24]

4. The 'ill times' of the gentry

The new regime, based on the county committee, included some members of major families, like Bussy Mansell of Briton Ferry (who had connections with the Earls of Pembroke) and William Lewis of Van (Wroth's pupil). The Prichards of Llancaeach were also sufficiently well established to have been represented on the Bench at the start of the century; and roundhead supporters included some minor offshoots of great families – like the Stradlings and Herberts, both from puritan Roath. However, the real core of the new ruling group in Glamorgan was drawn from an intermarried clique of lesser gentry, who were chiefly from west of the river Tawe, in Worcester's lordship of Gower. These families were 'gentry', but only in the Welsh sense of 'gentlemen', defined largely by pedigree. At the centre of this clique was Philip Jones of Llangyfelach, a petty squire of this type, who had loyally supported parliament throughout. Some traditions also describe him as a servant and protégé of Sir Lewis Mansell, the elusive but influential puritan squire. Jones and his family won their reward in 1648,

Table 16: *The roundheads*

(Cromwellian leaders are underlined)   John Price of Gellihir

    William Price   Prudence = Thomas Llewellyn

Philip Jones = Jane   John Price   Catherine = Colonel Henry Bowen
(1618 – 74) |
                          Ann = Evan Lewis

when they were among the few trusted government supporters in the area, and his group came to dominate South Wales. His ruling clique was as closely intermarried as was the leadership of their 'ultra' opponents (see Table 16).

For ten years, Philip Jones can only be described as dictator of South Wales, and power was only shared within a narrow clique – for instance with his baptist friend Rowland Dawkins, a 'Major-General' in local memory. Nor could the Pembroke influence moderate this dictatorship, for the Earls paid little attention to the county after 1645, and their local agent was the radical Michael Oldisworth.[25] Professor Underdown's study of changes in county government between 1645 and 1660 often has cause to mention that Welsh events were very different from English and this cannot be sufficiently stressed.[26] Wales experienced a true revolution after 1648, a real transfer of power to a military puritan clique who wished to create a society as radically different from the old order as the 'New England' their allies had sought to create in America.[27]

Puritan rule left the gentry with a very powerful memory of a 'dark age' – a time in which they had been excluded from power,[28] in which their mansions had been searched and plundered.[29] Jones's regime also left memories of extreme corruption. Naturally royalist propaganda would exaggerate this, and would seize on every example of landowners expropriated, juries rigged and court judgments ignored; but there is also a great deal of contemporary evidence to confirm the essential core of the charges.[30] Also, about 1709, details of anglican sufferings were collected for a martyrology of the anglican clergy, and this supplemented contemporary manuscripts by the family traditions of Francis Davies and Edward Mansell, both from 'suffering' lines.[31] Here, Jones is portrayed as a robber baron in the Vale, with servants like Evan Lewis as bandits and cattle-thieves rather than soldiers or politicians. Philip Jones's seizures of Glamorgan lands were paralleled in most parts of Wales, especially by the Earl of Carbery, who made his peace with Cromwell and 'hath set up and maintaineth an interest in most counties of Wales'.[32] Jones's allies, like Rowland Dawkins and Edmund Thomas, similarly found puritan convictions to be no barrier to personal aggrandisement. Conquered Ireland was a new field of enterprise for Welsh roundheads like Colonel Henry Bowen of Gower and William Cadogan of Cardiff, both of whom founded landed estates there – and the Cadogans would be earls in the next century.[33]

The justification for this military dictatorship was that the local roundheads were a tiny clique of the righteous in that great sea of popery, ignorance and indifference which was Wales, and that government by the 'godly' needed rigid enforcement to survive. As Fleetwood remarked, 'There are some precious good people in Wales, though very few. The generality of people in those parts, I fear, are little better than the Irish: they have invenomed hearts against the ways of God.'[34] In barbaric Wales, it was said, 'men will rule if they be not ruled'.[35] The regime lived in constant fear of risings, and riots often arose from popular hostility to the excise.[36] It is an index of the success of dictatorship that although puritan rule was harshest in Glamorgan, there were no insurrections here after 1648. Force, however, could only be a short-term solution, and wider measures were required for the remodelling of government in the interest of the 'godly'. In the 1650s the puritan lawyer Evan Seys was examining the charters of some Glamorgan boroughs, perhaps with the intention of altering the structure of power in favour of his party;[37] but in the long term the real solution was to broaden the popular base of support by converting Wales to radical protestantism.[38] Conversion was the policy from which would flow all the reforms desired by radical theorists: in education and the legal system, in the extension of social justice, and in a soundly protestant foreign policy.

In a sense it was partly an advantage that Wales was so little touched by protestantism, for it was seen as a *tabula rasa* in which the boldest experiments could be tried, as in New England.[39] Philip Jones and his Welsh allies were close to Hugh Peter, and this circle evolved the idea of the 'Commission for the propagation of the Gospel in Wales', to fulfil the old puritan ambition of a mission to the 'dark corners' of the island.[40] However, it was also seen as a radical experiment for the future 'godly' government of Britain. It was feared that the commission was less interested in saving the souls of the ignorant than in preparing a power-base for Major-General Harrison, who is often mentioned in connection with the radical Welsh groups. He had been friendly with Welsh puritans like Cradock and Vavasor Powell, and he dabbled in the affairs of Welsh towns like Monmouth and Haverfordwest. Indeed, he was such a familiar figure that in their correspondence, he is simply referred to as 'M.G.H.',[41] while the propagation measure was known as 'Harrison's Act'.[42] There was a substantial Welsh millenarian element in Barebone's parliament, which was the culmination of these attempts at far-reaching social reform, but its failure by no means marked the end of the effort of 'propagation'. It continued until 1660, although it was widely accused of being only a mechanism for the transfer of Church funds to Philip Jones's circle, after it had lost its religious *raison d'être*. The 'Court of Triers' continued to meet at Llantwit Major to examine ministers, and it was administered by the moderate squires Deere and Humphrey Wyndham; but 'behind the door' was Philip Jones, and outside, his satraps waited to seize herds of cattle.[43]

After the radical failure in 1653, Harrison was followed into opposition by some of his Welsh followers, notably Vavasor Powell, and who carried on a republican propaganda campaign in Wales and Ireland.[44] Philip Jones, Dawkins and their Glamorgan allies did not accept his position, despite extensive links with the opponents of the Protectorate, and no doubt they were influenced in their decision by sheer love of power and wealth. But they were not entirely cynical, for many puritans thought that Cromwell could still achieve 'godly' rule, involving low taxes, the extirpation of popery and the militant expansion overseas of the Gospel. Also, the paucity of loyal men in Wales meant that the local puritans needed the support of the central government as constantly as that government relied on them. The Glamorgan roundheads therefore stayed true to Cromwell, and won their rewards. Cromwell counted Philip Jones and William Erbery among his close friends, the former becoming Comptroller of the Household, while Evan Seys became Attorney-General. When Cromwell formed his 'upper house', the new 'Lords' included Philip Jones, John Jones of Merionethshire, and Edmund Thomas of Wenvoe, whose extensive family connections included Edmund Ludlow, and the new 'Lords' William and Walter Strickland.[45] Radical criticisms of the new 'courtiers' appeared justified when Philip Jones urged Cromwell to accept the crown, and offered to make him financially independent of parliament. Locally, however, Jones's circle was as radical as it had ever been, and Propagation continued apace, in the effort to undermine the traditional religious order.

The new religious regime was based on itinerant ministers, many of whom were described even by the nonconformist martyrologist Calamy as being of low birth, immoral, illiterate, and sometimes monoglot Welsh speakers.[46] Independents and baptists predominated, and soon established themselves in areas previously little acquainted with puritan ideas. The strength of later puritanism in areas like upland Glamorgan was attributed both by contemporaries and later commentators to the 'Grand Rebellion', when the 'hydra of sectaries' 'multiplied apace'.[47] Also, these conversions took place in areas without much experience of even generally protestant teaching, and soon still more radical sects arose whose heresies reflected older traditions of popular scepticism verging on atheism.[48] Both Independent and baptist congregations were troubled by secessions to such extreme ideas, as at Merthyr Tydfil where there emerged sects of ranters and quakers. In the baptist church in Gower, the roundhead Colonel Bowen came to reject the whole supernatural world, accepting agnostic opinions which sound like those of a ranter – although his sister was a quaker.[49] Such dissensions were especially common in Erbery's congregation at Cardiff, for Erbery had come to doubt the certainty of almost all religious dogmas, including the divinity of Christ.[50] He became a 'Seeker', waiting in spiritual darkness for God's enlightenment.[51] Critics saw him as a 'seducing quaker', and his followers often found the enlightenment he had sought in this new sect, although they followed the extreme 'Naylorite' wing of the movement. When Naylor made his messianic entry into Bristol, he was accompanied by Erbery's daughter Dorcas, and by Timothy Wedlock, who settled in Loughor.[52]

The leadership of the local quakers included at least five officers from the Cardiff garrison, old puritans like the man 'who hath been a commission officer in the service of the Commonwealth nine or ten years in England and Ireland'.[53] There was also Matthew Gibbon of Moulton, a parliamentary captain who had lost an arm 'for the Good Old Cause, the liberty of conscience', and Major John Gawler, a member of the Cardiff congregation. Gawler, like Bowen, had formerly been part of Philip Jones's clique.[54] At last puritanism was winning wide popular support in Glamorgan, but in a form which many traditional 'godly' men found repulsive. Leading baptists in Wales and the Borders now denounced quakers in the same terms as papists. Accounts of quaker sufferings in Glamorgan list the chief persecutors, who included once-radical puritans like John Herbert of Roath, or baptists like Rowland Dawkins. Also for the first time, a puritan sect made a large impact on the arable areas of the Vale of Glamorgan, traditionally a squire ridden country with an acquiescent peasantry. Now, however, the demands of conscience led the sectaries to attack the 'hireling priests', who were the Independent or baptist ministers in the villages. A vision of the tenantry rebelling against their civil and ecclesiastical superiors – under the leadership of roundhead veterans – was terrifying for both the old and new ruling elites, and an attack on tithes could lead to a refusal to pay rents. The savage and widespread reaction against the quakers by ruling classes both old and new tends to confirm Dr Barry Reay's view about the importance of the tithe issue in the opposition to early quakerism.[55]

5. Shades of royalism

Even before religious developments appeared to be moving towards the destruction of all established norms, the traditional community of county society was deeply alienated from the regime. The extreme royalist position was upheld by the Aubreys, Kemys's and Jenkins's, who maintained episcopalian clergy and who avoided the universities. There was a flourishing underground tradition of anglicanism throughout South Wales from about 1644, when refugees had established themselves at St Donat's, Llantrithyd and (Carbery's seat) Golden Grove.[56] They were led by Francis Mansell, and included both present and future bishops as well as Oxford scholars – major anglican figures like Jeremy Taylor and Gilbert Sheldon. Such refugees maintained the traditional services, but they also taught a new generation of loyalists, under the protection of gentry like the Aubreys of Glamorgan, and counterparts throughout Wales and the Borders. It was through the patronage of such high anglican families that Leoline Jenkins began his friendship with leaders like Sheldon who would gain power at the Restoration, and thus commenced a career which led to his becoming Secretary of State in the 1680s. In terms of religious belief, I have argued elsewhere that it was these Welsh circles which largely succeeded in passing on the tradition of Great Tew to Restoration governments.[57]

Other royalists were equally determined to preserve the old order. Some fought on until the last campaigns, and then fled abroad to serve the exiled Court. This group included, from Glamorgan, members of the Bassett, Carne and Gamage families, who did not return until 1660. Even among those who remained, royalist zeal continued unabated. The funeral of one puritan leader in 1659 was prevented by the episcopalian Richard Seys, who used his sword to ensure that Swansea's church should not be polluted by the corpse.[58] But anglican loyalty required more than such physical resistance. Both abroad and at home, catholics made great efforts in these years to win converts from the wreck of the Church of England, and some gains were made, like the Carnes of Nash.[59] For the old Church of England, the double threat from puritans and papists required constant vigilance, and the best that could be hoped for was survival, albeit in ever diminishing numbers.

The Welsh were regarded as 'the forwardest and greatest promoters' of the Stuart cause, but not all ex-royalists remained aloof from the new order.[60] Philip Jones, for example, was served by some gentry who had been 'malignants', even catholics, but who were now completely dependent on him. These included major Glamorgan gentlemen, like Richard Lougher, 'one that submitted in all government' and David Evans of Gwernllwynchwyth, 'a dark-lantern man that never stuck at anything in the ill times', and they had counterparts throughout South Wales.[61] On the other hand, it is uncertain whether the most flagrant 'turncoats' were cynically seeking wealth and place, or else trying to support any government which offered peace and order, regardless of ideological considerations. Such a view would appeal to the 'moderate' party of the Civil War, who hated war and feared social chaos, and sympathised with the Protectorate's attempts at moral reform. The Cromwellian regime was also a defence against the fanatics to the 'left' of the baptists, for by the mid-1650s even Philip Jones's circle seemed preferable to the quakers.

These 'moderates' are typified by Sir Trevor Williams in Monmouthshire, a defector from the king's cause who was by the 1650s patronising bitterly anti-radical clergy like John Cragge. He earned the favour of the Protectorate despite the hostility of local Army authorities. (In the same way, Worcester had favoured his execution in the 1640s, although the Court trusted Williams until the last days.[62]) Naturally there is a tendency to see such figures as simple 'trimmers' or turncoats, but they appear rather to represent a consistent party, changing sides more on the basis of ideological belief than of simple self-interest. I would suggest that one common pattern of political development began with moderate puritanism, moral reform and anti-popery before the Civil Wars, continued with moderate royalism in the 1640s and presbyterianism in the 1650s, and led to 'country' opposition by the 1670s. When we examine the whigs of the 1680s, we often find that their families had passed through most of these 'moderate' stages. Examples were the Harleys of Herefordshire, and Arthur Owen of Orielton in Pembrokeshire, who was regularly denounced as a traitor by both political extremes. Certainly presbyterianism was a reasonable 'moderate' position at this time: Cardiff had provided the presbyterian – royalist cause with its great martyr Christopher Love (executed in 1651), and the presbyterian clergy were as violently anti-quaker as the most conservative squire could wish.[63]

This 'moderate' course of behaviour is exactly what we find in

Glamorgan with the career of Sir Edward Mansell of Margam, son of the puritan Sir Lewis. Edward was the nephew of the second Earl of Manchester, the leading presbyterian with whom he spent much time in the Interregnum. Margam had been royalist in the wars, but the Mansells would ultimately follow their Pembroke patrons into the service of the Commonwealth. By 1657, Mansell served on one of the Protector's committees – to examine the effectiveness of sumptuary laws – and it was about this time that he and his 'moderate' allies began to be represented once more on the county committees.[64] Here they allied with those ex-Cromwellians who had long opposed the corruption of the Propagator clique, and there began a new attempt to impeach Jones which was greatly facilitated by the death of Cromwell. By 1659, these 'moderates', on either side, were allied, and they looked increasingly to the Stuarts to end the Republic. Turncoats of 1645 like Sir Trevor Williams and Thomas Morgan of Machen were allied with moderate royalists like Mansell of Margam and Gwynne of Llanelwedd, and with ex-Cromwellians like Evan Seys and Humphrey Wyndham. This alliance was formed to defeat Philip Jones and religious extremism, but the foundations were now laid of a movement which would be important long after the Restoration, although then its members would be challenging the extremism of the opposite, catholic, party.

Their initial prospects were excellent; for by 1660, the roundhead commander Bussy Mansell, 'early repenting', was negotiating with the Stuarts.[65] Philip Jones's clique had generally been excluded from office by 1660, and only well-timed benevolence to the Mansells and the Earls of Carbery prevented his exile or execution. Throughout South Wales, the committees fell to 'cavaliers or at best neuters', in the words of Edmund Thomas of Wenvoe.[66]

Of course, this 'moderate' triumph depended on national affairs, and there were considerable vested interests which stood to lose everything by a Stuart return. The defeat of Booth's rising appeared to make a Restoration impossible, so in 1659 it seemed at least as likely that the future lay with radical republicans, particularly the quakers. Lambert at least seemed to be directing his policies to the manipulation of such a movement. Certainly, republicans did not lack schemes for a tolerant commonwealth, based on the 'Good Old Cause' of religious toleration, and other radicals evolved ideas not unlike later secular whiggery: toleration, equality before the law, parliamentary sovereignty and no standing armies.[67] The apparent revival of radicalism had a special impact in the old royalist areas, where the puritans felt themselves to be an especially small and threatened minority. Power appeared to be passing to baptists and quakers, and in Wales the main castles were placed in the hands of Vavasor Powell's men, still strong although his congregations were much troubled by defections to quakerism.[68] In Glamorgan, it seemed as though the quakers were about to fulfil all the worst royalist fears: the quaker ex-officer John Gawler asked Fox's advice whether he could accept Fleetwood's offer of a colonelcy in the militia, under a superior who was 'loving to Friends'.[69] Another veteran, Matthew Gibbon, wished to become a captain, and the congregation were sympathetic to him, hoping he might thus be 'serviceable for Truth'. Fox discouraged their enthusiasm, but (as Dr Cole rightly noted) pacifism was by no means a definite quaker trait in 1660.[70] This illustrates the great potential loyalty on which a radical republic could draw. On the other hand, the republic was weakened by a grave economic crisis, and the extremists lacked a serious alternative leader, for Lambert never fulfilled his early promise. The military grandees could destroy any government, but they could not construct anew. When Richard Cromwell indicated his unwillingness to continue his dynasty, the only alternatives were a Stuart Restoration or a radical commonwealth, and the latter went by default.

Even so, no royalist could afford to be sanguine about the permanence of the Restoration, and throughout 1660 there were attempts at organised opposition in most counties of Wales, often under experienced ex-officers.[71] A strong current of opposition continued for some years, and government fears were exacerbated by the possibility that plots in 1661 and 1663 might have regional offshoots, notably in Vavasor Powell's areas of Wales. Until about 1666 there were constant fears of regional and national plots. Militant puritanism was very strong in all the South Wales boroughs until the 1680s, for parliamentary 'captains' and 'colonels' were well represented in corporations no less than in conventicles. There was also thought to be a threat that old roundheads would serve as a 'fifth column' for Dutch invaders. Only the lack of such outbreaks in the war of 1665 – 7 went some way to calming these fears.

6. 'The southern flames': the royalist reaction 1660 – 1675

The Welsh gentry took vigorous action to establish the new regime, and often used violence of a degree beyond even that permitted by the draconian legislation of these years. All dissenters were seen as potential rebels – particularly quakers and baptists – and repression was endemic through the 1660s.[72] Ministers were repeatedly charged with seeking to coordinate seditious activities in Glamorgan and south-west England, and these charges were substantiated by the existence of congregations straddling the Bristol Channel. The baptists of the Vale and Swansea were close to those of Somerset, while the Gawlers' quaker congregation at Cardiff shared ministers with the Friends of Bristol, the 'Quakers' Jerusalem'.[73] Such a relationship must have seemed to the anglican gentry like part of a national conspiracy. No doubt the severity of Philip Jones's rule made the Glamorgan gentry especially fierce against dissent, and the number of ejections in 1662 (twenty-four) was the highest for any Welsh county. When Colonel Carne disrupted a Merthyr Tydfil conventicle in 1668, he was asked by what authority he acted, whereupon he 'laid his hand upon his sword, and said that was his authority'.[74] In 1670, the puritan James Owen was relieved to flee from 'the southern flames' of persecution, to the relative peace of North Wales.[75] The fanaticism of some sections of the anglican gentry was demonstrated in 1672, when Colonel Thomas Stradling of St Donat's ordered his army company to punish the citizens of Huntingdon and Sawtry as 'Roundheadly rebellious rogues' deserved, because Huntingdon was the home of the 'rebellious rogue', Cromwell.[76]

The great sense of danger felt in the early years of the Restoration united the various sections of royalist opinion in this extreme position. Notable among the persecutors of dissent in this period were, naturally, families who had suffered heavily for royalist activities, and were also close to the Marquis of Worcester. Among these were Sir John Aubrey, Sir John Carne, Sir Richard Bassett and David Jenkins. But Pembroke's family was back in full strength in Glamorgan: the fifth earl was *Custos* from 1660, and his son was county MP from 1661 to 1669. The new president of the Council of Wales was equally 'moderate', for this was that Earl of Carbery who had defected to parliament in 1645, and had kept his county loyal to Cromwell. Other 'trimmers' now active in persecution included the Gwynnes in Radnorshire and Herberts of Cherbury, the latter being especially severe against the quakers.

Another prominent moderate with wide authority after 1660 was Sir Edward Mansell of Margam, who was a deputy-lieutenant in all the South Wales counties. Throughout the difficult period of the Dutch wars, he won the government's gratitude as an efficient Vice-Admiral of South Wales and colonel of the militia, and he provided useful accounts of local families and their political inclinations. As early as the 1670s, admiring high church clergy assumed that so zealous a man must have been the son of a royalist martyr killed by the roundheads; but in fact, Mansell royalism had been no means as unbending as that of Aubrey or Jenkins. In his militia work, he now cooperated with other old 'moderates' like Carbery, George Gwyne and others in south-west Wales.[77]

The need to prevent a return to the Republic made the gentry accept normally unpalatable measures, like the role of the Somersets of Raglan in defending the new regime in the Borders, or the dominance of the region rather than the county in militia organisation. In the north and west of Britain, the new order was to be based on well-defended castles like Carlisle, Chester, Ludlow and Chepstow, the last of which was said in 1663 to dominate four counties; and it was in the hands of the former Earl of Glamorgan, now Marquis of Worcester. Once the immediate danger had passed, many gentlemen raised an outcry against the threat of tyranny represented by Chepstow Castle and the Somerset dynasty, but in the 1660s this extraordinary power was accepted as necessary.[78] To return to the terms of the 1640s, this represented a renewal of that royalist coalition of moderates and extremists. Although unlikely to be stable for long, it lasted long enough to secure the restored order.

The Glamorgan gentry were very close to Restoration governments, and especially when the men who gained power in Church and State were often those who had taken refuge in South Wales during the Interregnum. Between 1660 and 1680, about five English and two Irish bishops were in this category, including Sheldon who was virtual head of the English Church from 1660 to 1677 – and he remembered old friends like the Stradlings and Bassetts.[79] The Duke of Ormonde's Welsh connections included Sir Edward Mansell and Francis Gwyn, and Mansell was also linked to the Court by his relationship with Manchester, who was now Lord Chamberlain. Moreover, there were powerful interests urging the government to make full payment of its debts and moral obligations to those who had served the Stuarts in adversity, and between 1660 and 1662 there were many such appeals for patronage or relief.

Royalist exiles requested pensions, often citing the misfortunes of themselves or their relatives in the 'ill times', as when Miles Button of Cottrell mentioned his relationship to the martyrs of 1648, Kemys and Poyer. Eight Glamorgan squires were to be enlisted in the proposed new order of 'Knights of the Royal Oak'.[80] Among more palpable rewards, Sir Richard Bassett was to be a Collector of Royal Tolls, and Sir William Bassett became a royal Chamberlain. Dr William Bassett was the mainstay of high Sheldonian settlement in the diocese of Llandaff, where yet another relative (Henry Bassett) became registrar. The Mansells of Margam became Chamberlains of South Wales; while a junior branch of the family became customs officers in Swansea. These were good years for royalist sufferers like the Aubreys, who won rich ecclesiastical offices in Breconshire; and Sir John Aubrey found it hard to believe that a lawsuit would be permitted to go against so loyal a servant of the late martyred king as himself.[81]

The shower of pensions and offices now received by old royalists throughout Wales made the Restoration a golden age in their history.[82] For instance, the return of traditional county society to government favour is strikingly demonstrated by military patronage. The colonels of regiments were usually peers or magnates in their own right, who used their patronage so that their officers were almost entirely drawn from the leading families of the areas they dominated. After the Restoration, the ascendancy of peers like Worcester, Carbery, Pembroke and Leicester ensured a wealth of commissions for the gentry of South Wales, and some officers who rose by such means later acquired their own regiments, thus continuing the local associations. Examples were Sir Thomas Stradling and Sir John Carne, both members of the Duke of York's catholic military clique.[83]

Links between the Glamorgan gentry and the government were especially close in the 1670s, as is suggested by the friendly correspondence between Secretary Williamson and the Mansells and Morgans. As 'Court' MPs, they were summoned to parliament at the beginning of the session and received government newsletters, but social contacts also lubricated the workings of effective government, and Williamson eventually visited Margam. The moderate clique around Mansell was not regarded as very loyal to the Court – including Sir Trevor Williams and the house of Tredegar.[84] However, Williamson was aware of the dangers of confirming favours to any one family or clique, so he also directed his diplomatic efforts to the old ultras – Sir Edward Stradling, Sir Charles Kemys and David Jenkins. This network was greatly extended with the rise in government of Leoline Jenkins and Francis Gwyn. Both were Court MPs and (among other offices) sometime Secretaries of State. Their acquisition of power was widely greeted in Glamorgan because they could now help their 'countrymen' from the very source of patronage. In 1679, Jenkins and Gwyn were asked by squire Morgan of Coedygoras 'whether there be in the disposal of either of you any place that may be in any way advantageous to his eldest son', and they were to be aided in this search for income by those other loyalists, Sir John Aubrey and Sir Charles Kemys.[85] In the

1680s, Francis Gwyn made repeated efforts to find places for his relations, but his requests laid less emphasis on their capabilities than on the loyalty of their families, and the fact that they were his kinsmen.[86]

7. Moderates and presbyterians

With so many bonds of affection and mutual interest, Glamorgan should have been one of the most firmly loyal counties, but as in the Civil War, the balance of parties was more complex than a simple twofold division between cavaliers and roundheads; and a very similar 'middle' party recurs, now standing above all for religious toleration. From the early years of the Restoration, the broadly 'loyalist' gentlemen appear to have been divided on the issue of persecution, and several of the leading families did not act against the sectaries. In 1664, the anglican gentry of the Vale complained that conventicles 'abound in the western parts, and that we could not well remedy the same without giving some disgust to the deputy lieutenants and justices of the peace of those limits'. Almost certainly, this criticism refers to the Mansells of Margam and Briton Ferry, and the Hobys of Neath.[87] Here they are accused of tolerating baptists, but there is still more evidence of gentry sympathy for those moderate Independents and presbyterians who were ejected in 1662. They were little troubled after initial fears for the Restoration had subsided, as their piety and moderation appealed particularly to those gentry families who had themselves been 'moderate' royalists in the 1650s.

The most prominent presbyterian of the area was Samuel Jones, who after ejection, 'taught academical learning in his own house, and had under his tuition some young gentlemen of good quality in that country'.[88] His pupils in the 1670s included Thomas Mansell, probably the son of Sir Edward, the over-tolerant deputy-lieutenant, and Samuel Jones's close friends included the Mansells' chaplain, the conformist vicar of Margam. Similar harmony existed in Swansea, which Stephen Hughes made a great centre for dissenting education, although he too was close to the local anglican clergy. Hughes followed in the tradition of evangelism among the poor long favoured by the Mansells; and he even edited the works of Rhys Prichard, the friend of Sir Lewis Mansell.[89] Again at Swansea, the Independent Marmaduke Matthews continued his ministry with the sympathy of the local magistrates, and of unspecified gentry who must have included the Mansells and the Hobys of Neath Abbey.[90] We have already observed the ambiguous loyalism of the Mansells, but the Hobys were equally 'moderate'. Philip Hoby was the son of a presbyterian member of the long parliament, ejected during Pride's Purge; and Philip's wife was a sister of the republican writer James Tyrrell.

With a few exceptions among the hill-gentry, Glamorgan squires did not join dissenting congregations after 1660. However, we can observe a whole opposition culture based on those like Edmund Thomas who conformed but remained sympathetic to dissent. Indeed, the Wenvoe family long retained these views, as the estate granted land for a dissenting chapel at Cardiff on extremely generous terms as late as 1696. At Briton Ferry, the journals of Bussy Mansell's steward at Briton Ferry in the 1670s record days of fasting and humiliation for the 'Popish Plot', as well as noting the murder of Sir Edmund Berry Godfrey, and the death of the presbyterian leader Thomas Manton.[91] There were other great gentry families, some members of which were at least half 'conventicler', and who invariably referred to the Sabbath as the 'Lord's day' rather than the profane 'Sunday'. In 1668, the much-feared Vavasor Powell came to Glamorgan,[92] 'hearing of the moderation of the gentlemen of these parts', but his meeting at Merthyr Tydfil was disrupted by soldiers, and even Edmund Thomas agreed with these draconian actions. Powell's biographer ironically reminds us that this was 'in Oliver Cromwell's time, Lord Thomas' – and Thomas's sister was living in exile with her husband, Edmund Ludlow, the regicide. However, Powell's hopes of 'moderation' were not entirely disappointed, for he was 'very civilly and mildly' treated by 'the chiefest of the deputy lieutenants, S. E. M. [Sir Edward Mansell]'. Mansell's attitude is all the more remarkable when it is recalled that Powell was one of the chief surviving links with the Fifth Monarchy tradition; when he died in 1670, he is even reported to have had a vision of three saints, 'Paul, Harrison and Cradoc'.[93] Surely Mansell could have felt no sympathy for him? But one recalls that Sir Edward's uncle was that Earl of Manchester who had even been inclined to leniency at the trial of the regicides. It is very remarkable still to find broadly 'puritan' squires in the bitter years of the 1660s, and acting so similarly to their fathers in the 1630s.

We may illustrate the nature and composition of the 'moderate' party by studying the actions of various squires during and after the Civil War. In Table 17, the first three columns indicate the royalist veterans of the revolutionary years, while the remainder indicate how these were split into distinct factions by the question of religious persecution. Mansell and the five listed after him often seem to act as a faction in county society, while similarly 'tolerant' patterns can perhaps be traced for Sir Edward Thomas,

Table 17: *Activity in religious persecution 1660 – 1688*

The columns denote:
1 Major compounder of civil war[a]
2 Proposed Knight of the Royal Oak 1660[b]
3 Deputy-lieutenant 1663[c]
4 Signed warrant against quakers 1661[d]
5 Active against baptists 1663 – 4[e]
6 Involved in arrest of Vavasor Powell 1668[f]
7 Investigated radical plot 1683[g]
8 Signed warrant to arrest suspected rebels 1685[h]

	1	2	3	4	5	6	7	8
Sir Edward Mansell			x					
Humphrey Wyndham								
Miles Button	x		x					
Bussy Mansell			x					
David Matthews, Llandaff	x	x						
Richard Seys	x							
Sir John Aubrey	x		x		x	x		x
Sir Richard Bassett	x		x	x	x		x	
David Jenkins	x	x		x			x	x
William Herbert			x	x	x		x	
Herbert Evans			x	x				
Sir Thomas Lewis			x		x			
John Carne	x					x		
Lamorack Stradling	x			x				
Richard Lougher					x			
William Bassett		x			x	x		
Sir Edward Stradling	x	x	x					x
Sir Charles Kemys	x						x	
Sir Edward Thomas	x		x					
Thomas Matthews, Castell-y-Mynach	x	x	x					

Source: [a] *Cal. Comp., passim.*
[b] Banks, *Antient usage*, pp. 170 – 2.
[c] PRO SP 29/88, fo. 95.
[d] GRO D/DSF/F/313/3.
[e] PRO SP 29/97, fo. 47.
[f] Bagshaw, *Vavasor Powell*, pp. 132 – 42, 177 – 82.
[g] *CSPD 1683 (June – December)*, p. 262; *1682*, p. 318.
[h] P&M 1137.

and possibly Matthews of Castell-y-Mynach. This 'tolerant' party has previously been identified as the followers of the Earl of Pembroke, and support for this view comes from a study of the earl's sale of his Glamorgan lands between 1666 and 1668.[94] He disposed of £12,000 worth of lands, and his local friends took great care to see that they went to politically safe hands – presumably at preferential rates. Sir Edward Mansell acquired one-third of the total, while 45 per cent passed to Evan Seys, Martin Button, John Wyndham and Bussy Mansell.

I believe that we are dealing with two distinct factions among the elite of county society, who were chiefly divided by attitudes to dissent. One party looked for support at Court to Wharton and Manchester; the other to Sheldon and Ormonde. The 'moderates' are clearly marked, while the order of 'Knights of the Royal Oak' may perhaps suggest the leadership of the 'ultras'. But whatever the exact meaning of this order, the broad pattern is clear. Furthermore, this division implied a major divergence in view about the obedience due to the central government and its representatives. It also seems probable that this lack of concern about the dissenting threat arose from the greater fears experienced by moderates about catholicism, even in the years of royalist reaction. As in neighbouring counties, some Glamorgan puritans were still tolerated by the 'sober part of the gentry', who were a powerful element in county society.

8. Anti-popery

From about 1666, the Stuart dynasty seemed securely placed on the throne, and there was some relaxation of severity towards ex-roundheads in most counties of South Wales, where they began once more to occupy official positions. This was especially marked after the fall of Clarendon and the disgrace of Sheldon, both in 1667. Frequent complaints were now heard of the 'old leaven' and their strength and arrogance, especially since they seemed to have powerful friends at Court.[95] Of course, there were such old Cromwellians who conspired against the new regime, but they were not responsible for the revival of gentry opposition to the Stuarts in the 1670s. Whiggery or 'country' opposition was widespread among those moderate gentry who had abhorred Philip Jones' rule, and who were now marked by their tolerant religious attitudes. The drift of moderates like Sir Edward Mansell into vigorous opposition was caused particularly by the increasing fear of catholic influences, both nationally and locally, after 1666. The threat of a catholic king seemed to presage religious persecution, or else a return to civil war and military despotism. In the 1670s, Glamorgan's borough member Sir Robert Thomas (lately a fervent royalist) was noted for the fierce bigotry of his parliamentary attacks on the king's papist advisers, among whom he counted Pepys.[96] He could best be described as an adventurer, not fully trusted by Shaftesbury, and he attempted to sell information on whig activities to Danby. Of greater significance was the growing alienation of the moderate royalists, classified as Court MPs in the 1670s, but perhaps even more violent than the ex-roundheads during the exclusion crisis. This transition was the result of specific local grievances, among which anti-popery was dominant.

As I have argued elsewhere, catholicism was a real popular movement on the Welsh Border, and Monmouthshire was second only to Lancashire in catholic loyalties.[97] Fear and hatred of catholicism were based on its overt nature, which led to exaggerated estimates of its numerical strength. When in 1668 Vavasor Powell was on trial before the Glamorgan JPs, he very shrewdly asked why they should bother to persecute a protestant dissenter like himself while popery was rampant.[98] This was precisely the question that many squires were beginning to ask themselves. Anti-popery was peculiarly strong in this area because of the instability of religious loyalties in the previous half-century. Gentry families were sharply divided between members of different faiths, and this apparently led to intense religious conflicts. The fanatical anti-papists and priest-hunters of the 1670s and 1680s regularly came from strong catholic backgrounds, and were often lapsed catholics themselves. In this area at least, whig loyalties were closely allied to anti-popery, and to a catholic past. This pattern can be discerned for many leading whigs, like John Arnold, the Morgans of Tredegar, or Edward Turberville. In Glamorgan, this was true of Sir Robert Thomas and of Marmaduke Gibbs, the whig lawyer who was instrumental in reconciling and drawing together the old 'moderate' and roundhead strands into a new whiggery.

Religious divisions in this area had to become party politics because of the traditional dependence of local catholics on the Marquis of Worcester's family at Raglan. Paradoxically, it was precisely because the marquis who succeeded in 1667 was a protestant that anti-catholic fears were renewed. He could not be excluded from office on religious grounds, and became the government's chief representative as President in 1672. He therefore added official sanction to his existing territorial power, and the military strength provided by his garrison at Chepstow. However, he was widely seen as a crypto-papist, still friendly with local catholic gentry, and related to catholic magnates in other shires. He also secured the position of

President by displacing Carbery, a noted 'moderate' whose record in the 1650s had been very much like those of the Pembroke party, so this could be seen a deliberate snub to the latter. 1672 was moreover the year of the Declaration of Indulgence, the French alliance against Holland, and the exposure of the catholic sympathies of Arlington and the Duke of York. At both national and local level, catholic conspiracy seemed obvious – and we now find Sir Edward Mansell tentatively moving into opposition to the Court.[99]

The strong anti-popery of South Wales was now directed against the King's representative in Wales, which was potentially dangerous, although rivalry was contained while the central government could be seen to be arbitrating fairly between the factions. Williamson succeeded in this difficult task, but the moderate gentry of South Wales were acquiring views and connections increasingly distant from those of the government. Primarily, they now regarded catholicism as a much greater peril than dissent, while the authorities had very different priorities. Straightforward anglican toryism was difficult when the choice appeared to lie between Worcester and the catholics on the one hand, and Shaftesbury's whigs on the other, and many gentry were driven to the latter persuasion.

In the 1670s, the opposition found a focus in the charitable educational work of the 'Welsh Trust', whose governing board included low churchmen like Tillotson and Stillingfleet as well as nonconformists like Baxter and Thomas Firmin.[100] Its aims were to spread protestantism by the dissemination of religious works and the skills to read them, which seems a continuation of the ideas of the 1630s and the 1650s. The attempt to evangelise Wales had been continued after ejection by the Taunton presbyterian, Joseph Alleine, possibly with the encouragement of Samuel Jones, and later efforts were fostered by the churchmen and dissenters friendly with Stephen Hughes. This essentially puritan scheme was fostered by Lord Wharton, a friend of Philip Jones and Edmund Thomas of Wenvoe, which latter married Wharton's daughter in 1674. The list of local lay supporters of the Trust reads like a roll-call of Worcester's enemies, and although some were ex-roundheads (like the sons of Philip Jones) the remainder had been Pembroke's moderate royalists. Supporters included Sir Edward Mansell, Sir Trevor Williams, John Wyndham of Dunraven and William Morgan of Tredegar. Anglican and nonconformist clergy, old roundheads and royalist 'sufferers' – only the perception of an imminent catholic threat could have stimulated such a close alliance between Church and dissent.

Between about 1675 and 1678, the 'moderates' were drawn into repeated conflicts with Worcester, and in each case we see the opposition as comprising the old 'presbyterian' followers of Pembroke – John Arnold, Sir Trevor Williams, Sir Edward Harley. They were the backbone of the parliamentary inquiry into Monmouthshire recusancy in 1675; they led the resistance to Worcester's enclosures in southern Monmouthshire in 1677;[101] and they were the targets of the Marquis's wrath when he tried to exclude them from the Bench and from parliament. To Worcester, there were no moderates: there were his partisans, and then there were round-heads. When he struck at protestants of such indubitable loyalty, he natur-ally confirmed fears of incipient catholic dictatorship – and this was suffi-cient to draw Sir Edward Mansell into alliance with Tredegar and the Monmouthshire opposition. An extremely complex network of marriage alliances now linked the opposition families of the two counties – Tre-degar with Margam and Llanbradach, Llangibby with Dunraven and Tre-degar, Dyffryn with Van. By 1678, Williamson was receiving fervent pro-tests from the Monmouthshire 'moderates' and their friends in Glamor-gan – neighbours who were also cousins and in-laws. The Pembroke party now had more cohesion than at any time since the 1620s.

It is most important to remember that these gentry and the faction they represented considered themselves as royalist throughout, and would ab-solutely reject the term 'whig' when it came into common use. When in 1677 Sir Edward Mansell prepared a list of the Glamorgan gentry describ-ing their political inclinations, he is contemptuous of Sir Robert Thomas, and very hostile to those like David Evans who had submitted to the Pro-tectorate for political gain. Roundheads like Rowland Dawkins are obvi-ously regarded as opponents, who 'raised [their] fortune in the ill times', and he praises royalist sufferers. However, the most interesting feature of this list is that several are described as 'true old cavaliers' or 'a fair behaved man, both to church and state', although they were from families bitterly opposed to Worcester, and several were ejected as whigs during the next few years. These included Bussy Mansell ('concerned in the late times, but early repenting'), John Wyndham, Martin Button, William Thomas of Llanbradach ('the son of a true old cavalier') and David Matthews of Llan-daff – again, the familiar litany of 'moderate' families. We are dealing with the curious phenomenon of a 'cavalier', 'royalist', or 'loyalist' faction – which included an old Cromwellian (Bussy Mansell) and a future dissenter (Button). It also comprised John Wyndham, who was married to the daughter of the presbyterian Colonel Strode, and whose Strode in-laws were not only whig MPs but active nonconformists.[102]

Worcester, understandably, found this confusing. Surely whigs and dissenters could not be old royalists? He charged his critic Richard Seys with a roundhead past, but Sir Edward Mansell could easily rebut this. Seys's property had been decimated along with that of the other 'cavaliers'. He might have added that Seys's uncle and namesake was the fanatical anglican who had tried to prevent the burial of a puritan leader in 1659.[103] The 'moderates' appeared to lack any consistency. In the 1680s, one of the county's leading whigs was Philip Williams of Dyffryn, an associate of the opposition families of Hoby and Mansell.[104] He wrote and collected bitter satires on Charles II, his epitaph is a classic of the 'Norman Yoke' theme; but he satirised 'whigges', and described himself as a 'royalist' or 'loyalist'.[105] Clearly, the political factions of Wales had evolved very differently from England – and in explaining this, I would place most emphasis on the ambiguous role of Worcester's family. By the 1670s, the Court appeared to have given the region over to catholic power; and the old royalists saw themselves as engaged in a counter-revolution.

9. The Popish Plot

All the old contests focussed in the 'Popish Plot' and its aftermath, and the intensity of religious strife on the Borders demonstrates the zeal on both sides, for only here was a catholic mission totally destroyed, with considerable loss of life.[106] As I have argued elsewhere, South Wales played a wholly disproportionate role in the 'plot', in the activities attributed to Worcester on the catholic side, and in the role of informers like Bedloe or Edward Turberville. Turberville's patrons were Philip Hoby of Neath, and the Swansea dissenter Marmaduke Matthews, so he was close to the Mansell party. There was a strong Welsh contingent in the parliamentary attack on the Duke of York (Worcester's special friend) led by Arnold, Sir Trevor Williams and Sir Rowland Gwynne. Gwynne's family had been allied with Sir Edward Mansell both in opposing Philip Jones, and securing the Restoration. Shaftesbury included Welsh MPs at the centre of the 'country' opposition, including Sir Edward Harley and the ex-Cromwellian, Evan Seys. Worcester's impeachment was rumoured, and 'loyalists' like Sir Edward Mansell adopted more extreme positions, so that Shaftesbury classified his whig fervour as equal to that of Sir Trevor Williams.[107] He was even seen as a more dependable ally than the dubious Sir Robert Thomas. Mansell was ejected from both the Bench and his militia command in 1680, along with men he might once have regarded as traitors, but the government continued to accept Worcester's recommendations for purges.[108]

Worcester's policies helped to create extremism, and the area's 'whigs' became as extreme as any outside London. Arnold was allegedly conspiring with Samuel Jones in 1680 for the establishment of a presbyterian republic, and Sir William Waller was said to be active in the area, which is possible in light of his family links with Briton Ferry. At lower social levels, old radicals re-emerged into the political arena, so we are not surprised to find a strong whig clique from the old puritan parish of Roath reappearing in the borough politics of Cardiff.[109] In the uplands, the leader of the quaker radicals reappeared as under-sheriff in 1679, to launch a ferocious hunt for priests and their sympathisers.[110] Worcester's opponents now developed a version of the powerful 'Norman Yoke' theory, once used by the Independent Erbery. In this view, the descendants of free Welsh princes were oppressed and reduced to 'Beaufordian servitude' (referring to Worcester's later title).[111] Moreover, the early Welsh were believed to have had direct contact with the apostolic church through Joseph of Arimathea, until these primitive protestants had been conquered by Saxon and Norman catholics.

In 1679, 11 of 27 Welsh MPs voted for Exclusion, including both Glamorgan members. The county MP was Bussy Mansell, whose Exclusionist son Thomas sat for Brecon borough, while the tory, Sir Edward Stradling, was defeated in Cardiff borough by Sir Robert Thomas. Another strong whig supporter was Sir Rowland Gwynne, who sat for Radnorshire but who held important Glamorgan estates. The political struggle was reflected locally, as when Sir Edward Mansell began a violent feud with his erstwhile loyalist ally Sir Charles Kemys.[112] By 1682 Cardiff informers regarded a speech in support of the house of Margam as tantamount to advocating parliamentarian rebellion against the King.[113] There could be no better index of the failure of Worcester's actions.

The return of peace by 1685 was aided by widespread realisation of the full implications of the conflict, with its dangers to law, social order and the anglican establishment. After mediation by Lord Elland (the son of Halifax), Sir Edward Mansell took the lead in submitting to Beaufort (Worcester's title from 1682). The Duke enthusiastically acknowledged this powerful ally in the struggle against whiggery.[114] He served as a 'steadying influence' on Tredegar, and the Earl of Pembroke undertook to reassure the government that the rumoured disloyalty of Cardiff had been greatly exaggerated.[115] Alleged (perhaps invented) plots helped to complete the triumph. A conspiracy in 1683 was said to involve Sir Rowland Gwynne with Vavasor Powell's followers in Breconshire and Merthyr Tydfil, as well as the quakers of the Glamorgan uplands. The quaker leadership fled to Pennsylvania, and a group of old 'moderates' took refuge in Holland, including Gwynne, Edward Matthews and Colonel Romsey.[116]

Corporations were remodelled with the aid of neighbouring gentry who secured borough offices, such as Sir Edward Mansell in Neath and Swansea, or Francis Gwyn at Cowbridge. The Bench was 'tuned' once more, this time without protest from those remaining, and an all-but royal progress through Wales confirmed Beaufort's position, providing the opportunity for loyalist demonstrations.[117] The seats of the leading tory magnates were included in the itinerary, and in Glamorgan Beaufort visited Margam and Cefn Mabli. The Duke's visit was partly conciliatory, as shown by his inclusion of several seats of gentlemen who had been classified as bitter enemies until the tory revival, like the Philipps' of Pembrokeshire or the Mansells themselves.[118]

The defeat of the whigs was not achieved without opposition, and one of the leaders of the Rye House plot was Colonel Romsey of Monmouthshire, whose family were intimates of Sir Charles Kemys and the Morgans of Tredegar.[119] He had been a royalist in the Civil War despite a family connection with the Earls of Pembroke, and like so many other Welsh whigs, he was said to be an ex-catholic, so he fitted well into the tradition of the 'moderates'. Part of the Rye House scheme was (allegedly) to seize the Marquis of Worcester and secure Bristol, while Romsey was one of the extreme republican elements among the leadership. In 1685, the threat of disorder was sufficiently real to make the justices arrest several old roundheads and dissenters (including Bussy Mansell), and to have the militia at full readiness; but such fears proved groundless.[120] On the other hand, Professor Dodd was not correct to say that 'the Duke of Monmouth's revolt... evoked no Welsh support, not even from old admirers, or fellow campaigners',[121] for at least one Glamorgan man was executed for his involvement. He was Edward Matthews of Llandaff, of a family royalist in the Civil War, and described by Sir Edward Mansell as 'true old cavaliers'.[122] His family had extensive catholic links, but they were not active in the persecution of dissent after 1660. Therefore, he was probably one of the 'moderate' gentry of the Mansells' party – but he was also the leader of the Duke of Monmouth's cavalry at Sedgemoor. He left an infant heir, and an estate that was apparently protected by Sir Edward Mansell during the minority; no doubt Mansell was aware how close he might have come to the same fate if matters had developed a little differently in 1682. Matthews was not unique: his transition to whiggery represents, albeit in an extreme form, the path taken by many families who suffered for loyalty to Charles I.

10. Towards revolution 1685 – 1688

By 1685, Matthews' actively whig views were rare, and both the accession of James and the Monmouth rising were occasions for the expression of great loyalty. Those anglicans who had supported Exclusion were now dismissed as 'protestant jesuits', and Beaufort could remove 500 men from Wales to defend Bristol. The solidly loyalist Bench of the new reign included Sir Edward Mansell, restored to his allies of the 1660s, and with the recent past forgotten. The ultimate result of the Exclusion crisis was ironically a triumph for Beaufort and his clients: 'ironically' because this success was only possible as a reaction to fears of civil violence, which fears were in very large part the disastrous results of his own mismanagement. But such 'tyranny' was only acceptable when landed society felt this was the last resort for securing order against a threat to more basic beliefs, secular and religious, epitomised by the slogan, 'religion, liberty and property'. That James failed to understand this, and mistook loyalty to the established order for unquestioning support for a stronger monarchy, has been frequently described, as have his truly revolutionary attacks on each aspect of the anglican establishment: Church, Army, universities, and finally the Bench of justices in each county.

The tory loyalists failed to support him: only one Glamorgan justice attended Beaufort to discuss the 'three questions' and he refused to consent to the first two. Sir Charles Kemys was a close friend of Beaufort, as well as of other servants of the dynasty like Jeffreys and Lord Craven, but even he was embarrassed at stories that he had agreed to the removal of the Test and Penal Acts, a slander also used against Colonel Sir John Carne.[123] Having alienated the loyalists by his extreme policies, James then proposed to replace Beaufort as President in Wales by the latter's catholic kinsman, Powis. This at once removed the Crown's firmest supporter in South Wales, and reawakened the ancient fear of a catholic 'fifth column' prepared to welcome an Irish invasion of Wales. The Crown's new power was to be based on men little known or liked in the principality, and Jeffreys' acquisition of the Pembroke estates by marriage gave him much influence in the south. He and Sir William Williams were to replace families who had supported the Stuarts loyally in the Civil War or Exclusion, but who were now ejected. Some kind of catholic interest could be created to replace

them in Monmouthshire, but elsewhere in Wales conversions had become
pitifully slow. In Glamorgan, the only certain case of conversion under
James was that of Colonel Sir Thomas Stradling, a younger son of the St
Donat's house.[124]

But without catholic justices, this only left the dissenters to provide an
alternative government – and James's policies here presented the paradox
of a catholic king apparently preparing the way for a new puritan dictatorship. In Wales particularly, the new justices were not only dissenters, but
the survivors of the most extreme baptist and millenarian sects, notably
those close to Vavasor Powell and the tradition of Harrison.[125] In Glamorgan, for example, the proposed Bench included old roundhead captains
like Henry Williams and Thomas Evans, both extreme baptists allegedly
involved in several plots since 1660, and leaders of the old radicals around
Merthyr Tydfil and Gelligaer. When in 1688 Philip Williams wrote a squib
against the 'new justices', he complained of the traitors of 1641, roundheads, fanatics and Swansea tradesmen, who would overturn the law and
subvert the Church and monarchy 'with their hot zeal for the commonwealth'.[126]

In 1688, Glamorgan overwhelmingly supported Williams' invasion.
The only 'jacobites' were the Carnes of Nash and Ewenni, although there
may have been some families who remained uncertain until the last moment. Sir Edward Mansell helped to delay or suppress Beaufort's orders to
the militia, and cooperated with Sir Rowland Gwynne, newly returned
from Dutch exile to help the Morgans to lead the insurrectionary forces.
Rumoured Irish invasions contributed to widespread popular violence,
especially directed against the property of Beaufort and Powis, but not
even fears of a new commonwealth and possible regicide could cause the
gentry to rally to the Stuarts.[127] This was a remarkable demonstration of
how thoroughly James had destroyed a power-base of greater potential
strength than a monarch had possessed for a century. By 1688, Sir Edward
Mansell's son Thomas 'thought that they [the Stuarts] had not a friend in
England without they were catholics and those very inconsiderable in their
number'.[128] This belief was confirmed that November by the defection of
Beaufort's own son to William, fragmenting that Welsh army of which
James had hoped so much.

Conclusion

The period from 1640 to 1690 has been described here as an 'heroic age'
because so many of its great conflicts entered political legend. But it was

also one age – a distinct period with a definite continuity. Assuredly, the balance of forces often changed – in 1645, in 1660, in 1682 – but the composition of those forces remained very consistent. I am not suggesting that family groupings or factions were rigid, but the broad three-party alignment remains a useful model for the interpretation of the whole period. In 1642, the moderates were allied with ultra-royalists, and that was the royalist coalition. In the 1660s, this alliance was restored, but in the 1670s the moderates joined the old parliamentarians against the ultras – and that was the first whig party. Still more shifts would occur in the 1680s, always under the pressure of religious threats. This pattern was common throughout Wales and the Borders: similar patterns can be found for Carbery in Carmarthenshire, Lord Herbert of Cherbury in Mid Wales, the Booths in Cheshire. All faced the same political dilemma as Glamorgan: could total loyalty be given to the Stuart dynasty if that meant 'soft' policies against catholicism – the religion of local peers like Powis and Worcester, and of perilously close Ireland?

In this context, we may take up the familiar question of exactly what was restored at the Restoration. Certainly gentry power came back; but in terms of party loyalties 1660 only implied a new shift in the balance of power. The most noticeable 'restoration' in the South Wales of the 1660s was the renewal of old conflicts. For instance, the moderates of both the 1630s and 1660s had tried to evangelise the poor, and resented the suspicion that such activities caused in the government or Church. By the 1660s, the Church was often made up of better-quality men who had proved their mettle under persecution – but dissenters were equally impressive, so why should both not ally to create a protestant society? The government responded by persecuting dissent and favouring Worcester: it was a pattern wearily familiar to survivors of Laud's time. For a Welsh protestant about 1670, high anglican politics meant supporting Worcester's clique – apparently a course far more likely to undermine the Church than tolerating dissent.

In Wales, the Restoration was not therefore decisive in changing party allegiances. Matters continued in roughly their old course, and the political battle lines of 1685 were very like those of 1645. Real change would only come in 1688 – that 'Glorious Revolution' which twentieth-century historians have viewed with much less awe than did their Georgian and Victorian counterparts. But, at least in Wales, this was the event which shattered the political mould, and made possible the assimilation of regional factions into the national structure of party politics.

6

Political history 1688 – 1790: the new order

Introduction

The events of 1688 were a 'revolution' in that they altered the basic issues of political life, both at national and county level, dispelling the shades of puritan or catholic dictatorship, and finally establishing parliament as an indispensable part of the constitution. Ancient fears of a catholic descent on Wales were removed by William's Irish victories. The flight of Powis and the self-imposed retirement of the Duke of Beaufort marked the end of the threat from catholic or crypto-papist nobles that had been a central issue in Welsh politics for decades. Both families were allegedly connected with occasional jacobite plots, but now there could be no doubt of the government's hostility to their machinations. The absence of Beaufort, in particular, destroyed the traditional government policy of rule through magnates, while in Glamorgan the removal of this aristocratic dominance confirmed the political supremacy of the Mansells and the other great gentry for seventy years.

The year also marked a complete realignment of parties, which can be closely observed in Glamorgan – where it is of particular interest because of the activity there by Francis Gwyn and Robert Harley's circle. The age of Harley was the period in which the great Glamorgan families found themselves closest to the centre of power, and therefore a Glamorgan historian is in an excellent position to observe not only the new party structures, but the development of the new forms of oligarchy based on patronage, which would change the national political landscape so fundamentally by the 1720s. By about 1712, it seemed almost inevitable that the Mansells were about to establish themselves as virtual rulers of southern Wales through a combination of traditional family power and the newer governmental authority. Such power was difficult to renounce gracefully. The tories resisted vigorously, and from 1714 to 1740 we shall observe the emergence of a sophisticated tory party organisation based on a very wide spectrum of opinions – from tolerant and congenial moderates like

Thomas Mansell to highly ideological jacobite extremists like David Morgan or Sir Charles Kemys. On the whig side, a study of Glamorgan also allows us to study the combination of temptation and coercion by which such recalcitrant local communities could be won over to the government's side. It provides a fascinating example of how a small oligarchy could secure its local power so absolutely, despite massive resistance.

We can summarise the major themes of this chapter as party, patronage, and the quest for peace and stability. However, this study differs from other regional examples of the 'growth of political stability' in important respects. Firstly, the county's industrial orientation gave a very firm economic footing to questions of war, foreign policy, religion and the succession – in short, of party loyalties. In this context, it is scarcely surprising neither that the county should have been an opposition stronghold in 1740 or the 1770s, nor that it should have been placid in the late 1750s. Secondly, Glamorgan provides a clear example of the demographic crisis which helped provide the basis for social and political oligarchy by the 1740s.

In this chapter, as in Part III, I will trace the stages by which the endemic political conflicts and threats of unrest of the seventeenth century gave way to a new stability. This was based on the reconciliation of local landed elites with the Court and government through the satisfactory allocation of power and patronage, the recognition of local independence, and the decline of fundamental, especially religious, issues. Ideological purity on both sides was no doubt weakened still further by attempts to form a 'broad-bottom' coalition of tories and opposition whigs in the 1730s and 1740s, while the events of 1745 symbolised a fundamental reordering of party politics. Both can be studied in detail in Glamorgan, and local events suggest how stability was achieved on a national scale.

Already the conflicts of the seventeenth century seemed like an appalling and distant dream. Even if there were still riots, who in 1750 could seriously imagine popular risings against the landed gentry, or a return to Levelling doctrines? Yet, in the last decades of our period, the apparently tranquil acquiescence to the new ruling class was under threat. This was at first an internal conflict on the old lines against the power of old-established magnates, but it was acquiring ominous overtones by the 1770s and 1780s. Radical gentry were allied with nonconformists and libertarians against both Church and Court and they had evolved sophisticated forms of structure and organisation (freemasonry), and of campaign (the Association). Still worse, there were threatening links with the old radicalism.

The radicalism of the hill-people never died – even the most extreme political views of the 1650s still found followers in the next century. Sometimes this tradition appeared in more acceptable forms of theological dispute rather than social rebellion. But a certain dissidence was always there, and it was soon to receive a great fillip from the growth of iron and coal undertakings in just those areas. The part of the county outside the gentry's world suddenly assumed enormous and frightening importance in the national economy, so that where once the squires had seen isolated hill-farms, they now saw jacobinical towns beyond the control of Church or State. The ruling class recoiled in fear from its radical allies and the election of 1789 was the last triumph of the new libertarian 'Patriot' alliance. This chapter will describe both the reconciliation of landed society with central government, and the appearance of new forces which threatened both.

1. The new whigs

When historians of this period wish to discuss the most obscurantist of backwoods gentry, the most fanatical tories, they commonly use Wales as an example. Professor Plumb writes that at their worst, 'the politically minded citizens of London could be as suspicious of authority as the squires of Wales'.[1] The natural assumption is that these were the most 'country'-minded, and therefore the most tory (or jacobite) under Anne. Professor Holmes has remarked on the difficulty of finding any whigs to serve as parliamentary candidates: 'In most of the Welsh counties the whig gentry were pitifully thin on the ground.'[2] Two objections can be made to such an idea. First, it is questionable whether any Welsh county was quite so badly placed, in the light of Professor Thomas's work on early eighteenth-century Welsh elections. Welsh ultra-royalism was a myth inspired by the memory of Judge Jenkins, and later of jacobite fanatics like David Morgan (executed in 1746). Second, it was less true of some counties than of others. The three most populous counties of Wales all had very strong whig interests: in Carmarthenshire, the gentry had no option but to dance to the tune of the aristocratic whig owners of Golden Grove – first the Earls of Carbery and then (after 1713) the Dukes of Bolton. In both Glamorgan and Monmouthshire, it will be argued that about 1700, whig great gentry were not much inferior to their tory counterparts in wealth and numbers. Welsh whiggery was a powerful force, which rapidly developed a modern party structure and methods.

The near unanimity of the 'county' opposition in 1688 could not be expected to survive very long, but the politics of South Wales in the next decade are marked by the activity of a number of firm whigs who would provide vigorous and consistent support for the new regime. There was Carbery in Carmarthenshire, the Vaughans in Cardiganshire – and in 1695 these were raised to the peerage as Lords Lisburne. However, the whig heartland of Wales lay on the Borders and in the south-east. Only 7 of 27 Welsh MPs supported William's governments loyally throughout the 1690s, but no less than five of these held their main estates in Glamorgan and Monmouthshire. Most were 'country' veterans ejected by Beaufort during the Exclusion crisis. In Monmouthshire, both Sir Trevor Williams and John Arnold retained their old views, and the latter was still connected with Titus Oates and the quakers in the 1690s, when most whigs had outgrown these past enthusiasms. He had still not been cured of his tendency to 'reveal' popish plots – this time, against King William.[3] The Morgans of Tredegar had also been ejected in 1680, but now returned to begin the establishment of a territorial power-base in three counties (including Glamorgan) which made them a mainstay of Welsh whiggery for a century. The party in Monmouthshire was strengthened by the return from the Mediterranean of the immensely wealthy Charles Williams of Caerleon, a close friend of the Mansells of both Margam and Briton Ferry.[4]

In Glamorgan, the old whigs who now found themselves close to the government included Bussy Mansell and Marmaduke Gibbs, the latter now a judge. There was also Richard Seys of Swansea, son of Evan the Cromwellian – and Richard's daughter married the whig Lord Chancellor, Peter King. There was therefore a strong whig network in west Glamorgan, in the area where Beaufort's territorial interest was strongest and most sharply resented. The radical group included the Hobys of Neath, and each whig squire carried with him the support of a network of kinsmen and dependents, mobilised by stewards like Philip Williams of Dyffryn.[5] Further east, Sir Rowland Gwynne had returned from exile to obtain both patronage and parliamentary status as a lieutenant of the Junto and 'one of the strongest whigs in the House'. He was the 'honest country gentleman' who proposed the Association of loyalty to William in 1696, but like Arnold, he was more radical and anti-clerical than many of his whig colleagues; and he was closest to extreme whigs like Rochford, Orford and Stamford. His zeal to protect the Hanoverian succession caused his flight to Germany in 1705, when one of his pamphlets offended the Queen.[6]

Whig strength was considerably reinforced in Glamorgan by the addition after 1690 of some very rich gentlemen who had been among the firmest tories before the Revolution, like Sir John Aubrey, Sir Charles Kemys, and Richard Jenkins of Hensol. These three families had often acted together in the past, notably in the Civil War when they had represented the most intransigent and incorruptible royalist faction of county society, and similarly during the persecution of dissent after 1660. They were all among the highest tories of the 1680s, and Kemys is still mentioned as a tory MP in 1690, a supporter of the 'Church interest' and a friend of Rochester and Beaufort.[7] Very shortly afterwards, this gentry faction was converted to whiggery and the new regime, and came to follow the Whartons as loyally as they had once fought for Worcester and the High Church.

Marriage alliances help to explain the change, for about 1677 Sir Charles Kemys had married the daughter of the puritan and whig, Lord Wharton, whose son Thomas was to become a key member of the Junto.[8] Moreover, Kemys stood to acquire a large Dutch estate from a kinswoman if he could only secure the favour of Portland or some other Williamite courtier. He retained his tory friendships, but his parliamentary voting in William's reign was identical on major issues to that of his old whig enemies Arnold and Sir Trevor Williams. When the whigs were in power, his connections with Wharton (and the latter's friends, like Devonshire) put Kemys in an excellent position for access to government favour and patronage. Sir John Aubrey similarly formed alliances with leading families at William's court, like the Lowthers and the Jephsons. He also married the heiress of the Boarstall estate in Wharton's county of Buckinghamshire, and in 1698 he sat for the Wharton borough of Brackley. After Aubrey's death in 1700, his widow married Sir Charles Kemys who also became a Buckinghamshire landowner, albeit briefly. After his death in 1702, the new Sir Charles Kemys was brought up as the ward of his uncle, Thomas Wharton, so the family links were close and numerous. There is less evidence for the transition of the Jenkins family of Hensol, descendants of the royalist hero, David, but they were certainly whig by the 1690s, and were friendly with Marmaduke Gibbs.[9]

Other whig families in Glamorgan included new men who had risen through government patronage, or else were connected with the 'moneyed interest' so widely hated by the gentry. Sir Thomas Jones of Bridgend rose from humble origins through a legal career, won a knighthood by his services to whig governments, and was added to the Glamorgan Bench, along with other lawyers like the Ogmore dissenter Robert Thomas. Sir Humphrey Edwin of Llanmihangel was a dissenting London merchant, and Sir

George Howell of Roath was a barrister who won the lucrative post of tax collector for South Wales because he was 'the greatest whig in England.'[10] Howell's background also reminds us of several major themes of the county's seventeenth-century history. He apparently came from a family still catholic in the 1670s,[11] and so fits the model argued earlier of transition from one political extreme directly to the other. Furthermore, he emerged from the parish of Roath, a radical hotbed where local political conflict was perhaps as intense as anywhere in the region. Roath also now provided another whig justice in Michael Richards.

Whig governments therefore had long-standing local traditions on which they could build support, even in areas apparently lost to diehard toryism. Supporters could be rewarded with the patronage provided by war and colonial expansion, and the whigs benefited greatly. Of about twenty greater gentry families in Glamorgan whose politics can be identified, about nine were whig at the start of the eighteenth century, which does not support the traditional image of Wales as solidly tory, if not jacobite.

2. King or country? The tories

Despite the conversion of some of the greatest tory families to whiggery, the tory interest in Glamorgan remained very powerful in these years. There had been few active jacobites in 1688, but tory traditions revived shortly afterwards among those who had only accepted the Revolution as a grim necessity; and the offer of the crown to William was a watershed. There were many who believed that 'parliament is doing a thing it has no power to do', in the words of a Glamorgan petty gentleman who fled rather than pay taxes for the Irish wars.[12] Among the 150 MPs who voted against the offer of the crown were Francis Gwyn, Richard Lewis of Van, Thomas Mansell of Margam, the Marquis of Worcester (son of Beaufort) and four representatives of other Welsh constituencies.[13] Some of those who refused to accept the new order became nonjurors, and Welshmen like William Thomas were prominent in the national leadership of the movement. Eighteen Welsh clergy refused to take the new oaths, including two in Glamorgan, and the movement had strong lay support among the greatest gentry of Wales. At the core of the new high toryism were several former servants of the Stuarts, who had often held office in central government in the 1680s, like the Wynnes of North Wales, or the Musgraves.[14] The example of Francis Gwyn was of particular importance for Glamorgan, as he was widely connected both with the leading local gentry, and the

Table 18: *The political connections of Francis Gwyn*

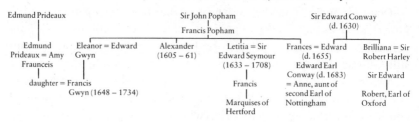

extreme national faction represented by his kinsmen the Earl of Rochester and Sir Edward Seymour. For example, it was through him that friendship developed between the Mansells of Margam and high tories like Edward Nicholas and the Musgraves. His power was greatly extended in 1690 when he acquired a large Dorset estate, and he was very active in the bitter elections of the West Country. His wide connections are illustrated in Table 18. Finches (Earls of Nottingham), Conways, Harleys, Seymours –it would be difficult to imagine a more prestigious list of kin, or one more central to the tory politics of the end of the seventeenth century. By 1705, Gwyn was seen as a tory 'firebrand' in the South-West, and 'Sir Edward Seymour's successor in his western Empire'.[15]

From about 1691, this high tory ground was strengthened by what was at first a tactical alliance with the 'country' opponents of William's regime, in which faction Robert Harley was increasingly powerful. Contemporaries were well-aware of the incongruity of this for many of the 'country' MPs regarded themselves as the firmest of whigs, and Harley himself represented a family long at the centre of Welsh opposition to the Duke of Beaufort, and to the Stuart dynasty which the Somersets had supported. Indeed, he was still friendly with Welsh whigs like Arnold, Sir Rowland Gwynne and Thomas Mansell of Briton Ferry – and he retained these links well after 1700. Feiling suggested that Sir Thomas Clarges was important in forging this remarkable 'country' alliance, but there is also a great deal of early correspondence between Harley and other tory leaders like Musgrave and, notably, Francis Gwyn.[16] Gwyn and Harley were both close to the Marquis of Halifax and were related through the Conway family, but the deep love each had for antiquarian studies may have helped to bring them together.[17] Both were friends and patrons of nonjuring scholars like Hearne, Hickes and Wanley, and it may have been through this scholarly interest that Harley formed his great friendship with Thomas Mansell of Margam.[18]

Whatever the true importance of Gwyn in its formation, the tory – 'country' alliance was presenting firm opposition to Court policies from the early 1690s, with the odd result that men like Gwyn and Musgrave 'have got the character of commonwealthsmen' (republicans).[19] Undoubtedly the protracted war was a vital element in the creation of this new opposition alignment, for the successful undertaking of war now required a much larger State machine, with all that that implied in the way of increased government patronage and higher taxes. The valuation of Welsh estates for tax purposes certainly erred on the side of under-estimation, but this did not prevent a large number of complaints that the gentry were being ruined by tax collectors. Of course, a properly fought naval war could have had enomous advantages for the gentry, but this was a whig war, fought with expensive armies.[20] Equally irritating was the fact that the gentry were allegedly being impoverished for the benefit of financial adventurers who secured government favours, like Sir George Howell.[21] In 1701, Thomas Mansell of Margam wrote of the whigs who 'came in beggars and have done all they could to make all of us so, while they have got both titles and estates'.[22] Continuing war also meant greater patronage through the expansion of the armed services and colonial bureaucracies, and seemed to infringe on the rights and safety of gentlemen by justifying actions of dubious legality against suspected traitors. In the early 1690s these issues were focussed by the parliamentary debates on new treason legislation, and the confiscation of the lands of Irish jacobites. Increasingly, the government seemed to represent the interests of foreigners and placemen against the rights and liberties of Englishmen, and notably of English gentlemen.[23] The campaign against such an administration could bring together a broad spectrum of political views. Tories like Francis Gwyn might not agree that 1688 was in fact a great opportunity to create a better constitution, but in practice they could easily act alongside the whigs who had felt this, and who now saw the Revolution as betrayed. It is a sign of the transformation wrought in political attitudes that, by 1694, the jacobite Court was urging its English followers in parliament to support the Harley faction in an attempt to elect Paul Foley as Speaker.[24]

The new political alignments were reflected in local partisan loyalties in Glamorgan, and some of the county's leading gentlemen were also involved in the 'country' opposition at national level. Thomas Mansell of Margam was one of the greatest acquisitions of the new alliance, because of the family's huge territorial wealth and their influence in south-west Wales. Throughout the 1690s, Thomas Mansell became increasingly alienated from his father, Sir Edward, who consistently supported William's government, and is best described as a whig. Thomas, however, followed the same policies as his friend Francis Gwyn, and they shared the same circle of 'high' friends, like Musgrave, Charles Fox and Edward Nicholas.[25] Both accepted the leadership of Rochester, who was in 1696 proposing to visit Margam and Llansannor, although this was cancelled at the last moment.[26] With Beaufort, they refused to sign the Association of that same year, which Mansell 'scorned and abhorred to be concerned in... and would not do such a thing for all the Kings in Christendom'.[27] Mansell was thus following the views of Rochester and Gwyn on this divisive issue, which seemed to endanger the coalition of country and tory interests, and his 'high' politics gave great concern to his father. Although in 1699 Thomas Mansell accompanied his whig kinsman the Duke of Manchester on an embassy to France, his father was still warning him against extremism which could plunge the family back into the disasters it had faced in the 1640s: 'neither would I have you give so clear a demonstration of being an enemy to the present government, which is protestant'.[28] In 1701, both Thomas Mansell and Sir Edward Stradling enthusiastically followed Gwyn and Seymour in supporting the impeachment of the whig ministers, much to the disgust of Sir Edward Mansell.[29] On such issues it is possible to see how far traditional ideological patterns had broken down. This family division represents the conflict of old and new 'country' opinion, the latter form being increasingly identified with pure toryism. Thomas Mansell was seen as a 'very violent tory' until friendship with Harley (and possibly the personal intervention of the king) led him to mellower views.[30] However, a friend still had to deny his jacobitism as late as 1707, and affirm that Mansell 'had always been for the Church taken in a right sense, and much averse to persecution'.[31] This remark carries conviction, for Thomas (like Harley) had been educated in a dissenting academy, and they sought to moderate anglican extremism in the government of 1710. It is possible that the growth of religion as a central political issue from about 1697 found Mansell somewhat alienated from Rochester's circles, and more inclined to seek refuge in Harleyite 'moderation', but the exact date of his conversion cannot be ascertained.[32]

3. The new Church party

The Mansells were neither unique nor eccentric in producing both 'country' opponents to the Stuarts in one generation, and tories in the next. Both the Harleys and the Foleys had long had presbyterian sympathies, as had leading Welsh Tories like the Trevors, or the Philipps' and Meyricks of south-west Wales. It is striking how many of the high tories under Anne were descended from earlier roundheads, even regicides: examples included Sacheverell, Sir William Whitelock, even Bolingbroke. In Glamorgan, the grandson of Colonel Philip Jones was by 1712 a high tory MP of jacobite inclinations in whose portrait gallery Cromwell and Ireton would soon be joined by the Old Pretender.[33] The highflying Sir Humphrey Mackworth of Neath was descended from Cromwell's Major-General in Shropshire, and the successor to 'Lord' Thomas of Wenvoe was a country tory, married to the daughter of the allegedly jacobite MP, John Howe. Partly, this transition may demonstrate that the continuing factor was 'country' opposition to any government, however party labels may change.

There was also a more positive element, a real drift towards the established Church. The 'puritan squire' was a rare animal in Glamorgan by 1700, at least in the sense of active dissenters, and the sons of Sir Humphrey Edwin were tories and anglicans. Also, the decline of the catholic threat after 1688 permitted the growth of high anglican opinions. As in Georgian Scotland or Ireland, the clergy of seventeenth-century Wales had rarely risked flirting with high church opinions when catholicism was so blatant a danger. But from the 1690s, we can at last observe the appearance of high-flying clergy in Glamorgan livings. The Stradlings appointed Thomas Hancorne to St Donat's,[34] the Lewises gave Merthyr Tydfil to Thomas Price; we find James Harris at Llantrisant, Thomas Davies in Llandaff. By 1710, Glamorgan would have a powerful Sacheverellite caucus. To take an extreme example of the drift from 'moderation' to high church opinions, it might be noted that the nephew of the Monmouthite martyr Edward Matthews was the jacobite and nonjuror activist David Morgan – who also died on the scaffold.

Of course, converts from broad 'puritanism' to highflying anglicanism retained some old sympathies, such as their zeal to spread the Gospel among the poor by means of education. 'Converts' like the Mackworths and Philipps' of Picton were at the centre of the Society for the Propagation of Christian Knowledge, which had a strong Welsh contingent. Resemblances to the old 'Welsh Trust' were increased by the presence of veterans like Arnold and Sir Edward Mansell in the new Society.[35] However, the SPCK was a more definitely anglican body, and many of its local contributors saw the struggle against dissent and quakerism as having equal

priority with the general missionary purpose. Of five high tory clerical justices appointed to the Glamorgan Bench between 1712 and 1714, at least
four were strong supporters of the SPCK, including Thomas Price and
James Harris the antiquary.[36] The high churchmen sought to remodel
society through moral enforcement by the appointment of active JPs
(preferably clergy), and through the old anti-papist devices of evangelism
and popular education. About twenty charity schools were founded in the
county in the first quarter of the eighteenth century, almost all under the
auspices of alleged jacobites – Roger Powell, Thomas Lewis of Van,
Cradock Wells of Cardiff, James Harris and others. The old puritan tactics
had now been transformed to fight dissent.

The hatred of dissent deserves emphasis, because it affected many old
'moderates'. By the 1690s, nonconformity had lost much of its gentry support and become more identified with the City, and therefore with whig
governments and policies. Also, the removal of the catholic danger meant
that the chief peril to the anglican establishment now came from the successors of those who had already overthrown it in the 1650s, so high
church views spread among those whose families had once favoured toleration. Pamphleteers recalled the suffering of royalist families under the
fanatics. Extensive researches into anglican sufferings at puritan hands
were carried out by Edward Mansell of Swansea, and his friends like
Thomas Davies of Llandaff.[37] The answers they received showed the deep
and widespread resentment surviving fifty years after the Interregnum.
Nor did appeals to solidarity with persecuted Continental protestants have
the appeal they once had. Protestants outside the established Church differed only from English roundheads in the degree of their heresy, so there
was clearly no enthusiasm for the government's attempt to settle German
refugees in Glamorgan in 1709. After all, as the gentry's representatives
said, the county had neither trade nor industry – a gross lie.[38]

Against these arguments, the whigs drew on the long anti-papist tradition, and cited especially the Irish massacre of 1641 and the misdeeds of
James II. It had been divines much venerated by the established Church
who had most bitterly opposed these aggressions. Whigs could also cite the
behaviour of dissenters after 1660 as justifying the highest anglican ideals
of 'passive obedience', and the no less embarrassing fact that so many high
churchmen were the sons of dissenters, while whigs were often from
royalist families.

To a remarkable extent, history was the currency of political argument
in this period, and Professor Kenyon has explored the growth of a tory

ideology based on memories of the Civil War Years.[39] But contemporary grievances also helped to make religious policy central to national affairs; English anglicans, for instance, would long remember the persecution of their episcopalian brethren in Scotland, especially when sufferers from the 'plaguey hypocritical Kirk' took refuge south of the border. When Union was negotiated in 1707 by a ministry which included Thomas Mansell, he received fervent anglican petitions against collaboration with persecutors.[40] However, the presbyterian sympathies of the whig party seemed only to be confirmed by the enthusiasm for Union shown by Welsh whig MPs.[41] Heresy and immorality were both blamed on whig governments. The presence of Toland and Gildon among the extreme whigs made it possible for violent tory partisans to identify whiggery with irreligion, and to blame it for the contamination of the local gentry by metropolitan scepticism. The growth of a deist group in Swansea under Anne naturally provided ammunition for local Sacheverellite clergy like Thomas Hancorne – but of course, as we have seen, scepticism had local roots, and did not need external influence.[42] From the mid-1690s moreover, a number of incidents seemed to demonstrate the growing peril from dissent and the government's unwillingness to help the Church to stand against it, so the tories' desire to defend the religious establishment became more clamorous, and central to their political ideology.

The main pillars of tory policy for the next generation were already apparent in the series of campaigns against the government between about 1694 and 1698, the bitterness of which was exacerbated by the grave economic situation. In parliament there were demands for an Occasional Conformity Bill to remove dissenters from positions of power, and opposition was expressed to government corruption and abuse of patronage. Of particular relevance to Wales was the legal assault on the King's land grants to the Earl of Portland, a campaign led by Beaufort's ally Robert Price (a friend of Francis Gwyn, Harley and Sir Charles Kemys).[43] Price again used the Welsh version of the 'Norman Yoke', even including a distinctively Welsh 'Original Contract', but underneath these whig terms was a deep tory hatred of courtiers and foreign favourites. It was also in these years that jacobite propaganda again seems to have been read in Welsh country houses, including Margam, although few gentry were omitted from the loyal 'Association' of 1696.

The issues underlying this partisan struggle were not received for a generation, and kept alive the broad conflict between whig and tory, however much these groups may have been split internally. For example, in

Glamorgan, the Harleyites were represented by Thomas Mansell and his dependents, the faction of Rochester and Seymour by Francis Gwyn, while most high churchmen looked to the Duke of Beaufort. This last group included Sir Humphrey Mackworth, Richard Lewis of Van and the son and namesake of Sir Charles Kemys, and these families retained their friendship for the Beaufort interest for decades. Mackworth, moreover, was a powerful high church politician in his own right, close to Seymour, Edward Nicholas, Harcourt, Musgrave and, especially, St John.[44] His 'Company of Mine Adventurers' was mainly a high tory concern, which brought peers like the Duke of Leeds into contact with Welsh jacobite leaders like Lewis Pryse and William Powell.[45]

4. Party or faction? Family feuds under William and Anne

There can be no doubt of the partisan zeal of many gentlemen during this age, when political opinions affected such matters of everyday life as investments, or preferences in books, plays, inns and wine. But it is not clear how far national loyalties were reflected at local level. An MP's neighbours took an interest in his parliamentary votes, and could decide to withhold their further support if he was unsatisfactory, as actually happened in Breconshire in 1690 and Carmarthenshire in 1714.[46] By 1689, there was sufficient demand for news to permit the employment of a professional reporter by the Morgans of Tredegar and several of their friends in Breconshire and Monmouthshire.[47] In 1695, Sir Charles Kemys attributed the opposition to his candidature in Glamorgan to a jacobite faction,[48] and others mention local whig and tory groups, which would suggest that county politics closely resembled those at Westminster.

On the other hand, there is no evidence that any of the feuds in Glamorgan during this period involved a clear division between whig and tory. Despite partisan vigour on both sides (and a large county electorate of 2,000), there was only one election between 1681 and 1727 which led to an actual contest at the polls. The considerable expertise in electoral affairs demonstrated in the correspondence of the Glamorgan gentry had often been acquired in other counties where they held interests, either in Wales or in the very hard school of Wiltshire's boroughs. Already in the 1690s they had learned the importance in an election of circular letters, a 'house to house' canvass, false rumours, and great demonstrations at the poll;[49] and what knowledge they lacked was rapidly acquired in the bitterly fought campaign of 1708. This sophistication belies the electoral stability of

Glamorgan, for heightened party zeal did not lead (as in many counties) to a great increase in the number of contested elections.

Gentry families were often involved in feuds, which might entail prolonged litigation or even armed violençe, but these virtually never concern national partisan divisions. Passionate commitment was much more likely to be aroused by the recurrent fears that Margam was seeking to monopolise both the county's seats, a threat with economic overtones because control of a borough affected the fights to trade, and to mineral exploitation. Simple disputes could easily develop into major contests involving electoral or commercial advantage, or assaults on the Margam supremacy, as over the issue of the rebuilding of Cardiff bridge in 1700. Both Sir Edward Mansell and Sir Charles Kemys were whigs, but the feud they engaged in was savage. Both factions used violence, placed their own men in borough offices, and made expensive efforts to win over the citizens. The contest eventually went to Chancery, and the strain of the lawsuit and the shock of defeat is said to have hastened Sir Charles' death in 1702. This was the culmination of a war that had lasted throughout the 1690s, and which had been manifested, for example, in attempts to fill a vacancy in the bishopric in 1690, or in Kemys' rumoured candidacy in the election of 1698.[50] The Cardiff bridge dispute has left a very large body of surviving correspondence and legal papers, including Sir Edward's remarkable appeal to Pembroke, reminiscing about the happy state of Glamorgan under Herbert rule – showing the amazing tenacity of his loyalty.[51]

A similar confusion of issues – personal, political and commercial – is to be found in the most prolonged and bitter feud of the period, which culminated in the contested election of 1708. The dispute ostensibly began in 1706, when Thomas Mansell refused to accept his brother-in-law Sir Edward Stradling as borough member. Stradling undertook to oppose Mansell's nominee for the borough seat, and Richard Jenkins of Hensol opposed him for the county, whereupon both factions began to campaign hectically, 'making of interest and spending of money as if the election was next month'.[52] Was this a party election? Professor Thomas has suggested that an important reason for opposition was Mansell's membership in the current ministry, and so the dispute can be seen as an attack on the government.[53] Even if the two sides could not be strictly seen as whig or tory, then might it be a battle of 'ins' and 'outs'? The answer is almost certainly not.

Both factions were extremely heterogeneous, and each included a fairly complete party spectrum, from jacobites to dissenting sympathisers. This was neither a contest between whig and tory, nor a test of ministerial popularity. Mansell himself was a Harleyite, and as we would expect in 1705 – 6, he had whig support including Sir John Aubrey (his nominee for the borough) and the Tredegar interest. But he was also supported by the high tory Edmund Thomas of Wenvoe, and the Tacker Francis Gwyn. This strange alliance also had its social manifestations, like the 'St Nicholas Club', where whigs like Aubrey met jacobites like Alexander Trotter. Talk of such a party club about 1708 led Professor Holmes to conclude that this was a group of 'devoted squires' keeping Glamorgan 'generally safe for the church interest' – in fact, they were only united by support for Mansell.[54]

On the other side, the group described as 'Mr. Jenkins' whig friends' included Sir Edward Stradling, a high tory who had defended the impeachments of 1701. Otherwise, there was the Tacker, Mackworth, and the jacobites, Beaufort and Lewis of Van: while among this company is found Sir Humphrey Edwin, whose nonchalant attitude to occasional conformity had directly provoked the tory campaign which culminated in the Tack. At the start of the affair, moreover, Beaufort was not felt to be committed to either side, and both factions requested his support.

However, the dispute is explicable in the context of local issues and personal enmities. Mansell's personal relationship with Stradling had never been good, and in 1706 they were engaged in legal action over Mansell's failure to pay a marriage settlement agreed in 1694.[55] There was also the issue of Stradling's alleged misappropriation of a valuable deed.[56] Of the other main opponents, Mackworth had been engaged in legal and industrial battles with the Mansells since about 1696. These were still continuing in 1707, by which time this struggle became part of a wider assault on the Mansell position, in which Mackworth's role as an organiser is continually mentioned. It is in this setting of economic self-interest that we must see the denunciations of Mackworth in Sir Edward Mansell's whig circles. William Philipps, of an old Exclusionist family, described Mackworth as a 'tyrant', aiming 'at nothing less than arbitrary attempts on the county', despite the efforts of Glamorgan's 'patriots'.[57] This well illustrates the debasement of political language after the heroic days of Exclusion. It also reminds us that whig support for the Mansells may have resulted less from Thomas's current alliance with a partly whig ministry, than from old loyalties to Sir Edward as a 'country' leader. This applied both to the election and to the Mackworth feud. The Mansells' allies included the whig partisans George Howells and Thomas Button, and that of Thomas Popkins who was a leading whig activist in Carmarthenshire.[58] Other old Exclusionists like William Philipps and Michael Richards of Roath were long Mansell supporters, showing the curious local repercussions of transitions in national politics.

5. A Mansell monarchy?

In addition, there was a political (though not partisan) justification for opposition to Margam, expressed by Jenkins himself when he wrote that 'the election was no man's birthright, and opposition of this nature was very common in other parts of the kingdom'.[59] His objection was particularly valid in 1706, in which year died both Sir Edward Mansell of Margam and Thomas Mansell of Briton Ferry, leaving Thomas Mansell of Margam in possession of both vast estates. He had a strong territorial interest in the west of the county, where most of the minor gentry were believed to depend on him. Just as significant as his consolidation of wealth and power was the fact that Mansell had three young sons, so it did not require great foresight to imagine a time when both Glamorgan's seats might well be held permanently by his line. The county's political stability depended on a correct balance between the families, which Mansell's wealth served to endanger. In the event, the opposing faction had crumbled before the election. Mansell joined Beaufort in an appeal to avoid the expense, rancour and possible riot involved in an election, as a result of which the great 'interest' of Lewis of Van now passed to Margam.[60] The opposition fell apart, and the restoration of political harmony took place on Mansell terms. Stradling accepted a loyal but subordinate role, holding the borough seat (with Mansell's consent) from 1710 to 1722. Mackworth's challenge ended with the collapse of his 'Mine Adventurers' amidst debt, charges of dishonesty and threats of impeachment, which he piously compared to the trials of Job. The scale of the victory was demonstrated by Mansell's new (albeit brief) dominance of Neath and Cardiff, while he was until his death a partner in the tory electoral alliance with Beaufort and Windsor that chose the county's MPs.[61]

This was the greatest period for the Mansells since the mid sixteenth century, when the family's founder had seemed destined to accompany the Herberts into the peerage. The new power was consolidated when 'Tom of Ten Thousand' held ministerial office from 1704 to 1708, and 1710 to 1714. The resulting influence and patronage were used to perpetuate the family's political dominance of the county, whether by securing favourable sheriffs when a contested election seemed likely, or else by winning votes with jobs in the customs or the many new fields made available by war and the growth of the executive. The use of patronage is demonstrated by the sheer bulk of correspondence on the subject when Mansell was in the ministry, but constant effort was needed to secure control of strategic local officials like postmasters, especially during faction struggles.[62] Patronage had wide uses. On the simplest level it meant the financial advantage of Thomas Mansell and his clan of dependents, and a solution to the problems of a large family of indigent cousins and in-laws for whom he felt a strong sense of responbility. Normally, he secured jobs or pensions for relatives, or was at least able to assist them in legal troubles arising from duels or less honourable scrapes.[63] Of far wider significance was the development of a substantial clientage within Glamorgan. Other landed families were bound to his interest by patronage as well as kinship, as were the Carnes, who began a relationship with the East India Company which endured throughout the century.[64] In 1707, it was sadly remarked that all recent army commissions had gone to members of parliament or their dependents and Thomas Mansell was close to the source of this patronage.[65] War had great uses for these politicians, who had risen by their opposition to taxes and placemen, and Mansell would have sympathies with a naval friend who bemoaned a peace which 'has given me great prospect of starving, and consequently terrible pain of the mind'.[66]

The height of Mansell's power came after 1710, with the tory electoral triumph caused by war-weariness and the Sacheverell fiasco, both of which evoked powerful sentiments in Glamorgan itself. The impact of the Sacheverell affair is demonstrated by the loyal petition sent by the county in 1710, denouncing the impiety and immorality existing under whig governments. That year's Assize sermon by Thomas Hancorne bore many echoes of Sacheverell's original sermon: he too chose to attack the 'licentious Deist' and the 'rude attempts of prophaneness on our religion', and actually used the familiar phrase 'perils among false brethren'.[67] Thomas Mansell's constituents included some exponents of the highest tory ideology, who saw him as their representative, and in 1710 a Cardiff tory praised him for his role in the 'late delivery out of the management of wicked and unprincipled men'.[68] Mansell was, however, an intimate of Harley – perhaps his greatest personal friend – and like Harley, he opposed the more extreme policies of persecution suggested by some in the ministry, including the Schism Act. Similarly, his use of patronage was not quite so rigidly partisan as would have been approved by his violent followers like Edward Mansell of Swansea whose martyrological works were designed to help the campaign for a Schism Act.[69] In 1712, this fanatical anglican advised the army officer William Lucas (of Gower) that he would be unwise to appeal for patronage to both Thomas Mansell and the whig Peter King: 'if it be about any preferment take this caution, that my Lord will have nothing to do with anybody that depends on Sir Peter (and God be praised). Sir Peter, nor no whig or fanatic, are in reputation here, times are altered.'[70] In reality, Lord Mansell was on excellent terms with Peter King, a fellow *alumnus* of a dissenting academy, and he was friendly with other strong whigs like General Cadogan, Jocelyn Sydney, the Earl of Berkeley, and Charles Williams of Caerleon.[71]

Mansell's wide local connections and use of patronage gave him a position whose only precedent in Glamorgan was the Pembroke ascendancy before 1640, and this was enhanced by Mansell's peerage in 1711. Under the tory regime the Bench was remodelled by the addition of Mansell followers like Alexander Trotter of Swansea, who had always looked more to Thomas Mansell than to Sir Edward. There also appeared Roger Powell and Thomas Price of Merthyr Tydfil, who followed the (jacobite) Lewises of Van. Seven of nine JPs added in 1714 were said to have been jacobites, and these included all the five clerical justices, who were a novelty in Glamorgan. Equally satisfactory for the tory partisans was the purge of the zealous whig George Howells, persecuted by some 'great man then in the ministry' (Francis Gwyn or perhaps Thomas Mansell). Howell was said to owe the government £10,000 from his tenure as Receiver-General of Taxes for four Welsh counties, and he was forced to mortgage his estate and flee the county, although even this did not prevent a stay in Newgate. Howell was regarded as 'a great sufferer by the late destructive ministry for his zeal to the succession in the house of Hanover'.[72]

Mansell's great power was also used constructively to try and create a new Welsh territorial base parallel to that of Beaufort and Carbery. This was a notable break with Glamorgan precedents, whereby such extensions of alliances and landownership more commonly took place across the Bristol Channel than in Wales. Possibly through Harley's Welsh crony Erasmus Lewis, he was on excellent terms with the tory gentry of Pembrokeshire and Carmarthenshire, as well as most of the Welsh judges.[73] He bought lands to increase his electoral interest in Carmarthenshire and Breconshire, and a Carmarthenshire friend suggested that 'being *custos rotulorum* likewise would very much add to the interest you already have (in Carmarthenshire), by yourself and your friends'.[74] This plan was proposed in 1713, after the Earl of Carbery had died, so presumably Mansell's interest was to supplant his. This growing strength was based on his powers of patronage, particularly in the customs, but the ability to choose sheriffs was also useful, because of their power to influence elections. Mansell was aspiring to the same dominance of South Wales which had earlier been held by Philip Jones or Beaufort, and pursued these aims with vigour. Moreover, his position as 'viceroy' in Wales in a tory Britain under Harley would be more secure than either of these precedents, because more firmly established by patronage.[75]

6. Sky-blue incorruptibles: the jacobite interest

Mansell was not the only Glamorgan magnate to benefit from the new tory ascendancy. Lord Windsor gained a new title (Baron Mountjoy) in the creation of peers to pass the tory peace treaty, and Francis Gwyn held office as a Commissioner of Trade, and later Secretary of War. Sir Humphrey Mackworth also found his request for patronage in the Cornish Stannaries favourably received by the new high church government, and Beaufort became lord-lieutenant of Hampshire and Gloucestershire. All of these four represented a more extreme form of toryism than that of Harley and Mansell. Beaufort was widely regarded as a jacobite leader, and from 1709 he organised the high tory 'Board of Loyal Brotherhood', which was based on the tory coffee-house of the Cocoa Tree. Jacobitism developed during Anne's reign because of the strength of the high Church, and Wales was seen as a particular danger to the Hanoverian succession. In south-west Wales, Stuart sympathies were widespread among the greatest gentry,[76] who looked for leadership to Lewis Pryse as much as to Beaufort, and Pryse's Glamorgan friends included Beaufort's clients, Kemys and Mackworth. In a sense, the jacobites had a far more justifiable policy than the moderate tories, for the regime of the latter was unlikely to survive the death of Anne, while at least the extremists had a possible alternative. However, the schemes of both factions collapsed in 1714, and the government favour on which Mansell's new power-block was to be based passed to the whigs.

The complex structure of Welsh toryism deserves emphasis. Professor Holmes' *British politics in the age of Anne* is one of the few studies to place Mansell and his circle in a national context, but even here, there is the questionable statement that the South Wales tories were 'grouped around the Mansells of Margam'.[77] In fact, the toryism of this area was divided between Mansell's Harleyite sympathies and the rigid High Church and jacobite views of Pryse and Beaufort. Mansell maintained links with such partisans – just as he did with extreme whigs. He was not the universally accepted tory leader: but what must strike us at this point is how very far matters had developed in only two decades. Before 1688, the Mansells led a substantial moderate party; by 1710, there had been a very marked 'rightward' shift, so that Thomas Mansell was doing all he could to temper the tory extremism of his old followers. I have explained the growth of Church politics in terms of the decline of the catholic threat, but whatever the reason, South Wales was now acquiring the vehement high church toryism for which it would long be celebrated. The collapse of 'moderation' was a dangerous portent for civil peace.

There was no Welsh participation in the rising of 1715, but the failure of the rebellion did not signify the end of the jacobite hopes. There was widespread rioting betwen 1715 and 1720, especially in Wales and the west of England, and in towns like Bath and Bristol which were dominated by Beaufort's family. Key jacobite dates like 10 June could be relied on to lead to political violence, as at Brecon in 1718.[78] Throughout South Wales, the few active supporters of the whig authorities were persecuted, with little chance of redress, because both justices and postmasters were jacobite, and spread Stuart propaganda among the common people. 'The greatest incendiaries and most disaffected persons in Wales' included magnates like Lewis Pryse and William Powell in the south-west, or Lord Bulkeley and Watkin Williams-Wynn in the north.[79] Around such men there existed a network of agents and messengers, often drawn from nonjuring clergy and lawyers. Serious plots for a French landing were under discussion in 1717, and in 1722 a conspiracy was said to involve Beaufort and his catholic neighbours in the Borders – a striking reminiscence of 1641 and 1678.[80]

Jacobite organisation was formalised by the mid-1720s into a series of clubs, like the 'Cycle' of north-east Wales, the 'Club of 27' in Montgomeryshire, and the 'Society of Sea Serjeants' in the south, the last of which comprised the old associates of Lewis Pryse. The same activists also dominated the new masonic lodges, who particularly overlapped with the Sea Serjeants. Indeed the first lodges (Carmarthen 1726, Haverfordwest 1741) were both in Serjeants' territory.[81] Even the Serjeants' emblem was an eight-pointed star, described by a modern historian of the society as a 'jacobite star' – but heraldry knows nothing of such a symbol. In freemasonry, however, it betokened the knights templar, the hypothetical predecessors of the cult. With all these manifestations of the 'fury and boldness' of Welsh jacobitism, it is not surprising that the whigs began to fear that the optimism of their opponents was not unjustified.[82]

There is not such definite evidence in Glamorgan of riots and the perse-cution of whigs, but there were jacobite murmurings after the Hanoverian succession, sometimes by yeomen wishing to shock their betters, but also by gentlemen at Cowbridge, and by respectable Cardiff tradesmen like the Purcells. These rarely demonstrate political views of any sophistication, beyond a hatred of the 'shit-sacks' (or dissenters).[83] There was little active support for rebellion, but it was not easy to destroy the tory consensus of county society, and the prevailing tone of Glamorgan politics by the 1720s was tory with a definite jacobite streak. Thomas Mansell was an excep-tion. He was friendly with jacobites like Mar, Wyndham, Musgrave and Bolingbroke, and his West Wales friends kept him informed of the early campaigns of the Sea Serjeants.[84] Despite this, he became disenchanted with politics after 1714, and would have retired altogether if not for con-stant loyalty to Harley, who persuaded him to subscribe his name to many of the Lords' Protests in the next decade.[85]

However, even his family had developed extensive jacobite links: his son Bussy married a daughter of the Earl of Jersey, thereby acquiring relatives (including Jersey and Lansdowne) who had titles recognised only by the Stuart Court. The other son, Robert, was at the exiled Court in 1717, and affirmed his loyalty to James in a message which 'the King took very kindly (and relies on his doing him all the services in his power)'.[86] In 1721, he was returned for Minehead in Sir William Wyndham's interest, and he spoke for Atterbury, expressing the tory fear that the plot would be an excuse to persecute gentlemen for alleged Stuart loyalties: 'no one knows how soon it may be his own case, and I believe everyone would expect their friends' attendance when their lives and estates are at stake'.[87] He chided his father for failing to participate in the defence. Robert Mansell led a jacobite fac-tion in Glamorgan, while other Mansell kin and dependents were credited with seditious views at this time. After the disasters of 1714 – 15, it seemed as if the moderate tories were wholly discredited.

Jacobite views are attributed in the 1720s to Lord Windsor, Francis Gwyn, the Joneses of Fonmon and Carnes of Ewenni, while all the Dukes of Beaufort retained Stuart links until the 1750s. Both the Glamorgan seats were held by alleged jacobites between 1712 and 1734 – Robert Jones and Sir Charles Kemys for the county, high church Stradlings for the borough. One indication of the strength of such views is a list drawn up by Stuart agents about 1721, listing possible supporters of a rebellion in each county. Of course, the significance of this is debatable. 'Redgauntlet' had few counterparts in reality, and the exiled Court was notoriously prone to over-optimism. However, the list is a guide to broad sympathies, even if those named would never in fact take up arms, or might regard a catholic monarch with trepidation if the prospect were examined more closely. Most of the Welsh counties were regarded as very promising, notably Montgomeryshire and Pembrokeshire; and the role of Beaufort's family is repeatedly mentioned, although the current duke was a minor. In Monmouthshire, a rising was to be led by Sir Charles Kemys, Lord Windsor and Beaufort's two stewards. The vast estates of the Somersets are a reason given for the 'honesty' (that is, jacobitism) of the people there.

From Glamorgan, those listed include Robert Mansell, Sir Edward Stradling, Thomas Lewis of Van and Jones of Fonmon, as well as Kemys and Windsor. Beaufort's steward Gabriel Powell also appears, and he had long played an important role in organising tory campaigns in Glamorgan, Breconshire and Carmarthenshire. He was influenced by Sir Watkin Williams-Wynn, and helped to preserve the interests of the tory house of Fonmon during a minority. Beaufort's friends and allies were thus united by political belief, but also by real economic interests, as these were just the families who in the 1720s were participating in copper exploitation in the Swansea area. Indeed, the more one examines the Sea Serjeants, catholics and nonjurors involved in the Lockwood and Morris copper concern, the more this looks like a jacobite conspiracy in itself.[88]

The 1721 list represented the greatest landed interests, who followed one of the two factions mentioned, under Robert Mansell or Sir Charles Kemys. Presumably, Kemys had succeeded to the leadership of Beaufort's followers during the duke's minority, but the status he held in his own right is suggested by his further inclusion in 1730 as one of four potential rebel leaders in the west of Britain. Sir Humphrey Mackworth's omission from the list is curious, as he was close both to Beaufort and Lord Digby, a patron of nonjurors. His son Herbert invited Robert Digby to visit him at Neath in 1721. Mackworth had extensive links in the near-jacobite society of the Midland gentry, but perhaps the exiled Court assumed his financial troubles would keep him out of active politics.[89] Economic considerations weighed heavily with him, and his only involvement in the crisis of 1715 was to buy a great many stocks 'venturing boldly at the time of the rebellion when stocks are low'.[90] Below the level of the greater gentry, it is still more difficult to assess political sympathies, but there were both lay and clerical nonjurors in several towns of South Wales.[91] Nonjuring ministers were used as emissaries by jacobites like Lewis Pryse, and they could rely on the patronage of the Duke of Beaufort in Monmouthshire, or Sir

Charles Kemys and his wealthy burgess friends in Cardiff. Here, the Wells and Purcell families both favoured the nonjuring congregation, which had its own minister and maintained jacobite traditions until the reign of George III.[92] In 1726, it was still possible for a confidence trickster to live off the Welsh gentry by posing as a nonjuring parson, but he gave himself away by his wealth and his too-worldly attitudes. In 1733, Cardiff whigs tried to argue that a tory election victory was invalid as both the new bailiffs were nonjuror followers of the Stradlings.[93] Cardiff would long be as great a source of offence to the whigs as dissenting Swansea was to the high anglicans.

Of course, opposition to the new establishment was not in itself a badge of jacobitism, although the government's propagandists often attempted to make it appear so. The old moderate Church–tory tradition was still vigorous and many of the government's bitter opponents had thoroughly demonstrated their loyalty to the accession of the new dynasty. Tory opposition in parliament particularly concentrated on old issues dear to the 'country' tradition, like army brutality, the Septennial Bill and the severity of the Treason or Mutiny Acts, as well as newer partisan issues like the impeachment of Harley, or attainder of Bolingbroke. On such issues, Mansell and Harley regularly joined with jacobites and the occasional opposition whig to attack the new measures. Toryism continued to be a broad coalition, with moderates allied to jacobites of varying degrees of commitment, in both houses of parliament. The tory opposition also had its own distinctive culture and social life, in London and the provinces, and political opinions still determined the coffee-house, inn or theatre which one attended. At Newport, Beaufort's steward wrote in 1720 that the duke's friends always used the Ship Inn, because it was run by a good woman whose 'ancestors have been sufferers for their loyalty, and her grandfather died a nonjuror'.[94] The tory gentry and aristocracy gathered for hunting and racing, which amusements became almost political badges. Magnates established race-meetings under their own patronage, which were political assemblies as well as sporting occasions. Tory gentlemen used tory attorneys for their legal work, and borrowed money from tory merchants like Colston of Bristol.[95]

After 1714, another tory centre was the University of Oxford, where some of the leading scholars were nonjurors, and where in 1721 'to call yourself a whig... is the same as to be attainted and outlawed'.[96] Colleges like Christ Church had a particularly 'high' reputation (Atterbury himself had once been Dean) and Glamorgan tories matriculating there between

1716 and 1718 included Francis Gwyn the younger, Bussy Mansell, Edward Stradling and William Savours. There was also Magdalen College, long frequented by the Digbys and Mackworths. Tory circles also favoured the same group of writers, like Thomas Yalden or Joseph Trapp, and subscribed to the same books.[97] In the absence of any definite party organisation, it was by such social and cultural manifestations that the tories maintained their unity and identity outside parliament.

7. Whig oligarchy

In the 1720s, toryism was strong in Glamorgan as in other areas, and it possessed a considerable extremist element. But obviously, there never was a widespread Welsh rising for the Pretender, and the remarkable fact of the next twenty years was not only the decline of jacobitism but the fragmentation of Glamorgan toryism, so that the whigs won elections fought on broadly party lines in 1734 and 1745. Throughout Wales and the Borders, we shall observe a clear pattern of governments attempting to control disaffected localities by the same policies. Firstly, local whig magnates were to be responsible for shires or groups of counties, from which they could keep the central government informed, and where they could act as channels of patronage to promote loyalty. Patronage implied office and pensions, but also security from being excluded from positions of local power. Finally, elections were heavily weighted against opposition candidates. Before studying in detail how these methods worked in Glamorgan, it is necessary to provide a regional context by showing how whig strength was promoted throughout the western tory redoubt.

Various ministries attempted to counterbalance tory power by distributing lavish rewards to loyal whigs. The power-base of high tories like Beaufort or Pryse was secured for the government by the influence of Lisburne in Cardiganshire, Winchester in Carmarthenshire, Coningsby in Herefordshire, or Herbert in Shropshire. In Glamorgan and south-east Wales the equivalent family was the Morgans of Tredegar who were already the most powerful Welsh family, and who grew in wealth and prestige during the century.

After 1714, the Morgans were loyal followers of successive whig ministries, and they were friendly with powerful peers like King, Sunderland and Stanhope.[98] Sir William Morgan married the daughter of the Duke of Devonshire, and the families remained close for decades.[99]. The family acquired honours for themselves, such as a knighthood in 1725, but they were also seen as agents from whom the neighbouring gentry could obtain government favour, and whose wishes had therefore to be respected. They could win for their neighbours useful prizes, such as college exhibitions or favour in legal disputes, or lucrative Customs posts in Glamorgan, while they were sufficiently strong to protect clients (and their jobs) from rival magnates.[100] Their power helped to secure the govenment's local support, and they were responsible for appointing the sheriff and *Custos Rotulorum* in their three counties of south-east Wales.[101] Tredegar was able to obtain a loyal petition from Monmouthshire during the critical year of 1722, despite Beaufort's enormous power in the county, and all the optimism of the jacobite Court, so their value for the government was immense.[102] Moreover, their power depended chiefly on government favour, so the family was rarely inclined to stray into political unorthodoxy. They voted with the ministry even on such unpopular issues as the Hessian troops (1730) and the excise (1733).

The Morgans demonstrate, albeit to an extreme degree, the use of government powers and patronage in creating a strong whig interest in predominantly tory areas. After 1714, patronage was also used to reward whigs who had suffered from the partisan vindictiveness of the tory government of 1710 to 1714. George Howell in Glamorgan was knighted and was restored to the county Bench, together with his son and namesake.[103] Sir Thomas Jones was added to the Bench because of his whig loyalties, and his influence in government was seen as an opportunity for his Glamorgan neighbours who had previously turned to Lord Mansell for advancement. He was also active in London in the organisation of the 'Society of Ancient Britons', for this expression of Welsh patriotism was also a focus of whig loyalties among Welsh *emigrés*, and its members included Lord Lisburne and office holders or placemen.[104] Other Glamorgan whigs who benefitted from the coming of the 'millenary year of Whiggism' in 1714 included Sir Rowland Gwynne, who now received a pension to relieve his growing economic distress.[105]

Of greater long-term importance for the political future of the county were the offices and honours received by those who, with Tredegar, would direct the fortunes of the whig interest for a generation. By the 1720s, we can observe a new political elite developing in South Wales, with power based on their position in the government, armed forces or judiciary – and all naturally loyal to the whig order. It is very reminiscent of the new whig Court and financial elite in Hampshire and Berkshire, as described by Professor Thompson. A typical example was Richard Carter, who in 1728 became Chief Justice on the circuit which covered the three counties of south-east Wales, and he was thenceforward the 'honoured friend' of the Morgans. His family later intermarried with the whig Aubreys of Glamorgan, and (with Tredegar) Carter determined the appointment of sheriffs and justices in these counties until the 1750s.[106]

Other leading whigs included Sir Edmund Thomas of Wenvoe, whose brother became a general and married the sister of the Earl of Albemarle. There was also Admiral Matthews of Llandaff, son of the martyr of 1685, and who settled in Glamorgan as a country squire from about 1724. He owed his wealth to a successful naval career and the tenure of valuable offices and diplomatic posts, while his son held high rank in the army. Government patronage was important in the career of the other local whig leader, Charles Talbot, who inherited the Hensol estate in 1721. The son of a staunchly whig Bishop of Durham, he was Solicitor-General and later Lord Chancellor, and between 1727 and 1730, he was one of the 'Select Lords', virtually part of the king's 'Cabinet'. As such, he had great powers of patronage, and friends like Secker and Benson received bishoprics shortly after he became Chancellor. He was able to raise his deist chaplain Rundle to an Irish bishopric in the face of heavy espiscopal opposition, although he failed to secure advancement for the still more radical Samuel Clarke, the arian.[107] Talbot's period of office was recalled with nostalgia by the whig gentry of Wales, particularly those of the Vale of Glamorgan, who now found it politic to 'dance attendance at Hensol' for 'peer's favours'.[108] The Glamorgan whigs grew in strength during the 1720s. In 1721, the opposition to Lord Mansell on the Bench had derived from only two major families, the Jenkins's of Hensol and Thomases of Wenvoe.[109] By contrast, there were several great families acting together in the whig cause in the 1730s, including the Aubreys, Morgans, Matthews of Llandaff, Talbots and Thomases of Wenvoe, each supported by clients among the lesser gentry. The whigs also mobilised popular support in the form of the dissenting interest, whose electoral power they were attempting to gauge from at least 1715. Nonconformists had become a wealthy group, and in 1734 the tory candidate sought to win their favour by denying rumours that he was of a persecuting nature.[110] However, they realised that they had everything to fear from a return to tory rule, and so rallied to the government's support even on a contentious issue like the excise.

While the whig interest was being strengthened considerably by government favour, the tories were suffering such serious blows to their morale as the exposure of the Atterbury plot, and the addition of petty whig families to the commission of the peace. Why should they continue to suffer such perils and humiliations? For tory politicians, the Stuart cause became increasingly a mixture of nostalgia and opportunism, rather than the cornerstone of their ideology. Few can have excluded entirely the possibility of a jacobite Restoration, but the accession of a second Hanoverian in 1727 must have shown that the new dynasty was not going to vanish overnight; and that must have caused the tory gentry much thought as to how much they were prepared to sacrifice for political purity. The whig monopoly of patronage, moreover, exercised great attractions, and there were some defections, like Colonel Vaughan of Breconshire.[111] Other potential rebels on the 1721 list were won over by government favour or actual bribery, including Thomas Lewis of Van who declared himself a true friend of Walpole in 1726. By 1730, he was an intimate of the whigs, Matthews, Morgan and Talbot.

Apart from those who turned their coats, some families died out in the male line, or else (like the Gwyns) moved out of the county, and this weakened the tory ascendancy. There were minorities in the family of Jones of Fonmon from 1715 to 1727, and 1742 to 1760, and in that of the Dukes of Beaufort from 1714 to 1728, and 1756 and 1765. The whigs were especially aided by demographic change via the decline of the Mansells after the first Lord's death in 1723. His jacobite son Robert predeceased him, so there now began a minority which lasted until 1740. In this time, the Margam interest was preserved by the heir's uncle, Bussy Mansell of Briton Ferry, despite the constant need to refer to the guardians before major decisions could be taken. Nor did uncertainty end when the second Lord came of age, for a dispute over the Stradling inheritance led to bad feeling between him and Bussy, and very nearly caused the loss of the county seat to the Edwins by default. The decline of the Mansell interest is suggested by their loss of control in boroughs like Cardiff, where the Stradlings were the main tory force by 1730, or Aberafan, which passed to the Mackworths.[112] By the 1740s, Bussy Mansell was closely following the lead of Beaufort – an alliance which would have appalled Thomas Mansell, still more a 'moderate' like Sir Edward. This extraordinary series of misfortunes, together with massive debts, effectively sabotaged the county's most powerful tory interest after 1723, and the family died out in the male line in 1750.

This largely fortuitous decline in tory strength coincided with a determined government policy to dominate the political fortunes of such opposition strongholds as the Welsh counties by, for instance, a highly partisan use of patronage. Whigs and dissenters were normally likely to succeed in appeals against appointment to the onerous office of sheriff, while this post could be allotted to those whose votes had been cast injudiciously during an election. The ministry's influence was often decisive in elections, for instance by the appointment of whig sheriffs solely to secure a favourable result, for the discretion they could exercise was considerable. 'Arbitrary and illegal proceedings' by sheriffs were blamed for whig victories in Glamorgan's county seat in both 1734 and 1745. In the earlier case, the sheriff was William Bassett of Miskin, cousin and heir of Sir Rowland Gwynne. Requiring office holders to vote for ministry candidates was also a powerful weapon in a maritime county where many had relatives in the customs service. In 1745, Charles Edwin's steward disobeyed orders to campaign for a tory, partly for fear of losing his job as a distributor of stamps.[113] When such means failed, the petition gave an additional opportunity to favour ministry candidates, and partisan decisions in 1727 alone secured the return of whigs in Flintshire, Cardigan and Brecon. Glamorgan tories were fortunate that the borough seat was so firmly controlled and rarely contested (two Mackworths held it from 1739 to 1790). Borough elections elsewhere in Wales permitted not only biassed elections, but also permanent revisions of the franchise in whig interests, as occurred between 1715 and 1729 in three counties. In 1732, Sir Edward Stradling was examining the precedents of Flintshire and Montgomery to defend the tory interest in the Glamorgan borough, where the 1734 election was bitterly fought.[114] Many burgesses were added and removed in Cardiff, and in the by-election of 1738, new burgesses appeared from Stradling parishes like St Donat's, Wick and Monknash. But such fears were temporary, largely confined to the 1730s. Even at the nadir of tory fortunes, whig petitions were not invariably successful, and there were counties where the full weight of government influence could not displace an opposition member. By such means, however, the number of whigs returned for the twenty-seven Welsh constituencies had risen from 8 in 1715 to 18 in 1734, and 14 of the latter were ministry supporters.

Whig electoral advantages acted as a supplement to patronage, both in providing the temptation of a secure parliamentary seat for the loyal, and in neutralising those opponents not attracted by offers of place or pension. The novel fact of likely opposition (even if ultimately unsuccessful) created many new problems, which could only be overcome by regarding the election as something akin to a military campaign. Men skilled in these affairs were very valuable, and their social status rose accordingly, which helped the acceptance into the county community of newly successful lawyers like Anthony Maddocks or the Tayntons.[115] A great disadvantage of the new political world was that the absence of electoral harmony meant that the voters (even of the lower class) came to realise the value placed on their support. They began to demand frequent election treats as of right, and at least in one case, they insisted on the recognition of disputed common rights before votes would be given. The worst feature of the new situation was that the cost of a campaign could rise to frightening proportions. Bussy Mansell spent £4,000 on the three elections of 1727, 1734 and 1737, although the last of these was uncontested, while in the first two, other expenses were borne by Beaufort and Kemys.[116] There was considerable incentive for even a great family like the Mackworths to avoid a contested election, either by not standing or by reaching a compromise with the whigs; and elsewhere in Wales, the Mostyns and the Myddeltons had suddenly become equally timorous. Sir Charles Kemys and his kinsman Edward Kemys have been described as 'rabid Welsh jacobites',[117] but in 1731 they agreed to support the Tredegar interest in Monmouthshire rather than face the disasters of a contested election.[118]

8. Tory survival 1720 – 1740

However, toryism could not be wholly destroyed, for the party never had fewer than 111 MPs during the reign of George II, while the total was as high as 144 in 1734.[119] Of course, it is only in retrospect that we realise the permanence of the Hanoverian settlement. The proscriptions suffered by some tories might only be a brief interlude before the acquisition of honours and rewards on the return of the Pretender; but this possibility diminished as the century progressed. On the other hand, politics was never simply an affair of self-interest, and tories maintained their opposition to the whig government for other less tangible reasons, like family tradition. Toryism had also a definite political ideology apart from any supposed jacobite links. Indeed, these latter became an embarrassment to those of the party who felt that traditions of monarchism and passive obedience should lead them to support the Hanoverians and the current establishment. But it was their vigorous suspicion of all governments (inheriting much of the old 'country' tradition) which kept toryism alive as a strong political force between 1714 and 1760, even when prospects of success seemed at their lowest. Their politics in these years can best be described as 'populist', and they had to remain close to the wishes of the constituencies which returned them: and Sir Charles Kemys-Tynte promised to be a 'slave' of his Glamorgan electors in 1745.[120] The tories had no access to government patronage to maintain their unity.

One important element in their ideology was loyalty to the Church, but issues could no longer be as clear-cut as in Anne's reign because now the hierarchy itself was whig. The bishops of St David's were whig statesmen, but they were conscientious men who regularly visited their diocese.[121] By contrast, holders of the poor see of Llandaff were notorious absentees who usually distributed their limited patronage to men from outside the county. Their promises of advancement to Glamorgan men were only 'froth and whipsillabub', so relations sank to appalling levels. It was an ironic theme of the 1720s and 1730s that the tory gentry who spoke so much of maintaining the Church interest would contribute nothing to prevent the literal collapse of Llandaff Cathedral.[122] This was left to the new 'loyalists', whig families like the Matthews, Buttons, Talbots and Lewises of Van. Some anglican clergy were so outraged by their lack of advancement that they campaigned against donations to the repair fund, while others wished that the county might produce a Sir John Pakington who would unite the theory and practice of his high church opinions. Only to a limited extent did the Church tradition remain a living force in politics and in domestic piety. Among the Sea Serjeants, both the Hancornes and the Gwynnes of Taliaris came from families for whom such ideas had long been the chief motives of political action;[123] but it will be argued below that much of the doctrinal and intellectual substance had been lost to this tradition. By the 1730s, the tories found it useful to attack critics of the anglican establishment, but the high church days of 1710 to 1714 had gone forever. All that could now be hoped was to fight off the worst manifestations of heresy and indifference.

Old fears of deist and arian assaults seemed confirmed by developments after 1714 with the presence of men like Talbot in government. Scepticism was widely expressed on issues like the divinity of Christ, or the existence of Hell or of angels. The height of arian influence in this period has been dated to between 1726 and 1733, in which years Talbot attempted to elevate to bishoprics the deist Rundle and the arian Clarke. This was also an age of widespread anti-clericalism, represented in Glamorgan by a libellous diatribe against the cathedral clergy of Llandaff and their courts.[124] In 1737, Sir Edmund Thomas of Wenvoe wrote a ferociously anti-clerical 'Short view' of the English clergy from 1066 to 1688, proving how frequently their interests had been contrary to those of the nation.[125] Tory defence against such assaults focussed particularly on the parliamentary efforts to pass laws for the toleration of dissenters, and on the Mortmain Bill which threatened the tory stronghold of the universities. This coincided with an attempt to relieve quakers of the burden of tithes, and the tory reaction was violent both in parliament and the country. In Glamorgan, for instance, there was a bitter literary controversy about whether tory clerics like James Harris had treated the quakers with kindness or severity in their exaction of tithes, and past persecutions were re-examined.[126]

Broad 'libertarianism' was also vital in continuing tory opposition, and this involved attitudes which had often characterised the most extreme whigs before 1688. Landed gentlemen were seen as representing the liberties of the subject against an over-strong state, and the despotism sought by a foreign dynasty aided by corrupt moneyed interests, courtiers and placemen, and by mercenary soldiers. This general conspiracy against liberty justified opposition to the government's foreign policy and its extravagant taxes, and it confirmed the tory gentry in their dislike of greater landowners and peers. Of course, the role of the Duke of Beaufort in tory South Wales prevented this hatred of magnates becoming part of tory ideology there. Resentments were particularly focussed on issues like the employment of Hessian troops in 1730, on which Bussy Mansell and six other Welsh MPs opposed the government. The terms in which this question was seen in the Mackworth family were so black and white as to permit no compromise between self-evident liberty and tyranny. There was the obvious conclusion that policies as abhorrent as those proposed by the government could only be supported by the greedy and self-interested; and Herbert Mackworth was strictly warned by his wife, Juliana Digby, not to compromise his honour by being marked in print for a Hanoverian.[127] Another such issue was the Excise Bill of 1733, the reaction to which was so violent that tories like Williams-Wynn became very optimistic about the prospects of Walpole's imminent destruction.[128]

Despite proscriptions and some defections, the tories continued to act as a vigorous opposition both in parliament and the country at large, and the party acquired a degree of organisation based on the informal lines which had emerged before 1725. For instance, newspapers like the *Craftsman*[129] helped to keep local tories informed of national affairs, but the key element was what we might call 'federalism'. The tory interest in each county or region was headed by some magnate, like Lord Gower in Staffordshire or Sir John St Aubyn in Cornwall, and these leaders met to discuss common policy or action. There was an important Welsh element in the leadership, including Lord Windsor, Sir Watkin Williams-Wynn, the Earl of Oxford – and notably the Dukes of Beaufort whose electoral influence was felt in at least ten western counties between 1710 and 1760. Social contacts and marriages consolidated the bonds between the various regional leaderships, and such interdependence was very useful when a weakness occurred in one area. Beaufort, for instance, was able to rely on the legal expertise of the Lancashire barrister Fazakerley during his disputes in Swansea and west Glamorgan.[130] In the Beaufort minority of the 1720s, the efforts of the family's clients and stewards to preserve his Welsh interests were supplemented by those of the Berties, Lord Gower and Judge Robert Price (acting for the Earl of Oxford). Beaufort's steward, Gabriel Powell, was helped by Williams-Wynn, and both Powell and Price were aided by Sir Charles Kemys in legal and electoral affairs.[131] Sir John Philipps of Picton played a like role in the affairs of south-west Wales, as in Cardiganshire where he, Wynn and Price were able to preserve tory fortunes through the minority of the heir of Lewis Pryse.

This organisation was formalised with the existence of societies like the Sea Serjeants or the Cycle, in the areas of influence of, respectively, Philipps and Wynn.[132] Although the history of both clubs is shadowy before the 1750s, there is no doubt that they were composed overwhelmingly of tory gentlemen, and their organisational role can be demonstrated in early elections. No Glamorgan men participated in the Cycle, and only a few in the Sea Serjeants, but the latter group included some leading gentry of west Glamorgan, particularly those close to the Mansells. These were the Swansea merchant, George Noble, and gentry like the Hancornes, Popkins's, Collins's and Williams's of Dyffryn. Eventually there was also the heir of Margam, Thomas Talbot.[133] Swansea became a frequent meeting place for the society, at least in its later days, for annual dinners were held there in 1749, 1752 and 1756, and Sir John Philipps stayed in the town.[134]

Such regional forms of party organisation were connected with the tory party on a national scale through quasi-social institutions like race-meetings. Jacobite agents took great comfort in the sentiments expressed at Lichfield Races in the 1740s, and in 1747 Beaufort invited Herbert Mackworth to attend Burford with 'our friends' like Sir Watkin Williams-Wynn or Sir Walter Bagot of Staffordshire, and many more.[135] Here they could discuss plans for the forthcoming parliamentary session. Academic occasions at Oxford University provided another venue for such meetings, while London's taverns and coffee-houses were the normal settings for tory gatherings. Perhaps the most important was the Cocoa Tree, with which Beaufort's 'Loyal Brotherhood' was associated. Welsh members of the latter included Sir Charles Kemys and his heir, Sir Charles Kemys-Tynte, as well as Sir John Philipps. In 1745 this was a party headquarters for co-ordinating the tory campaign in the Glamorgan election, where national leaders met local gentry like Tynte or Herbert Mackworth.[136] Another form of tory organisation by the 1740s was the 'Independent Electors of Westminster', whose members included Sir John Philipps and (from Glamorgan) Tynte and the jacobite lawyer, David Morgan.

Charles Edwin of Llanmihangel was actually elected for Westminster through the efforts of the Independent Electors, and in 1745 they played an important role in dissuading him from splitting Glamorgan's tory vote by his candidacy.[137] Edwin was the grandson of the nonconformist Lord Mayor of London, Sir Humphrey, and it is curiously appropriate that he should have been active in a club which belonged to the tradition of urban radicalism. This even led some contemporaries to regard him as a highly idiosyncratic whig as late as 1740. But Edwin and the radicals were allied in the tory interest, in a society believed to be deep in jacobite conspiracy. Nor had the transition carried the Edwin interest smoothly with the family head. At the beginning of the century, the whig Edwins had chosen stewards of their own political persuasion. By the 1740s, these men were still whigs – like Maddocks and the Tayntons – and they attempted to sabotage the tory campaign they had been ordered to promote. In the correspondence of the tory managers like Mansell and Tynte,[138] there are repeated expressions of concern about such 'subversion'.

9. 'Broad-bottom': the tories and the opposition whigs 1730 – 1745

During Walpole's long dominance, there was a strange mingling of the various opposition strands and ideologies, like that found in the Independent Electors. From the mid-1720s, the jacobite danger had faded sufficiently to permit a working alliance of anti-Walpole whigs with the tory opposition, and this despite the wide disparity on some views, notably religious. From the early 1730s, this alliance presented the ministry with regular and effective opposition, and the overlap between whig and tory was reflected by curious alignments at local level. One of Walpole's strongest opponents from about 1735 was the son of Lord Chancellor Talbot, who succeeded to his title in 1737, and was associated with the whig circles at Stowe.[139] He was noted for religious unorthodoxy and extreme political views of a near-republican nature. His immorality was also celebrated, and his close friends included other 'rakes' like Jocelyn Sydney, and especially Charles Edwin of the Independent Electors. Edwin and Talbot now became central figures in creating a new opposition alliance.

Talbot can only be described as a radical whig, but in the 1730s and 1740s he became a powerful influence on the second Lord Mansell – the grandson of the Harleyite Thomas Mansell and the son of the jacobite Robert. Lord Mansell had attended the high church centre of Christ Church, Oxford – yet in the early 1740s, he appears alongside Talbot in the regular anti-Walpole protests in the House of Lords. Mansell's correspondence is striking testimony as to how far traditional loyalties had crumbled, for his intimates included other undoubted whigs like Edward Coke and the Marquis of Hartington.[140] He had not become a traitor: it was just that Walpole could only be removed by an alliance stretching from the extreme whig Talbot to the jacobite Beaufort. Equally striking were the connections of Lord Mansell's high tory uncle, Bussy. He had cooperated with Beaufort and Sir Charles Kemys in the elections of the 1730s, but he was also close to the Prince of Wales's Court, to Pulteney and to his own Hervey relatives.[141]

The new alliance was powerful in South Wales. The Marquis of Winchester who had preserved the whig interest in Carmarthenshire in the 1720s was, by the 1730s, that Duke of Bolton who opposed Walpole so bitterly. There were other defections among Welsh whiggery, including the MP for Brecon and Thomas Wyndham of Dunraven, who married a sister of Charles Edwin.[142] Edwin was in very good odour at the Prince's Court, enough to win a chaplaincy for his client John Wilkinson – but only limited patronage could be acquired here. Following the Prince only made sense in the hope of the great rewards to be won at his accession to the throne. On that day, there would be spoils – but also a new position for the tories. I have argued elsewhere that the Prince of Wales's initiation into freemasonry in 1737 represented a sealing of his alliance with the tories, which had largely been negotiated by Talbot;[143] and from this point, opposition hopes seemed to attain a new realism. In the 1730s, the correspondence of extreme tories like the Kemys's eagerly notes the growing disaffection of whigs like Hervey, Winnington, and especially Pulteney, who was becoming the great jacobite hope.[144]

Herbert Mackworth of Gnoll provides an excellent illustration of the development of political opposition during this period, and especially the manner in which Walpole's enemies drew together in the 1730s. His inclinations were high tory, reflected in his attendance at the Cocoa Tree and

Table 19: *The connections of the Mackworth family*

(a) *The Digbys and Somersets*

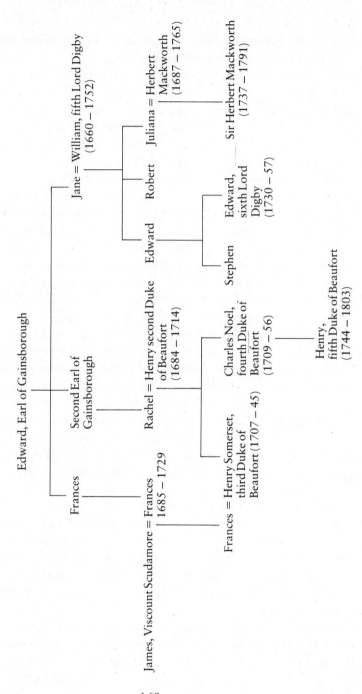

(b) *The Digbys and Foxes*

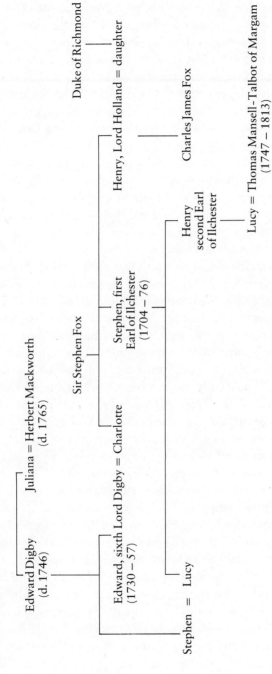

Edward Digby
(d. 1746)

Juliana = Herbert Mackworth
(d. 1765)

Edward, sixth Lord Digby = Charlotte
(1730 – 57)

Sir Stephen Fox

Stephen, first
Earl of Ilchester
(1704 – 76)

Duke of Richmond

Henry, Lord Holland = daughter

Charles James Fox

Stephen = Lucy

Henry
second Earl
of Ilchester

Lucy = Thomas Mansell-Talbot of Margam
(1747 – 1813)

his very close friendship with his wife's kinsmen, the Dukes of Beaufort. There were a great many letters between the families, and visits were often exchanged, for personal influence played a vital part in the maintenance of the tory interest during the years of exclusion from government, when loyalty could not be secured by the spoils of office. Through marriage into the Digby family, Mackworth was also connected with the high tory gentry of Dorset, Warwickshire and Staffordshire, and his correspondents in these counties include many families regarded as potential jacobite rebels in the 1720s.[145] However, his political associates in the 1730s were opposition whigs. Perhaps his most frequent correspondent was Charles Cotes, a whig MP for Tamworth who supported the attack on Walpole, and who followed Henry Fox. From about 1714 the Digbys also grew closer to the Fox family (their Dorset neighbours) and this friendship was reflected in marriages, so Mackworth became connected with this whig line. Their relationships are given in Table 18.

Throughout his life, Mackworth was involved with charitable organisations like the SPCK and the Georgia Society, both of which reflected the contemporary alliance of opposition groups. They included tories of formerly puritan families like the Mackworths themselves, the Philipps' of Picton.[146] There were also high tories like Edward Digby, and opposition whigs, notably Lord Talbot and the family of Lord Egmont. Talbot's connections have already been examined, but Egmont's social circle was equally mixed politically. He was friendly with Edmund Thomas of Wenvoe, a mainstay of the Prince's Court, but also with Lord Mansell, and with many close to the Mansells – men like Sir William Heathcote. Egmont's son, moreover, was Charles Edwin's colleague as MP for Westminster. The two normally followed the same political line, although each was constantly on his guard against treachery by the other.[147]

By the late 1730s, the opposition alliance was well established, and had an organisational structure through freemasonry and certain charities, as well as the unofficial social intercourse of the metropolis. How had it altered loyalties in the shires? The answer is mixed. Mackworth had extensive social and political links with opposition whigs, and in 1738 he was favoured by Glamorgan's whig 'caucus' (led by Talbot) to succeed to the borough seat.[148] This suggests that he was seen less as a tory than as a broadly acceptable 'country' opponent of the ministry. However, the old allegiances had not quite diminished sufficiently for Mackworth to accept this if it implied any dispute with Beaufort, so his election was secured through the traditional alliance of tory borough patrons.[149] The new *rapprochement* did not wholly submerge older rivalries.

The campaign against Walpole sought to replace his rule with a 'broad-bottomed' administration, with some tories. The prospect raised whig fears of an arbitrary and extreme regime on the lines of that of 1710, endangering the dynasty and even the protestant religion itself. Despite this, Walpole's regime was progressively undermined from about 1739, and the assault involved Welsh politicians like Beaufort, Wynn, Philipps and Talbot. Glamorgan squires were naturally concerned about the war crisis – which erupted from disputes over the West Indies, an area so dear to the interests of their friends and financiers in Bristol. Moreover, it coincided with an agrarian crisis which placed a new premium on their industrial and colonial interests. One of the vital parliamentary votes in securing the government's fall concerned the election at Chippenham of Sir Edmund Thomas of Wenvoe, an opposition whig, so there was much Glamorgan interest in the crisis. By 1742, Walpole was out of office and the new government included some tory elements. This had the encouraging result that some whig petitions were defeated after elections, as in Cardiganshire and Denbighshire. There were also great hopes for a new distribution of patronage, and in Glamorgan, clerical justices returned to the Bench in 1743, for the first time since 1717; but contradictions between the former allies began to make themselves felt.[150] Beaufort wrote to Herbert Mackworth of the new administration, adding 'It is not the change of men but of measures that can contribute towards the good of our country.'[151]

It was in this atmosphere of political confusion that one of the most important Glamorgan elections of the period took place, when, in January 1745, the tory Tynte and the whig Matthews contested the county seat. The government played little part in this except in offering Matthews the security of an alternative seat, should it be required. So the tories stood an excellent chance. The abundant correspondence of Tynte's circle demonstrates the tory organisation working efficiently, so that his party was confident of success until the last moment. Beaufort justly remarked that 'If there is not exceeding foul play, I should imagine that Sir Charles would carry it.'[152] Several members of the Sea Serjeants had useful interests in the county, and Tynte was supported by Wynn, Beaufort and Windsor. There was also Bussy Mansell, who by now controlled the estates of Margam, Briton Ferry and St Donat's. The tories had no lack of people skilled in electioneering, notably Mansell himself who claimed to 'write and think' for Tynte,[153] while Beaufort sent a man skilled in the electoral tricks of Wiltshire to instruct his allies.[154] He also wrote personally to the county's squires making it difficult for them to refuse such a request without insulting him. Tynte gained the interests of the Gwyns, Mackworths and

Turbervilles of Ewenni, while Charles Edwin was won over by the Independent Electors. On the other side, the chief interests were those of Lord Talbot and of Matthews himself – but it was Matthews who won. It is remarkable that it should still have been impossible in 1745 for a well-organised tory campaign to make headway against the whigs' traditional advantages, notably the decisive role of a biassed sheriff. Although Talbot and his whigs had long been allied to Beaufort's circle, different criteria appear to have applied on national and local levels, and whig – tory rivalries held good at the latter.

10. Towards stability: the aftermath of 1745

This election was crucial for the tory interest in Glamorgan. Tynte shared expenses of over £2,000 with Beaufort, Windsor and Mansell, but the damage was greater than merely financial. Mansell's disillusion at what he believed to be another corrupt election made him withdraw from politics until his death, and Beaufort had to concentrate more on Monmouthshire, where his family's position had been undermined by the whigs since 1727. Tynte now switched his energies to Somerset, where he was county member from 1747 to 1774, and the leading tory protagonists were thus diverted from their Glamorgan interests. The change was not revolutionary, for these families were very important in Glamorgan long afterwards, but it was a landmark in that the county's MPs would in future be drawn from newer families. None of Glamorgan's borough MPs after 1734 was descended in the male line from a family established in Glamorgan before 1680. None of the county members from 1745 came from a family who had previously represented a seat there: these were the Matthews's (1745 – 7, 1756 – 61), Thomases of Wenvoe (1761 – 7), Vernons (1767 – 80) and 'Edwins' or Wyndhams (1747 – 56, 1780 – 1814). It was also Glamorgan's last hard-fought election for several decades, and it marked the end of a generation of highly partisan contests. The reasons for such an apparently abrupt change therefore deserve detailed consideration, as it derived from both immediate circumstances and long-term trends.

I would suggest that this may be best understood by a detailed study of local responses to the 1745 Jacobite rising, and the way in which tory gentry saw themselves as working within the Hanoverian system in the ensuing decades. Politics had become the bloodless quest for patronage so thoroughly analysed by Namier, but to state this is to describe an effect of change, rather than to list its causes. Religious changes certainly had their effects, as will be seen from attitudes to catholics, dissenters and methodists, while other explanations might be sought in the concentration of landed wealth. Furthermore, governments were finally fighting the kind of wars which worked in favour of gentry interests. But whatever the exact causation, we can see 1745 as symbolising a real change in the nature of party conflict, one unparalleled since 1688.

A major aspect of the new social and political stability was the complete failure of Wales to aid the jacobite cause in 1745. Whigs feared that the 'Broad-bottom' scheme of these years represented a jacobite 'Trojan horse', and tories like Philipps and Wynn did indeed have strong links with the exiled Court. Dr Eveline Cruickshanks quotes in her *Political untouchables* a French report in 1743 claiming that Wales and Monmouthshire were '*entierèment soumis*' to the Duke of Beaufort and his brother, to Powis, Bulkeley and Wynn, and that the country was merely awaiting Barrymore's call to ride to arms.[155] However, the tory leadership rallied to the government cause in 1745, raising troops and arresting traitors, while tory members were summoned to parliament in terms echoing the most fervent whig propaganda: 'everything that is near and dear to us is now at stake', so all must attend 'who have any love or regard for their country, and the preservation of the constitution'.[156] This loyalty was reflected at lower levels, and the Loyal Association from Philipps' county of Pembrokeshire was 'unanimously' signed by the gentry, no doubt including many Sea Serjeants.[157] In Glamorgan, tory justices and deputy-lieutenants like Herbert Mackworth met to suppress disturbances and to put into effect the laws against papists and nonjurors.[158]

Real jacobite supporters were not wholly lacking in Wales, as was shown by the Vaughans of Courtfield. The only Glamorgan jacobite who sought to join Charles was David Morgan, a member of the Independent Electors (and a close friend of Wynn) who was executed in 1746. His political ideas, as shown in a document written shortly before his death, unite the themes which had long kept alive high toryism: indefeasible dynastic right, a 'country' attack on armies and taxes, combined with a nonjuring anglicanism which had already rejected Luther as well as Calvin.[159] During the debates which followed the march on Derby, he urged Charles to march into Wales and mobilise the support he had there, a move which the government desperately feared.[160] In October 1745, a nonconformist minister in Swansea believed 'that the rebels' hopes from Wales do not appear to be without some foundation'.[161] In December, a group of West

Country catholics were said to be attempting to take ship to Glamorgan, with the intention of joining the Pretender in Wales.[162] Moreover, the existence of some latent support among the Welsh gentry is suggested by jacobite poems associated with the Cycle and the Sea Serjeants, and apparently written during the rising itself.[163] Perhaps some members of these groups were not content with the 'trimming' of Wynn and Philipps, and would have approved a more adventurous policy, which the Pretender's presence would have justified. Such phenomena tend to support the argument of Dr Cruickshanks, who argued that the tories still had a strong and authentic jacobite streak in the 1740s, and that 1745 represented a real opportunity for a gentry rising.

But grave qualifications must be made about such a view. As Dr Linda Colley has shown,[164] the actions and the personal correspondence of leading tory gentlemen point to overwhelming opposition to Charles's enterprise. The venture is usually seen (for instance by Mackworth's correspondents) as a Scots civil war which developed into a purely foreign invasion of England.[165] It was an assault by alien and barbarous Highlanders rather than a coup by a British political faction: Charles led 'a banditti crew of vagabonds, whom no one would ever have thought could have surprised so brave a nation as this was once'.[166] The foreign element was exaggerated by its association with a rumoured French invasion, especially feared in Wales and the West, and actually said to have taken place in January 1746.[167] Very few of the contemporary letters lay much stress on fears of an internal 'fifth column', and the 'jacobitism' of the Welsh gentry appeared very different from the cause of the papist Highlanders. When the latter entered England, an atmosphere of near-panic developed: people observed the poor quality of the English army, and realised that the rebellion might develop into a larger-scale civil war, with all the bloodshed and division that implied. Moreover, this suffering appeared to have been brought capriciously to a peaceful country by an ambitious Pretender, and this could not be justified by all the propaganda against 'oppression and tyranny' and 'extravagant taxes'. The invasion threatened to introduce the depredations of alien armies and necessitated the concealment of treasure and even flight as refugees. This was a very different matter from the dream of restoring the Pretender on the terms of the English tories, while in 1745 there was also the possibility that the rising would only cause the party to lose the hard-won foothold in government they had recently obtained. The Welsh evidence strongly tends to support the view of Dr Colley about the rhetorical nature of the jacobitism of the 1740s.

Effectively, Welsh jacobitism died with David Morgan. Some gentlemen continued to profess older sympathies, but that was all. Both the Cycle and the Sea Serjeants survived, but the latter had begun their evolution into a respectable dining club with a ladies' section and (by the 1750s) a loyal oath to Church and King. However, if jacobitism was no longer a force, tory-ism remained, and Sir John Philipps was still central to party organis-ation, corresponding with leaders throughout England and Wales.[168] Gower's defection certainly caused some loss of morale, and it was dis-couraging to return to the old impotence so soon after 1745. When Beaufort summoned Mackworth to parliament in 1747, he ended with the pessimistic remark, 'not that there is the least probability of being success-ful'.[169] On the other hand, the party's ability to organise wide popular sup-port was apparent in several hard-fought elections and local feuds of the 1750s. Indeed, 'jacobites' were said to be active in faction struggles in sev-eral Welsh counties. These included the feud for control of Carmarthen borough, or the opposition to Crown grants of lead-mining rights in Cardiganshire; and in various contests in Anglesey, Breconshire and Monmouthshire.[170]

In some cases, old tory interests were actually strengthened in this period. Beaufort was on excellent terms with more moderate tory leaders like Oxford, with whom he had earlier had some disagreements.[171] He strengthened his territorial power in west Glamorgan by legal victories over a gentry faction which had tried to infringe his mineral rights.[172] The Duke's position was also improved in 1750 when Margam passed to the Rev. Thomas Talbot of Wiltshire: Talbot's rectory of Collingbourne was adjacent to Beaufort's seat at Netheravon, and this neighbour also had jacobite antecedents, so Margam was in even safer hands than under Bussy Mansell.[173] In 1752, this was clearly shown when Talbot broke all Mansell precedents by joining the Sea Serjeants. In 1754, Glamorgan also acquired two masonic lodges, which were almost certainly centres of high tory party organisations, so the decline of the Serjeants did not weaken party struc-ture too greatly.

The Duke was also friendly with Sir Charles Kemys-Tynte, and it was this interest which chose Glamorgan's county members in the 1750s – re-spectively Charles Edwin and the son of Admiral Matthews. Beaufort's power in west Glamorgan benefited when in 1745 he established a scholar-ship at Oriel College, to be a prize for loyal families. This helped cement the loyalty of gentry like the Talbots of Margam or Llewellyns of Ynysgerwn, and (further afield) of the great north Welsh squire John Pugh

Pryse. Swansea families benefited especially, as did the sons of those vital stewards and lawyers on whom electoral success depended – men like Windsor's steward Thomas Edwards, or his own Gabriel Powell.[174] Beaufort's local power certainly remained undiminished in the 1750s, and dukes made 'progresses' to Swansea in 1749 and 1756.[175] It seemed as if little had changed from the disaffection of the 1720s, or the optimism of the 1730s.

Neither was the national situation entirely black. There were still about 111 Tory MPs in 1747, and the chance of a tory role in government was revived by conspiracies with the Prince of Wales's Court at Leicester House. Beaufort was prominent in these on the tory side, as were his electoral managers and political allies, including Herbert Mackworth.[176] On the whig side, Lord Talbot was still one of the main protagonists, while the connection of Sir Edmund Thomas with the Prince's Court dated at least from 1742, when he was appointed Groom of the Bedchamber. However, the Tories suffered serious blows from 1749, with the deaths of Wynn and the Prince. A nine-year minority followed the death of the fourth Duke of Beaufort in 1756, and the political interests of both the Edwin and Windsor families were in the hands of minors for many years after (respectively) 1756 and 1758. Fortunes revived in the late 1750s with the new 're-versionary interest' of another Prince of Wales, again supported by Talbot and Thomas of Wenvoe. Moreover, even the remaining jacobites were encouraged by the entry into government of Pitt, whose war policies represented the traditional tory 'blue-water' theories, which suited the commercial orientation of the south Wales gentry. Herbert Mackworth's tory circle viewed Pitt as the person who would 'pour balsam into the wounds of his bleeding country', and (interestingly) as the successor to Beaufort, who had died 'when men of such true patriot principle are so exceeding scarce'. Dr Brewer has explored Pitt's inheritance from the 'Patriot' opposition, but it is still remarkable to find him viewed in such a near-jacobite context.[177]

The tory tradition therefore continued with varying fortunes, and would soon reap considerable benefits at the accession of George III. However, an important change had taken place in the nature of political conflict which had already been foreshadowed in the virtual unity of landed society against Charles's invasion in 1745; and which meant that the toryism of the 1750s had changed fundamentally from the older 'country' tradition. Civil peace resulted from a change in the substance and intensity of political issues. Gentlemen like Tynte or Mackworth may have disapproved vigorously of the whig settlement, but the government made no efforts to interfere with their property, local independence, or authority over the lower orders. For example, whig magnates were just as concerned as their tory neighbours about the upsurge of rural crime and protest from the 1720s and and 1730s – if only because such a movement attacked the property of both sides alike. Whig leaders like Talbot may still have played with old republican notions, but this naturally never led them to sympathise with the saboteurs who struck at their estates. Except in the view of the most implacable tories, whiggery had long ceased to be synonymous with fanaticism.

11. The crisis of confessional politics 1720 – 1760

Wider social changes tended to remove the issues which had so often driven the country near to rebellion and civil war, and the lessening of religious tensions was central. It seems as if the decline of religious orthodoxy within the Church encouraged this growing peace, but this is difficult to trace, given the habit of squires to parrot 'Church in danger' through the reign of George II. A tentative picture can be given of these changes. Firstly, the tories became much less enthusiastic about a Church governed by whig bishops, and so tended to withdraw their sympathy and material support – a phenomenon bemoaned by Llandaff clergy from the 1720s. Who then were the 'Church party' under George II? The cathedral clergy of Llandaff did indeed find whig support – but the Glamorgan whigs are a striking affirmation of three decades of tory propaganda about the heresy and irreligion of whiggery. The whig leadership in the 1730s included the arian Talbots, the deist Rowland Gwynne, and the anti-clerical Thomas of Wenvoe. By the 1750s, the county's MP (supported by both whig and tory) was Admiral Matthews' son, who thought the Bible was only a barbarous record of ancient tribes. From the 1730s, tories and opposition whigs were drawing closer both in parliament, and in the masonic lodges, which were based on mutual tolerance and a broad theism.

By the 1750s, foreign travellers to England had doubts whether anyone there really believed in difficult doctrines like Hell, the Trinity or the Atonement. Of course there were orthodox anglicans, like the Rev. John Nicholl, who in 1752 had to prepare all his sermons from the defensive point of view that 'scepticism [is] a professed and reigning principle of this age'. Everything not 'objects of sense' needed elaborate philosophical justification, and certainly one could not speak of 'aetherial beings' like angels without the fear of mockery. Most gentry had passed to 'pure and rational religion' – deist or arian views which emphasised tolerance and benevolence.

So by the 1760s, the gentry of Glamorgan included many freemasons, like Thomas William Matthews (the sceptical MP), or his friends Richard Knight and Christopher Bassett. There was Herbert Mackworth, who came from an old high tory family, but who was sufficiently liberal by the 1760s to attend a presbyterian service in Edinburgh; and there was Robert Morris, son of a nonjuror, who wrote in 1764, 'Can more be expected than that a man should act up to the dictates of his conscience in morality? Can more be expected in religious opinions than that a man should believe according to the light that is in him?' Few of his fellow gentry would have disagreed – and no strong opposition could have been expected from the clergy, as the Llandaff registrar at this time was a fellow mason, and the new bishop in the 1780s was Richard Watson.[178] There were still orthodox christians – the Edwins, some of the Joneses of Fonmon – but even the houses which had welcomed Wesley in the 1740s were in the hands of sceptics or rakes by the 1760s. They would neither die for their creed, nor persecute for it.

Religious animosities had declined dramatically by the 1750s, despite some indications to the contrary. For instance, it sometimes seems as if anti-popery were still as potent as ever. In 1756, the methodist Howell Harris joined the army to fight France out of concern 'lest our privileges and liberties should be taken away from us, especially the liberty of the Gospel, which, should the Papists succeed, we should be robbed of'. Such ideas also existed in much higher social strata, but the causes of such virulent hatred had diminished. The last two major families of catholic gentry had left the county by 1710, and by the 1760s Glamorgan had only a handful of catholic seamen, a doctor and a steward.[179]

In the brief revival of anti-popery about 1745, the county had 'not one gentleman... of any figure or fortune that is a papist or nonjuror, and we are told that there are but very few of the meaner sort'.[180] The collapse of the threat from catholic Ireland, which had once seemed so very immediate, permitted domestic recusancy to be seen in a more realistic context. Professor Plumb is rare in giving due emphasis to this major factor promoting stability after 1700.[181] In gentry letters of the eighteenth century, Ireland is no longer a threatening catholic presence, but a potential source of patronage, and an area in which to expand one's landed interest.

The 'old dissent' also seemed less perilous. Its followers were numerous, but they were concentrated in a few large upland parishes, remote from the gentry, so the Vale seemed restored to anglican acquiescence. In Swansea, dissenters were many, but they represented mercantile respectability rather than roundhead zeal. Throughout the area, dissent had come to represent what seemed to the gentry much more sober and rational views. 'Enthusiasm' had been widely condemned after the affair of the 'French Prophets' under Queen Anne, and from the 1720s many dissenters had adopted increasingly rationalistic opinions, reflected in the drift of congregations to arminian or arian ideas.[182] When, in 1746, a non-conformist squire requested not to be made sheriff because of his opinions, he showed little of the staunch puritan refusal to betray his conscience by taking forbidden oaths.[183] He merely wrote apologetically that his father had been a dissenter and so, through no fault of his own, was he; and he therefore reluctantly requested exemption from service. This decline of religious zeal fitted the sceptical mood of many gentry.[184]

Nonconformity became much less associated with social and political rebellion, and by the 1740s it was no longer seen as the peril which had mobilised tory opinion for so long. Indeed, it was even a firm ally in the campaign against the dissolute and undisciplined life of the lower classes. From this decade, however, the most terrifying features of old puritanism seemed to be revived with the spread of methodism, especially in its Welsh calvinist form. Once again there were itinerant preachers, often drawn from village craftsmen or pedlars, who denounced the pleasures of the gentry at their races and cockfights, and criticised the squires for wasting money on election contests at a time of crop failure. As in the 1650s, there was also a temptation for plebeian methodism to lead to more extreme and eccentric religious forms, including those of the 'Jumpers' and (very often) quakers.[185] The Welsh revival coincided with the English, but had independent origins, and it developed very different traditions – notably the apparent social radicalism represented by the communitarian experiment at Trefecca in the 1750s. This was led by one of the greatest Welsh preachers, Howell Harris, whose background was in a chapel founded by Vavasor Powell, and under teachers whose own masters had followed the great republican saint. There was certainly material here for the widespread anglican propaganda which denounced the new sect as levellers and potential regicides, and the bitter opponents of the methodists were high tory leaders like Wynn, Lord Hereford, Beaufort, and Thomas Talbot of Margam.[186]

But the rise of methodism did not involve a return to the central role of religion in political life, nor great fears of a new 'rule of the saints'. In much of coastal South Wales, particularly Pembrokeshire and Glamorgan, methodism first took root in its Wesleyan form, and was patronised by gentry families of puritan ancestry, who had become as high tory as Wesley himself.[187] In Pembrokeshire, the Philipps' of Picton were a clear example of such continuity. In Glamorgan, Robert Jones of Fonmon was 'truly inclined to piety' and influenced both his family's dependents and relatives, the latter from old whig houses like Wenvoe, Llandaff and Llanbradach. The Edwins, yet again, had been dissenters before 1700 but had become tory by the mid eighteenth century; and Glamorgan's leading methodist clergy normally held livings in one of the Edwin parishes around Bridgend. Charles Edwin's wife Charlotte was an especially active patron of methodists and a friend of Lady Huntingdon; Charles's sister actually joined the Moravian sect.

Glamorgan methodism in its first decades did therefore represent a return to older puritan traditions, but the relatively respectable ones which encouraged the gentry to spread religion and morality among the poor. There were even lesser branches of the gentry – such as the Bassetts and Popkins – who became methodist ministers. It is not therefore surprising to find the methodist leadership of the Vale very conservative on issues like the American and French revolutions, and still willing to preach on old conservative texts like Romans XIII. Not until the end of the century did puritan traditions of radicalism or political activism revive in the Vale.[188]

12. The triumph of patronage

Growing religious peace coincided with a consolidation of landed wealth, which may also have contributed to growing stability in mid-century. At least, the landed oligarchy would need very great provocations to risk all on political adventures, and the government's great achievement was to ensure that such provocations did not occur. It was therefore against a favourable social background that the government was able to create a stable relationship between the central administration and hostile localities. While the later Stuarts had mainly relied on the power of territorial magnates, patronage was now the chief weapon to secure the dominant element of landed society directly to the government by means of the strongest bonds, those of mutual self-interest. So the continuing tory tradition conceals a change in the substance of political conflict. Despite occasional manifestations of fervent party feeling at elections, issues of principle were now much more likely to be subordinated to personal contests, and access to government patronage was overwhelmingly the greatest prize of political life.

No principles appear to have been sufficiently strong to prevent applications to the Duke of Newcastle, the great dispenser of patronage, whether the petitioners were tories or opposition whigs like Sir Edmund Thomas.[189] The correspondence of Bussy Mansell with Newcastle in the later 1740s demonstrates a harmony amazing in the light of Mansell's friendship with Beaufort – but both Mansell and Newcastle were Sussex magnates, duty-bound to preserve the 'harmony of the county'.[190] So, Glamorgan whigs and tories presented a united front in 1748 to petition that Judge Carter be replaced by Probyn – and Mansell led the representations.[191]

There had always been 'parliamentary beggars' whose sole aim in pursuing a political career was financial survival, and some for whom party and principle were of no importance, even in times of bitter ideological conflict, but in the mid eighteenth century such attitudes appear to have become the norm. Those who were disappointed in the quest for official favours turned to Leicester House to await better times. As a Glamorgan squire suggested on the death of Prince Frederick, none had ever followed him except in the hope of 'great preferments'.[192] This cynicism was true nationally, but ordinary voters were also prepared to give their support to the parliamentary candidate who promised them the best sinecure, regardless of clientage or supposed 'feudal ties'.[193]

In this political world, the greatest rewards went to those families who had given long service to the government, and especially to families with useful electoral and parliamentary influence – so on both counts the whig magnates in Wales stood to benefit. The Morgans of Tredegar secured the greatest rewards as the main government agents in three counties for a generation, and a family of immense influence in their own right. They were key supporters of the whig interest in Glamorgan and throughout Wales they were a bulwark against both tory and whig opponents of the ministry. To Lord Egmont and the Leicester House opposition, both they and their Hanbury allies were 'very sour and real enemies', among the 'most obnoxious' of the Pelhams' friends. Morgan influence locally was especially strong in the choice of officers like sheriffs who could decide elections for 'the King's friends in the three counties'. Throughout the 1750s they successfully petitioned Newcastle for themselves and their friends, so that Thomas Morgan of Ruperra became Judge Advocate of the Forces and

another Morgan a general, while friends received posts as Customs officials or receivers of taxes.[194]

There were also those whose public careers suggested more consistent
opposition to government than did their private letters. John Talbot,
brother of the opposition Lord, sat for the Morgan borough of Brecon for
twenty years, and when he lost this in 1754, the government contributed
£1,000 to his election at Ilchester.[195] The 'opposition' whig Matthews sat
for Glamorgan at Beaufort's behest – but he helped the whigs in Carmarthen borough break the power of the Sea Serjeants, and the government rewarded him accordingly. By 1757, he was able to secure places for
Glamorgan voters in the Navy and excise.[196] An equally ambiguous pattern emerges with Sir Edmund Thomas, an opponent of the ministry who
was prepared to compromise himself to seek relief from a troublesome and
extravagant relative. To solve the problem, he approached government
loyalists like General Townshend or the diplomat Andrew Mitchell.[197]

Elsewhere in Wales, there was a little-opposed golden age for the
families who had preserved the whig interest since the 1720s, and now
contributed the votes of their parliamentary cliques – the Herberts in the
Welsh Borderland, the Wynnes in North Wales. Perhaps the most striking
of the new men was George Rice in Carmarthenshire, whose marriage to a
daughter of Lord Talbot gave the house of Hensol a network of Welsh alliances comparable only to that of Tredegar. The Talbots now established
the dynastic alliances, which by the next century would bring their descendants the immensely wealthy earldoms of Shrewsbury and Dynevor.

'Namier's world' – in which the quest for patronage overshadowed
party labels – was therefore well established by the 1750s. As Dr Clark has
shown, the political infighting between 1754 and 1757 served to erase
many of the remnants of earlier ideologies.[198] The accession of George III
merely admitted a new clique to power and patronage – broadly, the old
and very heterogeneous followers of the Prince's Court. Sir Edmund
Thomas, George Rice, Lord (now Earl) Talbot and Sir John Philipps all
held office in the new ministry, for whom the Cocoa Tree became a kind of
ministerial club. Even a lifelong tory like Sir Charles Kemys-Tynte was in-
duced to support the government from 1764, through friendship with Sir
Edmund Thomas – and in the hope of a peerage.

Initial fears that the 'new' toryism might conceal arbitrary intentions
were soon dispelled, and old Crown servants like George Rice and Marmaduke Gwynne continued to support this regime as firmly as they had
that of the Pelhams.[199] Patronage (rather than ideology) was still the key to

political life. The new Welsh element in government seemed promising to those seeking advancement in the colonies or the armed services. In 1762, Henry Knight of Tythegston could ask his Glamorgan patrons to request that the weighty influences of Talbot, Rice and Sir Edmund Thomas should be used on his behalf.[200] Herbert Mackworth, a tory, looked hopefully to the many job opportunities created by the diplomatic efforts of 1761 – 2; and many other long-standing opponents of the whigs supported ministries consistently after 1760.[201] Reports of political news still made it appear that the older struggles were continuing in new guises, but this was deceptive, for the older broad parties of whig and tory now meant little.[202] Greater stability, and a decline of partisan conflict, were also observable at the level of local politics, and although an individual might profess himself a strong whig or tory, these factions had little to do with the national issues. During the Seven Years War, squires of most factions cooperated on programmes of defence (the militia) and internal improvements – especially the new turnpike roads. Ministers like Talbot and Thomas were supported by tories like Mackworth – and the strong popular opposition found leadership only in the populist radical Robert Jones, and the old paternalist Richard Turberville. The gentry had attained a remarkable unity, which was best exemplified in electoral politics. When Sir Edmund Thomas began to seek the county seat in 1759, his closest allies included the 'Margam interest' and the tory Tynte, against the old whig Matthews.[203] Thomas sat from 1761 to 1767, and despite some unpopularity over the Cider Act, there was no party element in the opposition which displaced him. Certainly Thomas looked to Bute while his opponent Vernon looked to Newcastle, but ideological differences between the two were little referred to, and would have been difficult to detect.[204]

The lack of party elections in Glamorgan between 1745 and the 1780s was a token of the county's being ruled by a narrow oligarchy of magnates which had already prevailed in the borough seat. Here, two Mackworths held the constituency from 1738 to 1790 by common consent of the four great landlords who controlled the electoral boroughs. All four had been firm tories but the chief considerations by the 1760s were personal esteem for the Mackworth family, and their almost hereditary right. From the 1750s a similar system emerged in the county seat, and the chief function of the county meetings was to balance the claims of established families like the Mackworths and Edwins against new men like Bute and Lord Vernon. Normally the seven leading magnates united in their choice of members despite their various party loyalties, as in 1780 when followers of Fox and Pitt combined to elect Edwin, to avoid causing division and expense.[205]

13. From jacobite to jacobin

Party principles were not dead however, and new forms of opposition were developing, especially with the revival of the old country tradition of the gentry, which opposed corruption and oligarchy. This was now allied with the renewed social radicalism of London. Both of these elements had appeared in whig and tory guises during the previous century. Their alliance was cemented once more by the Wilkes agitation of the 1760s, and Wilkes's circle included several who would later be important in struggles against the magnates of South Wales. Several Glamorgan squires were at least friendly with members of the 'Hellfire Club' at Medmenham, and actual membership can be proved in the case of Sir John Aubrey.[206] He long supported the most radical positions on issues like Wilkes, America, Ireland and parliamentary reform. Other 'monks' were the Vansittart brothers, one of whom became recorder of Monmouth – and this town was accordingly visited by various colleagues from these rakish and radical circles. Wilkes's other close friends included Robert Morris of Swansea and Sir Watkin Lewes (heir of the Popkins estate). Both of these remained in the forefront of radical agitation for decades, in their home localities as in metropolitan affairs. The industrial families of the Swansea area were especially prolific in producing Wilkites – Lewes, Morris, and the MP James Townsend, son of the entrepreneur Chauncy. But their friends included many Vale families hitherto outside the ranks of the older gentry, but who were in the process of establishing themselves as landed squires by the profits of stewardship, commerce or legal careers. Such families were the Curres, Deeres, Edmondes' and others who would also be involved in later opposition to Glamorgan's landed oligarchy.

I have argued elsewhere that the new gentry radicals found an organisational structure through masonic lodges, which were customarily built on the ruins of old jacobite societies like the Sea Serjeants.[207] The two movements had long been closely associated, which explains the continuity of jacobite slogans and significant dates into Welsh freemasonry. With striking consistency, we can observe a pattern whereby the high tory families of the 1730s became the Wilkites of the 1760s. For instance, this was true of Robert Jones of Fonmon, Robert Morris, or John Pugh Pryse (in North and West Wales). Through the masonic cult, they became allied with old whigs and deists, like Thomas Matthews of Llandaff – but the movement was very successful in uniting radicals both from the gentry and the 'middling' classes. Masonry rapidly made deep inroads into the county establishment. In the Vale, for example, by 1765 it could claim several of the greatest squires, influential attorneys, the county coroner, and the master of Cowbridge school. The number of Welsh lodges rapidly increased, from six in 1760 to sixteen by 1771.

Freemasonry provided a common ground for anglicans and members of the new dissenting opposition. It was a very remarkable fate for the old tory families, but they now found themselves cooperating with members of the 'old dissent' who had become exponents of rationalism and extreme theological liberalism. This tended to develop into political radicalism from the mid-century, because such 'enlightened' and 'rational' men could see no reason why full toleration should not be granted. Their arminian or unitarian views were congenial to other political radicals like Robert Morris or Thomas Matthews, and older religious issues seemed to revive somewhat when liberals demanded revisions of the Creed. Old alignments and conflicts stirred in 1772, when the new liberalising efforts were condemned in a parliamentary sermon on King Charles the Martyr's Day, by Thomas Nowell.[208] He was a high anglican from the old nonjuror centre of Cardiff, and a follower of Beaufort's, who had attended the duke's college of Oriel. Clearly he was attempting to become a new Sacheverell, and he succeeded sufficiently to force a parliamentary debate in which the Civil War issues seemed to live anew. Not all the substance of the old toryism had been lost.

Equally, it is also possible that the radical and democratic implications of dissent had not been wholly forgotten, but were rather lying dormant in the mid eighteenth century. Some ministers read Gerrard Winstanley, others in the 1770s were reading Vavasor Powell and Morgan Llwyd.[209] Perhaps the best example of a link between old and new radicalism was Dr Richard Price, a unitarian radical and also a freemason, who became Grand Master of a new Bridgend lodge in 1777. He derived from a family of Glamorgan petty gentry whose puritanism probably dated from the Interregnum, and Price's study of Harrington also connected him to the movements of those years.[210]

The alliance between political and religious radicals developed rapidly from the late 1760s. In 1769, Morris and Lewes attempted to raise petitions for Wilkes throughout the counties of South Wales, including Glamorgan. Such local activity is described by Professor Rudé as very rare; but of course, Lewes' circle had a great tory tradition to draw on in attempting to spread consciousness of national issues at national level.[211] Once they had looked for guidance to the Cocoa Tree or the Independent Electors – now it was the Society of Supporters of the Bill of Rights, and Wilkes himself. But whereas earlier tories had tried to resist the encroachments of dissenters, the Wilkite petitioning was supported by Richard Price, 'renowned in matters of liberty' in his own county no less than in London.[212] There was also the Caerphilly baptist David Williams, who was close to the deist circles of Benjamin Franklin, and whose radicalism also extended to social and educational theories. He knew the theory of the 'Saxon Yoke' and was sufficiently liberal to include catholics among his candidates for toleration. This group was brought closer to involvement in national political life through friendship with the unitarian group meeting at Essex Street in London, whose Glamorgan associates included the plebeian radicals John Bradford and Iolo Morgannwg.[213] By about 1772, Price had become connected by such means with the Earl of Shelburne, whose political mentor he long remained, especially on theories of 'economical reform' and the treatment of the colonies. Shelburne was also acquainted with David Williams, and the Earl's Buckinghamshire interests were largely managed by Sir John Aubrey.[214]

The various radical elements were brought together by national political issues, especially the American Revolution. It was in 1776 that Price achieved enormous international celebrity by his much-translated pamphlet, *Observations on the Nature of Civil Liberty*. A new libertarian ideology was emerging, but it was also deeply rooted in economic interest. Of course the squires were deeply concerned by rebellions in America, in Ireland or the West Indies – these were their markets, and the sources of raw materials for west Glamorgan's metallurgical industries. They found their natural leader in Shelburne, who had come to realise the need to secure peace with America on the basis which would result in the best commercial relations with the new state.[215] Considerations of sovereignty had to be secondary.

Colonial and commercial policies alienated many local gentry from government in the 1770s. But the radicals were increasingly involved in disputes more directly relevant to Glamorgan. These involved a prolonged campaign against the handful of immensely rich magnates who now held political sway. Such conflicts were obviously inspired partly by local grievances, but the elections which resulted in several Welsh counties nevertheless occasioned a broad rhetoric, asserting the rights of the small freeholder against great landlords, and calling for full religious toleration.[216] Shades of earlier struggles were evoked by the central role of the Duke of Beaufort as a villain, whose associations with both religious persecutions and jacobitism were recalled as late as the 1780s.[217] In Glamorgan, the first stirrings of such broad opposition to oligarchy were already apparent in the 1770s, and in 1789 the 'Patriots' and 'Independents' won a hard-fought election which called forth a greater volume of propaganda than had any previous elections. Pamphlets appeared in English and Welsh, appealing to all manner of grievances. In Swansea, the slogan employed against the duke was 'Down with the enclosures', and Price and Iolo showed much perception in singling out issues of concern to the common people. They attacked tithes and the Game Laws, militia service and feudal dues like heriots; while at the same time denouncing colonial oppression and slavery. Voters were asked in summary whether the fate of Glamorgan was to be decided by a clique of decadent aristocrats bargaining at a gaming table in London. In this combination of real and symbolic issues, the radicals produced a rhetoric remarkably like that of contemporary French dissidents or Dutch 'Patriots'.[218]

14. The great reaction

These events, however, marked the end of a political tradition, and at the end of the century there emerged a completely new set of issues to divide the political community. Industrialisation, notably, had called into existence a new and unrepresented class of entrepreneurs, whose political demands were soon heard, while an entirely new factor was the jacobinism developing in working-class communities like Merthyr Tydfil.[219] David Williams, Richard Price and Iolo all greeted the French Revolution, and Welsh dissenting congregations were profoundly disturbed by the new movements.[220] At the same time, the propertied classes were turning in fear to defensive conservatism, a 'maddened church-and-Kingism' reflected in the societies created to oppose levellers and jacobins in towns like Swansea. Such attitudes were reinforced by the presence in Glamorgan of refugees from the French and American revolutions, and by the invasion threat of 1797. The rise of military patronage, and the wars at the end of the century, served to bind the gentry still more closely to the established order. Some squires complained of the new wealth of government contractors or service officers, but there were many Glamorgan squires who profited even from this potential crisis. Llansannor, Fonmon, Wenvoe and

Llantrithyd all produced generals and admirals during the French wars after 1793. The implacably reactionary toryism of the end of the century was epitomised by Sir John Nicholl of Merthyr Mawr, a judge and MP opposed to any relaxation in the defences of the establishment – especially in matters of religion.

Throughout South Wales, the 1790s marked the beginning of three or four decades of extreme electoral stability, despite the radical undercurrents. Glamorgan was typical: after the death of Charles Edwin in 1756, his estates passed to his Wyndham brother-in-law, so the Llanmihangel and Dunraven estates were now combined. With such a political interest, it is not surprising that the county seat at the end of the century should have been dominated by members of the new dynasty – Charles Edwin (MP 1780 – 9) and his son Thomas Wyndham (1789 – 1814). Similar factors – demography and the concentration of landed estates – had established in very few hands the representation of most Welsh seats. From 1790 to 1840, Welsh MPs were overwhelmingly from aristocratic families, like Bute or Beaufort, or from commoners, like Mostyn, Philipps, Wilkins, Johnes or Williams-Wynn: not so much the especially prudent, as the survivors of the long demographic game of Russian roulette. Given the alternatives to their power, such families would oppose parliamentary reform at any cost.

'Old Corruption', middle-class parliamentary and religious reformers, working-class jacobins – we have clearly moved far from dynastic politics, and can already glimpse the factions and issues of the nineteenth century.

Conclusion to Part II

In the latter part of the eighteenth century, the gentry found themselves facing a new range of political challenges. What was especially disturbing was that social conflict was also increasing even in those areas little touched by industrialisation, in the gentry heartland of the Vale. Possibly, this was partly resistance to the new county community, which was felt to have abandoned local beliefs and loyalties. Lower-class resistance to this 'desertion' did not express itself in forms as direct as those of the 1650s. It was rather to be seen in the new types of crime and riot, the spread of popular methodism (rampant by the 1780s), and the new assertiveness about Welsh linguistic and cultural traditions which – at least by implication – the ruling class had betrayed.

At the end of our period, rulers and ruled represented two worlds of life and thought, religion and language – in the most literal sense, 'two nations'. Taking into account the new dangers from dissenters, jacobins and middle-class reformers, it is scarcely surprising that the gentry saw themselves as in peril; nor that their response was that 'Great Reaction' which lasted from the 1790s to the 1830s. I wish to suggest that the landed classes were very fortunate in achieving political stability during the early eighteenth century; but it was exactly the means by which this was achieved which contributed to the very divisive nature of politics at the end of that century. From the 1790s, it often seemed as if the new order would not be strong enough to withstand the new challenges it had created.

PART III

Society and culture

Introduction

The traditional gentry community had been firmly embedded in local traditions, local justifications for their power and existence, local expectations
of what they owed to their neighbours and inferiors. However, in the course
of the eighteenth century the old community fragmented, while rapid
economic change contributed to widening class divisions. The gentry community increasingly tended to share the views of ruling groups from
elsewhere in Britain and like them, they adopted a new common culture
emanating from London.

In this final section, I want to analyse what gentility meant in this period,
and how it was affected by the social and demographic changes of the early
eighteenth century. Change was very considerable, for several reasons.
Firstly, there was the disappearance of the old families, and with them the
patronage of art, culture and the other ways in which gentility had once
been proclaimed to the world. Secondly, we observe the coming of new
standards, which condemned many traditional forms of gentility as vulgar,
barbaric or ostentatious. Following on from this latter critique was the
question of how leisured gentlemen justified their existence if work was
godliness, and social use was the highest goal? It no longer sufficed to say
that the gentry served a social purpose by practising indiscriminate charity
to the poor, when this was seen as an irresponsible and archaic means of
promoting idleness. Equally, the duel was a key component of gentry
'ideology' because it reflected the need promptly to challenge any insult to
honour – the highest value of the class; but in the new perceptions, duelling was murder and traditional 'honour' was very much like vanity. Finally, traditional social hierarchy had been firmly underpinned by religious dogma. By the mid eighteenth century the gentry themselves were bitterly attacking religious orthodoxy – but could a vague deist cult of benevolence serve as an ideological buttress for such a social system? If one
abandoned Trinitarianism and the literal truth of the Bible, how could one
hope to preserve Pauline notions of subjection and social hierarchy?

In this section, we will observe the dialogue between traditional and neo-puritan standards, and the complex amalgam of these views which developed into a new gentry ideology in the eighteenth century. When the traditional standards were attacked, we might have expected the gentry to respond with simple scorn or resentment. But these new views were also those associated with the most esteemed metropolitan culture, the attractive sophistication of the *Spectator* and the novels. So, new justifications for gentility were evolved, and ostentation was curbed. The gentry did attempt to live up to the new aspirations, and become cosmopolitan where once they had been provincial, *dilettanti* where once they had studied heraldry and genealogy. This in turn drew them further away from the local community towards a national standard, reinforcing the demographic trends we have already described. In matters of culture and education, this change may be studied closely and may be represented by the supplanting of the local grammar school with the 'great' or 'public' school, where the children of all aspiring to the new gentility were educated. Similar trends can be observed in higher education and in the realm of culture and literature, where the decline of the local community had the disastrous effect of destroying a flourishing antiquarian school.

One does not therefore need to be a fervent Welsh nationalist to believe that the process I am describing is one of desertion – one by which the ruling class in a few decades detached themselves from the values and culture of the local Welsh community – and, much more important, from its language. Edmund Thomas of Wenvoe, the Cromwellian lord, could talk freely to his tenants and poorer neighbours in Welsh; his descendant and namesake in the 1750s would have required an interpreter – a fact of enormous significance for social relationships. In turn, the culture abandoned by the gentry was promoted by lower class groups, among whom it acquired plebeian and radical overtones. Culture, language and religion, all conspired to separate landlord and tenant more thoroughly from the late eighteenth century than in any part of England. Within a few decades of the eighteenth century social relationships had come to resemble those of Ireland.

Among the gentry themselves, resistance to the new ways was an equally interesting phenomenon. On the one hand, we can study the enormous extent to which the London ways influenced every particular of their new everyday life. Their local towns must possess a miniature Vauxhall, an Ascot, even a Drury lane. Their houses were remodelled after those seen in Soho or Bloomsbury – and family life changed to the 'affectionate inti-

mate' model hitherto familiar among the aristocracy and 'middling' classes. We will study the sources of this influence, how exactly each facet of the
new culture was seen and then lovingly copied; how ideas and styles which
originated at the French court or in burgher Amsterdam were first seen *in
situ* on the Continent, in London, Bristol or both, or copied at second hand
in a palace like Badminton. In turn, they spread from Margam or Hensol to
the humbler houses of the neighbourhood.

But having said this it was a strange conquest – at once absolute in the
degree to which it affected the trivia of life, but very limited in the vital aspects of gentry ideology which remained untouched. A whole opposition
anti-puritan culture emerged, proclaiming an image of traditional country
'virtues' – fox hunting and country sports, racing and carousing. That
such behaviour was so emphasised in as 'civilised' and sophisticated a setting serves to illustrate a dramatic conflict between tradition and modernity. From this conflict emerged the remarkable hybrid of the 'Georgian
squire'.

7

The idea of a gentleman

Introduction

When an observer like Blome attempted to describe the number of 'esquires' or 'gentlemen' in an area, what criteria did he apply? This chapter will analyse what was required of an individual before he was perceived as belonging to the 'gentry'. How much was social status a matter of ostentation, how much a matter of community recognition – and if this were the case, what reciprocal obligations were implied? The question then raised is what happened to the 'legitimacy of gentility' when these justifications were altered? I will define the perceptions of the world characteristic of this class, their sense of themselves and their family, their sense of honour and duties of kinship. The chapter will discuss gentry views of this world and the next, their duties to community and nation, and how all these changed fundamentally in the eighteenth century.

1. Display

In earlier chapters, the definition of 'gentry' has been taken in broad terms, as those who were accepted by contemporaries as belonging to this group. This criterion avoids the pitfalls of 'inflation', both literal and metaphorical. For example there was the problem that the great gentry in 1660 might have incomes of £500 and a title like 'esquire', while these same accomplishments might only mark a shopkeeper in 1780. 'Devaluation' of title can be observed in a list of Swansea's portreeves, all of whom appear as 'gentlemen' from 1708, and as 'esquires' from the 1780s, though these titles had once been real signs of distinction.[1] The aim of this section is to determine what set gentlemen apart from other groups.

The basic division in society concerned leisure, for the 'gentle' were those wealthy enough to have no need to perform manual labour, but income alone was never sufficient to determine 'gentlemanly' status. This might never be acquired by, for instance, substantial merchants or industrialists, and even if such men were known as 'esquires' they would not necessarily be regarded as part of the gentry community in the county in which they lived. A merchant might moreover remain in this position despite being on excellent social terms with local squires or lords, or perhaps a partner with them in a commercial or industrial venture. When, in 1774, two squires were to fight a duel at Swansea, the suggestion that a wealthy local apothecary should serve as a 'second' was rejected because he was not a gentleman; and an attempt by the portreeve to prevent the conflict was accompanied by many bows and obsequious apologies for interfering in the affairs of the gentry.[2] The key to higher status was landed wealth, which was the essential investment made by a businessman who sought social acceptance. It was possible by such means to enter the landed society, although the gentry community *per se* was a still narrower group, conscious of social differences which separated them from other landed families who enjoyed similar wealth. There were other conflicts between peers and squires, the 'Gothic haughtiness'[3] of the former being reciprocated by the jealous dislike epitomised in literature by Squire Western. Such feuds existed in Glamorgan, although diminished somewhat because of the long identity of political views with tory magnates like Beaufort and Windsor. The relative poverty of Glamorgan clergy may have inhibited their acceptance into the county community, which was only gradually accomplished during the eighteenth century. Absorption of new industrial wealth was perhaps more easily accomplished in this area than in some others because of the long established commercial orientation of the gentry, but there was nevertheless some hostility to *nouveaux riches* even after they had purchased an estate.[4]

Landed income was the essential prerequisite for a member of the gentry community. For example, it conferred the right to hunt, one of the rare legal privileges officially enjoyed by English gentlemen (in contrast to their better-treated European counterparts). This accordingly became a proudly borne badge of distinction. But wealth had to be used to maintain the particular style of life which characterised a gentleman. Lavish spending was required so that all one's possessions proclaimed extravagance and excess, or else one would be condemned for churlishly failing to live up to social obligations. In 1683, Thomas Morgan of Tredegar defended his heavy expenditure on travel, clothes and gambling: 'To enjoy a little of the fortune wherewith heaven hath favoured me, I hope will not be thought profuse... and therefore I hope you will not think it amiss if I do give myself a little liberty to enjoy what my birthright hath given me, who do resolve to live according to my quality.'[5]

A great country house was a vital element in the conspicuous consump-

tion which marked a gentleman, and in the later seventeenth century the
size of house (as shown by the number of hearths taxed) closely corresponded to one's position in the elaborate hierarchy of county society.
When newly rich families were attempting to gain acceptance in the county
community, a mansion with its grounds was a basic investment. In
Glamorgan, the great ages of building country houses were between 1560
and 1630, and 1760 and 1810, in both of which periods new and wealthy
elites were establishing themselves; and the successful families of the latter
period included industrialists like the Morris's and Crawshays. Moreover,
houses had to be in the latest fashions, and imitation of the latest Italian
style – as at Llandaff or Fonmon – conspicuously showed the extent of
one's travelling. If one did not travel then styles could be studied in books
like Campbell's *Vitruvius*, or else copied from the works of major ar-
chitects employed by local magnates. For instance in the 1770s, Lord
Mountstuart used Holland and Capability Brown at Cardiff Castle, and
they were in turn employed by Peter Birt of Wenvoe, and by Sir Charles
Kemys-Tynte. There was a constant pattern whereby styles and patterns
were imported into the county by a great man like Mansell or Beaufort,
and widely imitated by his followers.[6] Gardens too were subject to the dictates of fashion, for they adopted French or Dutch models after the Restoration, but loudly proclaimed the apparent absence of artifice by the mid
eighteenth century – as in the picturesque environments of Penrice in
Gower or Piercefield in Monmouthshire.[7]

Wealth and power were reflected by the ceremony maintained inside the
great houses, where the number of servants again corresponded to one's
position in the social hierarchy. There were 46 at Tredegar in 1674, 38 at
Margam in 1712, 33 at Fonmon in 1706, and 28 at Llantrithyd in 1713.[8] If
we estimate that few great squires would have had less than 20 servants at
once, and few small squires less than 10, the gentry's domestic servant
population in Glamorgan about 1710 must have exceeded a thousand –
some 2 or 3 per cent of the whole population. Gaining access to a great
squire like Sir Edward Mansell was described in terms more appopriate to
a royal court, with 'so many days to be spent in waiting for an opportunity
of perhaps but half an hour's converse',[9] for he 'locks himself up from all
approaches by the multiplied formalities of attendance'. Other tokens of
status included a coach, which under Charles II was the prerogative of the
greatest gentry families, like the Mansells, Morgans, Stradlings, Lewises,
Gwyns and Herberts. Like others of this elite, Sir Charles Kemys owned
several coaches and carriages, the best of which was expensively gilded.[10]

Status was demonstrated by the ownership of large quantities of gold or silver plate, the amount and value increasing as families became richer.[11] A gentleman's rank could immediately be perceived from the quality of his house or his clothing, which showed the wearer's status by the inclusion of costly materials like silk, lace or gold thread.[12] The richest gentlemen also had to maintain an establishment in London, where they had the costly duty of keeping up with the latest fashions, and it need occasion no surprise that such a style of life led many into debt. Dignity and state were to be maintained in death as well as life, for funerals were also vast and costly affairs normally involving a display of the family's escutcheons, and a suitable monument could cost a hundred pounds.[13]

2. Honour

A gentleman was marked by his whole style of living, and the number and quality of his material possessions, but his status also demanded allegiance to a code of duties and obligations. For instance, he had to demonstrate his firm independence, in a society based on clientage and patronage, and in 1706 Roger Powell threatened a duel with a man who falsely charged that he owed his power and even his vote to his patrons at Van.[14] In 1774, William Franklen of Llangyfelach left his job in a copperworks, 'his plan is to make something more of a gentleman in case he should succeed to a fortune'. It was not the element of trade which made his employment unsuitable, it was rather the subordinate position it entailed.[15] Maintenance of local independence against central control was a recurrent theme of the political history of the period. It was also imperative to prefer 'death before dishonour', in the words of the Bassett family motto. A gentleman should regard his word of honour as sacred once it had been given, even if his promise had been made on the basis of false information or assumptions. Election correspondence sometimes reveals the inability of the greatest magnates to force a petty squire to go back on his word.[16] Imagined insults were bitterly resented, and could lead to feuds lasting years, with far-reaching effects on factional politics or party opinions.

Sir Edward Mansell of Margam (1636 – 1706) well demonstrates the gentry's sensitivity on points of honour, and the practical effects this could have when his orders were refused by social inferiors, for he assaulted the Mayors of Neath and Cardiff when they opposed him.[17] His kinsman Sir Richard Mansell had to be extricated from legal difficulties which resulted from the death (from fear) of a creditor he had threatened with a sword;[18] while Sir Richard's brother (Sir William) posed other problems by killing men in duels.[19] The defence of honour or self-interest often implied a resort to violence, and if the offending party was of too high birth to be merely beaten or mobbed, then a duel could result. Gentlemen wore swords, were portrayed with them in paintings, and were expected to use them in affairs of honour. When Sir Charles Kemys declined a challenge from Sir Edward Mansell, he was thought to have forfeited his honour, and Mansell symbolically broke Kemys's sword.[20] Duels were frequent when the code of honour was so sensitive, and the situation was exacerbated by the political bitterness of the later seventeenth century, when partisan rivalries caused many fights involving some of the greatest families of Wales. At the time of the Exclusion crisis, Sir Charles Kemys was engaged in feuds with his whig opponents Mansell and Arnold, while the political struggles under Anne gave new grounds for insult and rebuff.[21]

The duel involved a detailed code of proprieties, such as the manner of the challenge, and the suitability of persons to serve as seconds. Formal letters of challenge are indeed among the best evidence for the gentry's sense of belonging to a clearly defined class with a code of beliefs to be defended quite literally to the death. Henry Knight of Tythegston challenged an enemy as a fool and a liar, 'which I am ready to make good as a gentleman ought'.[22] Christopher Talbot of Margam took great offence at the treacherous behaviour of Robert Morris, and insulted him 'but I require no satisfaction that may disgrace a gentleman'.[23] The situation had simply reached a point in which both men would be compromised if violence did not resolve the matter, and the importance of maintaining one's position as a gentleman in the view of the public is continually stressed. Christopher Talbot of Margam intended to justify his actions by a pamphlet, while Thomas Matthews of Llandaff published a defence in a Bath newspaper.[24]

Many such disputes were resolved before the resort to violence, as was that of Talbot and Morris, but deaths did occur, so some incidents led to the scattering abroad of several gentry. One of the Aubreys was killed in an affair of honour at Brecon in 1679,[25] and fatalities were not confined to the earlier part of the period when the gentry might have been less 'civilised'. The last of the Stradling line died in a duel in 1738 while on the Grand Tour, and others killed included Frederick Thomas of Wenvoe, in 1783. The second Lord Mansell was brought up in the aristocratic society of the metropolis in the 1720s, but in 1741 he was sufficiently conscious of the traditional codes to urge a friend violently to resist insult.[26] His uncle Bussy almost earned some historical notoriety when he threatened to kill Lord

Hervey.[27] Indeed, it may not only be the result of improved sources that there is so much evidence of duelling in the latter part of the century – often by members of the greatest families. Between 1760 and 1790, duels involved Lord Talbot, Sir John Aubrey, Frederick Thomas of Wenvoe and Christopher Talbot, as well as the experienced and aggressive duellists, Thomas Matthews, Henry Knight and Robert Morris. Perhaps the revival from the 1760s of deeply divisive political issues contributed to this new series of conflicts; and a diary of Cardiff life in the 1790s shows the frequency of such contests, among both old and new gentry.[28] The duel epitomises one of the most important and enduring elements of the gentry's ideology throughout the period.

3. Kinship

Another recurring theme in the history of the gentry was the overwhelming importance of the idea of family, which added to the sense of continuity and stability already created by possession of an ancient house and estate. The older Welsh concept of gentility (still extolled by the bards) emphasised noble descent rather than wealth, and created the paradox that poor hill-farmers might view themselves as more 'gentle', if not royal, than their richer neighbours and landlords. But genealogical studies were vigorously pursued and patronised until the 1720s by greater gentry families like the Aubreys, Herberts and Mansells, and aristocrats like the Somersets.[29] When Philip Jones became a Cromwellian peer, he purchased a castle, commissioned a portrait of himself, and ordered the drawing-up of splendid and ornate genealogies.[30] Similarly in 1712, when Thomas Mansell became a (tory) lord, he celebrated the event by considering a new classical mansion at Margam, ordering a portrait – and commissioning three detailed genealogies of his line.[31] With these studies so popular, it was not difficult to discover exactly how any given individual belonged to this ancient continuum, which showed one's relationship over many centuries to a particular area or house – and which might involve royal descent. One's ancestors were a visible presence in the form of a long series of family portraits such as survive for the families of Mansell, Mackworth, Aubrey and Jones of Fonmon; but lesser houses were also making such collections by the eighteenth century, as at Aberpergwm and Pwllywrach. The greater families still managed however to remain a leap ahead of their imitators by employing the best and most fashionable artists of the day: Lely, Wissing, Hogarth, Allan Ramsay and Reynolds.[32]

A sense of continuity was stressed after death by the existence of family mausolea in particular churches traditionally linked to a gentry 'dynasty'. The best surviving example in Glamorgan is probably that of the Mansells in Margam Abbey, but a 'Herbert Aisle' is mentioned in Cardiff, as well as a 'Dunraven tomb' at St Bride's Major, and a 'Radyr tomb' in Llandaff Cathedral.[33] Burial in such tombs was a bitterly defended privilege, and the family tradition in such churches was reinforced by the existence of long genealogies in monumental inscriptions. Royal descent was claimed by the Powells at Llanharan and the Joneses of Fonmon at Penmark – and more recent scholarship has tended to confirm the authenticity of such claims. Squires' genealogies really did go back to men like Caradoc Vreichvras, a historical late Roman princeling who ruled the area before the time of King Arthur – and before the English set foot on the island. Other genealogies specifically claimed links with the county's 'foundation legend' of Norman conquest and Welsh resistance.[34] Examples were the tombs of Philip Williams' family at Cadoxton-juxta-Neath, and of the Restoration sheriff Richard David at Penmaen, both of which refer to the last Welsh king of Morgannwg, Iestyn ap Gwrgan.[35] Epitaphs were moreover an excellent summary of the 'ideology' of a gentleman, frequently mentioning the virtues of charity and hospitality, but placing greatest visual emphasis on the coats of arms which epitomised the dignity and continuity of the dead man's family.

Apart from placing an individual firmly in his historical and geographical context, the stress on family loyalties also contributed to real political and economic power by providing a strong framework of potential alliances. In the political history of Glamorgan there were many occasions on which party links were either caused or cemented by marriage, as in the 1670s when the opponents of the Marquis of Worcester became linked by an elaborate network of relationships. Acting as godparents at baptism was another nexus which might be important in later political life, as a godfather was often a noble patron of the squire whose newborn son was being 'made a better Christian'.[36] The godfather of Francis Gwyn's son was his patron the Earl of Rochester, while the Marquis of Worcester accepted the same role for the son of Sir Charles Kemys.[37] Those who had the same godparents were, in a sense, brothers, with at least some obligations to each other, so even the most detailed genealogy cannot give a full picture of the widespread ties which motivated men's actions. Family links were strengthened over many generations of friendship, so that a very complex structure of kinship was developed, and 'cousin' might be the best (or only) term for a kinsman who might be related in several different ways at once.

Table 20: *The Aubrey and Jephson families*

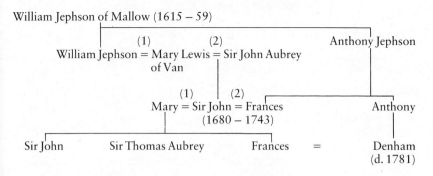

One example is the close links between the Aubreys and Jephsons shown in Table 20.[38] Equally dense networks of relationship bound the Mansells, Carnes and Bassetts, as a result of numerous marriages between 1500 and 1700.

Very distant relationships were often remembered and taken into account when assistance was to be claimed, or patronage distributed. The far-reaching repercussions of such obligations may be illustrated by the genealogy of the Mansell family, probably the best represented by surviving correspondence (the point would be equally valid for the Kemys's, or any other great house). Table 21 represents in skeleton form the connections of the Carmarthenshire branch of the Mansells with the main branch at Margam. Anthony Mansell was not even a second cousin of Sir Edward, but he was staying with his Margam kinsmen when he died in 1679, and was buried in the Abbey. Both Sir Edward and his son went to great trouble to help Sir Richard and Sir William out of their legal difficulties, and the latter often importuned the Morgan family for financial aid. More usefully, Sir Edward of Trimsaran supported his distant cousins in Glamorgan in the bitter elections of Anne's reign, but outlying branches of the family were more often the source of difficulty and expense rather than assistance. Lord Mansell was reminded that 'As you are the head of a noble family, you must bear the trouble of application to you from your relations and those who have dependence on you',[39] and such dependents also required the 'head's' services as arbitrator in their private disputes. Family, or name was often used in a sense not unlike 'clan', and the head of the widespread Matthews family defended the interests of very distant kin in this spirit.[40] The Joneses of Fonmon also provide a remarkable example of a distant dependent seeking help on the strength of his relationship to

Table 21: *The Carmarthenshire Mansells*

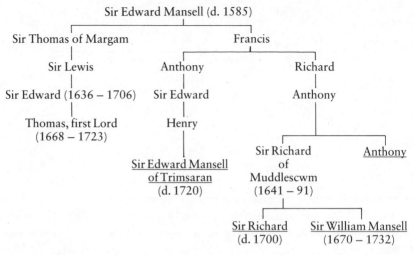

powerful gentry. When in 1755 the head of that 'clan' received a petition[41] from the very aged Philip Jones of Carmarthenshire, the appeal was accompanied by a genealogy showing the exact relationship of the supplicant. Jones did not appear to think that his case was weakened by the fact that he was appealing on the strength of a very distant relationship: in fact, he and the current squire of Fonmon shared a common ancestor who had died perhaps 150 years earlier.

Impartial generosity to kin, even in this very wide sense, was a greatly praised aspect of a gentleman's character, mentioned for example in epitaphs; although of course, obligations could be ignored. When Edward Mansell of Swansea was assailed by his creditors, his protectors included his Margam relative Thomas Mansell, but not the latter's father Sir Edward, one of the debtor's severest enemies. Bussy Mansell in the 1730s 'declined the trouble' of becoming guardian to his nephew Lord Mansell, although the alternative was that the latter should be brought up by the alcoholic John Ivery Talbot.[42] Again, family feuds often involved violence, theft and deception, as occurred in the 1670s when the unfortunately named brothers David and Jonathan Nicholl struggled for the living of Llanblethian.[43] More generally, wide consciousness of kinship did exist, and did more than merely encourage charity. Such obligations had real political force, well demonstrated by the relationship of the extreme royalist family of Stradling with the leading republicans, Ludlow and Oldisworth.[44] Neither side compromised its political principles, but the sense of family caused the radicals to protect the Stradlings in the 1650s, while in turn the Stradlings saved Ludlow's life at the Restoration; although this may have cost George Stradling a bishopric. The role of kinship in society meant that the head of a gentry family was the leader of a broad phalanx of potential supporters in his personal or factional disputes. This could ultimately determine the side they took in civil war, and was often said to make the impartial administration of justice in Wales virtually impossible.

4. A community of belief

The hierarchical structure, which existed in the broad framework of the family, was also perceived in society at large, and gentlemen were felt to have obligations to social inferiors as well as to poorer kinsmen. It would of course be wrong to suggest that a benevolent paternalism motivated the gentry at some unspecified period of the past – perhaps before the Civil War – while their degenerate successors accepted only the value of the market, and the cash nexus between man and man. Both historians and contemporary critics often claim that a certain period marked the transition from a traditional order, when good lordship won the loyalty and affection of tenants. Such a fragmentation has variously been assigned to most centuries from the tenth to the twentieth, which casts doubt on its likelihood. But even if such an account of past society is untrue, the existence of this historical myth still demonstrates the aspirations of an age which accepted it, and widely credited fictions may yet affect actions in the real world.[45]

Furthermore, there is some evidence that in Stuart times the Glamorgan gentry shared the social and intellectual commonplaces of their inferiors to a much higher degree than would be the case with their eighteenth-century descendants. Above all, this century was the last in which all classes of Glamorgan society spoke the Welsh language,[46] including great gentry like the Herberts, Gamages, Lewises and Kemys's, who had high regard for 'our ancient, copious, learned British tongue'. The gentry still maintained their ancient role as patrons of bardic poetry, the political ethos of which was accordingly anglican and high tory. The bards extolled the traditional Welsh values of gentility, and praised the possessions of squires (like their mansions or their hounds) no less than their accomplishments or virtues. At the beginning of the eighteenth century, lavish patronage was still received from some of the leading families, notably those connected with the Mansells of Margam and Briton Ferry, but also those at Beaupre, Hensol and St Donat's. Even a new English lord of a Glamorgan estate felt a duty to learn the Welsh language, or at least to favour the bards.[47]

The cultural homogeneity of society was also apparent in attitudes to the supernatural or irrational, for tales of omens or ghosts would attract as much attention from the 'gentle' as from the common people throughout the seventeenth century. In the Neath and Swansea of the 1690s, stories of local omens, hauntings and poltergeists (past and present) were popular with all classes and political persuasions.[48] There were atheists, deists and sceptics – but ironically, we often hear of their opinions only because their blasphemous views were said to lead to hauntings or curses.[49] It will be re-called that one of the striking problems about the world of Sir Edward Mansell of Margam was that someone could accept so many ancient superstitions and yet be such a progressive entrepreneur in economic mat-ters. However, he was not regarded as eccentric for this: one of the Mar-quis of Worcester's household wrote of the fall of Raglan in 1646, 'Never was there an old house so pulled down by prophecies, ushered into its ruin by predictions, and so laid hold upon by signs and tokens.'[50] Worcester had been wont to study such omens in an ancient book of prophecies. Like others of his age and class, Mansell merely shared the older beliefs on such matters, which views were also those of the 'lower orders', although they were being increasingly questioned in metropolitan society.

In so far as paternalism existed, it depended on the common acceptance by lord and tenant of a code of economic morality, which placed less em-phasis on profit than on good social relations and the maintenance of hereditary clientage. The self-interest of a landlord in turbulent times re-quired a substantial and loyal tenantry to act as supporters in feuds, and this idea was carried over into the elections of the seventeenth and eighteenth centuries. The old families were very reluctant to evict tenants except for a grave sin against social obligations like voting against one's landlords. Not until the 1740s did the Margam estate breach this code by evicting for simple arrears a family that had been tenants for over a century – but this was done by order of the second Lord, who had been brought up outside the county.[51] The older code generally held. Of course, there were many examples of harshness and injustice by 'traditionally' minded landlords, including the plunder of wards who were the heirs of neighbours and clients. Many such breaches of traditional loyalties were no doubt involved in the rapid growth of great estates from the mid sixteenth century; and some squires left an appalling reputation among poorer farmers.[52] In turn, claims that the gentry in the Civil War were able to 'lead the common people which way they pleased', should not be accepted without realising that the lower classes often joined the rebellions of their superiors only when it suited their own interests to do so. They were also quite capable of refusing to fight even after being led to battle.[53]

But many did accept a paternalistic code of obligations like Thomas Mansell of Margam (1668 – 1723) who regarded his efforts at arbitration among tenants and neighbours as having failed if any felt the need to go to law afterwards.[54] Lavish donations of corn were made regularly to the poor of the Margam neighbourhood,[55] and such charity was to be indiscriminate rather than using the later criterion of the 'deserving' poor. The Marquis of Worcester who defended Raglan in the Civil War had also been a model of 'paternalism', and in the great South Wales floods of 1607 he had not only helped the distressed with boats, but had gone 'himself unto such houses as he could that were in extremity, to minister unto them provision of meat and other necessaries'.[56] (It is a marvellous irony that this touching account of such a 'father of his country' was probably written by William Wroth, the founder of the Welsh puritan movement that would ultimately destroy Raglan.)

The gentry patronised the feasts and celebrations of the poor, and shared in their amusements, like cockfighting, which appalled urban and 'godly' writers by this 'promiscuous mixing'. The reactions of the lower classes to these gestures are obviously difficult to gauge, but occasionally we hear of examples like Bussy Mansell, 'hospitable Bush', 'of blessed memory' among the poor decades after his death in 1699.[57] Certainly, acts of injustice were usually blamed on the lawyers or stewards who represented the gentry, and with whom they commonly came into contact, so that the gentry themselves could be assumed to be ignorant of any wrong. Expressions of class hatred by the 'lower orders' in this period usually concerned members of the professional classes, like corrupt lawyers, grasping clergymen or corn dealers, and their complaints were often echoed by the gentry themselves. For example, both rich and poor alike saw lawyers as scavengers battening on the misfortunes of others, and attempting to steal their wealth. Particularly hated were great attorneys like Anthony Maddocks, Hopkin Llewellyn and the three Gabriel Powells of Swansea.[58] There was popular rejoicing at Cardiff in 1764 on a false report of the imprisonment of Thomas Edwards;[59] and Maddocks earned permanent notoriety by becoming the villain of the folk-tale of the 'Maid of Cefn Ydfa', a largely fictional story which is accurate chiefly in recalling the detestation in which the lawyer was held.[60] Popular protests – threats or sabotage – were especially directed against such men, in Glamorgan as in much of South Wales.

Similar unity was produced by hostility to new gentry families, who were sometimes whigs or dissenters, and linked to City commerce. Older 'paternalistic' gentlemen could deplore the harsh activities of dissenting landlords like Humphrey Edwin or John Watkins.[61] Political hatred for such men was especially strong when they had established themselves on the basis of the expanded government patronage at the end of the seventeenth century. The tory gentry, like the common people, opposed the high taxes associated with war, and found themselves allied in their common hatred of *nouveaux riches* lawyers and tax collectors, from George Howell in the 1690s to Anthony Maddocks a generation later. There was a surprising harmony of interest between the highest and lowest classes of Glamorgan society, so that 'paternalism' might be both well-intentioned and favourably received.

5. Loyalties

A gentleman therefore had a definite social ideology which emphasised duties to kinsmen and social inferiors, but loyalty was also required to the wider community of gentry, expressed in the county. This was more than a mere geographical or administrative unit, as it was tightly linked by family relationships among the gentry. For example, Sir Edward Mansell's 'cousins' included the Aubreys, Carnes, Bassetts, Wyndhams, Stradlings and Edwins, while his daughters married members of the Stradlings of St Donat's and Morgans of Tredegar, and his network of kinship was also widespread among lesser squires. Mansell's strong attachment to this community is apparent in his comments on the county's gentry in 1677,[62] where one squire is only 'a stranger to his country, living in Berkshire', while another, more promising, is 'not yet settled in his country'. A sense of county 'patriotism' was strengthened by common activities such as horse-racing or hunting, in which one participated together with 'fellow countrymen' who were, moreover, relations. In cockfighting, great combats took place between counties, which occasioned great 'patriotism'. There was a duty to subscribe to works by county authors, especially if they concerned local history, and it was felt that the gentry had an obligation to support the county's schools, notably Cowbridge, and to maintain its public buildings. With the Quarter Sessions, the county even had a form of parliament and administrative autonomy, and the loyalty expressed in the writings of poets and scholars sometimes verges on chauvinism.[63]

The strength of such loyalties is well demonstrated by the violent hostility to attempts to divide the county, on any issue, for this was the same as sowing discord among friends, neighbours and kinsmen. County 'neutralism' in the Civil War depended on this sentiment, that problems could be solved between neighbours, if only strangers would not interfere. After the Restoration, national dominance of local affairs had unpleasant connotations of extremism, which heightened still further the emphasis on local particularism. In elections, one of the gravest charges was that a candidate had gratuitously attempted to raise opposition and divide the 'harmony of the county'. This cry was heard much more often than that of 'whig' and 'tory' in surviving correspondence, whatever the views on national issues of those concerned.[64] Lawyers, again, were 'to be feared in nothing but in sowing sedition between great persons', and neither the whig Matthews nor the tory Beaufort were prepared to 'encourage any lawsuit between gentlemen',[65] thus dividing the community. These at least were their aspirations, although in reality they might raise opposition in elections, or pursue vindictive litigation. Problems arose if gentry owned lands in more than one county, as did most of the greater families, for loyalties might be divided, and they would serve as sheriffs and justices elsewhere. But the vigorous support for works of county history and genealogy demonstrates the remarkable cohesion of the community in the seventeenth and early eighteenth centuries.

County loyalties coexisted with the wider consciousness of belonging to a region, an account of which is complicated by the problem of deciding whether Wales, with its very different culture, was regarded only as a region rather than a nation. The gentry spoke Welsh, patronised Welsh music and literature, and proudly described themselves as 'Welshmen' or referred to 'my own country of Wales'. At the end of the seventeenth century, such terms were used by some of the greatest gentry families, like the Kemys's, Gwyns, Carnes and Thomases of Llanmihangel, as well as by that 'mountainous Welshman', Sir Edward Mansell.[66] They also favoured the appointment of Welsh clergy, and opposition to the transfer of the see of Llandaff to Cardiff about 1718 derived partly from pride in Welsh history.[67] It was 'small sin' in a Welshman 'to applaud and commend [his] own country', and compatriots applied for favour to magnates like Pembroke, Mansell and Carbery on the strength of their 'Ancient British' stock. Welsh sympathies even thrived among these aristocrats, for it was Carbery who led a West Wales movement in the 1670s to secure the appointment of a 'King's printer for the British tongue'.[68] The second Earl of Oxford regarded himself as Welsh as late as the

1720s, and the Somersets were patriotic Welshmen throughout the Stuart period.

In the 1640s, Worcester certainly spoke Welsh. He decorated his home at Raglan with 'Ancient British' stories on the tapestries, and a later member of the family was a student of Welsh genealogy; but he was also sufficiently far from being a backward provincial to translate Corneille for the stage.[69] St David's Day was joyously celebrated in the 1640s, and early in the next century the feast was used for political purposes by the whig 'Society of Ancient Britons', by Welsh jacobites and freemasons.[70] There are some examples of anti-English prejudice, as among the Glamorgan peasants who joined the Clubmen in the 1640s, and attacked anyone they believed to be English.[71] Commanders on both sides had continually to take into account the cordial hatred which existed between the Welsh and their neighbours in Somerset and Gloucestershire, and conflict long survived the war. Genealogists had little sympathy for English marriages, even if the writers were sophisticated scholars like Sir John Aubrey in the 1670s. The other John Aubrey – the antiquary – proposed to include Welsh on the curriculum in the Comenian college he wished to create at Van. In the 1670s, how could a gentleman hope to be civilised without knowing the British tongue, which was as old as Latin or Greek?[72]

National sentiment was partly political and religious, for the Welsh were celebrated (or notorious) for high Royalist views, and roundhead sentiment could be attributed to the influence of English immigrants.[73] On the other hand, Welsh sentiments must not be exaggerated, for they seldom had real importance except in political rhetoric. Actual nationalism or separatism was so rare as to be quite insignificant.[74] The same men who called themselves 'Welsh' on some occasions describe themselves as 'true Englishmen' on others,[75] including Thomas Stradling, Thomas Mansell, Francis Gwyn, Sir Charles Kemys and Sir Edmund Thomas, all of good Celtic stock. Even Richard Price the nonconformist was campaigning in 1776 for true 'English liberty'. The name of their nation was England rather than Britain, and despite loyalties to shire or region, national patriotism was a real force, particularly in time of war. Naturally it usually focussed on the monarchy, and the exertions of many Welsh gentry for the Stuart dynasty have already been described. In the 1640s, Francis Mansell's exertions for Charles I overrode both personal gratitude to the Earl of Pembroke, and his family loyalties to his orphaned nephews, whose goods he devoted to the royal service.[76] Moreover, the efficacy of the royal touch for the 'King's Evil' was fully accepted. It took many years of neglect, foolishness and gratuitous insult before this dynastic loyalty was forfeited.

Finally, political loyalty to magnates has frequently been remarked on, and was extremely long-lived. The Kemys's and Mackworths were loyal to Worcester's family for generations, while 'Pembroke's party' acted as a coherent force in county politics for most of the century. Such adherence often overshadowed partisan views: the Mansells' old whig friends in and around Neath continued to support the house of Margam decades after it had become a tory mainstay in Wales, and such survivals were common. Not until the 1760s did many of these old family factions vanish, to be replaced by newer party cliques. While certainly not denying the strength of whig and tory parties throughout, it would be equally unwise to believe that these wholly supplanted family traditions.

6. Religion and hierarchy

However, neither the nation state nor the monarchy itself were the ultimate focus of loyalty, particularly in the seventeenth century, when the great issues concerned supra-national conflicts between religious sects and ideas. Catholic gentry were loyal to an international Church, and had wide European contacts through their relatives in continental schools or religious houses, or perhaps the armed forces of France or Spain. They often married co-religionists from other counties, and served Catholic peers like the Marquis of Powis or Viscount Stafford, who otherwise had little contact with Glamorgan. On the other side, the puritan squire was not a common figure by the end of the seventeenth century, but international protestant solidarity continued to be exploited to aid continental refugees. In the 1750s, the military successes of Frederick the Great briefly revived the sense of sharing in a protestant crusade, even for worldly whig courtiers like Sir Edmund Thomas, who named a son after the Prussian hero; and for the lower classes, the Seven Years War was to some extent a religious struggle.[77] Throughout the period, the anglican Church was the most influential factor in determining political loyalty. Loyalty to different concepts of the Church, and hence to the dangers threatening it, led many to accept extreme courses, with the concurrent risks – death in battle or on the scaffold, or economic ruin.

But the religious disputes of the eighteenth century should not conceal one vital fact. Threats to the power of the Church were seen as socially dangerous throughout, which explains why the eighteenth-century gentry were still prepared to fight for it – especially against methodists or other enthusiasts. But I have argued that doctrinal loyalty to the Church had changed fundamentally between about 1720 and 1760, so that few gentry by the 1760s believed much more than a minimalist deism. There is a strong impression that Christian references in memorial inscriptions by the 1760s often had no more substance of real belief than did the references to Cynthia and Apollo in poetry. For the first time in British history, a large section of the landed magnates had entered a phase which we can describe as sub-Christian, if not post-Christian. Their ethics were as likely to be drawn from Seneca or Cicero as from St Paul – and once again, we can observe a severe blow being struck against the community of belief and principle. Professors Hay and Thompson have made the excellent point that it was precisely such a decline of traditional sanctions for power that made the ruling class extol the new ideology of the 'rule of law',[78] the supremacy of an apparently neutral code that would defend the land and property of rich and poor alike. We have already noted the problem the gentry faced in imposing such a code on a more old-fashioned tenantry – but enlightened men could not hope to revive older ideas of natural hierarchy.

7. Justifying gentility

The gentry were subject to other powerful forces which would undermine their older system of beliefs and loyalties. In the seventeenth century, their most radical critics had been quakers or other sectaries like Erbery or Llwyd, who had attacked the waste, excess and idleness which characterised the class, and regarded the duel as simple murder rather than an affair of honour. For them, usefulness was the only justification of gentlemanly status – if, for example, wealth and leisure were employed for good works. By the end of the century, such 'puritan' opinions were no longer the prerogative of a proscribed group of politically abhorrent extremists, but were widely held among anglicans, like the great Welsh writer Ellis Wynne.[79] It was now men like this who demanded that gentlemen should justify themselves as social and moral reformers.[80] Formerly puritan families were now among the strongest upholders of the established church, and were well represented in the anglican SPCK, which stood for a newer 'ideology' of gentility.

One index of the new standards was the attempt to prevent duelling. SPCK supporters like Sir John Philipps and Sir Humphrey Mackworth both refused challenges, although this represented a gross betrayal of duty to more traditionally minded gentlemen. The new ideas came to be widely accepted in the eighteenth century, with the spread of 'middle-class' values from the metropolis, and numerous anglican sermons reinforced these ideas, 'proving slowness to anger the truest gallantry'.[81] In the 1760s, Lewis Morris simply wrote of a duellist who had killed his opponent as a 'murderer' and Frederick Thomas of Wenvoe accepted a challenge in 1783 with severe qualms; and his words were quoted approvingly by Boswell. He had been forced to it, 'by the rules of what is called honour' and apologised to God for this step taken 'in compliance with the unwarrantable custom of a wicked world'.[82] The attack on the older view of honour was only one aspect of the new culture. At Bath, its apostle was Richard Nash of Swansea, 'by birth a gentleman, an ancient Briton... born to govern' who none the less opposed the duel and sought to enforce higher standards of gentility.[83] He stressed the error of supposing 'every man in a laced coat to be a gentleman', for this status was acquired by correct manners and moral behaviour. Ostentation became unfashionable, not least in tombs and monumental inscriptions. Many of these, from the early eighteenth century onwards, demonstrate the love of simplicity for which their subjects wished to be known.[84]

8. English and Welsh

Glamorgan gentlemen came to be increasingly divided from their social inferiors, for instance by intellectual commonplaces. Gentry culture now emphasised science, rationality and scepticism, and the new ideal was the *dilettante*, a widely travelled and fully rounded connoisseur, equally conversant with modern science and classical antiquity. This was the great age of 'medagliomania' – the obsessive collection of Roman coins – and the popularity of scientific toys, microscopes and optical devices.[85] These 'virtuosi' had little sympathy for the older superstitions of the countryside. The new outlook was suggested by the case in 1763 when a man was accused of having a wizard's teats: the result was neither a duel nor a witch-persecution, but a wager, to be decided by Dr Bates of Cowbridge.[86] More important were the changes in language, symbolised by the rapid decline in patronage for Welsh culture from about 1710. In 1726, a gentry lady living in the *Blaenau* had to explain that she did not speak Welsh, as she had been brought up at Nash in the Vale – presumably this was thought to be an adequate explanation.[87] Fashionable contempt for Welsh speakers as ignorant provincials no doubt reinforced the influence of new forms of education, for there were charges that gentlemen deliberately feigned an inability to understand Welsh.[88] In polite circles, 'Welsh' was often a synonym for drunken, ignorant and superstitious, so in the 1750s the Duke of Beaufort described his gentry opponents in west Glamorgan as 'Welch ragamuffins'.[89]

Interestingly, there was also a decline of traditional Celtic culture in contemporary Scotland, where Gaelic poets – like their bardic counterparts – blamed the trend on slavish imitation of French and English fashions. Dr Burke has described this upper-class desertion of popular culture as characteristic of much of Europe in the late seventeenth and early eighteenth centuries, and Welsh events are reminiscent not only of those in Scotland but also of Norway, Bohemia, Languedoc,[90] and perhaps Ireland.[91]

We are clearly dealing with a widespread phenomenon, and in 1975 Professor Hechter attempted to study the decline of these Celtic cultures in his study of *Internal colonialism*.[92] He describes 'the cooptation of local elites' into the mainstream of an English ruling class, and interprets this as part of a colonialist process, whereby the metropolitan South-East imposed its values on the periphery. This is an attractive hypothesis, but it is inadequately developed for Wales. Firstly, the anglicisation of the Welsh gentry is described as all but complete by 1640 – absurd even in the most anglicised counties; and Wales is also seen as a simple unit – which it was linguistically, but certainly not politically or geographically. Finally, eighteenth-century phenomena like unchallenged gentry rule are viewed as peculiarly Welsh when in fact they applied equally to most of England.

It is very unfortunate that Professor Hechter discusses Wales before the nineteenth century in such general terms, as something like what he wishes to prove can be clearly seen in eighteenth-century Glamorgan: the gentry are joining 'Britain', while the common people were joining 'Wales'. I am sceptical about whether a 'colonial' model can in fact be applied here, as this surely implies anglicisation through state action – unthinkable by the eighteenth century. A much more important factor was demographic, the profound alteration in the composition of the gentry community from about 1720. The older gentry families died out, to be replaced by new lines, often English, who had little sympathy for the traditional ways of the county. Among the last Vale squires to support the bards were Richard Jenkins (died 1721) and Edward Stradling (died 1726).[93] A good example of the transition was at Briton Ferry where the line of 'hospitable Bush' resided until 1706, and which another Bussy Mansell occupied from 1723 to 1744. Stewards lived here in the interim, and again from 1744 to 1757 when it passed to Lord Vernon of Derbyshire, a frequent absentee denounced for his poor hospitality. By the end of the century, absentees were occasionally opposed by 'native' families like the Morgans of Tredegar, whose electoral propaganda stressed their ancient character, and made great play of the 'home-brewed ales of Tredegar'.[94] However, lines which could truly claim such continuity were increasingly rare, as were (idealised) 'plain, honest' gentlemen like Richard Turberville (died 1765) or William Bassett (died 1771), both with appropriately 'Norman' names; and the latter was mourned in a Welsh elegy.[95]

New social divisions were reflected by cultural changes, as the weakening of the traditional community meant a decline in patronage for literature, genealogy or 'county' antiquarianism, as well as more tangible indices like building. All declined into insignificance between about 1720 and the 1760s, but they revived after 1760 with the establishment of a new county society. Even funerals reflect this pattern: in mid-century, gentry had been buried on their English estates, as the Mansells were in Kent, the Tyntes in Somerset, or the Aubreys in Buckinghamshire. From the 1760s, we once more find splendid tombs in Glamorgan, and the state of funerals became greater and more impressive, with over a thousand people following the coffins of John Morgan of Tredegar (1792), Thomas Mansell Talbot (1813) and Thomas Wyndham (1814).[96] Also in the years of decline, Welsh literature had ceased to be the preserve of anglican and royalist bards, and was now rather associated with radicals and deists like the artisan circles of Iolo Morgannwg. We may contrast the greatest Glamorgan bards of the Restoration – firm royalists like Edward Dafydd of Margam – with those of the Glamorgan literary revival of the 1720s and 1740s. In the latter movement, a rich culture developed based on the newly revived eisteddfod – but the poets were upland dissenters, like the carpenter and leading Independent Lewis Hopkin, or the deist weaver John Bradford.

The national culture of Wales was becoming a weapon to be used against the ruling classes. In the early nineteenth century rioters would use an idealised version of the medieval lawcode of Hywel D da to justify popular squatting rights and 'moral economy'.[97] John Walters the lexicographer applied the idea of the 'Norman Yoke' to those tyrannical invaders who had become Glamorgan's gentry, yet who would not favour the Welsh language. They, 'being Welshmen by birth, have lately commenced Englishmen',[98] and the radical nature of his criticism will be apparent when it is realised that the 'true' Welsh gentlemen he praised could refer only to a small handful like the Prices of Penllergaer and Williams's of

Aberpergwm.[99] Already in the 1770s, there were glimmerings of the
nineteenth- and twentieth-century ideas that the 'true' Wales was peasant,
Welsh-speaking and nonconformist,[100] with corresponding contempt for
its English-speaking and episcopalian traditions – the world of Sir Edward
Mansell and the poet Henry Vaughan. Already, it was often possible to tell
social class by language, but also by Christian name, as the lower classes
were more likely to bear exotic Biblical names (a development especially of
the mid-century). Among the gentry, even the patriotic 'David' was little
used as a name after 1700.

By the later eighteenth century, Glamorgan's ruling elite had come to
have much more in common with the elites of other counties, or of aristocrats and city merchants, and this was true in language, culture, economic
morality, or social and intellectual commonplaces. These were precisely
the points which had come to divide them from the lower classes of their
own county. The aim of the following chapters is to examine various aspects of that transformation.

8

Education and culture

Introduction

The effects of changes in the concept of gentility are apparent from educational developments. Schools and colleges had greatly increased in number in the century before 1640 as a result both of new professional needs, and of a highly intellectual ideal of gentility, and Welsh gentlemen had shared fully in this flowering. However, by the eighteenth century, more emphasis was placed on manners and social polish, and a surfeit of academic learning was condemned as pedantry, although some slight acquaintance was required with many aspects of art, literature and science. As 'virtuosi', the landed classes had acquired new educational needs which could not wholly be satisfied either by the skills taught or the methods used in the traditional system. A solution was found by a renewed emphasis on old-established methods of private and informal instruction, like the domestic tutor, and wide experience of foreign travel. Glamorgan will be found to provide strong support for Professor Stone's account of the 'educational depression' from the 1670s, and especially his view that the Welsh kept older patterns alive a little longer than their English counterparts.[1] Older institutions like the universities declined accordingly, because of new fashions, but also as a result of political fears that the over-production of educated men before 1640 had increased social unrest. Only in one significant respect does Glamorgan diverge from the national pattern: post-Restoration royalists tended to suspect grammar schools as havens of sedition, so these normally declined in the late seventeenth century. Glamorgan however greatly expanded its grammar schools precisely during the tory reaction of the 1680s, a phenomenon that will require explanation.

Otherwise, the county now entered a long depression in formal education, which may be epitomised as the attempt by the great gentry to distance themselves from their lesser neighbours. If the 'gentlemen' went to Cowbridge or Jesus College, the 'esquires' went to Westminster or Christ Church; but increasingly it came to appear that the only way to avoid contamination was to desert formal education altogether.

These educational trends helped to detach the gentry from local loyalties. Other historians have noted that during the eighteenth century, public schools helped the provincial elites to lose their 'barbarous' local accents, and gain a Home Counties tone – but in Wales, we are not merely talking about a change of accent, but the loss of a language, and the culture and social relationships which accompanied it. This theme will recur in the following discussion on culture, which will suggest how the gentry of the eighteenth century found themselves in a much more cosmopolitan world of reading, one profoundly influenced by the latest fashions of London.

However, this change cannot wholly be regarded as gain. The culture which had existed before about 1710 had had justified claims to scholarship, and to scholarship of a more intellectual and empirical kind than that of the Georgian *dilettanti*. Antiquarianism had represented the finest flowering of gentry culture from Elizabethan days until about the 1720s, largely because it was a celebration of the community, and its local roots. The work done here about 1710 was of a quality and perspicacity unparalleled until the mid nineteenth century. As with so many aspects of the old gentry culture – literature, bardic poetry, music – we find a last flowering between 1660 and 1720, and then a tragic collapse which we can associate with the demographic crisis. When these arts and sciences revived towards 1760, it was in a new guise, radical and mystical. 'Traditional' Welsh culture was reinvented on a wholly new social base, while the gentry had departed for the new national culture of manners and Enlightenment.

1. The grammar schools

Only about 10 per cent of gentry boys were educated at a major English school in our period, so most of the remainder were probably educated locally – although we do not have good admission lists for the grammar schools of either Cowbridge or Swansea. It is however possible to form some impression of the numbers attending these schools – especially Cowbridge, a Jacobean foundation established by the Stradlings. In the 1670s, it probably had about thirty pupils at any one time, but it grew sharply in the generation after its virtual refounding about 1683, so that it may have had about eighty boys at the end of the century. Such a growth was most unusual in this period, for the century-and-a-half after the Restoration was generally a period of decline for the grammar schools.[2] However, the main agent in this restoration was Leoline Jenkins, aided by his many high anglican acquaintances in Church and government. Many of these had taken refuge in the Vale of Glamorgan during the Interregnum, and they now paid their debt of gratitude to the community which had sheltered them.[3] At Swansea, the county's other major school was founded about 1683 under the will of Bishop Hugh Gore,[4] who had also been an ejected clergyman in the 1650s, and had taken refuge in the town.

The great age of these schools therefore coincided with a general 'educational depression', which might suggest that the Glamorgan gentry would have retained their zeal for formal education longer than their English counterparts. At least half the Cowbridge admissions in the mid eighteenth century were from Glamorgan; and the headmaster Daniel Durel (who held office from 1724 to 1766) maintained a vigorous campaign to ensure that the gentry sent their sons there. His success seems to be confirmed by the remark made in 1795 that 'a majority of the Glamorganshire gentlemen' have been educated at this 'neat' and 'fashionable' school.[5] On the other hand, Durel's friendship with great families like the Mansells, Aubreys and Stradlings was not reflected in the attendance of their sons at his school. The wealthiest pupils were from rich 'secondary' families like the Dawkins's of Kilvrough, Powells of Swansea or Bowens of Gower. Other pupils were the sons of Swansea professional men, Cowbridge aldermen or local clergy, who could well afford the annual fee of forty shillings. Some of the greater gentry may have attended the school in the seventeenth century, but it is most unlikely that many did after 1700.

Nothing like Durel's informative correspondence survives for the Swansea school, but the available evidence suggests a similar picture. It was under the patronage and favour of the Mansells of Briton Ferry (Gore's trustees) but its pupils were sons of 'respectable gentlemen' from Swansea families, like the local petty branch of the Mansells. In the 1760s it normally had about 60 to 70 pupils, many from lesser gentry families in neighbouring counties, where it was 'in much celebrity'.[6]

The syllabus of these schools was heavily oriented towards classical literature. In 1694, Edward Kemys asked his relative Sir Charles Kemys to find him some sort of employment 'for I thoroughly understand the Latin tongue and much of the Greek one, which I am sure makes me qualified for most employments', and he even understood 'most of the rules of arithmetic (by whole numbers)'.[7] His view of the sufficiency of classical subjects for most careers was widely held. Despite complaints, Durel's long regime at Cowbridge had much in its favour, for the school taught geography, French, writing, arithmetic and dancing, besides the essential classics; and corporal punishment was used very sparingly. Durel was a considerable scholar in his own right, whose closest friends were prominent Oxford orientalists. Cowbridge's library included many works from the collections of the Stradlings, the Mansells and of Leoline Jenkins, and Durel was a member of the local book society, whose purchases were at the disposal of the school.[8] Cowbridge represented some of the best aspects of the traditional system, so the school was in marked contrast to those severely criticised by contemporaries for their failures to produce either men of taste, or worthy clergy.[9]

But if the local schools had these advantages, why were they not better patronised by the elite? The major reason is that gentry parents were often more concerned with features of education other than the purely academic. They had long sought to separate their children from association with inferiors, notably servants, by sending sons away to travel, or to stay with aristocratic friends. Only thus could they be saved from acquiring 'rude' or 'clownish' speech and behaviour from country children, as Mary Prichard of Llancaeach wrote in 1649.[10] In a small area like the Vale, where most of the greater gentry lived, Cowbridge was perhaps *too* accessible, and proximity to the town boys was cited by Thomas Wyndham of Dunraven as his reason for not sending his son to the school in 1740.[11] In the eighteenth century, there was the additional incentive of striving to attain a 'correct' English accent, for which purpose parents in outlying counties sent their children to school in London or the Home Counties. The Welsh grammar schools were also intended to be centres of anglicisation, but at Cowbridge Durel had to introduce English lessons for the nearly monoglot Welsh sons of petty gentlemen.[12]

2. The 'great schools'

Glamorgan families had widespread contacts in South Wales and south-west England, and a little use was made of schools in this wider area. The Lewises of Van had important interests in Wiltshire, so sent their sons to school at Salisbury. Generally, however, if a major family had enough wealth and social incentive to keep its sons at school in England, it chose one of the nine 'great schools' which would by the early nineteenth century serve as models for the new 'public school'. Five of these took a total of fourteen Glamorgan pupils during the eighteenth century, and others probably attended Shrewsbury. But by far the most frequented English school was Westminster, with 31 Glamorgan pupils between 1628 and 1812, and 18 between 1660 and 1760.[13] Education here was expensive, costing between 50 and 60 pounds a year, and 20 of the Glamorgan pupils derived from just eight families from the elite of county society. Westminster's curriculum was not so hidebound as to exclude fashionable skills like dancing and fencing, but the school's chief attractions were not its formal subjects. Busby's headmastership had made it fashionable for aristocrats and gentry who would otherwise have attended their local grammar schools, and pupils came from the greatest gentry of Wales. Useful friendships of political value could be made there, for the tradition of loyalty to fellow pupils of one's school was already strong. The eighteenth-century Dukes of Beaufort were keenly aware of their obligations to their 'chums', the word itself being a coinage of the 'great schools'.[14]

There is also some evidence of the idea that attendance at a 'great school' was one criterion of gentility, and this was part of the process whereby a rising family was accepted into the gentry. Lawson and Silver attribute this to the Victorian period, but there are strong signs of it in our period.[15] For instance, the Margam steward Hopkin Llewellyn sent his son to Rugby. When in the 1760s the *nouveau riche* steward Thomas Edmondes wished to make his son a gentleman, the first step was a 'liberal education', followed by the purchase of a commission in the Guards.[16] In the Westminster admission lists are other sons of men who had just risen to wealth, like Sir John Nicholl or Richard Franklen of Clemenston, and in neither case had any previous member of the family attended the school.

The 'great schools' did however have serious drawbacks, for moral supervision was lax: the last squire of Friars, Thomas Herbert, was led into marriage with a servant girl while he was at Eton about 1720. Westminster had all the temptations of London at hand, and in addition it was described by Chesterfield as 'the seat of illiberal manners and brutal behaviour'.[17] Some boys were educated in London at academies which had the advantage of being located in or near the capital, but avoided the pedantry and savage birchings of Westminster. They could also provide a select social environment. The Mansells used such schools at Cheam and St James's, and others are known in Mortlake, Twickenham and Wandsworth.[18] Herbert Mackworth's son was sent to a Wandsworth school in the 1740s, when his fellow pupils included the sons of the Duke of Richmond, Lord Falkland and the Earl of Pembroke, as well as members of the Fox family, Herbert's political allies.[19] It was in such institutions that the girls of the gentry class were educated, if they received any instruction other than in the home, or from local schoolmasters.[20] Women's education was more in 'feminine skills' like music or needlework than academic subjects and not until the end of the eighteenth century did writers satirise the bluestocking, with her scientific pretensions.[21]

3. Private education

The existing system of formal education seemed to perpetuate brutal pedantry, which Aubrey the antiquary sought to eliminate by applying Comenian methods in a series of colleges to be established throughout Britain. He proposed to establish such an institution for South Wales and south-west England at the Van, in Glamorgan, where several of the greatest landowners showed sympathy for this experiment, including Worcester, Pembroke, Leicester and Sir John Aubrey.[22] The scheme failed, and in the absence of such a college, any gentleman wishing to introduce new subjects or gentler methods into his children's education had either to undertake it himself, or else to employ a tutor. There were undoubted advantages in this latter course, especially in the eighteenth century when parents were increasingly reluctant to let their children leave home at too early an age. Moreover, teachers available locally were often men of remarkable scholarship, like William Thomas of Michaelston-super-Ely, with his interests in statistics, botany and archaeology, or the poet Dafydd Nicolas, who was tutor at Aberpergwm in the 1730s. The Mansells of Margam used in this capacity the fine antiquary John Williams and the lexicographer John Walters; and this use of local clergy may explain Durel's complaints that the gentry were deserting Cowbridge school to patronise nearby curates.[23]

The availability of scholars was increased by the political and religious struggles of the age, and the recurrent proscriptions and ejections which provided many unemployed graduates. In the 1650s, South Wales was a refuge for leading anglicans who often maintained themselves by teaching, and ejected puritan clergy adopted this course after the Restoration. Samuel Jones the presbyterian, 'a pretty good orientalist', had several gentry pupils including Thomas Mansell of Margam, whose own son had a nonjuror as his tutor.[24] Tutors were not of course a new institution of the later seventeenth century – indeed William Lewis of Van had been taught by the puritan Wroth about 1620. Lewis's own son had three tutors, one each for the Latin, French and Welsh languages.[25] The use of tutors almost certainly increased after 1660.

If the sons of the greater gentry attended neither Cowbridge nor an English school, they must have been educated somewhere, and tutors seem the most probable explanation. Also, some form of educational change during the seventeenth century is suggested by the fact that the Glamorgan gentry ceased to speak the Welsh language, as it is most unlikely that this could have been accomplished in the Welsh environment of Swansea or Cowbridge. It therefore seems likely that from the later seventeenth century, the education of this class was often supervised by tutors, who took great care to eliminate the unfashionable Welsh language among their pupils.

4. The universities

Glamorgan men attending university showed a massive preference for Oxford, 410 matriculating here between 1621 and 1800, in which period only about 3 Cambridge admissions can be traced.[26] The former figure represented an average of about twenty-three matriculations per decade, although there were considerable fluctuations in patterns of attendance, and these illustrate changing attitudes to higher education. For instance, Glamorgan played its part in the expansion of the universities in the century before 1640, sending over 60 students to Oxford between 1621 and 1642. In this period, only 90 attended from the three counties of south-west Wales combined.[27] Matriculations in each decade are given in Table 22. Admissions fell off sharply in the Civil War and Interregnum, but there were certainly some Welsh royalists undertaking academic study at Oxford who deliberately refused official contact with the university. This group was in high favour at the Restoration, especially in the Church and universities, and Welsh friends were remembered. Glamorgan men returned to Oxford in full force, and the matriculation figure for the 1660s was the highest for any decade before the nineteenth century.[28] A slump in admissions at the time of the Exclusion crisis led to a period of 'deep and prolonged decline' for the university at large, but Glamorgan attendance was affected only gradually. As Professor Stone suggested, the Welsh seem to have retained their zeal for education long after the 'depression' had begun in England, for they continued sending students at the pre-Civil War rate until well into the eighteenth century. But there was some 'depression' in that the greater gentry tended to desert the university. Between 1621 and 1690, 31.4 per cent of Glamorgan men matriculating at Oxford came from greater gentry families; between 1721 and 1780, the figure fell to 9.4 per cent.[29]

New ideas of gentility contributed to this disenchantment. In contrast to

Table 22: *Glamorgan matriculations at Oxford*[30]

Decade	Matriculations
1621 – 30	28
1631 – 40	29
1641 – 50	5
1651 – 60	13
1661 – 70	41
1671 – 80	27
1681 – 90	26
1691 – 1700	24
1701 – 10	27
1711 – 20	24
1721 – 30	25
1731 – 40	25
1741 – 50	16
1751 – 60	28
1761 – 70	24
1771 – 80	20
1781 – 90	15
1791 – 1800	12
TOTAL 1621 – 1800	409

the intellectual aspirations of the Renaissance, many after 1700 would have agreed with Chesterfield that 'the deepest learning, without good breeding, is unwelcome and tiresome pedantry'.[31] The universities became increasingly unpopular as they could not provide the social polish which the gentry sought. They had also become the resort of students of low status, often Welsh. Even if the great gentry of Glamorgan did attend university, they tended to keep at arm's length from their humbler compatriots by choosing colleges other than Jesus. The proportion of great gentry among Glamorgan men attending Jesus between 1621 and 1700 was 55 per cent; between 1701 and 1780 it fell to 32 per cent. By contrast, other more select colleges attracted a wave of great squires. Matriculations at Christ Church in particular were chiefly of greater gentry families like the Mansells, Stradlings and Gwyns, and these continued at a rate of between two and four per decade for most of the period.

The gentry who came to Oxford sought there social rather than intellectual improvement, and it was complained that the educational aspects of the institution were damaged by such 'scholars only in masquerade'.[32] Oxford's social life after 1660 was that of a foxhunting squire or society aristocrat transposed to a university setting, and many who here acquired recreations beyond their means later faced serious financial difficulties.[33] The temptations of drink and prostitutes were both frequent complaints, and lax religious supervision permitted undergraduates to fall into scepticism – or worse, popery. But if Oxford and Cambridge were far from satisfactory, the gentry do not seem to have used other universities as alternatives. Some Glamorgan students matriculated in Holland, Ireland, Scotland or America, but the numbers concerned were tiny until the end of the eighteenth century, when the Scottish institutions enjoyed their great flowering. Thomas Matthews of Llandaff and Sir Thomas Stradling both attended Leyden about 1731, and there must have been other Glamorgan students here, but the evidence is very difficult to use.[34]

5. Other forms of higher education

Britain itself had a 'third university' in the form of the Inns of Court, which had benefited greatly from the pre-war educational expansion, and which were still more heavily dominated by peers and gentry than were the universities. In the 1650s, Francis Mansell had described the ideal sequence of education for his gentry pupils at university, followed by Inn of Court, and then foreign travel.[35] A total of 135 Glamorgan men were admitted to the Inns between 1601 and 1780, of whom 80 (59 per cent) attended before 1660. Changing patterns of attendance are described in Table 23, which attempts to give the total number receiving higher education throughout the period (although problems of studying matriculations in Ireland, America or Holland make such estimates tentative).

With these figures, it may be seen for example that the abstention of the gentry from the universities in the 1650s was compensated by increased attendance at the Inns as well as 'informal' attendance at Oxford – a pattern also noted among the Cardiganshire gentry.[36] Again, the slowness of the decline after the Restoration becomes more apparent. Some families continued to make zealous use of the traditional institutions throughout the period, suggesting that these were adequate for some (mostly professional) lines: 17 Gamages were at university between 1621 and 1760, all of whom became clergy, and who normally succeeded each other in the county's richest livings.[37]

There were many criticisms of the university syllabus, and its neglect of 'modern' subjects like languages and sciences. These were not wholly justified, and the university was a thriving antiquarian centre in the time of Edward Lhuyd. During the eighteenth century, work of merit was done in

Table 23: *Attendance at university and Inn of Court*

Decade	Only attending Oxford	Only attending Inn of Court	Attending both	Total
1621 – 30	22	4	6	32
1631 – 40	23	9	6	38
1641 – 50	5	9	0	14
1651 – 60	7	13	6	26
1661 – 70	39	4	2	45
1671 – 80	24	4	3	31
1681 – 90	22	7	4	33
1691 – 1700	19	7	5	31
1701 – 10	23	4	4	31
1711 – 20	19	6	5	30
1721 – 30	23	2	2	27
1731 – 40	21	3	4	28
1741 – 50	14	2	2	18
1751 – 60	21	1	2	29
1761 – 70	24	3	4	31
1771 – 80	18	0	2	20
TOTAL	329	78	57	464

astronomy, languages and literary criticism, and in 1759 Herbert Mackworth attended Blackstone's lectures on law.[38] If official encouragement was lacking, gentlemen could make progress through their own efforts, or with the help of a tutor, as was demonstrated by the orientalist efforts of Erasmus Philipps of Pembrokeshire in the 1720s.[39] However, many contemporary comments seem to justify the criticisms of both the students and the university, and especially by contrast with the more 'modern' and scientific tone of the dissenting academies. The school at Brynllywarch became the nucleus of the eighteenth-century academy at Carmarthen, and other institutions close to Glamorgan included those at Tewkesbury, Shrewsbury and Abergavenny. Furthermore, the methodist seminary of Trefecca (Breconshire) was founded in 1768. There is little evidence that Glamorgan gentry frequented the academies after about 1700, although possible examples of continuity are the Prices of Tynton and the Buttons.[40] It does not appear that those gentry who did not attend university made up for this at the academies. This again suggests that academic learning was a lesser consideration in education than were social advantages.

6. Foreign travel

The informal education used in place of the schools and universities was characterised by domestic tutors and by foreign travel, which latter was by no means a new element in higher education. Aubrey the antiquary traced its popularity to the parents' desire to cure their children of the influences of low company, to which they resorted when alienated by parental severity. Grand Tours can be traced at least from the 1630s and all the heirs of the elite families would apparently have participated. Between 1715 and 1740, for example, we can find evidence of European travel by all three sons of the first Lord Mansell and by his grandson the second Lord;[41] by Edward and Thomas Stradling, by Robert Jones and Thomas Matthews.[42] As new families like the Lucases moved into the elite by the 1770s, so they too adopted this form of education and entertainment.[43]

Perhaps exile in the 1650s served to increase interest in the countries visited, and the Tour became a well-established institution by the end of the century; although Mary Kemys was rare among women in having accomplished it, in the company of her Wharton brothers.[44] In the most-frequented cities, there developed a profession of guides who chiefly survived on the income from English 'students'. Several aristocratic families used the services of the Scot, John Clephane, including the Mansells, Cokes and Cavendishes.[45] His educational role is hard to categorise except that it partook of tutor, physician, guide, diplomat, moral preceptor and literary adviser; and contemporaries briefly summarised it as 'bear-leader'. These were often men of high calibre: Clephane was a close friend of David Hume, while a Monmouthshire counterpart was John Turberville Needham, a catholic antiquary, orientalist and scientist. The Tour usually followed well-tried routes to cities where there already were English colonies, like Paris, Rome, Florence, Venice, Angers and Montpellier, and British travellers patronised the same small group of Italian painters. There were long lists of the correct buildings to see in each area, and in 1739 Lord Mansell was provided with such a list of Italian villas, palaces and churches, which were duly marked as the journey progressed.[46] Parents tried to stress the strictly educational aspects of the journey, and urged their sons to note carefully the details of the countries they visited, especially the 'laws, customs, governments and the products or manufactories of each particular place'.[47] In 1692, an account of George Stradling emphasised that the purpose of his wide travels in the 1630s had been to study history and politics, and not merely to seek 'old walls, ruined amphitheatres and antiquated coins' as did many young gentlemen.[48]

The Grand Tour was a very considerable investment, and the Tour of a young aristocrat could cost seven or eight hundred pounds for each of three or four years.[49] This widespread institution was not, however, without its critics, who complained that little could be learned of foreign customs by those who invariably frequented their own compatriots, in the usual handful of well-established expatriate communities. Chesterfield wrote that young English travellers were celebrated for disorderly and immoral behaviour, while their ignorance of foreign languages made learning difficult.[50] Even if well-intentioned, they only saw the usual tourist round; they might also acquire foreign vices, and Clephane warned Lord Mansell of the prevalence of black magic in European cities.[51] Adulterous behaviour no longer tolerated by the English upper classes might well be indulged in Italy, where Lord Mansell's whoring was notorious.[52] More dangerous might be the political contacts made abroad, catholic or republican before 1688, and jacobite afterwards. Passports (or at least parental orders) might forbid travellers from frequenting dangerous company among English exiles, but visitors to the Stuart court in the 1720s included Robert Mansell, the Dukes of Beaufort, and probably Robert Jones of Fonmon.[53]

As early as the 1650s, Francis Mansell was dubious about allowing his charges to travel abroad, and the Tour had other critics in the next century.[54] There was also a growing call for the addition of a British tour to European travel. In 1730, Robert Jones of Fonmon was advised that a young gentleman should see his own country before travelling abroad, or else foreigners would regard him as ignorant.[55] At the end of the eighteenth century, war forced British gentlemen to discover their own country, reinforcing the trend away from foreign travel, but the Grand Tour never wholly faded as a central part of upper-class education.

7. The political element

Natural concern for the sound education of one's children was greatly strengthened in this period by the omnipresence of political considerations in such matters as the choice of a college or the appointment of a tutor. Certain colleges had strong reputations as havens of puritan or royalist views, and associations here were long enduring. The origins of Sheldon's

Welsh circle were to be found in his period as Warden of All Souls in the 1630s,[56] and it has been argued above that the early gentry puritanism of the Lewises and Mansells was equally an 'Oxford Movement'.[57] This could also be illustrated by the methodist tradition which resulted from the association of some Glamorgan squires with the Oxford 'Holy Club' of the 1720s. At local level, schoolmasters were often drawn from the substantial yeomen and artisans, whose role as articulate leaders of the village community sometimes led them into radical politics or religion. Local teachers were often dissenters, catholics or quakers, and were accused of spreading sedition, so control of education was politically necessary.[58] Restoration bishops were anxious to prevent seditious teaching, and a tory work of 1713 urged parents to supervise their children's reading closely, to see whether their books were 'of the Church or the conventicle'.[59] Accordingly, changes of national regime were closely reflected locally.[60]

Concern for ideological safety led to numerous battles over patronage.[61] Moreover, posts in schools or colleges were often valuable prizes, and the ability to confer them on dependents extended one's power. Even the establishment of a petty charity school created one more job with which to confirm one's authority at parish level, as did the ability to obtain a Cowbridge monitorship or Oxford servitorship for the son of a tenant or servant. Maintaining a poor but talented neighbour was an act of laudable charity, but it was also an investment, as he might later be a useful client. The Aubreys found this with Sir Leoline Jenkins, as did Beaufort with the anglican preacher Thomas Nowell. In Durel's correspondence, a vacant monitorship was the occasion for letters and petitions from the greatest men of the county, like Sir Thomas Stradling, Sir John Aubrey or Bussy Mansell.[62] Such men attached enormous importance to minor details in the preservation of their local influence, and the role of a magnate as a channel of patronage is a recurrent theme in the correspondence of (say) the first Lord Mansell. Beaufort's exhibition at Oriel was a very useful reward or bribe. At least 13 Glamorgan men attended this college between 1745 and 1780, representing about 16 per cent of total county matriculations for these years (by contrast, only six Glamorgan men had attended Oriel between 1621 and 1744, before the foundation of the scholarship). The appointment to this exhibition involved the exercise of influence by the county's magnates, like Lord Vernon and Sir Charles Kemys-Tynte.[63] Academic considerations took second place to the demands of politics and influence in deciding who received education, just as social factors dominated in moulding the forms of education available. The deep partisanship

of the early eighteenth century must have contributed still further to the
decline of the traditional institutions of learning, and reinforced trends to
private education.

8. Libraries

Politics, social fashion, demographic change, all conspired to change very
considerably the intellectual attainments expected of gentlemen. Now, it
should be possible to illustrate this from the library catalogues occasionally found in collections of gentry papers, and to show that the squire educated at Cowbridge and Jesus bought and read very different books from
his son who had experienced private tuition and a spell at Christ Church.
Unfortunately this cannot be done with precision, but certain trends can be
observed. Firstly, gentry library catalogues are rarely found before the
1740s, and I have not been able to locate any from the later seventeenth
century. In eighteenth-century Glamorgan, we have a good sequence of
Margam catalogues, but otherwise only a really detailed list from Penllergaer.[64] Another problem is that ownership of a book did not necessarily
mean that its recorded possessor had himself acquired it, and even if he had
it is difficult to prove that the book was ever read. Subscription lists and
chance references in correspondence indicate more definite interest, but
the former evidence is rare. Allowing for these difficulties, some tentative
conclusions may be drawn about the nature of the gentry libraries, for instance about their size.

   This evidence tends to disprove Macaulay's charge that the squires of
1685 were semi-literate, and studied only the Game Laws and a few ro-
mances. At the end of the century, secondary gentlemen like Richard Herbert of Cilybebill or Thomas Price of Penllergaer each possessed libraries
of about 100 books, and these were undistinguished squires not especially
noted for learning or culture.[65] Among the great families, Margam had
1,850 volumes in the 1740s, a total which increased to over 2,500 when
the estate passed to the Talbots in 1750.[66] Two or three thousand volumes
was a normal size for the libraries of the greatest gentry, both in Glamorgan and other Welsh shires.[67] Even Margam may not have been the largest
library in Glamorgan. The Stradling library at St Donat's was celebrated
from Elizabethan times until its dissolution after 1738, and was probably
greater than Margam, although we have no detailed record of it. Considerable libraries would certainly have existed at Miskin under William
Bassett, a Doctor of Laws offered the headship of Jesus College, Oxford, at

the Restoration. Presumably, Hensol possessed an excellent collection under the very learned Judge Jenkins, and there must have been good libraries at the houses of wealthy antiquaries like Evan Seys of Boverton and Francis Gwyn of Llansannor. In the 1640s, Humphrey Matthews of Castell-y-Mynach owed £500 to the London dealer Thomason for a collection of manuscripts.[68] Below the greater gentry, there were certainly many books and manuscripts at Dyffryn and Llanharan, and the former was the seat of Philip Williams, a much-consulted scholar and antiquary. Books were therefore numerous and accessible among the Glamorgan gentry, and they could readily be obtained from a number of sources, inside and outside the county – for instance at Newport, Monmouth, Abergavenny, London, Bristol and Oxford, as well as Continental cities.[69]

9. Reading and scholarship

Given the limitations of the available evidence, do the booklists support the hypothesis about a major cultural transition after the 1720s? In one area, it seems they do not, and that is the remarkable absence of Welsh material before any presumed cultural shift. Neither Margam nor Penllergaer owned so much as a Welsh Bible or Prayer Book in the early eighteenth century, nor did the presbyterian minister Samuel Jones, although both Brynllywarch and Penllergaer were in overwhelmingly Welsh-speaking areas.[70] This seems a paradox, especially when we know that Sir Edward Mansell was a considerable patron of the bards. The answer to this seems to be that even in the most solidly Welsh counties – like those of the north-west – the seventeenth-century gentry simply had never owned Welsh books (nor written Welsh letters), so this cannot be used as an index of 'Welshness'. Unfortunately, it also means that a lack of Welsh reading after 1740 cannot be used to illustrate cultural change.

We also find that although Glamorgan had a strong Welsh culture before the 1720s, it was considerably separated from that of other shires. Glamorgan was probably the most populous Welsh county by the early eighteenth century, yet it was very poorly represented on subscription lists to works by Welsh authors. Eighteen such lists are known between 1707 and 1731, but Glamorgan names occur on only six of these – and on four they formed 1 per cent or less of the total.[71] Similarly of 140 Welsh writers identified between 1660 and 1730, only two originated in Glamorgan.[72] On the other hand, a proposed English – Welsh dictionary by Thomas Richards of Coychurch attracted massive Glamorgan support in 1753, nearly all its 158 subscribers being from the county – and this included 36 JPs, about half the Bench.[73] This may reflect a growing academic interest in the Welsh language long after it had ceased to be the normal medium of speech for the gentry; but more important was the feeling of county solidarity, and the wish to support the work of a county writer.

This evidence in itself does not allow us to conclude that the loss of the old community meant a severe blow to Welsh culture. However, it does show that the gentry of the age of Sir Edward Mansell were a community of considerable learning and scholarship. We may recall the portrait of Sir Roger de Coverley's library which consisted chiefly of the very dry works of Restoration anglican divines; but for the gentry, anglicanism was often much more than a simple matter of conservatism and prejudice. The squires of Margam, St Donat's or Penllergaer read very widely in the works of divines covering a broad theological spectrum, from Ken to Stillingfleet, from Sancroft to Chillingworth. In the writings of high churchmen, like George Stradling, Sir Humphrey Mackworth, Leoline Jenkins or Rees Powell of Llanharan, orthodoxy is a well-reasoned and ably defended proposition, often based on a huge corpus of texts.[74] In political matters too, tastes were very catholic. The tory Mansells of the 1740s read *Cato's Letters*, while books by Toland, Ludlow or Harrington regularly appear in the possession of the most orthodox tories. Collectors of political pamphlets or satires like the whig Philip Williams made sure to gather a full spectrum of views, from near-republican whiggery to unreconstructed jacobitism.[75]

The last generations of the old community – those of the early eighteenth century – appear to have been an extremely well-informed group, on history, theology, and current affairs. They provided an avid market for the spate of books on exotic lands and monarchs. Margam in the 1740s had works on Turkey, Africa, India, China and Russia – and 6.5 per cent of the library comprised accounts of other countries. In the 1730s and 1740s, a striking number of gentry display some awareness of the new orientalism, perhaps inspired by the presence of Durel at Cowbridge.[76] Francis Gwyn corresponded with his kinsman Humphrey Prideaux about the latter's *Life* of Muhammad, and contemporary religious debate often shows real awareness of Eastern Christianity or of Islam.[77]

We often find groups of gentry very much aware of current literary and intellectual developments. The poet Henry Vaughan had extensive Glamorgan links including the Mansell's chaplain John Williams the antiquary.[78] To take another example, about 1690 Sir Charles Kemys was in

London discussing a new translation of Pascal by his friend Robert Merrett.[79] His other great intimate was Beaufort's son, the Marquis of Worcester, who was engaged in translating Corneille for the stage. Sir Charles's wife Mary kept up her own learned correspondence with both puritan divines and agricultural improvers.[80] The gentry patronised scholars and poets, but also wrote themselves: Philip Williams was especially prolific as a satirist and poet – who even experimented with the use of Welsh verse-forms in English poetry.[81]

By the 1730s, the Glamorgan gentry were a remarkably cultured society. The poet Savage found a number of patrons at Swansea in 1739 and the squires readily accepted the new culture of novels and magazines. The fourth Lord Mansell had *Joseph Andrews* and *Clarissa Harlowe* soon after publication, while letters and catalogues show how widely were read journals like the *Spectator* or *Tatler*, the *Gentleman's Magazine*, the *Craftsman* or the *Independent Whig*.[82] Such journals were the means of disseminating a national culture based on London common to all propertied groups, no matter how bitter their mutual hatred; the *Gentleman's Magazine*, for instance, received contributions from squires, from tory clergy – and from nonconformist ministers like Thomas Morgan of Swansea.[83] The novel was an equally universal taste.

But again, these were the last years of the old society. The gentry of the 1730s combined such modern tastes with some considerable learning, as may be seen from a remarkable example which allows us to see a large group of Glamorgan gentlemen choosing books by mutual agreement. At Cowbridge in the 1730s, about twenty gentlemen (including seven justices) agreed to subscribe to a common fund for the purchase of books, and their selections are recorded.[84] Between 1737 and 1740, 33 books were ordered, including 8 on religion and 6 on geography or accounts of distant lands, such as Muscovy, Tartary, Nubia and China. Other works were biographies (of Peter the Great, Kubla Khan and King David) and history, the high moral tone perhaps reflecting the central role in the society of Durel, the headmaster. Philosophy was especially well represented, by Bacon's *Works*, Newton and Cudworth's *Intellectual System* and his *Morality*, works very popular in gentry libraries. This variety is a good reflection of gentry taste, and shows that this community was not hidebound in its literary tastes. They were prepared to accept new themes and forms in literature, although older interests and beliefs remained strong.

By contrast, it is much more difficult to find such scholarly interests after the passing of the old community. In the 1760s, the gentry's cultured society was largely engaged in writing poems and occasional pieces for the *St James's Magazine*.[85] The culture of Robert Morris of Clasemont was largely that of the novel: he had read all the major works of Defoe, Smollett, Fielding, Sterne and Richardson, as well as Percy's *Reliques* and the poems of Gray. Sir John Philipps read Swift, Smollett and Richardson, Robert Jones read Voltaire's *Princess of Babylon*.[86] Of course, this exhibited excellent taste, but the gentry of fifty years earlier had combined literary interests with some scholarship and much original work. That culture had now perished; and this change will become apparent when we study the development of antiquarian interests in the county.

10. The antiquaries

It is appropriate that the selections of the Cowbridge society should have included five of the finest works of antiquarian scholarship[87] for historical study was perhaps central to the intellectual life of the gentry community. It was a sphere in which original scholarly work of real and lasting merit was done in the county at this time. Moreover, it demonstrates how academic study at the local and national level both reflected and stimulated each other, at a period when the sophistication of historical and archaeological work was higher than at any period before the mid nineteenth century. Many major books were published on the subject of British antiquities between 1670 and 1740, including county histories in the tradition of Lambarde and Dugdale, and editions of major medieval texts and chronicles. The greatest monument to this antiquarian school is probably the 1695 edition of Camden's *Britannia* by Bishop Gibson, with excellent contributions and additions by (among others) Plot, Lhuyd and Nicholson. Also at this time, material remains of the past were noticed and examined anew, especially by Stukely and his followers. South Wales was very richly endowed with the remains of antiquity – it had over eighty castles – and chance finds of the Roman and prehistoric periods are often recorded. Historical study may also have been stimulated by the use of ancient documents for contests over elections or landownership.

   Much of the evidence for the Glamorgan antiquaries comes from the work, and particularly the correspondence, of Edward Lhuyd. His interest in Welsh archaeology, manuscripts and natural history undoubtedly stimulated a local response, but such studies had flourished before Lhuyd's inquiries permit us to see them in sharper focus. In Elizabethan times, Glamorgan had produced in Rice Merrick one of Britain's first county historians, and manuscripts had been collected by the Mansells, Stradlings and Earls of Worcester. A much-studied part of the traditional history of Glamorgan was the county's 'foundation legend' which told of the last Welsh King Iestyn, conquered by the twelve (mythical) Norman knights through the plots of 'Einon the traitor'. This splendid tale of lust and treason had fascinated the Elizabethan scholars, partly for its intrinsic merits of drama and colour, but also because it gave the gentry community an origin myth little inferior to those of whole nations; and it concerned *local* places and families. Antiquarianism was clearly a subject worthy both of their class and their community.

The tradition is less easy to trace through the following century, but work was extensive, so that the libraries of the Stradlings and Wilkins's of Llanblethian included some of the most important collections of Welsh poetry. In the 1640s, Ussher found his enforced retirement at St Donat's very profitable. Renewed stimulus to study was provided by the Civil Wars, in which old records had to be saved from destruction; and defeat gave excluded royalists the leisure to study antiquities. About 1654, Sir John Aubrey entertained at Llantrithyd his Wiltshire namesake, who began there his long antiquarian career. The two John Aubreys remained friendly for decades, and the second baronet supplied his kinsman with Roman coins and with information about Caerphilly Castle. He also aided the publication of the *Templa Druidum*.[88] Other historical scholars included George Stradling, Evan Seys of Boverton, Sir Charles Kemys, Francis Gwyn and the Lewises of Van, so antiquarian interests were widespread in Glamorgan before Lhuyd's first contacts with the area in 1693.[89] His role was to act as a focus for these diverse studies.

Originally intending to gather information for the 1695 revisions to Camden, Lhuyd was drawn into the great project of a comprehensive *Archaeologia Britannia* by the request of the Glamorgan gentry, who were throughout his most loyal supporters and most vigorous campaigners for subscriptions. Francis Gwyn was very active in this, but the *Archaelogia* was finally dedicated to Thomas Mansell of Margam, 'so much the author of the undertaking from the beginning'. Mansell's role is repeatedly stressed, as the centre of a large circle of friends, dependents and relatives, and six Mansells occur among the subscribers to the *Archaeologia*.[90] Mansell's chaplain John Williams was one of Lhuyd's most important Welsh correspondents, while in turn Williams's relationship with the families of Seys and Evans of Eaglesbush provided Lhuyd with useful contacts. However, the project evoked far wider support than merely that of the Mansell circle for it drew on feelings of county loyalty and solidarity, which was also loyalty to the 'county' community of landed society; and it was such considerations that caused Francis Gwyn to urge Lhuyd to place more emphasis on genealogy and heraldry in his work. Twenty-nine of the subscribers came from Glamorgan, including 15 of 27 JPs. Moreover, minor gentlemen who contributed to Lhuyd's 'Parochalia' often emerge as shrewd and knowledgeable observers, although we would otherwise know little of them beyond the fact of their existence.[91]

Antiquarianism was so popular partly because it brought together so many of the other intellectual preoccupations of the gentry. Undoubtedly, the religious and constitutional struggles of the seventeenth century had fostered an interest in the past, particularly the history of the Church in England, and when religion and politics were inseparably linked it was inconceivable that history should be politically neutral. For instance, high tories like Francis Gwyn concentrated on medieval studies, which radical whigs found uncongenial because too monkish, and so they preferred to look to an idealised pre-Roman commonwealth. Similarly the apostolic foundation of the British Church was widely accepted, but different parties drew very different conclusions from this. This distinct Celtic origin of Welsh Christianity was used by catholics to prove that protestantism was a foreign creed imposed by violence, and by protestants to argue that Saxon papists had overwhelmed the primitive protestantism of Wales. The protestant theory of the 'Saxon Yoke' was accepted by the leading whig scholar Philip Williams, who was anxious to demonstrate that the origins of Margam Abbey were Celtic rather than Roman and Cistercian.[92] Here, religious, political and nationalists concerns were combined, but Williams and others of Lhuyd's circle were normally sufficiently scholarly to prevent such bias from interfering with their work. Lhuyd, a proud Welshman, nevertheless sought to write the civil history of Wales 'as far as it may be retrieved and purified from the fabulous traditions of our own countrymen'.[93]

As befitted contemporaries of Plot and Stukeley, the quality of this historical and archaeological work was remarkably high, excellent in its own right and incomparably better than the 'Druidical' fantasies of later years. Excavations seem to have been rare, none being certainly known in Glamorgan before 1750, but normally a great virtue of this period was the close attention paid to topography and the geographical context of a site.[94] John Williams's observation that the Gower megalith known as 'Arthur's table' was intended to mark a boundary shows very shrewd historical reasoning, and similar conclusions were reached by some of Lhuyd's other contemporaries.[95] The quality of observation in Lhuyd's 'Parochial Queries' is striking, for correspondents like Philip Williams actually walked along a Roman road, or visited the site of alleged wonders, before reporting them – while their successors might not be so fastidious. Nor did the Bible constrain their hypotheses about the more distant epochs, for their accounts of fossils suggest appreciation that the world was far older than a mere five or six thousand years.[96]

In the 1695 *Britannia*, Lhuyd's discussion of the possible Roman origin of Caerphilly Castle shows sanity and logic all too rare in archaeology for another two centuries and his opinions here may have been influenced by those of the two Aubreys.[97] The accuracy and number of drawings in this work is also a model of its kind. The very high quality of work seems to have influenced more than just a gentry elite: it is remarkable to find a Fonmon steward marking the great Dark Age fortress of Dinas Powis on an estate map at this time, with the note that it was a 'Danish camp'. He was wrong by three centuries, but it was a wonderful surmise.[98] Finally, the sense of responsibility shown by such men is remarkable. Lhuyd and others received generous help from the gentry, and were able to consult or borrow charters and manuscripts, but this was certainly not because their value was underestimated. They tried to preserve what they found, and there was not as yet the tendency to despise all monuments other than Roman. Lhuyd, like Camden, has long accounts of Dark Age memorial stones, although these are disregarded even by a fine scholar like Horsley and by the 1730s members of the Society of Antiquaries sought to apply the inappropriate criteria of Roman architecture to Caerphilly Castle.[99]

The local antiquarian school did not vanish on Lhuyd's death in 1709, although the nature and location of the sources both change.[100] There were still individual squires like Francis Gwyn and Herbert Mackworth who pursued these studies, and scholars like Wotton, Willis and Lethieullier visited Glamorgan. Indeed, there was a vigorous school of antiquaries among Llandaff Cathedral's tory clergy, like James Harris or Thomas Davies, who maintained Lhuyd's traditions into the late 1730s. However, there was a definite decline, shown by the neglect of old mansions and of the cathedral itself. The disregard of old manuscripts was much lamented from the 1720s, and scholars of national repute could no longer find local correspondents of such quality as hitherto. No doubt the demographic decline of the old community contributed to this, but it was also part of the much wider collapse of 'county' culture, the transfer of loyalties from the local to the national sphere.

When antiquarian studies revived from the 1760s, they had some support from the major gentry, but actual research and writing had become the preserve of middle-class antiquaries. Scholarship was pursued: early Welsh texts were edited, and a new series of county histories appeared, often of high quality. The gentry naturally had some interest in supporting such studies, especially when emphasis on the long continuity of an estate like Margam or Cefn Mabli might distract attention from the question of how recently the current proprietors had gained the property. They helped the new community acquire a false veneer of antiquity.

But this was a very different sort of antiquarianism – loftier in some ways, more trivial in others. For instance, the gentry of the later eighteenth century did indeed notice the county's wealth of antiquities, but this only inspired them to infinite absurdities in the way of follies, grottoes, or 'druid temples' – and all the leading houses succumbed: Gnoll, Penrice, Bonvilston, Stouthall. Real monuments like Arthur's Stone seem to have provided an irresistible impulse to initiate and 'improve'. Equally, the new social context of antiquarian study was not congenial to the sober research of Lhuyd or John Williams. The new works contained many questionable elements such as an almost mystical obsession with Celtic languages or druidism. Furthermore, craftsmen like John Bradford and Iolo Morgannwg gave a distinctly radical tone to the new antiquarianism. Bradford was a rationalist weaver, Iolo a unitarian stonemason – and the radical nonconformist David Williams published in 1796 a model *History of Monmouthshire*.[101] Such men now gained prestige from acting as the last torchbearers of an ancient culture which had seemed on the verge of ruin. The eighteenth century saw the high culture of Wales transformed from serving the interests of local magnates to being a weapon of radicalism and (often) neo-puritanism. The landed classes did not achieve their new wealth and power without grave social cost.

9

The spread of metropolitan standards

Introduction

Perspectives were changing rapidly – social, geographical, intellectual. Changes no less profound also took place in the gentry's everyday life, their manners and their standards of domestic comfort; and it was London that provided the ultimate model in each case. The country gentry had long placed a high value on their firm independence from the metropolis, from the aristocratic corruption associated with the Court, and the sordid money-making of the City. But in the eighteenth century it was precisely the Court and the City which were so influential in spreading to the province's new values of 'politeness' in language, literature and forms of entertainment. As the gentry were the political masters of the shire, it was to be expected that they should have come into contact with the Court periodically, and tried to emulate its manners. More curious is the tremendous influence in this period of the way of life of the professional and commercial classes, especially those of London, who seemed so far removed from landed society in their attitudes and commonplaces.

From the later seventeenth century, such 'middle-class' views were expressed in a vigorous and popular literature and art, the market for which had only recently been created by new economic forces. Expanded trade, notably in the colonies, greatly enriched the commercial classes, and helped create a larger and wealthier home market among 'middling' groups, who could now afford more consumer goods, and a higher level of domestic comfort. Greater leisure in turn created a need for new forms of entertainment, met by magazines like the *Spectator*, and by the emerging novel. The unprecedented scale on which the new literature was produced and read created a greater homogeneity of outlook between readers in the capital and those in remote areas of the country. A flourishing provincial press, read by such 'middling' groups as well as the gentry, drew much of its material from London, and thereby contributed to the establishment of a national public opinion on major issues.[1]

239

The values on which this national culture was based show the social commonplaces of its 'middle-class' market and its puritan origins, although this was a very secularised and diluted puritanism. The new literature was realistic and didactic in spirit and praised industry and humanity. It was hostile to the libertine traditions of the more aristocratic theatre of the Restoration which seemed to extol wit and breeding to the exclusion of morality; and it was true to its puritan origins in praising married love, requiring that marriage should be based on comradeship and mutual affection. Sexual immorality was condemned, and greater reticence about such matters led to the banishment from 'polite' conversation of previously permitted words and subjects, which often led to prudery in language and behaviour.

'Moral' writers had little sympathy for traditional views of gentility, but the disparity between the two cultures was not so wide as might appear from their criticisms, or from the gentry's reciprocal hatred of religious extremism. 'Middling' groups aspired to imitate the gentry by buying lands or educating their sons in fashionable schools, and there was great demand for goods modelled on upper-class luxuries, only in cheaper materials. Landed society was in turn influenced by the manners and style of life which had once distinguished the 'bourgeois' or 'puritan'. New wealth and new fashions together transformed the local environment of the gentry, as Professor Mingay has shown. They remodelled their neighbouring towns and even their domestic life in imitation of the fashionable life of London. Greater commercial sophistication, improved communications, and increased availability of luxury goods all helped diminish the difference between town and country in such matters as ideals of material prosperity and domestic comfort, and access to the new forms of entertainment. The resulting amalgam was a national culture, based on wealth and social class rather than region. The purpose of this chapter is to examine the means by which standards ultimately derived from London patrician society (whether courtly or mercantile) permeated one county community, and the effects of an environment at once richer and 'politer' on traditional modes of life.

Firstly, we will examine the means of contact with the new ideas – through London, through provincial capitals like Bath or Bristol, or direct to Continental sources of the new manners. Next, we will examine how the local environment was thoroughly remodelled in accordance with the new fashions – the towns and public buildings, next the private houses, and the whole domestic world, a process especially visible in matters of leisure and entertainment. Changes so thoroughgoing both echoed and influenced more subtle changes affecting private life – in the structure of the family and the status of its members. Glamorgan again resembled the wealthier English provinces in the speed with which it adopted the new culture, and became a market for the 'commercialisation of leisure' of which Professor Plumb has written.

This chapter concludes with an account of the creation of a myth-figure – the Georgian squire. We have seen how the gentry of the later seventeenth century were men of considerable learning and taste, possessing no small political acumen and a zeal for economic improvement that would have delighted Samuel Smiles. The squires of the mid eighteenth century had many of the same qualities, together with a rapidly growing sophistication of domestic life and family relationships. Yet were the earlier squires really the barbarians described by Macaulay, or the later ones all like Squire Western? It seems to us paradoxical – and this may not only be the result of two centuries of hindsight: many contemporaries noticed the paradox. It will be suggested here that some of the 'barbarism' of the late Stuart and Georgian squires was to some extent deliberately cultivated: that the image of the hard-drinking, violent, boorish foxhunter was an assertion of class values, a rejection of the metropolitan conquest which was transforming their lives. Of course I am not suggesting that a real-life Squire Western would occasionally put aside his sporting obsessions and provincial prejudices to revert to his true cultured and cosmopolitan self: but the provincialisms did have their social function. The image of the foxhunter and the dilettante, the entrepreneur and the barbarian chieftain – all serve to remind us of the extremely complex nature of this class and its ethos.

1. London

London's dominance was not remarkable when it is considered that its population was roughly one tenth of the whole of Britain in the seventeenth century, and that it was, throughout the period, the political, economic, legal and social capital. Above all, there were the ancient attractions of the Court. Younger sons of gentry families also tried to make their fortunes in London's commerce or industry, and sometimes succeeded so well that they were able to found new estates in their original localities. Such Welsh activity continued to be important in the eighteenth century, when the Bassetts and Bevans of Glamorgan made successful careers there as apothecaries, and others became rich as lawyers and merchants. Some gentry were connected by marriage to city lines whose prosperity derived in whole or in part from mercantile enterprise, especially with the expansion of colonial trade after 1660. Of the marriages made by heads of greater Glamorgan families in this period, 8 per cent were made with the daughters of Londoners. Between 1670 and 1710, Glamorgan gentlemen who succeeded in marrying the daughters of rich citizens included the Mansells of both Margam and Briton Ferry, Stradlings, Aubreys, Joneses of Fonmon and Lewises of Van.

Apart from immediate political and economic interests, London's social attractions were already sufficiently strong for us to perceive some evidence of the 'season' well before 1640, and a few Glamorgan gentlemen had houses there.[2] In the Interregnum, a government proclamation exiling 'malignants' from the capital was a blow deeply resented by squires well established there, like Sir John Aubrey, Sir Edward Mansell, Sir Charles Kemys and Sir Edward Stradling, and others from the richest gentry of South Wales.[3] The chances of winning advancement in London increased with the extension of government patronage after 1690, and the consequent possibility that valuable jobs or pensions might be won by political services. There was also an increase in the number of elections, and a greater likelihood that a local squire would be in parliament for at least some part of his life, especially since the Glamorgan gentry were sufficiently wealthy and widely connected to sit for other counties and boroughs besides their own. The frequent need to be in London would have justified the purchase or rental of a house in the capital.[4] Moreover, the gentry were heavily concentrated in the fashionable parts of London. Under Charles II, this meant Soho, but by the 1720s there was a migration to the new West End – Bond Street, Berkeley, Hanover and Leicester Squares. When the centre of fashionable life moved to Bloomsbury under George III, so did the homes of the Welsh magnates. Mayfair had become as much the home of the Glamorgan magnates as the Vale itself. Between 1725 and 1750, for example, Sir Edmund Thomas, Sir Charles Kemys-Tynte and Robert Jones of Fonmon all had houses off Hanover Square; Charles Edwin and Bussy Mansell were in Upper Grosvenor Street. Lord Windsor was in Albemarle Street, Lord Ashburnham lived off Berkeley Square, Lord Mansell was to be found in St James's Street, and Charles Noel Somerset in Brook Street.[5]

Once in London, the greater gentry were sufficiently wealthy to participate in aristocratic society with its balls, masques, private concerts and dinner parties. In the 1730s, Lord Egmont's diary mentions his frequent meetings with Lords Mansell and Talbot, and a concert he patronised in 1733 was attended by Thomas Stradling and Edmund Thomas of Wenvoe.[6] Vauxhall and Ranelagh were the scenes of extravagantly popular balls and assemblies, the success of which is demonstrated by the zeal with which the country gentry imitated assembly rooms and pleasure gardens in their own provincial capitals. Of course, the social attractions of the capital were often open to a far wider circle than merely the few leading families, for this was the great age of theatres, coffee-houses and tavern clubs, amusements patronised by the 'middling' groups of metropolitan society, and well within the reach of the poorer country gentlemen. There were few interests, social or intellectual, which could not be indulged in the tavern and coffee-house society of London. There were clubs for whigs and radicals, clergy and freemasons, gamblers and chess-players. Glamorgan gentlemen were active in jacobite coffee-houses, and they dabbled in societies with aims as diverse as colonial development, charity, science, antiquarianism or the promotion of manufactures. This was the social milieu of many of the attempts to promote the Welsh language and preserve its literature, and visiting Welsh squires had their distinctive haunts like the Somerset coffee-house and the 'Welsh Clubs'.[7] The account books of Herbert Mackworth, Robert Jones of Fonmon and Sir Thomas Aubrey in the mid eighteenth century show how fully they used these opportunities.[8] All regularly attended plays and oratorios as well as the assemblies of Vauxhall and Ranelagh, and visited a great variety of fashionable coffee-houses. London offered an enormous range of goods and services either not available in the country or greatly superior in quality, and local squires used the professional skills of metropolitan doctors and lawyers throughout the period. Among material items purchased in London, we hear of clothes, hats, wigs, gowns, shoes, furniture, china and jewellery, as well as harps and spinnets, clocks and wallpaper.[9]

For the greater families, the capital was their home for at least part of each year. Of course, London was bleak out of season,[10] but for a few months of each year, deprivation of metropolitan life, of 'London company and London claret' was a source of misery.[11] In the 1720s and 1730s, it was necessary for Glamorgan people to write to London to obtain news of virtually all the wealthy gentry who owned so large a proportion of the county. 'People of fashion' did not want to be left in the countryside, confined to the society of 'squires, parsons' wives, visiting tenants or farmers'.[12] The regularity with which the leading families resorted to London is suggested by the astonishment of Sir Edmund Thomas in 1734, on learning that his neighbour Sir Charles Kemys would miss the whole season.[13] By the 1760s, minor gentry enjoying the season included the Knights, Edmondes', Franklens, and Prices of Penllergaer.[14] Close acquaintance with London could not fail to have its effects on life in the localities, and some now saw a country existence as a tedious and regrettable interlude: the 'exiles' received advice from friends on the best way to stave off 'the ennui of the country', by sports, or by the use of a large library.[15] As Mary Jones of Fonmon wrote to her brother Robert after a series of balls and masquerades in 'Dear London', 'you'll not know how to spend your time in your old castle after so much politeness'.[16] The city had become the fixed centre of the gentry's life, by which criterion other environments were judged.

Apart from actual residence, there were many other means of contact with the metropolis, for instance through newspapers, and Welsh advertisements were placed in the London *Evening Post* or the *St James's Chronicle*, while local men contributed to London magazines. Also, gentry remaining in the country were kept informed by friends of changing London fashions, notably in clothes – and these might well be recent French modes.[17] In turn, new fashions would influence those who had only seen them locally, so the gentry became a medium of transmission for metropolitan ways. Moreover, the Duke of Beaufort's seats at Troy or Badminton were well known to local gentlemen who could afford the journey to London but rarely. Here, they could see new styles of dress or manners, as well as works of art (Canaletto, or the equestrian works of Wootton) or interior decoration: successively, Grinling Gibbons, Chinoiserie and Chippendale. If a trip to Badminton was too difficult, no one in the Vale of Glamorgan was more than a few miles from a great gentry house which might be entered on business or as supplicants, if never on social terms. There was a continuous process by which the way of life which characterised only the very rich in one generation would soon be imitated by lower social groups, including the petty gentry and professional classes.

2. Provincial cities

Virtually all levels of Glamorgan society were influenced by contacts with towns across the Bristol Channel, foremost among which was Bristol – in 1700 perhaps the second city of England. It could not compete with London in social amenities, but it had a flourishing theatre in the eighteenth century, and the spa at Hotwell was used by several of the leading families

in the century after 1680. Glamorgan people, from the great gentry downwards, used Bristol to buy almost any form of material goods required by
the new fashions in dress, diet, interior decoration or any other aspect of
everyday life, and particularly items for the colonies. Here they bought tea,
spices, sugar, fine linens, blankets, furniture, tobacco, gunpowder, books
and writing paper.[18] Bristol had a central post office, which facilitated the
wide distribution of the city's newspapers, 'from Liverpool to Plymouth,
through Wiltshire, Dorset, and all South Wales'.[19]

Because of the ease with which Glamorgan's inhabitants could reach
Somerset or Gloucestershire by water, they were very well placed to benefit
from the rise of Bath as a resort after 1660. In the early days of its celebrity,
it was chiefly known as a place to recover one's health, and presence there
was regarded as at best unfortunate, or at worst ominous.[20] The town already had some 'idle diversions' in the 1650s, but the growth of Bath as a
centre of fashion took place only gradually during the latter half of that
century.[21] From the 1690s, the town benefited from some royal visits, and
its entertainments were systematically reorganised by Beau Nash.[22] His
biographer attributed the development of Bath to the desire of fashionable
London society to find a resort outside the usual London season, and his
improvement of the town's facilities fulfilled these needs. Soon after 1700,
most of the leading peers were frequenting the town, and Nash succeeded
in overcoming the 'Gothic haughtiness', which had prevented them from
mixing with the gentry. Bath attracted visitors of very different religious
and political persuasions, including radical puritans, quakers and
catholics, and its jacobite tone in the eighteenth century did not discourage
whig attendance. Now, these very diverse groups came under the influence
of the orthodoxy of politeness and manners established by Nash. His biographer described his efforts to eliminate peccadilloes like men smoking
in public, or ladies wearing aprons and boots in society, but of greater
general importance was the ethos of moderation, humanity and 'politeness' which he sought to inculcate into the upper ranks of both sexes.

Virtually all the major Glamorgan families were at Bath at some time
during the period, so it was sometimes necessary for rival political factions
within the county to seek support there during elections.[23] Bath was much
less expensive than London, so by the mid eighteenth century it was a second home for many minor Glamorgan gentry, as well as 'middling' people
like lawyers and stewards. It was very popular with the clergy, and became
a centre from which was organised the fashionable methodism of the
Countess of Huntingdon and Charlotte Edwin.[24] In the ecclesiastical

sphere, no less than the secular, preferment was likely to be available where so many people of quality were gathered. Bath's attractions were so great that several families appear to have moved there permanently, including the great 'squarson' Gervase Powell of Llanharan, and the son of Admiral Matthews of Llandaff.[25]

The people of Glamorgan were acquainted with other towns offering activities like those of London, although in miniature. Hereford and Gloucester were the best examples, and both were influential through their widely disseminated newspapers.[26] Another point of contact with newer tastes and manners was through attendance at university, especially Oxford, while the Grand Tour brought the richer gentry to the Continental sources of many of the fashions which themselves influenced wealthy society in London. Holland above all was the long-established centre of many of the 'middle-class' fashions in dress, art or house styles adopted by British provincial society from London and the South-West. Traditions of direct contact with the Low Countries long preceded the eighteenth-century vogue of the 'Tour'. Holland was identified with sound protestantism, with religious and intellectual liberty, and these attractions were little affected by the sporadic outbreaks of hostility between the two countries. Many Welshmen knew the area well through service as soldiers of fortune, or study at Dutch universities; and cities like Amsterdam were well known as tolerant havens for refugees in time of persecution, to which came catholics as well as whigs. Such contacts sometimes led to marriages with Dutch patrician ladies, and this became more common after the establishment in England of William III's courtiers as peers and men of influence. The legal connections thus incurred necessitated further travel and litigation between the two countries by later generations of the families involved. Relationships formed by the marriages of the half-Dutch Anna Morgan led to legal disputes for decades after her death in 1699, so Dutch affairs were vital to the fortunes of at least the estates of Wenvoe, Cefn Mabli and Ruperra.[27] There were close and direct contacts between Holland and South Wales, even if they were not invariably peaceful.

3. Remodelling the towns 1750 – 1790

Through such means, virtually all the inhabitants of Glamorgan above the ranks of the very poor were acquainted to some degree with the new tastes and ideas. There were also many in the county sufficiently wealthy to afford the social activities and material possessions which were now necessary to maintain a fashionable, or at least, 'respectable' way of life. Apart from the gentry, there was also a substantial 'middle class' in the county, which group grew richer after 1690 with the expansion of both trade and government patronage. They aspired to the refinement and civilisation of the major gentry, seeking to reproduce the metropolitan way of life in their own localities. As the greater families came to regard London as one pole of their existence, so the lesser gentry and professional or trading groups based their lives on the nearby towns, and their increased facilities for 'polite' entertainment. The work of development was undertaken by such 'middling' families in the process of establishing themselves as gentry, like the Franklens or Edmondes' at Cowbridge. At Cardiff and Llantrisant the leading 'improvers' had similar backgrounds, as with the Birds, Trahernes, Llewellyns and Powells of Llanharan.[28]

In 1700, only Cowbridge among Glamorgan towns could compete as a centre of fashion with Carmarthen and Pembroke, as it had a popular grammar school and substantial inns. Most of the other towns were market or industrial communities which lacked social amenities like theatres, and in 1760 Bridgend could not offer one inn which could cater for the carriage of a London visitor.[29] The towns were also badly built, so Wesley in 1758 remarked on the ease with which a rainstorm could turn the streets of Swansea into rivers.[30] Some towns (like Aberafan) improved little, but progress was generally well advanced by the middle of the century. Cardiff acquired a new town hall in 1741, as did Llantrisant in 1773, and in the 1760s and 1770s Cardiff, Swansea and Bridgend were paved and lit after the model of London.[31] Social amenities expanded to accommodate a wealthier local society with higher ideals of civilised entertainment, so that by the 1750s there were regular assemblies and balls at Neath, Swansea, Cardiff, Cowbridge and Bridgend.[32]

Cowbridge was the best-established gentry centre, and it developed most rapidly under the new stimulus. An advertisement for its schools in 1770 could praise its 'polite and social neighbourhood' with justification. It could offer races, a library and a book society, and local wits described its 'school for scandal' as comparable to anything described by Sheridan, with 'incessant whispers and hints' at the town's 'rout, masked ball and dear ridotto'.[33] It had a new assembly room by 1758, Glamorgan's first printing press in 1771, and, in 1774, a traveller remarked that its 'broad and handsome' main street was superior to most in Wales'.[34] Polite entertainments improved through South Wales, notably at Monmouth, which could attract English visitors by the 1770s; but by this time it was only one of many such resorts in the area.[35] Strolling players or wandering lecturers could expect a wealthy and appreciative audience of minor gentry and middling people at half a dozen towns in South Wales, besides Cardiff and Swansea. In the 1750s and 1760s, Cowbridge was visited in turn by strolling players, freak shows of giants and dwarves, mountebanks, puppet shows and at least one popular lecturer.[36]

By the end of the eighteenth century, rapidly developing industry enriched the middle classes still further with larger opportunities for investment, more banks and insurance companies, better communications and more legal work for the growing profession of attorneys. A new 'shopocracy' came into existence at Merthyr Tydfil, and the word 'respectable' came not only to imply great praise, but also to denote the social status of the professional people who dominated the boroughs. The strength of the middle classes was reflected in the rapid expansion of Wesleyan methodism and freemasonry from the 1750s, both of which were supported by the 'respectable' people of the towns, especially Cardiff, Cowbridge and Brecon.[37] Widespread public building (again particularly in the towns) provided abundant patronage for John Nash the architect and William Edwards the bridge-builder; and the improvements of towns, houses and communications in Mid Wales have recently been studied by Mr Richard Haslam.[38] Swansea, Carmarthen, Newport and Merthyr Tydfil were now wealthy centres of commerce and industry, so the role of Bristol as 'metropolis of the west' became anachronistic. As Professor Daunton has pointed out, Bristol men had probably followed policies very detrimental to the long-term good of the city in promoting industrial growth so far outside its immediate hinterland, and now Bristol was to feel the consequences of this.[39] Swansea in particular became the capital of a new economic region in South Wales, and the county's communications began to orient themselves directly towards London.

Swansea's cultural maturity was demonstrated by the publication there at the end of the century of the first indigenous Welsh newspapers – notably the influential *Cambrian* (1804). In 1814, the first Welsh-language newspaper appeared here. The town's social tone greatly improved from the 1760s as both traditional and newer gentry families built villas around the bay, and squires from neighbouring counties moved permanently to houses there. As before, amenities for culture and entertainment expanded in proportion to the wealth and aspirations of Swansea's ruling elite, and the town now possessed facilities for which it had previously been necessary to go to London. From 1771 there were attempts to make the town a resort on the model of Weymouth with seabathing as an attraction besides the customary theatre and assembly rooms.

South Wales became a social and economic unit in its own right, rather than part of a wider province based on Bristol. It now developed direct links with the South-East, and these helped to increase the absorption of local elites into the new national culture. Undoubtedly, the expansion of the road from Cardiff to Swansea was important in increasing mutual awareness, so aristocratic travellers were a common sight in the southern half of the county by the 1780s. In 1771, Smollett's *Humphrey Clinker* mentions the towns and gentry houses of Glamorgan and Monmouthshire, which are described as if south-east Wales were a perfectly normal and anglicised part of provincial Britain. The area was a comfortable base from which to venture out into newly fashionable wild scenery, and tourist resorts began to flourish in the later eighteenth century – at Tenby, Pembroke, even tiny Oxwich in Gower.[40] Perhaps Wales's greatest attraction to visitors was the new interest in the 'picturesque' and Romantic, and the very influential writer Gilpin visited Glamorgan in 1770; while in 1806, Richard Colt Hoare wrote that 'Wales has of late years become the fashionable tour of the man of fortune, and the more instructive one of the artist'.[41] From the 1770s, many topographical paintings depict Glamorgan; Wales was the setting of some Gothic novels, while the apocalyptic images of the new industries attracted tourists. Professor Klingender's classic study of *Art and the Industrial Revolution* appropriately suggests that the first of many poems on the glories of the new mines and factories was Yalden's account of Neath and Mackworth, about 1710 – and this new sensibility soon became widespread.[42] The county's juxtaposition of ancient and modern provided ideal sites for the 'sublime'. At Neath Abbey, for instance, a Tudor mansion was vanishing under the depredations of copper-smelting and mining, and the result was a landscape worthy of Bosch.

Tourism became an institution on the strength of the 'picturesque', and the new antiquarianism. Many guidebooks were available in print or in manuscript, and noteworthy sites like Caerphilly or Pontypridd acquired professional guides, encouraged by local innkeepers and town corporations.[43] By the 1780s, every major town could offer at least one substantial inn as good as those of the English provinces, like the Bear at Cowbridge, the Mackworth Arms at Swansea, the Wyndham at Bridgend or the Ship and Castle at Neath. Good roads and inns were described by Arthur Young as essential to the 'grand chain of prosperity', and were also instrumental in the process of anglicisation.[44] By the end of the century, 'many strangers of consideration are daily drawn by the attractions of the county (Glamorgan) for residence therein', and visitors to Swansea included Landor, Southey and Mrs Fitzherbert. Early in the eighteenth century, Wales had been regarded as an obscure refuge for *roués* and debtors, hidden by embarrassed relatives far from the temptations of fashionable life. Richard Savage the poet was perhaps the most famous example, but the Verney correspondence shows how an 'incorrigible' relative died here in 1707, in the care of Richard Seys of Boverton. At best, it would provide a rural retreat for those tired of their English homes, like the antiquary William Cole. By 1800, people from south-east England knew Wales much better, but regional differences had so diminished that the country they now discovered was quite similar to the areas of Britain from which they came. In 1774, Dr Johnson found that 'Wales is so little different from England that it offers nothing to the speculation of the traveller'.[45] Tourism itself helped to further the process of assimilation.

4. Domestic gentility

Professor Mingay has remarked that in Wales and some outlying areas of England, the eighteenth-century gentry often lived in old and unfashionable houses by-passed by metropolitan sophistication.[46] This was certainly true for most of Wales, for impoverished counties like Radnor or Cardigan, but, as so often, Glamorgan represented a very different pattern. The effects of greater wealth and new fashions were felt in the towns and public buildings, but also in the smallest details of the gentry houses. Increasingly, the gentry sought to transplant the environment familiar from the West End or Bloomsbury to the countryside of the Vale or of Gower.

Traditionally, the great families had sought to express their wealth and status by the magnificence of their houses, but impressive display was often accompanied by cold, discomfort and squalor. At Margam in 1678 a visit by the Secretary of State was ruined by a plague of rats, and this was the first house in Glamorgan.[47] From an aesthetic point of view, the preponderance of native woods like oak made for monotony and a certain ruggedness, although lavish tapestries and hangings were also important in interior decoration. The 'Ancient British' themes on Raglan's tapestries in 1642 have already been mentioned, and they were very suitable for a society obsessed with genealogy and bardic poetry. The houses of the gentry were distinguished in the inventories by their numerous rooms, and the possession of luxuries like silver plate and ivory, together with vast quantities of pewter and linen. From the later seventeenth century, the houses of this class were built or remodelled with other purposes in view besides the maintenance of public state, and comfort and privacy were now high priorities. Better glass permitted improvements in window design and lighting, and rooms became more suited for private family life, with tradesmen or inferiors being consigned to ante-rooms. The changes could perhaps be summarised as the supplanting of the Great Hall by the drawing-room.[48] Dutch and Italian styles were imported, in room design, plasterwork and staircases, and wallpaper was among the most popular of the new fashions. Early use was recorded at Cefn Mabli in the 1680s – predictably, by the very modern-minded Mary Kemys.[49] Margam soon succumbed to the vogue, and the introduction of wallpaper was one aspect of the large scale remodelling of Gnoll after the death of Sir Humphrey Mackworth in 1727. His heir employed his London-born steward and housekeeper to make the vast damp mansion more habitable by the standards of contemporary 'politeness'.[50]

By the end of the seventeenth century, the houses of the gentry were marked by a much wider variety of materials in construction and fittings, such as marble from Purbeck, or Italy, and high quality woods from France or Holland. Commercial adventures in exotic lands permitted the adoption of new woods, like ebony, Virginian walnut, or mahogany,[51] and therefore of more elegant furniture to appeal to a more sophisticated market. In the inventories of the greatest Glamorgan gentlemen, like Lord Mansell or Charles Edwin, mahogany is one of the commonest woods mentioned, and Margam in the 1740s had several dozen items of furniture in this material.[52] Plate, especially silver, was still an important symbol of status, but the inventories now record other valuable items, revealing wider tastes, and the extent of contacts possible in an age of commercial expansion. In 1756, Charles Edwin of Llanmihangel owned Indian pictures, Persian curtains, carpets from both Turkey and Persia, and large quantities of damask and mahogany.[53] Other families owned oriental china, Spanish or Indian furniture and Russian towels, but the houses of the prosperous also contained goods by English craftsmen, including Kidderminster rugs and a number of clocks and mirrors.[54]

Increasingly the type of goods which had once been available only to the very rich were now accessible to lower social groups, including the professional classes of Cardiff or Swansea, but also the more substantial farmers and tradesmen, and indeed all but the poor.[55] Many could now buy good pewter and some silver, clocks and good linen, and makers of maps and prints found a thriving market among those who wished to imitate the

gentry by owning pictures. Tastes and comforts once regarded as aristocratic luxuries became everyday necessities.

. The increase in the variety of available goods was also apparent in matters of diet, with many new kinds of fruit and vegetables introduced from
the Continent or the colonies. Imports of sugar and spices developed until,
by the eighteenth century, they represented a major element of British
trade. As ever, the gentry benefited most from these changes, and they
could experiment with growing oranges or lemons on their own estates,
but the popularity of the new goods at all levels of society permitted a
widespread alteration in the types of food which could be prepared and
preserved. The spread of tea, coffee and chocolate from the mid seventeenth century is a good illustration of the process of change. Of course, the
gentry and aristocracy were the first to have access to these goods, and con-
trived to buy the best varieties from the most reputable dealers of London
and Bristol. In 1751, Herbert Mackworth spent £21 on Boheva, Souchong,
Pekoe and Green tea, chiefly from the firms of Twinings and Mawhoods.
At a much less exalted level, there is no doubt that yeomen and artisans
were using these drinks extensively by the mid eighteenth century, and this
provided an incentive for manufacturers to produce china and metalware
to imitate still more closely the material goods of the gentry. In Cardiff,
teapots and coffee-sets became commonplace in inventories from about
1710. In 1720 the standard terms on which a Swansea lodger took rooms
specified the necessities of life which she was expected to provide for herself as tea, coffee, chocolate, sugar and spices.[56] Material standards were
improving for at least the 'middling' groups of Glamorgan's society, because of the county's general prosperity, and its proximity to Bristol.

Both for the gentry and the merely respectable, Glamorgan was much
more advanced than its Welsh neighbours. While the goldsmiths and mer-
cers of Cardiff were investing in silver tea-sets and linen napkins, the gentry of Cardiganshire were still 'eating in gentlemen's houses out of cups
and spoons of wood', which perhaps reflected the weakness of middle-
class groups noted in many Welsh counties.[57] Indeed, Cardiganshire forms
an interesting contrast to south-east Wales, and demonstrates that there
was some truth in the English stereotype of Wales. This county was not untouched by the new developments, for at Nanteos in 1752 there were great
quantities of arras and damask, plate and marble, and Indian goods; but
generally, the county of Cardigan was noted for being 'pitiful poor'.[58] In
1684, it was said that the 'rich are happy and high... the vulgar here are
most miserable and low... both to an extreme'.[59] The squires – apart from

a few like at Nanteos – were 'a shocking prospect of poverty and idleness, neglect and ignorance', and similar terms were used of the clergy.[60] But even here there was some industry, and by the end of the eighteenth century a fashionable social life was to be found in the developing towns of Cardigan and Aberystwyth, where Nash the architect was active.[61]

The desire of the middle classes and lesser gentry to follow their betters in imitation of London was no less apparent in domestic pastimes and amusements, where the capital decided the types and rules of the games played in the regions, as it did for dress and manners. Whist, billiards and chess grew in popularity, and backgammon enjoyed a great vogue in the mid eighteenth century.[62] The magnates acquired new tastes directly – as when Sir Charles Kemys brought a billiard table back from France in the 1670s[63] – but the less wealthy had access to numerous guides to pastimes. As Professor Plumb has described, the appearance of game-manuals like Hoyle's was part of a general 'commercialisation of leisure' during the eighteenth century, as tradesmen sought to meet the needs of the new provincial market.[64]

Music, for example, had long had an important role in the lives of even the poorest hill-gentry, who might own keyboard instruments but devoted more attention to the traditional harp, and skilled harpists were men of great status. Tastes changed from the late seventeenth century, with more access to performances of music in London or at the universities, and this was reflected in domestic life. In Glamorgan inventories, spinnets and harpsichords are very common during this period, so the claim in 1730 that these instruments were 'used in most families of the nobility and gentry of this kingdom' does not appear unreasonable.[65] By this date, both violin and hautboys are met with far more frequently than the harp. It became fashionable at social gatherings to perform popular musical works, each member of the company being required to play, as at Bridgend in 1770 when the gentry of Merthyr Mawr and Tregroes were the main participants.[66] In 1784, Lord Newborough's invitation to Herbert Mackworth specified that he should bring his flute, to accompany the host's daughter on the harpsichord.[67] Musical talent was a desirable social skill, especially for a young lady, and Sir Humphrey Mackworth boasted in 1713 of the ability of his 'daughter and musician'.[68] Lesser groups sought to imitate this fashion of the greater gentry. In the 1790s the chief patron of music in Cardiff was John Bird, from a family of craftsmen and stewards.[69] There was sufficient interest in Glamorgan by the 1750s for Cardiff to maintain 'an organ-master and a shopkeeper, as also an instructor here and there of young ladies, to play on the spinnet and dulcimer, etc.'.[70]

The interest in fashionable music met a ready response from the tradesmen of London, from whom the instruments were often bought, and who helped to disseminate metropolitan tastes still further by the development of a music publishing industry. In the mid eighteenth century, the library of Juliana Mackworth included a large collection of sheet music, as well as books of songs, operas and country dances, and many books were available from which to learn to play the flute or harpsichord.[71] The institution of the family harpist never disappeared altogether. The Duke of Beaufort had one in his retinue in 1684, Margam had a harpist in 1711, and Richard Jenkins of Hensol was a leading squire who actually played the harp himself. However, Jenkins's death in 1721 marked the virtual end of patronage from the greater families in the Vale.[72] There are occasional references to the hire of harpists for feasts, and some old-fashioned families in the uplands continued to employ them as retainers, as at Aberpergwm and Energlyn; but it was no longer possible for a professional harpist to earn his living by wandering between the great houses.[73] This change in musical patronage coincided with the abandonment by the greater families of their support for bardic culture. Ironically, both revived together in the 1760s when it became fashionable to take an interest in Celtic antiquities, and literary works extolled the culture so recently abandoned by many Welsh gentry as outdated. It was the romantic and antiquarian Walters family who had a harpist at their feasts in 1778; but later, gentry would again employ household harpists – and these included wealthy anglicised houses like Cefn Mabli, Tredegar and Llanofer. As with poetry, however, harping now tended to be associated with the plebeian radical culture, and its great centre after 1800 was Merthyr Tydfil.[74]

The local gentry might have access to the theatre in London or Bristol, at university, or through a strolling company in their own neighbourhood, and the popularity of drama increased greatly during the eighteenth century. Plays were frequently read in the household, and some were certainly purchased with the intention of performing them in home theatricals. In one of the earliest examples, at Neath in the 1680s, a group including Philip Williams used the *Gloriana* and *Sophonisba* of Nathaniel Lee, but also heroic works of his own composition.[75] Normally, the plays performed were recent successes of the London stage, which accordingly expressed values of the metropolitan society which patronised them, whether rakish or respectable.

Together, the gentry and middling groups of the county tried to acquire the accomplishments of polite society, including those amusements like conversation or elegant letter writing, for which no entrepreneur or trades-man could cater. The new forms of domestic life, however, involved social changes more far-reaching than merely an increase in material prosperity or a growing sophistication in commercial marketing. Many of the changes in amusements or comfort were directed at a differently imagined family unit than hitherto, one that participated together in plays or con-certs; for this was a period of transformation in family structure no less than in many other matters.

5. Redefining the family

In traditional theory, the family unit was based on an economically inde-pendent man exercising patriarchal authority over a large household which included servants, clients and dependents. The same ideal held good at all levels of society at which economic independence was feasible, al-though the size of households was proportionate to wealth and status. There may have been some diminution in the size of households over the period, but there were still very large numbers of servants in gentry houses in the eighteenth century. The great change was in the concept of the 'fam-ily' itself, and the word came to have something more like its modern meaning, of a married couple with their children.[76] The new ideals were best portrayed in art by the eminently 'bourgeois' Dutch, and in England by the conversation pieces and portraits of painters like Hogarth, Arthur Devis and Allan Ramsay. They appealed particularly to the 'middle-class' market, but Ramsay painted the Mansell children about 1740. Robert Jones of Fonmon had himself depicted in the finest aristocratic mode by Solimena, but also commissioned Hogarth to paint a conversation piece which is a model of 'middle-class' art.[77] For tory or whig, the 'family' had come to mean the domestic nuclear unit; servants were to be excluded from familiarity with members of this inner group, and perhaps the fash-ion for black slaves owed something to the problem of imposing this new relationship on traditionally minded retainers.

Changing domestic standards reflect the new concepts, for life was not only to be more comfortable but also more private, so that new emphasis was laid on the division of functions between rooms. Houses now had elaborate staircases with bedrooms and nurseries in the upper storeys. New ideals of the family are well represented by the popularity of drawing-rooms which were suitable for intimate conversation rather than public display. All these features are common in the greater gentry houses of Glamorgan from the later seventeenth century, and the alteration they represent may be seen by contrast with Ewenni and Beaupre, neither of which changed greatly after the Restoration.[78] More numerous forms of polite culture and entertainment in the provinces provided social life either for a family participating together, or else specifically for women and children, who became a substantial new market for 'commercialised' forms of leisure. Higher material standards and new social ideals developed alongside one another, so it would be difficult to distinguish whether, or how, one of these trends affected the other. But it is certain that their combined effect on the everyday life of the provincial elites was far-reaching, and this particularly affected the women of the gentry and 'middling' classes.

In the later seventeenth century, the ideal wife was one who stayed at home, and whose reading did not extend beyond the Bible and the *Whole Duty of Man*, both frequently mentioned as female literature in wills. With so few social or cultural amenities in the nearby towns, there were few alternatives to this life except for those sufficiently wealthy to mix with the courtly circles of London; and in 1685, Richard Carne of Ewenni rejoiced that most Welsh women were sufficiently responsible and home-loving as not to flock to the capital for a great event like the coronation.[79] Macaulay's account of the life of gentry women at this time suggested that their existence was dominated by the management of the household, the supervision of children and servants, and the collection of recipes and medical remedies.[80]

Of course, such a picture was exaggerated. A woman could have considerable social and financial independence if she were a widow or dowager, or mother to the infant heir of an estate – and about one in ten gentry families were undergoing a minority at any given time. Again, when Eleanor Carne of Nash was widowed, she began to travel all over Europe and remained abroad for many years until her death in 1765.[81] In times of war or political upheaval the wife of a man in exile or on campaign might have charge of the family's lands. Women in this position, like Mary Kemys, were often efficient stewards, and some became active in industrial or commercial development.[82] When they succeeded to their husband's rights of directing the political interest of the estate, their favour had to be sedulously courted by gentlemen seeking election. Often educated and well read, women could have strongly independent views in politics and religion. They were usually among the major supporters of persecuted religious sects – episcopalians in the 1650s, dissenters and catholics thereafter – and they tried to direct the views of their husbands towards tolerance.[83]

Throughout the period, women were given in marriage as an element in political or economic alliances, for instance with a view to consolidating landed estates. The idea was never seriously questioned, but it was usually realised that the daughter's consent was needed. By the 1690s, the Mansells were displaying an unusually callous attitude when Sir Edward had promised a daughter to one man, while Thomas separately offered her to another.[84] Within that context, it is difficult to perceive the exact nature of relationships – when, for example, marriages assumed the 'affective individualist' model described by Professor Stone.[85] We do have evidence from the later seventeenth century of such a pattern in the marriages of some Glamorgan gentry – but only of a handful of puritans. For instance, the letters of Mary Kemys show a very romantic and companionable attitude to marriage; she often mentions her grief at her husband's absence, and recalls their tearful parting. Pet names are used, rather than the formal 'my lord'.[86] Mary's relative Elizabeth Thomas of Wenvoe was equally loyal and loving – but she was also a strong puritan, and the wife of Edmund Ludlow.[87]

Obviously, the extremely chancy survival of evidence makes it impossible for us to argue that close marital affection in the later seventeenth century was a puritan prerogative. All that can be said is that such attitudes were present, and were not a complete innovation of the eighteenth century. Whatever the origin of the new view of marriage, it became very widespread after 1700. Already in 1713, Sir Humphrey Mackworth was expressing a cliché when he wrote that 'Matches are made in heaven.'[88] In the 1740s Herbert Mackworth and Bussy Mansell both risked losing elections because they refused to leave perilously ill wives. When we do hear of occasional gross maltreatment in marriage, it is usually because it is widely regarded as unacceptable barbarism – as when Jocelyn Sydney of Coity locked up his wife to make her give up an inheritance, and then set a mob to recapture her when she escaped.[89] In the eighteenth century, affectionate and friendly correspondence like that of Mary Kemys becomes much more common.

Gentry women now enjoyed a higher status in the home, and benefited from the new prosperity. In particular, they were helped by the expansion of social life in the provinces, for they could participate locally in activities for which they would previously have had to go to London. One suspects that Richard Carne would have been appalled: not only were Welsh women rushing off to London society, but London society was coming to them. Magazines and papers like the *Spectator* had a great appeal for women seeking to acquire the new politeness, metropolitan standards being the criterion in behaviour, morality or literary tastes. A French author boasted of the superiority of the novel in his country because of the greater emancipation of French women, and their activity in patronising literary salons. In England, a female market was also very important in encouraging the growth of the novel after 1740, but this was not merely a matter of a few individuals and their salons, but a mass market in the capital and provinces, who were gaining increased wealth, leisure and social aspirations.[90]

The novel was equally designed to meet these new needs, both of a prosperous middle class, and of gentry women with a similar cultural outlook. Dr Johnson attributed the popularity of Milton to Addison's efforts, and claimed that he had been so successful that no one with any pretensions to gentility could admit to ignorance of *Paradise Lost*. Milton's works are indeed very common in the libraries of the eighteenth century, among the tory gentry as much as the clergy of the established Church, or of dissent, and his poetry was another aspect of this common culture spread by metropolitan influence.[91] Literary tastes helped spread manners and 'civility', and polite society implied mixed company. The final transformation of the Sea Serjeants into a social club for the leading gentry was marked in 1752 by the choice of a Lady Patroness and some female members. In such company, the language which it was permissible to use became limited by polite convention, so previously common words were excluded as obscene. Juliana Mackworth could only refer to excrement as 'nastiness', and was appalled by verses 'too gross for nice ears': 'we could not get a face to hear them and we were forced to go behind the fan, or look down upon the floor'.[92]

Nothing could change some unpleasant features of a woman's life, and without effective contraception wives might be pregnant for much of their child-bearing life. Birth intervals that can be established with certainty are those in the Seys family between 1640 and 1654 (18 months), in the Powells of Llanharan between 1704 and 1725 (20 months) and the Franklens between 1728 and 1750 (24 months).[93] On the other hand, it was now possible to lead a fuller and more interesting life less confined to household duties, sharing one's social life with other members of the immediate family, which developed into a closer and more self-contained institution.

It is intrinsically likely that influences sufficiently powerful to change matters as basic as the domestic environment, or standards of speech and behaviour, would also have affected the moral assumptions and commonplaces of local society. The most likely area in which to seek the influence of newer ideas, more 'middle class' and puritan, is in sexual habits; but these are very difficult to assess, and even when changes can be demonstrated, the sources and influences which produced them may well be unclear. There are references to 'gentlemen's harlots' or the seduction of domestic maids, but such cases are only likely to be recorded when they involved public scandal, and they are of little use as evidence for changing standards. Illegitimacy among the upper ranks of society may be taken as one index of attitudes to sexual morality, but statistics here are extremely difficult to obtain. The diary of William Thomas (written 1762 – 94) suggests that it was common among the gentry, for he attributes bastards to great families like the Williams's of Dyffryn, Turbervilles, Gwinnetts of Cottrell, Bassetts of Miskin, Hursts of Gabalfa and Bowens of Merthyr Mawr.[94]

On the other hand, the few examples we possess of extreme and scandalous sexual licence tend ironically to support the theory of a general tightening of moral standards. Such activities were characteristic of a self-conscious coterie of rakes, who apparently wished to demonstrate their freedom from clerical restraints, and their awareness of the mores current in the *demi-monde* of France or Italy. This was a form of 'conspicuous consumption' showing wealth and fashion, and this sophistication denoted the great families, who could appreciate the pornographic poems which circulated in Latin or Italian.[95] Often, immorality was combined with political and religious radicalism, as with the circle of Lord Talbot in the 1730s, when his friends included Jocelyn Sydney and Lord Mansell, aristocratic adventurers close to the Prince's court. All were involved in major scandals in the 1730s: Talbot broke up the marriage of the Duke of Beaufort, Jocelyn Sydney was notorious in Glamorgan for rakish behaviour, as well as cruelty to his wife; and the other Welsh opposition peer, the Duke of Bolton, was separated from his wife in 1732. In the 1760s, there were also the local associates of the Medmenham 'Hellfire Club'. The masonic radical Robert Morris caused a major scandal in 1772 by eloping with his ward, a fourteen-year-old heiress, and a rakish career punctuated by numerous duels necessitated frequent exile abroad.[96]

In such cases, the attitudes of the scandalised public are more representative than those of the clique of rakes who publicly scorned the moral commonplaces of their inferiors; Charles Edwin, John Wilkinson and Robert Morris were all ostracised from 'society' because of their turpitude. The new respect for the intimate family unit was accompanied (as we would expect) by an emphasis on the strict sanctity of marriage. In the Aubrey family about 1700, the third baronet was apparently forced to marry a servant girl whom he had made pregnant; but in the stricter moral climate of the next generation, this same man disinherited his son for committing the same offence.[97] Earlier, this would have been a peccadillo, but sexual activity outside marriage was now very reprehensible, and bitter punishment was reserved for those who overtly flouted this convention.

6. Parents and children

Changes in family structure particularly benefited children. Traditionally, they had often been viewed alongside the servants and menial dependents of a householder. In an age of high infant mortality, it was perhaps unwise to invest too much emotional capital in a child, who was therefore little loved, and whose death was chiefly to be regarded as regrettable when it endangered the male succession to an estate. When Sir Edward Mansell lost his eldest son in 1693, he expressed grief, but wrote that he could accept this as long as the 'issue male' was preserved, and he used the incident to exhort his remaining son to have children.[98] In the seventeenth century, children were sent away from home to be fostered, even in the greatest families like the Mansells, for Sir Edward (born in 1636) was brought up in the house of a nearby gentleman for his first six years.[99] Other leading squires had sent their sons to learn gentility in Worcester's castle at Raglan.[100] Ideas of original sin reinforced the desire for absolute submission to the parental will, so discipline was often savage. Religious ideas of the depravity of youth led to recommendations of extremely strict 'patriarchal' discipline by presbyterian writers like Manton and Daniel Williams, or the high anglican Erasmus Saunders.[101] Physical and psychological severity created barriers between children and parents, so that Aubrey the antiquary wrote that before the 1650s, 'the child perfectly loathed the sight of his parents, as the slave his torturer'.[102] The family hierarchy reflected the structure of society in which 'rebellion was as the sin of witchcraft', and one element in the attack on religious sectaries (papist or puritan) was that their tenets undermined both the state and concomitant parental authority. Domestic insurrection was one of the greatest sins. When a client of the Mansells attempted to turn Robert Mansell against the latter's father,

Robert 'told me with a grave face that it was a great sin, and I ought to think how I shall answer it at the dreadful day of judgment'.[103]

The problem of an aged father with an adult son arose more rarely in a time when great longevity was rare. In fact, the venerable patriarch was so highly esteemed partly because the type was so scarce: in 1677, of thirty-one heads of great estates in Glamorgan, only two were over 70, another three were in their 60s, and sixteen were between 40 and 59 years old. But the relationship of parents and adult children could present serious difficulties, as we can see from the Margam letters of the 1690s: Sir Edward Mansell was in a vigorous old age, and his son Thomas was over thirty, married, and a politician of some stature. Still, submission was expected, and Sir Edward expressed amazement that his son should wish to contradict him when, for example, the son was ordered not to go abroad, or to stand for parliament.[104] Similar problems occurred with the aged Sir Edward Thomas of Llanmihangel in the 1670s, when his son Robert was an MP. Robert was reported to parliament for his disobedient and corrupt behaviour towards his father, and contemporaries noted that this radical also betrayed family loyalties:[105] he was 'to his wife nor his king never true'. Perhaps the most intriguing example of a psychological link between family rebellion and political radicalism was that of Roger Seys, elder brother of the Cromwellian Attorney-General. Roger was disinherited for striking his mother, whereupon he left the country to enter a jesuit college. He returned as a priest in the 1620s – but by the 1640s he had veered to the opposite extreme, and become an itinerant puritan minister of radical views. Perhaps contemporaries were not so far wrong in seeing links between royal authority in Church and State, and patriarchal power in the home.[106]

While the structure of the seventeenth-century family was certainly authoritarian, it was by no means as loveless as was suggested by Professors Shorter or de Mause.[107] It is not difficult to find examples of a deep sense of personal loss felt on the death of a child, or great joy at the birth of a daughter or younger son. Not all puritans were as strict as Daniel Williams, as can be seen from the copious letters of the aristocratic whig Mary Kemys.[108] She clearly had a 'sentimental concept of childhood' by the last quarter of the seventeenth century, although Ariès suggested that this was an innovation of the mid eighteenth century. He suggested that only then does the correspondence of parents become obsessed with the doings of children, the 'modern taste for domesticity', but this is precisely what we see in Mary's letters of the 1680s. She wrote to her husband about the progress of their infant son and daughters, whether they could open doors or remember names; and there are even attempts to reproduce baby-talk. The growing tenderness of family relationships was a gradual development over the whole seventeenth century and this 'humanisation' should not be placed too late. On the other hand, the eighteenth century was indeed a time of considerable change in this sphere as in many others, and new fashions spread rapidly.

In contrast to the earlier practice of fostering, parents became reluctant to allow children to leave home, even for the purpose of attending school. Juliana Mackworth was so attached to her children in the 1730s that she was 'content to play with them all day long, for though it be ninny, 'tis very natural and quite in her character'.[109] She bitterly resented an attempt to entrust their education to a governess, feeling capable of undertaking this herself, and wanting 'to be sole mistress of my children'. Epitaphs now praised the indulgence of parents, although earlier moralists had specifically denounced this trait as leading to the damnation of both father and child. The death of Sir Humphrey Mackworth in 1727 caused his son Herbert a long and bitter period of melancholy, and Herbert's death in 1765 was in turn much regretted by his son,[110] suggesting relationships difficult to conceive if the attitudes mentioned by Aubrey were still present. Paintings of children increasingly presented a soft and sentimental image, the subjects being portrayed in flowing robes and accompanied by pets, rather than the earlier concept of adults in miniature, with the clothes and weapons of their elders. For 'miniature adults', we may study the St Fagan's painting of about 1700, which depicts Charles Kemys and Edmund Thomas. We can contrast this with the sentimental pictures of the Button family (about 1750) and that of an Aubrey girl of the 1770s at Chilton.

Children acquired their own bedrooms and had a much greater variety of manufactured toys, as commerce realised the size of the new provincial markets. Well-illustrated books appeared, to add greater interest and pleasure to learning, and book lists include song books specifically intended for children. Juliana Mackworth noted that her children enjoyed Aesop's *Fables* – assuming that Herbert would be interested and pleased by their reading. In the 1750s, the Nicholls were ordering a series of books including Watts' *Songs for children*, a 'New method to teach children to read', and a 'pretty little book of pictures'. In the Aubrey family at this time, the children had their own nursery, and on their trips to Cowbridge they were entertained by plays, a freak-show with a giant, and their own musical instruments. Toys now became a regular item in lists of purchases. Families made special visits to places of architectural or historical interest explicitly for educational purposes – as in 1699 when Mary Kemys particularly specified that her children should visit Eton and Windsor *en route* to London. By the last quarter of the century, accounts of children's lives are much easier to find – suggesting that their activities were thought worth recording – and a very attractive picture emerges. Daniel Walters spent his teenage years around Cowbridge in the late 1770s in a very undemanding round of fishing, shooting, playing 'bandy' and reading; and he read magazines, travel books and Shelvocke's memoirs of his life as a pirate. Of course parental authority was still to be firmly respected, and gross cruelty or physical brutality were still possible, but generally the life of a child improved greatly.

If Aubrey had been correct in asserting that severe discipline had alienated children and made them associate more with domestic servants, then the general improvement in relations should have diminished contacts between the gentry and their domestics, and increased the distance between social classes. When in the eighteenth century the gentry complained of over-familiarity between children and servants, the latter term normally referred to a chaplain or tutor, probably a 'gentleman' but certainly not fit to be a relative. Foreign travel, or some other means, might still be necessary to prevent contacts which might lead to disaster: in the demographic circumstances of the time, the adventurer might even win the heiress to an estate. Failure to take such precautions had terrible consequences for the Mansells in 1721, when their daughter married the chaplain; and for the Aubreys in 1726, when Sir John's daughter was 'debauched' by a clergyman 'perverted in his principles'.[111] The diminution of parental severity did however mean that children were less tempted to associate with menials, and probably became more distant from their customs and superstitions. When there was no need to converse with the humbler members of the household, there was little cause to know the Welsh language, which declined among the gentry from about 1710.

7. 'Foxhunters'

Given the profound impact of metropolitan ways of life and thought on the smallest details of provincial life, it is curious that the ancient literary tradition of the coarse, bigoted and semi-literate country squire continues so strongly throughout the eighteenth century. Macaulay's celebrated picture was only the culmination of 200 years of this idea, that the gentry were distinguished by 'a gun on their shoulder, a leash of dogs at their heels, and three or four scoundrels for their bosom friends'. This was also the way in which the squires sometimes presented themselves. About 1684, a 'Lampoon on the Glamorganshire gentlemen' by Philip Williams depicts his friends in very much these terms, with their alleged obsessions with women and wine – even in the case of the puritan Bussy Mansell.[112]

'Women and wine' did not exactly constitute Macaulay's 'unrefined sensuality', but it is strange that the gentry were so often prepared to present themselves as backwoodsmen. Why is it that Sir Edward Mansell should happily describe himself as a 'mountainous Welshman', or that his son should see himself as a mere 'Ogmore squire'? There is an obvious discrepancy between such a portrait and the wide intellectual and artistic interests demonstrated by the books and paintings bought or patronised by the Glamorgan gentry, and particularly their antiquarian studies. Sophisticated urban contempt of provincials is common to many cultures, but the frequent references to the bibulous hunting squire give no idea whatever of the great social changes under way in the countryside, and especially among the gentry. Of course, landed gentlemen did not abandon their traditional culture, even when most affected by the new values, so there was a recurrent paradox in their attitude to the metropolitan way of life. It was the families whose lives were most completely based on London who most glorified the county and its traditional ways, in what may have been a deliberate reaction to the standards of the city. Classical reading, especially Horace and Juvenal, fostered the cult of the simple and peaceful retirement to the country. The absence from London bemoaned by poorer gentlemen was extolled as a wise and deliberate policy in, for example, the epitaph of Sir John Stepney who preferred 'the innocent repose of rural retirement to the noise and hurry of a more busy, active scene of life'. In the papers of the Kemys family, correspondents often refer to their hatred of the town, and their desire to return to their 'good neighbours... in the enjoyment of the innocent contemplations and recreations of a country life'.[113] While in London, Sir Charles Kemys was 'continually remembered in a glass of pure ale, which I think will agree better with your constitution and mine than the nasty wine of the town'.[114] The 'country' was the symbol of moral superiority as much as of manly health. The fullest expression of these advantages was in rural sports, above all hunting, which became the token both of a social class and a political creed.

Attitudes to the metropolis were ambivalent, for against the permeation of the countryside by urban values must be set an almost obsessive interest

in the older rural pastimes. The appellation of 'Nimrod' was given to gentlemen from the greatest and most 'urbanised' families like the Edwins who
cultivated hunting as almost their sole preoccupation.[115] Great amounts of
time and money were expended in seeking to improve the breeding of
horses and hounds, and the greater families employed staffs of huntsmen
and feeders who were paid little less than the best bailiffs and stewards. Together with the purchase of guns and other accoutrements from the
craftsmen of London and Bristol, participation in gentry hunts was an expensive affair. Fascination with hunting is reflected in the works of art patronised by local gentry,[116] and poems in both Welsh and English com-
memorate in conventional terms the excellence of a squire's hounds and
horses – and, at least until about 1710, his hawks. There was a wide range
of books to expound the mysteries of hunting, and these are as commonplace in the great libraries as manuals on the Game Laws.

The Glamorgan gentry were peculiarly well-placed for the fulfilment of
this obsession, in a county 'equally fine to any in England' for its 'very great
variety of rural pleasures' and 'uncommon plenty of all sorts of game'. In
1741, Edward Coke of Holkham expressed envy for Lord Mansell who
could hunt in a rich country with 'the best horses in the world for shooting
or travelling', better than those of Norfolk.[117] Glamorgan was capable of
accommodating changes in hunting fashion with its many kinds of game
birds – woodcock, partridge and golden plover; and Thomas Mansell-
Talbot earned the gratitude of his neighbours in the 1770s by introducing
the pheasant. The county was very suitable for the vogue after 1700 for the
pursuit of the 'stateliest of beasts', the fox. Foxhunting in particular involved a wide section of landed society, from peers down to petty gentry
and clergy, and by the mid eighteenth century sportsmen were organised
into broadly supported hunts on a regional basis, as in Carmarthenshire,
or at Chepstow and Llangibby in Monmouthshire.[118] The sport was popular with all ranks of landed society, but the Game Laws severely controlled
the social status of participants. A high qualification of freehold land
naturally excluded the majority of country people from shooting, even on
their own land, although this right was regarded by the gentry as an essential part of their own liberty. These laws made hunting the preserve of
landed society, and almost acted as sumptuary laws, as only the gentry or
nobility could legally include game (like venison) as part of their diet.[119]
Friends and kinsmen among the landed classes often exchanged venison or
woodcocks, which gifts also served to remind clients or other inferiors of
one's wealth and status.[120]

Hunting was an essential part of the culture and ethos of landed society, of the 'county' community as well as of 'country' politics, for it generally encouraged 'vitality, cohesion and stability' among the gentry. It was pursued regardless of occasional feuds which arose from accidental encroachments on a neighbour's estate, or criticisms that it was beneath the dignity of a gentleman.[121] The sport also aggravated the relationship between squires and their tenants, and much time was spent in enforcing the Game Laws. Iolo Morgannwg, the son of a farmer, wrote of 'those kinds of sad dogs called foxhunters, who import foxes into the country for the savage sport of hunting them, or breaking their tenants' gates and fences and otherwise injure them. Fortunately for the world, they sometimes in breaking down a five-barred gate break their own necks.'[122] Such attitudes may have prompted the poisoning of Lord Talbot's hounds at Hensol in 1733, or the burning of Capel Hanbury's Monmouthshire game-heaths in 1759.

But hunting continued to flourish, and the identification between landed gentlemen and foxhunters was so close that virtually all the leading members of a hunt might be justices.[123] As in Borrow's day, the characteristics of a Glamorgan squire were that he should be both a 'justice of the peace, and keeper of a pack of hounds'.[124] Identification with the 'county' had strong political implications, which from the 1690s tended to be tory. Words like 'foxhunter' and 'tantivy' came to denote a tory political creed, although there were always whig country gentlemen like the Aubreys and Matthews who rode to hounds. The archetypal squire was 'the good-natured foxhunter who spends his days on horseback, and his evenings eating and drinking';[125] but against this pleasantly bucolic picture should be placed Addison's remark in 1716 that the 'greatest enemies' to the safety of both King and government were 'that rank of men who are commonly distinguished by the title foxhunters'.[126]

8. Horseracing

Hunting was exceptional among gentry amusements for the degree of its social exclusiveness, for the landed classes were also attached to other sports which involved so much social mixing that they drew criticism for this promiscuity; yet these become as much a part of the 'country', and of gentry culture, as hunting itself. Horseracing, notably, developed in the seventeenth century under the auspices of a closely interrelated group of leading families, so such early events at Ogmore or Cowbridge were as much family' affairs as county occasions.[127] The amount of popular support in these early stages is uncertain, but during the eighteenth century there developed more formal organisation and wider appeal. Changes came both through contacts with south-east England, and imitation of aristocrats. Certainly, Newmarket or Epsom were well known to the greater Welsh family from Restoration times, and both were presumably visited while the gentry were in London, at Court or for the season.[128] Horseracing developed from the later seventeenth century through the work of certain peers in Yorkshire and the Midlands, and its growing popularity in South Wales may be connected with links through clientage and kinship with lords like Beaufort or Wharton. As with the growth of assemblies in imitation of Vauxhall, so local race-meetings emerged on the model of Epsom or Newmarket, one of the best being under Beaufort's direct patronage at Monmouth, from 1717.[129] Beaufort's equivalent as chief of the tory interest in south-west Wales was Sir John Philipps, a member of the Jockey Club, and whose family patronised the meetings at Haverfordwest. These races, from the 1720s, drew 'vast numbers of people to lay out and expend in the said town great sums of money'.[130]

In Glamorgan, the great expansion came in the mid eighteenth century, with a complete reorganisation of older events. At Cowbridge the venue was changed in the 1740s to a fixed site at Stalling Down, where there were to be separate prizes for squires, freeholders and other groups. All the chief gentry attended here, like the Matthews of Llandaff and the Joneses of Fonmon, together with rising families like the Nicholls, Edmondes' and Morrises. Cowbridge so thrived that by 1760, horses were competing from Yorkshire itself. Cardiff developed on a smaller scale from the 1720s under the special patronage of the gentry of Llandaff and Tredegar, and the scale of popular interest here is indicated by races in the 1760s which culminated in rioting between the Welsh and the English.

Better organisation coincided with dramatic improvements in the breeding of horses, and the emergence of the modern thoroughbred with the spread of Arab and Turkish blood. At least one Turkish stallion was brought back by Welsh catholic gentry who had served as mercenaries in eastern Europe, and some of its offspring were in Glamorgan by 1700. The diffusion of these strains illustrates the working of patronage in society, for stallions obtained by peers like Wharton or Devonshire were loaned to the stables of their kinsmen, friends and dependents. In turn, the greater gentry could grant the use of their stallions to the stables of the lesser families, and requests for the use of a Margam Arab came from both Glamorgan and neighbouring counties.[131] Race-meetings were the resort of 'high and low', and were not confined to the ruling elite; but they received strong support from the gentry, and lists of subscribers resemble a roll-call of an area's leading families. They attracted other forms of gentry entertainments, both polite and traditional. At Monmouth in 1726, the races were accompanied by 'balls, plays and assemblies', and meetings were a great opportunity for travelling players. Cowbridge offered cockfighting and other forms of gambling, for the pursuit of 'vice and ruin'.[132]

As 'county' occasions, races also provided a venue for political gatherings or sedition. Meetings sometimes reflected whig opinions, but their tone was more often 'country', which from the 1690s normally meant hatred of all whiggery. A tory complexion may have been intensified by the sport's association with the 'exile' of the gentry from power, notably in the 1650s when the royalists cultivated 'the innocent recreation of Ogmore Downs'.[133] Similarly after 1714, magnates like Beaufort and Sir Watkin Williams-Wynn held 'tory congresses' at meetings like Burford and Lichfield. It is ironic that the same circles who were in some respects so receptive to the new social standards of the urban classes and whig magnates, were so bitterly opposed in their political rhetoric both to aristocratic domination and to City merchants. The irony is doubled when the outlet they found for their rage was a sport which could not have reached its maturity without the influence of sojourns in London, and the influence of the peerage.

9. The 'country' resistance

Other popular sports were not especially confined to the countryside, but nevertheless demarcated a broadly 'puritan' and 'middle-class' outlook from that of traditional society, whether urban or rural. Cockfighting, for example, was notably 'democratic', and aroused the anger of the 'respectable' for this reason, among others. Glamorgan gamecocks were much sought after as gifts from as far away as the West Indies, and the skill of Welsh 'feeders' or trainers was well known. Indeed, Howell Morgan of Pentyrch was enough of an authority to be consulted by the king of Denmark; and manuscript manuals on this art were widely read.[134] Patrons of the sport in Glamorgan included the wealthiest peers, like Beaufort, Plymouth and Talbot, as well as wealthy gentry like the Joneses of Fonmon and Morgans of Tredegar, and many clergy. When a cockfight was arranged at Neath in 1703, the list of supporters included virtually every squire and gentlemen of any substance whatever from the town of Neath or the Neath valley – the gentry of Forest, Aberpergwm, Dyffryn, Tynton, Ynyscedwyn, and many others.[135] The sport brought the leading members of landed society into social contact with lesser parish gentry, but also with minor yeomen, sufficiently far removed from the intellectual commonplaces of their betters to employ wizards and cunning men in pursuit of victory.

The wide appeal of cockfighting lay in its drama, violence and unpredictability. The great excitement generated by a match sometimes developed into riots among the spectators: violence, gambling, and a general appeal to the 'baser emotions' ensured that the pastime would be condemned by the puritanically inclined, but these were precisely the attractions which brought people from great distances to participate. Matches were so well supported that they involved competitions between regions, with gentry and lower groups combined against those of a different area, and the force of county loyalties was well demonstrated on such occasions. In 1763, Robert Jones of Fonmon allied with the Devon men to defeat those of Monmouthshire in a great tournament, and such regional events may have been very common.[136] Violence and passionate excitement were the great attractions of other sports which united the traditionally minded of town and country, like bear and bull-baiting, or prizefighting.[137] On the issue of amusements, the gentry had more in common with their humbler neighbours than with the urban middle classes, whose culture they shared in so much else.

Contemporary caricatures of the country squire rarely omitted to mention heavy indulgence in alcohol as one of his features, and this seems to be confirmed by the vast consumption of wine at gentry gatherings, like races or Quarter Sessions. Some of the greatest gentlemen literally drank themselves to death.[138] Traditionally, hospitality had been one of the most praised gentry virtues, and heavy drinking at least proved that one was not a supporter of the canting fanatics. This helps to explain the admiration with which the satirist Philip Williams portrays heavy drinking in the leading royalist gentry in his 'Lampoon'. For instance, if Sir John Aubrey had his way, 'None of the King's foes / That true drinking oppose / Should sit or eat at his table.' Francis Gwyn, similarly, had been fortunate enough to leave his post as Secrtary of State to return to the country, 'to ply women and wine.'

As Dr Malcolmson has argued, the 'country' culture had definite political purposes. Restored deerparks were as clearly symbols of the Restoration as were maypoles, and accounts of dissenting ministers recount their persecutions at the hands of ungodly gentlemen whom they encountered at worldly pursuits, like hawking and hunting.[139] The gentry of Glamorgan patronised the semi-pagan wakes or 'mapsants', and actually created new ones as customs in villages which lacked them, as at St Fagan's and St Andrew's – in the latter case, the innovation can be dated to about 1714, the time of the tory revival.[140] Of course some gentry long sympathised with dissent, and many more favoured broadly 'puritan' attitudes to morality. Frequently, gentlemen fostered the 'puritan' evangelisation of the countryside, but otherwise pursued the sports which had become an integral part of the way of life of their class, and so were less than fully integrated into the 'respectability' of their inferiors. In the 1690s, when the Edwins were attempting to establish themselves in the county community of Glamorgan, their acceptance of toryism and the established Church was confirmed by enthusiastic participation in the hunting and horseraces[141] of that society, again suggesting the political element in the traditional sports.

The SPCK and similar bodies opposed some aspects of gentry culture, but landed society could support these organisations as they were distant and dependent on their local correspondents, and so could not impose their ideas. The rise of methodism caused the basic divergence between 'puritan' values and the gentry way of life to become an immediate problem, as it was itinerant preachers within the county who attacked race-meetings or cockfights for their 'noise and rioting'. Methodists seemed to endanger cockfighting by converting skilled 'feeders', who then renounced the use of their talents. Puritanically minded justices found themselves in an ambivalent position, as when Howell Harris asked Capel Hanbury of Pontypool why his efforts were directed to persecuting methodists instead of joining them to stamp out violent and cruel sports.[142] Hanbury, from a family of quaker origins, might well have found the question seriously embarrassing. There was always a paradox in the concept of the puritan squire, and the issue of immoral sports tended to find the gentry cast in the image of sinners and persecutors, on the same side as the unregenerate 'mass' of the lower classes, in solidarity against preachers or moralists. Gentlemen led or exhorted the mobs which assailed Wesley and the Welsh evangelicals. In 1740 both 'high and low' followed the Duke of Beaufort and his tory clients in assailing the methodist Howell Harris, who had come to Monmouth races to preach against 'their balls, assemblies, horseraces, whoredom and drunkenness'.[143] Racing, hunting, cockfighting and other sports were powerful symbols which preachers criticised at their peril, and on such matters both 'county' society and the 'country' in general were remarkably united. Their continuing vigour also marked the limitations of the conquest of the countryside by metropolitan values.

Conclusion to Part III: 'Conspicuous antiquity'

The history of the Glamorgan gentry in the eighteenth century is over-whelmingly a story of detachment from local culture and loyalties, and the adoption of metropolitan ways: only by pursuing racing and hunting could they emphasise that they had not entirely lost their 'country' identity. But at the end of our period, we can observe a curious irony. From about 1760, fashionable society discovered a new subject for literature, and a model for artistic styles, in Celtic and medieval antiquities. When the real political threat from the old Celtic areas had subsided after 1745, it became possible for the rich of south-east England to turn their sympathies and studies to the forgotten corners of the island – Scotland chiefly, but also Wales. Iolo's druids of the 1790s provided ample material for this proto-romanticism, and the remote valleys of Glamorgan became an appropriate setting for novels – books like *The Fair Cambrians* of 1790.

So just as the Glamorgan gentry were rejecting the historical and architectural heritage of their county, so others were discovering it. In the 1780s, Lord Torrington remarked disparagingly on the Glamorgan squire who built classical houses overrun with 'fashionable' Italian paintings, while letting their own family homes decay. He was particularly thinking of Thomas Mansell-Talbot, who at this time was demolishing the Mansell house at Margam and creating a complete 'picturesque' environment for his new home at Penrice in Gower. The gentry soon realised that 'fashion' meant adopting the whole tinsel culture of follies, grottoes, of Strawberry Hill Gothic – and the deliberate antiquarian revival reflected in the patronage of Welsh harpists and singers. Also in the 1770s and 1780s, we first find electoral propaganda stressing that candidates were simple, old-fashioned squires with strong links to the soil, men of ancient descent – 'honest country gentlemen' who drank 'home-brewed ales'. Of course, all this had been true of Sir Edward Mansell or Sir Charles Kemys, but they had never needed to assert it. Antiquity and Welsh culture became social and political assets under George III – and the new gentry assumed them with enthusiasm.

This can be seen clearly in the building activities of the gentry, who now started building new houses in thorough Gothic or Tudor styles. Llandaff had a Gothic summerhouse in the 1760s, Bonvilston a Gothic folly. A new family at Swansea created Singleton 'Abbey' in 1784, and Clyne 'Castle' followed about 1800. But it was in the 1820s and 1830s that the houses of the Glamorgan gentry became most 'medieval', and the squires most overtly conscious of 'Welsh' antiquity. New Gothic castles on an immense scale appeared at Cyfarthfa and Hensol, both on the orders of new industrial families, the Crawshays and Halls. The wives of great industrialists – Lady Llanover and Lady Charlotte Guest – now explored the folk-culture of Wales with an omnivorous enthusiasm for every aspect of sham antiquity in 'traditional' Welsh songs, recipes or costumes. More usefully, they edited great medieval texts – like the *Mabinogion* – and the industrialist L. W. Dillwyn founded an archaeological 'Royal Institution of South Wales' at Swansea. This was the first great age in which the *eisteddfod* attained its modern reputation of a national congress of Welsh culture. The new upper classes of Wales were beginning to discover – and to invent – the tourist Wales of the modern postcards.

The paradox involved in all this was the rediscovery of a culture so newly lost, and so recently thriving. But this 'Gothic irony' was nowhere so delicious as at Margam, where the Elizabethan house had been demolished in the 1780s. Four decades later, Christopher Rice Mansell Talbot decided he needed as fine and authentic an old castle as the Crawshays had at Cyfarthfa; and he needed an appropriate seat for the eagerly anticipated day when he would gain the title of Lord Mansell of Margam, with seniority in the Lords dating back to 1711. So he built a new castle at Margam – a new great house, on the site of Sir Edward Mansell's, and in Elizabethan Gothic. Only a very new community needed to be so anxious to display its antiquity.[1]

Aftermath: towards the Victorian world

The antiquarianism of the early nineteenth century had much in it that was sham, and this becomes apparent when we see how far Glamorgan had strayed from supposedly 'traditional' Welsh patterns. From the mid eighteenth century, the county appeared to be developing social patterns akin to those of any English province – and they also foreshadowed the way of life we can call 'Victorian'. This was characterised by (for instance) the flourishing London season, prudery in high society, or the cult of the public school, attendance at which marked the arrival of the middle classes into 'gentility'. The gentry themselves had already acquired those tastes and aspirations which distinguish the characters of Jane Austen from those of Fielding: we are in the world of the Weymouth of *Persuasion*, the Bath of *Northanger Abbey*. There were also thriving provincial towns under the patronage of increasingly wealthy middle-class groups who speculated in banking and industry, and whose prosperity was closely linked to the Empire. Already by the 1770s names like Dowlais and Cyfarthfa, Guest and Crawshay, foreshadowed the 'Victorian' world coming into being. It was a world the gentry had done much to create, whether as innovators, consumers, or as transmitters of urban ways, even if they did increasingly try to retreat into an imaginary world of castles and medieval barons.

But, of course, the gentry did not simply retire after fulfilling any supposed historic role. The Glamorgan gentry continued to exist and flourish so that in 1873, there were 28 private Glamorgan landowners each with over 3,000 acres, together owning about half the county's land. The largest (with over 10,000 acres) were peers, like Bute, Windsor and Dunraven; but Margam was once again headed by an 'overgrown commoner' in Christopher Rice Mansell Talbot, with his £44,057 a year, and 33,920 acres. The remaining landlords still lived at ancient seats like Kilvrough, Dyffryn and Penllergaer. Generally, the great families from the late eighteenth century now owned between four and six thousand acres, and had incomes of three to five thousand pounds a year. Moreover, they still held a very large share of political power, albeit in alliance with newer Crawshays and Guests, with whom they usually shared similar economic views.[1] There were disputes – over Reform in 1832, or the Corn Laws in the 1840s – but both groups were aspiring to create the same sort of world. Unlike the ruling elites of Stuart times, they were also attempting to govern in alliance with the metropolitan power; and this bond was cemented after 1790 by the radical threat, and by the new wealth from military patronage and industrial growth. MPs of commercial and industrial backgrounds began to represent the county between 1814 and 1820, and by the 1830s, one seat was usually held by a Guest, a Vivian or a Dillwyn; but this was in conjunction with landed members. Nicholls, Wyndhams and the Bute line were all represented, but the century was dominated by C. R. M. Talbot, county MP from 1830 to 1890.[2]

Landed and industrial power worked closely together, stimulated by a common threat from the new populations gathered together by the economic forces they had set in motion. Everything seemed to divide the employing classes from the new workforce. Religious control had already been lost: in Merthyr in 1851 the anglicans had only 14 per cent of places of worship and 11.7 per cent of sittings. (This compared with a county total of 22.6 per cent of sittings in the possession of the established Church.) The new communities had grown up in Welsh-speaking areas which looked to the uplands of Breconshire and Monmouthshire, and so the population of Merthyr lacked the 'coastal' orientation of the great gentry.[3] Religion, language and geographical outlook all tended to divide rulers and ruled.

Squires joined the industrialists in the defence of property, as in 1816 – 17 when riots and disturbances in the hill-country were suppressed with the aid of the squires of Tythegston and Hensol.[4] In 1831, a still more serious crisis was met by the Marquis of Bute, and gentry militia officers with well-born names like Franklen, Penrice and Bruce. Any rivalry between old and new elites had to be tempered by considerations of the greater threat that lay altogether outside respectable society; and the ruling class closed its ranks accordingly.

Conclusion: from Civil War to Industrial Revolution

To return to my initial question: why did the world of Beaupre die? – or indeed the world of Llantrithyd or Van, all now standing as magnificent ruins in fields. This 'classical' gentry society flourished in the first decades of the seventeenth century, and was largely supplanted by the late eighteenth century. Already by 1800 the ancient lines of Bassett, Turberville and Mansell had either vanished from the county or had been reduced to a very minor status. Glamorgan was now the county of iron and coal, of the great industrialists; but there was still a gentry, wealthier and more powerful than ever, with a wholly new social and geographical outlook, new relationships with social inferiors, new justifications for their existence and power – and this was a widespread phenomenon in England and Wales. It is an obvious temptation to associate these changes with the one great political upheaval of the period, the Civil War and Interregnum, to argue that the old gentry were irretrievably crippled by 1660, and that the new gentry arose on the new post-war social foundations. Few would now see the Civil War as a straightforward bourgeois revolution, although it might well be claimed that it laid the foundations for a later bourgeois triumph, which in turn led to industrialisation. The revolutionary decades would thus be seen as a necessary prerequisite for Britain's economic take-off after 1760; therefore it was not merely coincidence that Britain should lead the world both in the 'English Revolution' – in the first great, distinctly modern political upheaval – and in the Industrial Revolution. We are overwhelmingly drawn to try and make some connection between the two, so that the century after 1660 acquires enormous importance as the period in which the politics and economy of modern Britain were created.

This model – particularly associated with the name of Christopher Hill – bears careful examination. It is straining credulity to believe that it was only coincidence that Britain became such a social and political pioneer in the seventeenth century, and such an economic leader only a century later. But what was the precise relationship? We encounter some paradoxes immediately: firstly, it is very difficult to choose a point at which the Glamorgan gentry can be said to have acquired a commercial or industrial orientation. They had always had this, and certainly were deeply involved in industry before 1640. Secondly, the revolutionary decades do not seem to have had that much long-term effect on the landed community. Apart from a handful of adventurers, the gentry community of 1720 was made up of very much the same families it had comprised in 1600; and equally important, the traditional culture and way of life which characterised this community were essentially unchanged. In 1720, there were still harpists and bards wandering from Margam to St Donat's and Llansannor, in which houses the pride of county society was expressed in antiquarian research of some sophistication. It was the world of 1760 that had seen the transformation, and the death of the society that had built Beaupre. I have argued that the demographic crisis contributed to the anglicisation of the gentry, their greater wealth, the new political stability and the new division in social relationships. Of course, I am uncomfortably aware that this explanation involves something very like a *deus ex machina*, but in each case I would stress that demographic change was only a contributory cause, and by no means the whole answer.

Furthermore, this cannot explain some of the important elements leading to industrialisation. I have stressed that the gentry of 1700 were culturally very similar to their grandfathers, but there were important differences. Industry and commerce grew rapidly from the 1670s, and by the 1690s Mackworth's 'invasion' of the county set off a period of extremely swift expansion in both scale and complexity. The pre-war gentry had run coalmines, traded, and acted as agents for Bristol merchants; the generation of 1700 were using the coal as a foundation of diversifying metallurgical enterprises, developing extensive links with the sources of ore in Cornwall, of finance in Bristol, of technology in the Midlands and Tyneside. Their attitudes had become those of entrepreneurs and true industrialists, and the developments initiated then continued unchecked until the industrial 'take-off' under George III.

Can we find any ways in which the events of 1640 – 1660 may be said to have led to industrialisation? The account which follows is extremely tentative, but it may begin to connect the 'English' and 'Industrial' Revolutions – at least in one region.

Incentives to industrialisation

In the 1650s the gentry incurred debts, taxes and losses of normal income which may have damaged the long-term financial health of their estates. This was aggravated by climatic problems associated with the cycle of the sun. The world passed through an especially cold period between 1645 and 1715, and this was reflected in poorer harvests and economic decline.[1] By the 1670s, the gentry found themselves heavily indebted, and in the middle of a serious depression. This was the background to the desperation which drove old royalists like Robert Thomas, Edward Turberville and Edward Matthews to political extremism in the 1680s; but other squires concentrated rather on saving themselves by economic improvement. There was considerable incentive to diversify their economic base by developing their ironworks and coalmines – while the 1670s was also an important decade for agricultural innovation. The scale of industry in south-east Wales suddenly changed, and the families undertaking development were the magnates: old royalists like Sir Charles Kemys, or moderates like the Mansells and Morgans. In Monmouthshire, Worcester's efforts to enclose land for timber to supply his ironworks was the source of bitter opposition about 1677 – but economic survival had to take precedence even over preserving one's political interest.

The puritan ethic

The industrial enterprises of the country were already under way when in 1687 there appeared in the county the man whose economic adventurism would revolutionise the complexity of local industry. Mackworth was a tory, but as he was son of a Cromwellian Major-General he may well be seen as a representative of the 'puritan tradition'. He was by far the most important case of a 'puritan' background to industrial progress, although we can find many more case histories of 'puritan' entrepreneurs. Bussy Mansell was a roundhead and later a whig, his cousin Thomas studied under a dissenting minister; and both were very active promoters of trade and industry. Mary Kemys was the daughter of a puritan peer, and she tried to promote agricultural development in Glamorgan. Such examples are easy to find, but their value is uncertain. I have suggested that few families retained absolutely consistent politics during the seventeenth century: there were conversions from catholicism or high toryism to whiggery, from puritan 'moderation' to high toryism. Most families by the early eighteenth century therefore had some experience of puritan influence at some time in their recent history.

It would be very difficult to argue that 'puritanism' or a roundhead inheritance necessarily predisposed a family to industrial innovation. On the other hand, exclusion from power (for whatever reason) did tend to drive the 'disinherited' to seek new sources of income, for instance in industry. This might explain for instance why the Dukes of Beaufort were so constantly involved in industrial progress, as the heads of the family were out of government favour for most of the period between 1640 and 1770. While they were excluded from power – for being catholics, tories or jacobites – they found themselves with the time to promote an industrial power-base in and around Swansea.

Equally, we often find the ejected whigs or dissenters creating industrial or commercial traditions, and this might be why we often find puritans in the lead in economic development. Veterans of the 1650s, and their descendants, were well represented among merchants, stewards and managers. A great improver of Cardiff in the later eighteenth century was one John Bird, from a radical family descended from a much-feared regicide sympathiser. In turn these middling families would during the eighteenth century become a sizeable market for consumer goods catering to new social aspirations, and so would provide more industrial demand. Old puritan families were especially concerned in the north and west of the county, and often provided the personnel for the whig expansion of the county Bench after 1714. This helped to expand the scope of those who could consider themselves as 'gentry', and who would have to buy the appropriate new consumer goods to fit that gentle status. It might be that the revolutionary years and later proscriptions created a more highly developed 'middling' class, who gained much wealth and power in the next century, and who would provide a market for consumer goods.

Demographic decline

Demographic crisis contributed to industrialisation by concentrating wealth among the Glamorgan elite, but can the crisis in turn be associated with the revolutionary years? Certainly it was the generation born between 1640 and 1680 which would commit the most heinous crimes against family continuity. Perhaps we may attribute this neglect to the period of instability in which they had grown up, a period in which the class had lost its essential confidence in the future. Equally, perhaps climatic changes may

indirectly have affected fertility; and again, the social effects of war and
revolution produced an anti-puritan ethic among the gentry, perhaps reflected in libertine views and habits hostile to marriage. But here, the effects of the Civil War must be seen as very tenuous indeed.

An ideology of reason

Scepticism became very widespread during the wars, perhaps as a result of
weariness with extreme religious conflict, or because of the decline of religious control and censorship. The affair of the 'French Prophets' under
Anne symbolised a major decline in older patterns of religion, those linked
with prophecy, mysticism, apocalyptic hysteria, 'enthusiasm'. The
eighteenth century was indeed an 'age of Reason', of deism, freemasonry –
the ideas which we have seen associated with the industrial improvers
under George III; so perhaps we can clearly see a Civil War heritage here.
By the early eighteenth century the decline of providential religion had led
to a new sense of empiricism and experiment, of the potential solubility of
problems, and therefore a Kuhnian paradigm change to views much more
suitable for industrialisation. Professor Anthony Wallace writes of the
basic change of scientific paradigm as occurring from about 1690: the Sav-
ery steam engine was invented in 1698, Newcomen's in 1705, and both
soon found ready markets among the coalmining gentry of South Wales.[2]
(We may recall here that a more primitive steam engine was invented in the
1650s by the Marquis of Worcester, who spent the Cromwellian decade in
exile or domestic disfavour.)

So, some case can be made for arguing that the long-term effects of the
Civil War contributed to industrialisation. But equally, industrialisation
can be explained in terms of factors which have little or no relationship to
the Civil War.

War

The events which made an enormous difference to the county's industrial
history were rather those French wars which kept demand for iron and
other metals so constant from 1689 to 1713, again in the War of the Aust-
rian Succession, the Seven Years War, and the wars against the American
and French revolutions. Industrial growth in the 1690s may be attributed
to the puritan background of Mackworth or to the new climate of

scepticism promoting research and inqury; but also of undoubted significance was the long war with Louis XIV and all it meant for demand and government contracts. War meant more colonies to serve as markets and sources of raw materials, and it meant more foreign foods to create and feed a market in Britain. In turn, it helped provide an incentive for technological improvements just as significant as the growth of empirical and secular thought. By the 1760s the armed services were also providing many of the key economic modernisers.

Political partisanship

I have argued that exclusion from political life tended to act as an incentive to economic improvement, and illustrated this by the case of Beaufort and his allies in and around Swansea – the catholic industrialist Rowland Pytt, the nonjuror Morrises. I have also suggested elsewhere that freemasonry arose at least as much from jacobite foundations as from any independent deist traditions. The Welsh lodges which provided so many of the improvers of the 1770s were overwhelmingly made up of old jacobite families. Only in the most tenuous and indirect way could the exclusion of jacobite gentry after 1714 be called an effect of the Civil War. England was distinguished by its intense level of party conflict, which frequently excluded people from access to central power, and left wealthy landed families free to pursue industrial development. This same party conflict ensured the frequent presence of gentry in London as MPs or courtiers, and here metropolitan standards were acquired at first hand, to be imitated later at home. So, the frequency of parliaments meeting under William III and Anne helped to expand the consumer market for goods, leisure and services.

Britain and Europe

The landowning elites of Britain were not unique in many of the factors which they experienced after 1660, and which can be seen to have contributed to economic growth. In other countries of Europe, popular culture declined in the eighteenth century, suggesting the same decline of noble patronage and perhaps a similar fusion into national ruling classes.[3] This was for de Tocqueville the major trend in French society during the eighteenth century: the standards of the metropolis became ubiquitous, differences diminished between aristocracy and bourgeoisie, and the land owners tended to abandon the countryside.[4] It may also be that similar demographic rises were very widespread in the Europe of the Enlightenment. Professor Richet noted that French Atlantic ports enjoyed a trade-boom from the 1680s, which contributed to industrial development further inland: a pattern which sounds very much like the relationship between Bristol and South Wales.[5] Again, both urban and landed elites throughout Europe developed the same social fashions for English polite culture – for journals like the *Spectator*, for novels, indeed for most things English. Freemasonry established itself throughout Europe during the 'Anglomania' which prevailed between about 1720 and 1750.[6] So, we might expect similar patterns of demand to stimulate similar consumer industries in other countries, and perhaps roughly simultaneous industrial revolutions.

There is a substantial literature on the question of why England achieved the first industrial 'take-off', but two major factors emerge here.[7] One is that English law had long encouraged trade and industrial development at many levels of society, from the aristocrat to the small farmer. It emphasised absolute ownership in land, the right to dispose of property as one pleased at death, the landowner's right to minerals found under his property; and it thus promoted enterprise and individualism. Secondly, it may well be that the landowners who emerged under such a system might have been much richer than many Continental counterparts. By the standards of an area like Toulouse or northern Italy, a petty Glamorgan squire of the 1770s was on a par with the wealthiest local aristocrat, and was consequently at least as able to mobilise capital for investment in industrial or colonial ventures.[8] If therefore the political climate provided Glamorgan gentry with an incentive to improve their estates, they had much more capacity to promote substantial change. If new social fashions required certain investments or purchases, then they had more disposable income to divert to that purpose. This was true of ninety or so estates in this one county, in addition to the staggering wealth of a magnate like Beaufort; so British industry was dealing with both a very large market, and a great potential for investment.

It might therefore be that after centuries of the operation of British land and inheritance law, a major economic take-off required only a slight stimulus. This occurred partly through the events of the 1640s, and the long political crises resulting from the failure to settle the religious issues arising from these years. European war provided further stimulus, and new markets were created by changes within landed society itself. By the

1750s, social and political factors were combining to create a truly 'revolutionary' economic situation.

Questions for future research

How may these speculative suggestions be tested? Certainly more local studies are needed for the years between 1660 and 1780, if only to see if other county communities were so thoroughly transformed under the first two Georges. In defining other questions, it is first necessary to decide in what areas our findings about Glamorgan may prove to have arisen from unusual local circumstances, and which conclusions may have more general validity.

It might be argued that findings about the loss of cultural homogeneity of Glamorgan would not be more widely applicable because this was mainly a Welsh-speaking county. This may be so, but the break-up of an earlier community of belief elsewhere could be observed through attitudes to popular culture and recreations (on the valuable model of Dr Malcolmson's *Popular recreations in English society*). Also, the development of a uniform ruling class accent might have had social consequences equivalent to those of the linguistic change in Wales. New economic *mores* and views of law and crime would be similar in English counties.

Geographical factors also make the Glamorgan evidence distinctive. Few counties were so sharply divided between a gentrified zone and one in which squires were almost unknown; few were such a juxtaposition of two areas, each wealthy in such a totally different way. Also, Glamorgan belonged to a distinct economic and cultural area based on Bristol. We would perhaps expect similar patterns in other gentry counties clustered around a commercial metropolis which was a major part of the Atlantic and colonial trade – around Liverpool, Whitehaven, perhaps even Glasgow. But the economic emphasis of each of these zones would differ from Bristol's. It would be interesting to find if belonging to one of these metropolitan areas also meant that there were definite economic reasons for tory loyalty in the eighteenth century. Was Glamorgan toryism of that period unique in being such an appropriate ideology for industrialists and entrepreneurs?

In studying economic development, I have laid particular emphasis on the activities of Sir Humphrey Mackworth in the 1690s, the reactions to his enterprises, and the influence of these rivalries on later industrialisation. Was the boom of the 1690s chiefly caused by the aggressive incursion of one man, or did other countries share a similar development at this time? If so, can this be used as evidence for the theory of technological paradigm change?

On political matters, Glamorgan did have definite peculiarities, which is an important fact if (as I have argued) the intensity of political partisanship influenced social and economic development. South-east Wales and adjacent English shires were very unusual because of the presence of the Somerset family, an immensely rich catholic or crypto-papist house who were sufficiently close to royal favour to be appointed the Stuarts' representatives in the area. This meant that there were political crises in which one could be a loyal protestant, or a royalist, but rarely both at once. Anglican royalism and toryism were therefore slow to develop, and political divisions in the area were extremely bitter. The fanatical politics of south-east Wales were unlikely to be paralleled elsewhere in England or Wales, except perhaps in Lancashire or Northumberland, where there were also violent confrontations between catholics and ultra-protestants. I have suggested elsewhere that in both political parties under William and Anne, there was an over-representation of activists from each of these areas (the Welsh Border, Lancashire and the North-East).[9]

This fact has wide implications. The presence of Worcester's power around Swansea meant that much early Glamorgan industry was developed by the political 'Right', by catholics or nonjurors. Was this the sole explanation for the high tory role in industry here? It also meant that there was a clear tory background to radical and masonic campaigns for economic and municipal reform in Glamorgan after 1760. More local studies are needed on the political background and connections of modernisers and improvers between about 1760 and 1800, to examine the role of radical toryism and of freemasonry. Dr John Money's study of the west Midlands in this period is a valuable contribution, but even here, the implications of masonic strength are not fully explored, and neither is the question of tory continuity.[10]

In the context of demographic change, I have argued elsewhere that Glamorgan was not unusual in the crisis endured by its gentry in the early eighteenth century. Such a phenomenon was common in other British local communities and apparently among landed elites in many parts of Europe. Was this indeed the case, or were only certain regions affected? If my findings here are generally applicable, we should find a dramatic cultural break in most shires between about 1710 and 1760. This would help to explain much about political and economic developments, about family structure and the new prestige of professional and commercial families. But why did the change occur? If the gentry had such a strong sense of family, of place and of continuity, why should they have committed family suicide? To take a specific example: Sir Charles Kemys died unmarried in 1735 at the age of 47, knowing that his sister's son would acquire the estate. Why was he prepared to do this? More important, why were there so many like him in this age?

The largest area for future research would be in the comparison of British and European local studies. If we really find the same demographic crisis of the gentry throughout much of Europe, then this is a fact of some importance. Again, we need comparative studies of landed estates and incomes, of the work and training of stewards, or the regional economic influence of great ports. Did Bordeaux or Nantes affect surrounding landed estates as Bristol affected its own neighbours? A study of two regions, one in Britain, one in France or the Netherlands, could illustrate much about the strength and composition of the professional classes, and their role as markets for consumer goods.[11]

In politics, what was the social impact of the unusual sophistication of party organisation and factional clubs in Britain? It might be, for instance, that the existence of national parties and regional structure contributed to the development of a sense of nationalism among the British ruling elite. Perhaps such party activism gave expertise and self-confidence to those 'middling' groups so essential in preserving a political interest – to a Marmaduke Gibbs or a Nathaniel Taynton. When British travellers exported the institution of freemasonry – in many ways, a familiar insular combination of social club and party cabal – it made an immense impact throughout Europe because of its total novelty there. Or, was Britain really so distinct? If it was, does this help to explain Britain's divergence from European patterns in other ways? It will be apparent that I am again utilising theories evolved to analyse contemporary modernisation in Third World countries. Did Britain modernise so early in part because of its bitter political struggles? This of course assumes that British ruling elites were unusually advanced in their consciousness of belonging to a national class. Comparative European studies might question this view.[12]

In summary, what is needed is for the century after the Restoration to be as well served with local British studies as in the period leading up to the Civil War; and a greater number of comparative studies is needed to place British developments in their European context. This book has suggested from the evidence of Glamorgan that what may divide the British provinces from their European counterparts was the great wealth and political sophistication of the former, the homogeneity and flexibility of the ruling class. Contemporary Europeans were astonished by the wealth and turbulent independence of the British gentry: perhaps more modern historians might investigate the consequences of these attributes.

Appendices

Appendix 1: Parliamentary service by Glamorgan landowners 1640 – 1800

Glamorgan county members

1640 (Long Parliament) Philip, Lord Herbert
1654 Philip Jones of Fonmon
     Edmund Thomas of Wenvoe
1656 (same)
1658 Evan Seys of Boverton
1660 Sir Edward Mansell of Margam
1661 William, Lord Herbert of Cardiff
1670 Edward Mansell (see 1660)
1679 Bussy Mansell of Briton Ferry
1681, 1685 Edward Mansell (see 1660)
1689, 1690, 1695, 1698 Bussy Mansell (see 1679)
1699 Thomas Mansell of Margam
1701 Thomas Mansell of Briton Ferry
1701, 1704, 1706, 1708, 1710 Thomas Mansell of Margam (see 1699)
1712 Robert Jones of Fonmon
1716, 1722, 1727 Sir Charles Kemys of Cefn Mabli
1734 William Talbot of Hensol
1737, 1741 Bussy Mansell of Briton Ferry
1745 Thomas Matthews of Llandaff
1747, 1754 Charles Edwin of Llanmihangel
1756 Thomas William Matthews of Llandaff
1761 Sir Edmund Thomas of Wenvoe
1767 Richard Turberville of Ewenni
1768, 1774 George Venables Vernon of Briton Ferry
1780, 1784 Charles Edwin of Llanmihangel and Dunraven
1789, 1814 Thomas Wyndham of Dunraven

Glamorgan borough members

1640 William Herbert of Cogan and Friars
1646 Algernon Sydney
1654, 1656 John Price of Gellihir
1660 Bussy Mansell (see county 1679)
1661, 1679 Robert Thomas of Llanmihangel

1681 Bussy Mansell
1685 Francis Gwyn of Llansannor
1689, 1690, 1695, 1698 Thomas Mansell of Margam (see county 1699)
1698 Edward Stradling of St Donat's
1701, 1704 Thomas Mansell of Briton Ferry
1706, 1708 Sir John Aubrey of Llantrithyd
1710, 1715 Edward Stradling (see 1698)
1722 Edward Stradling of St Donat's
1727 Bussy Mansell of Briton Ferry (see county 1737)
1734 Herbert Windsor of Cardiff
1739, 1741, 1747, 1754, 1761 Herbert Mackworth of Gnoll
1766, 1768, 1774, 1780, 1784 Herbert Mackworth of Gnoll
1790 Hon. John Stuart
1794 Evelyn James Stuart
1802 William Stuart

MPs for other counties or boroughs

Sir Thomas Aubrey	Wallingford 1784
Sir John Aubrey	Brackley 1698 (see borough 1706)
Sir John Aubrey	Various constituencies 1768 – 1826 including Bucks. 1784
Charles Edwin	Westminster 1742 (see county 1747)
Samuel Edwin	Minehead 1717
Francis Gwyn	Various English constituencies 1673 – 1727 (see borough 1685)
Francis Gwyn	Wells 1741 – 54
Edward Prideaux Gwyn	Wells 1727 – 9
Sir Rowland Gwynne	Radnorshire 1678 – 85; Brecon borough 1689, 1698, 1700
Sir Leoline Jenkins	Hythe 1671; Oxford University 1678, 1679, 1681
Sir Charles Kemys	Monmouthshire 1685, 1695; Monmouth 1690
Sir Charles Kemys	Monmouthshire 1713 – 15 (see county 1716)
Sir Charles Kemys-Tynte	Somerset 1747 – 74; Monmouth 1745
Richard Lewis of Van	Westbury 1679 – 1700
Thomas Lewis of Van	Various constituencies 1708 – 36, including Hampshire 1713
Sir Humphrey Mackworth	Cardigan 1701, 1702, 1710; Totnes 1705
William Mackworth-Praed	St Ives 1734 – 41
Robert Mansell of Margam	Minehead 1721
Thomas Mansell of Briton Ferry	Brecon 1678, 1679
Thomas William Matthews	Carmarthen 1747 – 51
Evan Seys	Gloucester 1661 – 82 (see county 1658)
Charles Talbot	Tregony 1719 – 20; Durham 1722 – 34
John Talbot	Brecon 1734 – 54; Ilchester 1754 – 6

Sir Edmund Thomas	Chippenham 1741 – 54 (see county 1761)
Walter Wilkins	Radnorshire 1796 – 1828
Thomas Wyndham	Truro 1721; Dunwich 1727

Appendix 2: The 'secondary' gentry families

Family	Estate	Title 1673 (1)	Number of hearths 1670
Aubrey	Bonvilston	Esq.	
Bennett	Pitt		8
Bowen	Kittle	Esq.	
Dawkins	Kilvrough		7
Evans	Eaglesbush	Esq.	
Evans	Gwernllwynchwyth	Gent.	6
Gamage	Bridgend	Esq.	
Gamage	Newcastle	Esq.	8
Gibbs	Llangynwyd		7
Herbert	Cilybebill	Esq.	
Herbert	Cogan	Gent.	8
Howells	Roath		
Lewis	Carnlloyd	Esq.	
Lewis	Llanishen	Esq.	17(6)
Lewis	Newhouse		10
Lewis	Ynysfargoed	Esq.	
Lewis	Ynysarwed		8
Llewellyn	Ynysgerwn	Gent.	8
Mansell	Henllys	Esq.	
Mansell	Penrice		
Matthews	Maesmawr	Gent.	9
Morgan	Llanrhymni		
Philipps	Penrhiwtyn		6
Price	Gellihir		15
Price	Penllergaer		14
Prichard	Llancaeach		
St John	Highlight	Gent.	
Seys	Rhyddings	Esq.	10
Stradling	Roath	Esq.	
Thomas	Llanbradach	Esq.	10
Thomas	Moulton	Esq.	
Traherne	Brofiscen	Esq.	
Watkins	Gower		

(1) Blome, *Britannia*

Appendix 3: The 'tertiary' families

Family	Estate	Title 1673	1735	Number of hearths 1670
Andrews	Cadoxton	Gent.		6
Aubrey	Pencoed	Gent.		
Bassett	Bonvilston	Gent.		
Burnett	Laleston			5
Cornish	Cowbridge		Esq.	
Deere	Ashall	Gent.	Gent.	
Deere	Penlline		Esq.	6
Deere	Roose			5
Edwards	Llandaff	Gent.		5
Evans	Llantwit			
Fleming	Penlline	Gent.		5
Gamage	Giblod	Gent.		4
Gibbon	Trecastle	Gent.		
Giles	Gileston	Gent.		6
Greenuff	Wern-y-domen	Gent.		
Harris	Bryncoch	Gent.		4
Herbert	Eglwys Ilan			
Herbert	Gyfylchi	Gent.		
Jenkins	Cowbridge	Gent.		5
Jenkins	Hendrewen			
Jenkins	Morlas			
Jenkins	Pantynawel	Gent.		5
Jones	Caerwigga	Gent.	8	
Jones	Dyffryn	Gent.		7
Jones	Gelliwastod			
Jones	Llantrithyd	Gent.		4
Llewellyn	Cwrt Colman			
Lucas	Stouthall		Esq.	7
Matthews	Flaxland	Gent.		
Matthews	Whitchurch	Gent.		6
Miles	Gabalfa	Gent.		8
Morgan	Abergorci	Gent.		
Morgan	Coedygoras	Gent.		
Morgan	Mynachdy	Gent.		5
Morgan	Rhiwbina		Gent.	7

Table – Appendix 3: The 'tertiary' families (*cont.*)

Family	Estate	Title 1673	1735	Number of hearths 1670
Nicholl	Ham			4
Nicholl	Llanmaes			
Perkins	St y Nyll	Gent.	Gent.	6
Popkins	Forest		Esq.	4
Portrey	Ynyscedwyn			6
Powell	Coytrahen		Esq.	
Powell	Energlyn		Esq.	6
Powell	Llandow	Gent.		5
Powell	Llanharan		Gent.	5
Powell	Llysworney			5
Powell	Llwydarth	Gent.		7
Powell	Maesteg	Gent.		8
Powell	Maydan	Gent.		7
Powell	Penyfai	Gent.		
Powell	Tondu		Gent.	
Price	Bettws			5
Price	Boverton			
Price	Cwrtycarne			
Price	Gellidarth	Gent.		
Price	Merthyr			7
Price	Pontypandy			
Prichard	Collenau		Esq.	
Rice	Llanpha	Gent.		
Stradling		Gent.		
Thomas	Baglan			7
Thomas	Brigan	Gent.		
Thomas	Cadoxton			
Thomas	Ogmore			
Thomas	Pwllywrach		Gent.	10
Thomas	Rudry	Gent.		
Thomas	Tredomen			
Thomas	Tregroes			8
Towgood	Wenvoe		Esq.	
Trotter	St Nicholas			
Wilkins	Llanblethian		Esq.	6
Williams	Aberpergwm	Gent.	Esq.	8
Williams	Blaen Baglan			9
Williams	Dyffryn	Esq.		
Williams	Pendoylan			
Williams	Park			
Williams	St Nicholas	Gent.		10

Appendix 4: The Mansell family and their connections with the greater gentry

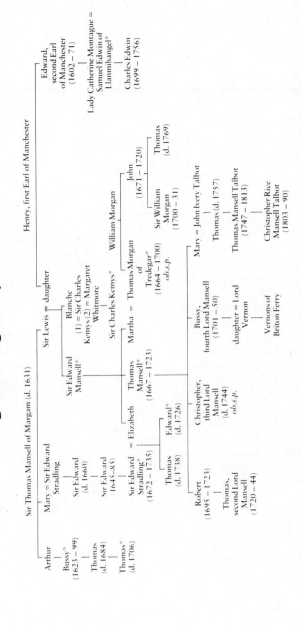

295

Note:

* Refers to those gentlemen who in 1694 signed an agreement regulating the horseracing on Ogmore Down (P&M 755). It specifies, for example, the weight carried, distance run, and value of the prize. Of ten signatories, nine belonged to the broad 'cousinship' of county society. The other, William Herbert of Friars, was almost certainly a 'cousin' of these families, but I cannot discover the exact relationship.

Appendix 5: The roundhead and puritan family links of the Thomases of Wenvoe

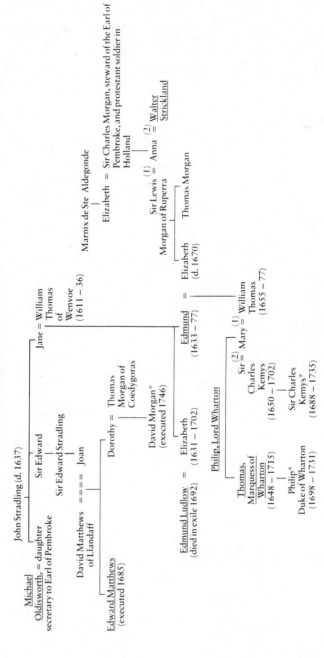

Note:
In this genealogy, puritan and whig leaders are underlined; prominent jacobites have an asterisk after their names.

Notes

General introduction

1 P. Jenkins, 'The origins of antipopery on the Welsh Marches in the seventeenth century', *Historical Journal*, 23 (1980), 278.
2 J. Baker, *A picturesque guide through Wales* (Worcester, 1795), p. 122.
3 *HMC Egmont MSS*, vol. 2, pp. 47–8; T. Dineley, *The official progress of the Duke of Beaufort through Wales in 1684*, ed. R. W. Banks (London, 1888), p. 314.
4 See below, Chapter 3.
5 *GCH*; Gareth E. Jones, 'The Glamorgan gentry 1563–1603' (MA thesis, University of Wales, 1963); M. Robbins, 'The agricultural, domestic, social and cultural interests of the gentry in south-east Glamorgan 1540–1640' (Ph.D thesis, University of Wales, 1974); H. A. Lloyd, *The gentry of south-west Wales 1540–1640* (Cardiff, 1968).
6 G. E. Mingay, *The gentry: the rise and fall of a ruling class* (London, 1976), and his *English landed society in the eighteenth century* (London, 1963); E. Moir, *Local government in Gloucestershire* (Bristol and Gloucestershire Archaeological Society, 1969), vol. 8; P. Roebuck, *Yorkshire baronets* (Hull University Press, 1980). See also C. W. Chalklin, *Seventeenth-century Kent* (London, 1965) and J. V. Beckett, *Coal and tobacco: the Lowthers and the economic development of west Cumberland, 1660–1770* (CUP, 1981).
7 C. Clay, 'Marriage, inheritance and the rise of large estates in England 1660–1815', *Ec.HR*, 2nd ser., 21 (1968); J. V. Beckett, 'English landownership in the later seventeenth and eighteenth centuries: the debate and the problems', *Ec.HR*, 2nd ser., 30 (1977). See also J. O. Martin, 'The landed estate in Glamorgan c. 1660 to 1760' (Ph.D thesis, University of Cambridge, 1978).
8 J. T. Cliffe, *The Yorkshire gentry from the Reformation to the Civil War* (London, 1969). J. S. Morrill, *Cheshire 1630–60* (OUP, 1974).
9 A. de Tocqueville, *The old regime and the French Revolution*, translated by S. Gilbert (New York, 1955), pp. 72 – 80, 120–37; M. Hechter, *Internal colonialism* (London, 1975), pp. 117–18.
10 The diary is available in facsimile form in CCL.
11 P. Jenkins, 'The demographic decline of the landed gentry in the eighteenth century', *WHR*, 11(1982), 31–49.
12 J. H. Plumb, *The growth of political stability in England* (London, 1967); G. Holmes, *British politics in the age of Anne* (London, 1967).

13 P. S. Fritz, 'Jacobitism and the English government 1717–31' (Ph.D thesis, University of Cambridge, 1967).
14 E. Cruickshanks, *Political untouchables* (London, 1979).
15 P. Jenkins, 'Jacobites and freemasons in eighteenth-century Wales', *WHR*, 9 (1979), 391–406.

1 Land and people

1 See below, Chapters 4 and 5, for political history. The Tawe was also the border between the dioceses of Llandaff and St David's.
2 The geographical account which follows is based on C. J. O. Evans, *Glamorgan, its history and topography*, new edn (Cardiff, 1945); W. Rees (ed.), *Glamorgan County History* (Cardiff, 1936), vol. 1.
3 These are typical comments from the numerous tories of the late eighteenth century. For 'Arcadia', see John Fox, *General views of the agriculture of Glamorgan, with observations on plans for improvement* (London, 1796), p. 15; John Thirsk, *The agrarian history of England and Wales* (CUP, 1967), vol. 4, p. 134.
4 S. Jones, 'Floods and sea defences', *Transactions of the Port Talbot Historical Society* (1977), 6–15. L579, L638, L768. Bodl. MS Willis 36, fo. 107.
5 J. Garsed, *Records of the Glamorgan Agricultural Society from the date of its establishment in 1772 to the year 1890* (Cardiff, 1890).
6 P. Jenkins, 'The roads of early modern Glamorgan', *Transactions of the Port Talbot Historical Society*, 3 (1981), 92–101.
7 A. H. Williams (ed.), *John Wesley in Wales* (Cardiff, University of Wales, 1971).
8 See below, Section 7, 'Radicals and dissenters'.
9 C. Hibbert (ed.), *An American in Regency England* (London, 1968), pp. 64–71; G. A. Williams, *The Merthyr rising* (London, 1978).
10 The south-western orientation is a frequent theme of gentry correspondence: see, for example, P&M; KT; ULS Mackworth; M. I. Williams, 'Some aspects of the economic and social life of the southern regions of Glamorgan 1600–1800', *Morgannwg*, 3 (1959), 21–40; M. I. Williams, 'Agriculture and society in Glamorgan 1660–1760' (Ph.D thesis, University of Leicester, 1967).
11 D. Moore (ed.), *The Irish Sea province in archaeology and history* (Cardiff, University of Wales, 1970).
12 In 1980, it was claimed that a site near Barry was the main late Roman naval base for the Irish Sea region, as vital a fortification as the 'Saxon Shore'-type castle at nearby Cardiff. 'Cold Knap', *Current Archaeology*, 7 (1981), 116–18.
13 NLW Add. MS 1689c, fo. 452.
14 PRO SP 36/76, fo. 440.
15 W. E. Minchinton, 'Bristol: Metropolis of the west in the eighteenth century', *TRHS*, 5th ser., 4(1954), 69–85.
16 *GCH*, pp. 342–3.
17 P. Smith, *Houses of the Welsh countryside* (London, HMSO, 1975), pp. 277,

341, 367, 487; B. Howells, 'The distribution of customary acres in South Wales', *NLWJ*, 15 (1967–8). For the disunity of Welsh history, see K. O. Morgan, *Rebirth of a nation: Wales 1880–1980* (OUP, 1981).

18 E. G. Bowen, *Saints, seaways and settlements* (Cardiff, University of Wales, 1977).

19 P. Jenkins, 'South Wales and Munster in the eighteenth century', *Journal of the Cork Historical and Archaeological Society* (1980).

20 L. Owen, 'The population of Wales in the sixteenth and seventeenth centuries', *TCS* (1959), 99–113; Williams, 'Agriculture and society', pp. 19–38. The Glamorgan hearth-tax is PRO E 179.221, fo. 294.

21 B. Ll. James, 'The Vale of Glamorgan 1780–1850' (MA thesis, University of Wales, 1971), pp. 1–8.

22 I. Soulsby and D. Jones, 'Historic towns of Wales', *Current Archaeology*, 53 (1975), 179–81. R. A. Griffiths, *Boroughs of medieval Wales* (Cardiff, University of Wales, 1978).

23 H. Carter, 'The growth and decline of Welsh towns', in D. Moore (ed.), *Wales in the eighteenth century* (Swansea, 1976), pp. 47–62.

24 James, 'Vale'; D. W. Howell, *Land and people in nineteenth-century Wales* (London, 1977).

25 Bodl. MS Willis 36, fos. 45–51.

26 S. Williams, *The Garden of Wales* (Cowbridge, 1961), p. 101; for deferential attitudes, see NLW Add. MS 6608E.

27 James, 'Vale', p. 165.

28 Ibid., p. 93; NLW Add. MS 13114B, fo. 85.

29 W. Davies, *General view of the agriculture of Glamorgan with observations on plans for improvement* (London, 1815), p. 215.

30 ULS Mackworth MS (BJ) 540; Fox, *General view*, pp. 45–7; Arthur Young, *A six weeks tour through the southern counties of England and Wales* (London, 1772), p. 166.

31 *GCH*, pp. 334–60.

32 Bodl. MS Willis 36, fo. 129 v, 131.

33 Although for the area's vagrant and itinerant population, see, for example, A. J. Johnes, *Essay on the causes which have produced dissent from the Established Church in the principality of Wales* (London, 1832), p. 10; and Iolo Davies, *A certaine schoole* (Cowbridge, 1967), p. 55.

34 B. Ll. James, 'The Welsh language in the Vale of Glamorgan', *Morgannwg*, 16 (1972), 16–37.

35 Clearly apparent in Williams, *Wesley in Wales*; and in the methodist correspondence preserved in the Cheshunt MSS at Westminster College, Cambridge (see, for instance, F/1/52).

36 NLW Church in Wales MSS, LL/CC/(G) series, for example, 183, 203, 218, 301, 657.

37 G. Grant-Francis, *The lordship of Gower in the Marches of Wales* (Cambrian Archaeological Association, supplement, 1861); H. Thomas, 'The industrialisation of a Glamorgan parish', *NLWJ*, 19 (1975), 194–209.

38 NLW Badminton MS 2183; P. Jenkins, 'Two poems on the Glamorgan gentry from the reign of James II', *NLWJ*, 21 (1979), 176–8.
39 NLW Badminton MS 2323; G. Grant-Francis, *The value of holdings in Glamorgan and Swansea in 1545 and 1717* (Swansea, 1869).
40 John Adams, *Index villaris*, 2nd edn (London, 1690).
41 Joan Thirsk, 'Industries in the countryside', in F. J. Fisher (ed.), *Essays in the economic and social history of Tudor and Stuart England* (CUP, 1961), pp. 70–89.
42 Such families in Llangyfelach were the Williams' (NLW Cilybebill MSS 72, 94) or Matthews (NLW Penllergaer MSS, bundle 4).
43 A. C. Davies, 'Aberdare 1750–1850' (MA thesis, University of Wales, 1963), pp. 16–18; John Davies, 'Glamorgan and the Bute estate' (Ph.D thesis, University of Wales, 1969), p. 35.
44 See below, Chapters 5 and 6.
45 NLW Badminton MS 2323.
46 NLW Badminton MSS 2321–414; J. O. Martin, 'Mineral property disputes', *WHR*, 9 (1978).
47 NLW Badminton MSS 2120, 2334.
48 M. Clement, *Correspondence and records of the S.P.C.K. relating to Wales 1699–1740*, Board of Celtic Studies, History and Law Series, no. 10 (Cardiff, University of Wales, 1952), pp. 12–64; Erasmus Saunders, *A view of the state of religion in the diocese of St. David's* (London, 1721).
49 R. L. Hugh, 'Annibyniaeth yng Ngorllewin Morgannwg 1646–1816' (MA thesis, University of Wales, 1945), p. 102.
50 P. Jenkins, '"The old leaven": the Welsh roundheads after 1660', *Historical Journal* (forthcoming, 1981–2).
51 M. Watts, *The dissenters* (OUP, 1978), vol. 1, pp. 507–10.
52 NLW Church in Wales MSS, LL/QA/1–2; SD/QA/1–2.
53 For example, *DWB*, 'Henry Davies' (1696–1766).
54 David Jenkins, 'The role of craftsmen in the religious history of modern Wales', *Welsh Anvil*, 6 (1962), 90–105; and numerous entries in *DWB*.
55 NLW Add. MS 398B; DWT, 28 July 1766.
56 P&M 9125.
57 E. T. Davies, *Religion in the Industrial Revolution in South Wales* (Cardiff, 1965).
58 For riots, see, for example, NLW Penllergaer MS 1153; P&M 6092; G. Roberts, *Aspects of Welsh history* (Cardiff, 1969), p. 68; P. Jenkins, 'A new source for the history of Monmouthshire in the eighteenth century', *Monmouthshire Antiquary*, 4 (1980), 47.
59 E. P. Thompson, 'The crime of anonymity' in D. Hay, P. Linebaugh *et al.* (eds.), *Albion's fatal tree* (London, 1975), p. 327.
60 D. J. V. Jones, *Before Rebecca* (London, 1973), p. 20.
61 Williams, *Merthyr rising, passim*. David Smith (ed.), *A people and a proletariat* (London, 1980), especially pp. 16–46, 72–93.

2 The gentry

1 A. H. Dodd, *Studies in Stuart Wales*, 2nd edn (Cardiff, University of Wales, 1971).
2 P. D. G. Thomas, 'Politics in Glamorgan 1700 to 1750', *Morgannwg*, 6 (1962), 52–78.
3 R. Blome, *Britannia* (London, 1673), pp. 460–2.
4 Adams, *Index villaris*.
5 Williams, 'Agriculture and society', pp. 49, 146–9.
6 L. and J. F. Stone, 'Country houses and their owners in Hertfordshire', in W. O. Aydelotte *et al.* (eds.), *Quantitative dimensions in historical research* (London, 1972).
7 BL Harl. MS 6804, fos. 180–1.
8 R. Symonds, *Diary of the marches of the royal army during the great Civil War*, ed. C. E. Long (London, Camden Society, 1859), pp. 216–17.
9 P&M 977.
10 Bodl. MS Willis 36, fos. 617–29. See Appendix 1 for MPs.
11 T. Nicholas, *Annals and antiquities of the counties and county families of Wales* (London, 1872).
12 Ibid., p. 5.
13 *Memoirs of Thomas Bruce, Earl of Ailesbury* (London, Roxburghe Club, 1890), vol. 2, p. 562. See Appendix 4 for the family's connections.
14 C. A. Maunsell and E. P. Statham, *History of the family of Maunsell* (London, 1917–20), vols. 1–4; A. L. Evans, *Margam Abbey* (Port Talbot, 1958).
15 J. B. Davies, 'The Matthews family', in R. Denning (ed.), *Glamorgan historian* (Cowbridge, 1976), vol. 2, pp. 171–87.
16 G. Williams, *Welsh Reformation essays* (Cardiff, University of Wales, 1967), pp. 91–110.
17 PRO SP 29/398, fos. 257–8.
18 A. G. Veysey, 'Colonel Philip Jones 1618–74' (MA thesis, University of Wales, 1958).
19 NLW Add. MS 6139C.
20 See below, Chapter 4 and see Appendices 2 and 3 for secondary and tertiary families.
21 J. Cule (ed.), *Wales and medicine* (Cardiff, 1975), pp. 190–223.
22 *DWB*, 'Sir Noah Thomas'.
23 P&M L1206.
24 P. Jenkins, 'The Gibbs family: law and politics in Stuart Glamorgan', *Morgannwg* (forthcoming, 1982).
25 See below, Chapter 6.
26 CCL MS 4.829; GRO D/DKT/1/73–6.
27 Ordination records in NLW Church in Wales MSS.
28 DWT, June 1764.
29 Roebuck, *Baronets*, pp. 272–88; Jenkins, 'Demographic decline'; T. H. Hollingsworth, 'Demography of the British peerage', *Population studies*, sup-

plement, 18 (1964); Lloyd Bonfield, 'Marriage settlements and the rise of great estates: the demographic aspect', *Ec.HR*, 2nd ser., 32 (1979), 483–94. For contemporary comment, see Bodl. MS Willis 42, fo. 245 v.

30 Martin, 'Landed estate'.

31 ULS Mackworth MS, Box N letter of Sir Humphrey Mackworth (1713).

32 H. A. Wyndham, *A family history 1688–1837* (OUP, 1950); Clay, 'Marriage'.

33 RISW, typescript, 'Swansea and Glamorgan calendar', vol. 3, p. 423.

34 See below, Chapter 7. The new houses built between about 1760 and 1810 were: Kilvrough, Wenvoe, Fonmon, Briton Ferry, Coedarhydarglyn, Stouthall, Gnoll, Clasemont, Penrice, Welsh St Donat's, Cardiff Castle, Singleton, Marino, Llanbradach, Dunraven, Glyncollen, Merthyr Mawr, Clyne and Baglan. J. P. Jenkins, 'The creation of an "ancient gentry": Glamorgan 1760–1840', *WHR* (forthcoming).

3 Economic development

1 W. Scott (ed.), *Somers tracts: a collection of scarce and valuable tracts from many collections, principally that of the late Lord Somers* (12 vols., London, 1809–20), vol. 10, pp. 596–7.

2 P&M 6668–82.

3 The houses of Van, Llantrithyd and Llansannor came to own more lands outside the county than in it.

4 Especially for Margam, Wenvoe and Hensol.

5 P&M L563; N. Luttrell, *Brief historical relation of state affairs* (6 vols., Oxford, 1857), vol. 6, p. 110.

6 Nicholas, *Annals*, p. 133.

7 PRO SP 29/398, fos. 257–8.

8 Symonds, *Diary*, pp. 216–17.

9 T. C. Banks (ed.), *The antient usage of arms by Sir W. Dugdale, Knight...* (London, 1811), pp. 171–2.

10 Robbins, 'Gentry', pp. 59–72; Martin, 'Landed estate', pp. 23–8, 202–10.

11 Mingay, *Gentry*, pp. 11–17.

12 NLW Tredegar MS 315; P&M 1926.

13 NLW Wynnstay MS C106.

14 A. MacInnes, *Robert Harley, puritan politician* (London, 1970), p. 19.

15 J. M. Howells, 'The Crosswood estate' (MA thesis, University of Wales, 1956), pp. 323–9.

16 For a typically poor Welsh country, see P. R. Roberts, 'The landed gentry in Merionethshire' (MA thesis, University of Wales, 1963), p. 96.

17 Bodl. MS Tanner 147, fo. 121 r; MS Walker C4, fos. 63–72.

18 See below, Chapter 4.

19 Martin, 'Landed estate', pp. 45–56. From numerous references in gentry correspondence, see, for example, P&M 332, L341, L449.

20 P&M 9368.

21 NLW Dunraven 1755, 12, will of John Wyndham, 17 August 1697.

22 P&M 9368.

23 See, for example, NLW KT, Mary to Sir Charles, 23 November 1689.

24 From many references, see GRO D/DN/230/2; GRO D/DF/F190; ULS Mackworth MS 380.
25 Martin, 'Landed estate', pp. 46–55; G. E. Mingay, 'The agricultural depression', *Ec.HR*, 2nd ser., 8 (1955–6), 323–8.
26 DWT, 25 January 1763; Jenkins, 'New source', pp. 48–9. For the 1740 riots, see T. S. Ashton and J. Sykes, *The coal industry of the eighteenth century* (Manchester University Press, 1929), pp. 118–21.
27 Mingay, *English landed society*, pp. 19–26; DWT, 23 January 1770, 1 May 1772; A. H. John, 'Farming 1793–1815' in E. L. Jones and G. E. Mingay (eds.), *Land, labour and population* (London, 1967), pp. 28–47.
28 Habakkuk, 'Landownership'; Clay, 'Marriage'; Beckett, 'Landownership'; G. E. Mingay, 'The large estate in the 18th century', in *Papers of the First International Conference of Economic History* (Stockholm, 1961), pp. 367–83.
29 Martin, 'Landed estate', pp. 202–89.
30 Jenkins, 'Demographic decline'.
31 A. H. Dodd, *History of Caernarvonshire 1284–1900* (Caernarvonshire Historical Society, 1968), p. 177.
32 P&M L811–12, L1560; for Bute, CCL MS 4.850.
33 James, 'Vale', pp. 35–9, 45–54. J. Britton, *Monmouthshire* (London, c. 1810), p. 26; D. W. Howell, 'The landed gentry of Pembrokeshire in the eighteenth century' (MA thesis, University of Wales, 1965).
34 J. Georgelin, 'A great estate in Venetia in the eighteenth century: Anguillara', in Marc Ferro (ed.), *Social historians in contemporary France: essays from 'Annales'* (New York, 1972), pp. 100–30.
35 R. Forster, *The nobility of Toulouse in the eighteenth century* (Baltimore, 1960), especially pp. 35–50.
36 James, 'Vale', pp. 35–54.
37 See below, 'Conclusion'.
38 H. M. Thomas, 'Margam estate management', in S. Williams (ed.), *Glamorgan historian* (1969), vol. 6, pp. 13–27.
39 From many examples, NLW Edwinsford MS 2881; P&M 2189; NLW Bute MSS, Box 93, J3.
40 Young, *Six weeks tour*, pp. 164–9; D. Thomas, 'Arthur Young in Wales', *BBCS*, 20 (1964), 413–21.
41 B. H. Malkin, *Scenery, antiquities and biography of South Wales* (London, 1803).
42 Mingay, *Gentry*, p. 84.
43 PRO SP 29/398, fos. 257–8.
44 NLW Add. MS 1914B; P. Jenkins, 'Mary Wharton and the rise of the new woman', *NLWJ*, 22 (1981), 170–86.
45 M. A. Havinden, 'Lime and agriculture in Devon', in C. Chalklin and M. A. Havinden (eds.), *Rural change and urban growth* (London, 1974), pp. 107–15. For enclosures, T. I. Jeffreys-Jones, 'The enclosure movement in South Wales' (MA thesis, University of Wales, 1936).
46 F. V. Emery, 'The early cultivation of clover in Gower', *Gower*, 26 (1975),

    45–52; see also P&M 2436, GRO D/DC/F2, GRO D/DN/230/1, CCL MS 3.618/3 – and many other references.

47 Young, *Six weeks tour*, p. 164; John Aubrey, *Brief lives*, ed. O. L. Dick (London, 1972), p. 52; Fox, *General view*, p. 32.

48 NLW Penllergaer MS 536; DWT, 1 February 1771, 16 June 1773; Bucks RO D/DR/8/13/3.

49 NLW KT, H. Richards to Sir Charles Kemys, 13 December 1695.

50 Fox, *General view*; Davies, *General view*.

51 Malkin, *Scenery*, p. 60.

52 P&M 2206; ULS Mackworth MSS 485–7; BJ480A; Add. MS IV.

53 Aubrey, *Brief lives*, p. 64; M. I. Williams, 'Further contribution to the commercial history of Glamorgan', *NLWJ*, 11 (1959–60), 342–3.

54 Mackworth MSS, Box P, letter of P. Courteen, 20 February 1741; Young, *Six weeks tour*, pp. 164–9.

55 For example, Fox, *General view*, p. 62; Davies, *General view*, vol. 1, p. 184, vol. 2, p. 485; NLW Add. MS 13114B, fo. 89.

56 Wyndham, *Family history*, p. 115.

57 A. H. John, *Industrial development of South Wales 1750–1850* (Cardiff, 1950), p. 129.

58 NLW Badminton MS 14448.

59 P&M 5971B.

60 G. E. Mingay, 'The eighteenth-century land steward' in Jones and Mingay, *Land, labour and population*, pp. 3–27; E. Hughes, 'The eighteenth-century estate agent' in H. A. Cronne, T. W. Moody and D. B. Quinn (eds.), *Essays in British and Irish history* (London, 1949), pp. 185–200; J. O. Martin, 'Estate stewards and their work in Glamorgan', *Morgannwg*, 23 (1979), 9–28.

61 From numerous references, see, for example, the NLW KT letters of the 1670s and 1680s; P&M 6007, P&M L591. ULS Mackworth MSS, letters of P. Courteen in the 1730s and 1740s.

62 CCL MS 2.716.

63 For the work of Beaufort's stewards in the west, see NLW Badminton MSS 1451, 2321–414; Martin, 'Mineral property disputes'; RISW, 'Gabriel Powell's survey of Gower 1764'.

64 Roebuck, *Baronets*, pp. 35, 258.

65 NLW Badminton MS 2323.

66 P&M L1282; Thomas, 'Margam estate management', pp. 13–27.

67 P&M 2587.

68 Martin, 'Estate stewards', p. 19.

69 P&M L1120, L1276–7, 2436.

70 PRO C5/508/48.

71 S. Williams (ed.), *Saints and sailing ships* (Cowbridge, 1962), p. 94.

72 See, for example, GROD/DN 268; NLWMS 11017E, letter of 21 January 1679.

73 J. T. Ward and R. G. Wilson (eds.), *Land and industry* (Newton Abbot, 1971); Mingay, *English landed society*, pp. 190–205.

74 W. Rees, *Industry before the Industrial Revolution* (2 vols., Cardiff, University

of Wales, 1968). A. H. John and Glanmor Williams (eds.), *Glamorgan County History: Industrial Glamorgan*, vol. 5 (Cardiff, University of Wales, 1980).

75 Lhuyd, 'Parochalia', p. 75.

76 For opposition to industry, see, for example, P&M 2600, 3249, 5508–9; ULS Mackworth MS 361; G. Grant-Francis, *The smelting of copper in the Swansea district* (London, 1881), p. 115.

77 Rees, *Industry*, vol. 1, pp. 90–109; L. W. Dillwyn, *A contribution towards the history of Swansea* (London, 1840) pp. 12–13.

78 B. M. Evans, 'The Welsh coal trade' (MA thesis, University of Wales, 1928), pp. 58–60; *The case of Sir Humphrey Mackworth and the Mine Adventurers* (London, 1705); P&M L1373.

79 Rees, *Industry*, vol. 1, pp. 300–2; L. J. Williams, 'A Glamorgan ironworks of the later seventeenth century', *NLWJ*, 11 (1959).

80 For the very uncommercial attitudes of the North Wales gentry, see, for example, NLW Brogyntyn MSS (Clenennau letters) 913.

81 *HMC Portland MSS*, vol. 3, p. 564.

82 E. Jenkins (ed.), *Neath and district: a symposium*, 2nd edn (Neath, 1974). Mackworth's developments are the subject of extensive papers and letters in the P&M collection, the NLW Donald C. Jones MSS, and, of course, the ULS Mackworth MSS. See especially P&M 3249.

83 R. D. Till, 'Proprietary politics in Glamorgan', *Morgannwg*, 14 (1972), 37–53; see below, Chapter 5; P&M 2600, 3249, 5558, 9023, 9028, L519–L529, and many others.

84 P&M L551.

85 Mingay, *English landed society*, p. 65; ULS Mackworth MSS, Box P, unnumbered French advertisement, 17 July 1724.

86 P&M L823, L1056; ULS Mackworth MSS 433, 522, 744; NLW Cilybebill MS 701.

87 J. Rowe, *Cornwall in the Industrial Revolution* (London, 1953), pp. 18–23; Grant-Francis, *Smelting of copper*, pp. 96–122.

88 ULS Morris MSS, 'History of the copper concern', fo. 21.

89 Ibid.; P&M L1253 for Mansell.

90 John, *Industrial development*, p. 5.

91 Martin, 'Mineral property dispute'; P. Morgan, 'The Glais boundary dispute', in S. Williams (ed.), *Glamorgan historian* (1973), vol. 9, pp. 203–210. P. R. Reynolds, 'Chauncy Townsend's wagonway', *Morgannwg*, 21 (1977), 42–68.

92 NLW Penllergaer MS 808; P. Morgan, 'The end of an elegant house', *Gower*, 23 (1972), 4–7.

93 P&M L791, L842, L896, L903, L1114, L1130.

94 John, *Industrial development*; J. Lloyd, *The early history of the old South Wales ironworks* (London, 1906); Rees, *Industry*, vol. 1, pp. 300–17.

95 D. R. Phillips, *History of the Vale of Neath* (Swansea, 1925), pp. 296–9.

96 W. J. Lewis, *Lead mining in Wales* (Cardiff, 1967), pp. 80–94; CCL MS 4.772 (18 February 1731) for Cottrell.

97 W. E. Minchinton, *The British tinplate industry* (OUP, 1957).

98 R. O. Roberts, 'Dr. John Lane', *Gower*, 4 (1953), 18–24.

99 ULS Mackworth MSS 602, 848.

100 J. Byng (Viscount Torrington), *The Torrington Diaries*, ed. C. B. Andrews (4 vols., London, 1970), vol. 1, pp. 295–305; DWT, 29 August 1791.

101 *DWB*, 'Wilkins'; CCL MS 2.716, vol. 2, fo. 9.

102 Mingay, *Gentry*, pp. 99–101; Beckett, *Coal and tobacco*.

103 K. Hudson, *Patriotism with profit* (London, 1972); DWT, 6 January 1763, 12 January 1764; Garsed, *Records*. For political disputes, see below, Chapter 6.

104 Fox, *General view*, appendix; Garsed, *Records*, pp. 5–8; CCL MS 2.344, fo. 106.

105 E. A. Wrigley, 'The process of modernisation and the Industrial Revolution in England', *Journal of Interdisciplinary History*, 3 (1972–3), 225–59.

106 David E. Apter, *The politics of modernisation* (University of Chicago Press, 1965).

107 ULS Mackworth MS 589; A. H. John, 'War and the English economy', *Ec.HR*, 2nd ser., 7 (1954–5).

108 John, *Industrial development*, p. 10; R. Davis, *The rise of the English shipping industry* (Newton Abbot, 1972), pp. 315–37. Mingay, *English landed society*, p. 65 for the 'great market'.

109 NLW KT, John Andrews to Sir Charles Kemys, 18 July 1698.

110 R. Burton, *A history of the principality of Wales* (London, 1695), p. 167. For the 1708 scare, see P&M L1607, L1442.

111 *CSPD 1667*, pp. 359, 424; P&M L721; GRO D/DN/232/11.

112 GRO D/DN/230/7.

113 ULS Mackworth MS 1236.

114 DWT, 31 August 1764.

115 John, 'War'; J. R. Harris, 'Copper and the shipping industry', *Ec.HR*, 2nd ser., 19 (1965), 550–68; L. J. Williams, 'The Welsh tinplate trade in the mid-eighteenth century', *Ec.HR*, 2nd ser., 13 (1960–1). L. Namier, 'Antony Bacon', in W. E. Minchinton (ed.), *Industrial South Wales 1750–1914* (London, 1969), pp. 59–107.

116 M. J. Daunton, 'Towns and economic growth in eighteenth-century England', in P. Abrams and E.A. Wrigley (eds.), *Towns and society* (CUP, 1978), pp. 266–9.

117 R. O. Roberts, 'Penclawdd brass and copper works', *Gower*, 14 (1961), 35; John, *Industrial development*, p. 8.

118 D. Williams, *History of modern Wales*, new edn (London, 1977), pp. 178–9. DWT, 19 September 1762, 29 December 1763, 19 January 1769; ULS Morris MSS, 'History of the copper concern', fo. 55.

119 ULS Mackworth MS 706; Davies, *Certaine schoole*, p. 57; *HMC 11th Report*, Appendix, pt. 4, p. 321.

120 GRO D/DF, vol. 81; Martin, 'Landed estate', pp. 251–71, especially 266–71. For gambling, GRO D/DN/22; 236/1.

121 DWT, 12 September 1767; G. J. Thomas, 'Family history of Thomas of Wenvoe' (1855), microfilm copy in CCL.

122 ULS Mackworth MSS, Box P, letter of Juliana Mackworth to Herbert, 30 May 1738.
123 DWT suggests a similar set of problems for many estates in the 1760s.
124 J. Broad, 'Gentry finances and the Civil War', *Ec.HR*, 2nd ser., 32 (1979), 183–200.
125 J. S. Corbett, *Papers and notes on the lordship of Glamorgan and its members* (Cardiff Naturalists' Society, 1925), p. 240.
126 *Cal. Comp.*, pp. 1276, 1355.
127 Jenkins, 'Two poems', p. 170; NLW Add. MS 11021E. See below, Chapter 5.
128 NLW MS 11021E.
129 Martin, 'Landed estate', pp. 251, 265.
130 For Colston and his circle, see, for example, P&M L219–20, L407, L423–4, L438; NLW Tredegar MS 323; NLW Bute MS 7468.
131 NLW KT, 21, Mary to Sir Charles, 18 February 1690; ULS Mackworth MSS, Box P, Juliana to Herbert, 30 May 1738.
132 P&M L479, L813, L941: see below, Chapter 6.
133 P&M L579.
134 P&M L691, L732, L747, L819.
135 DWT, June 1764, 10 June 1765, GRO D/DN/232/11. See above, pp. 37–8.

Conclusion to Part I

1 T. Birch (ed.), *Collection of state papers of John Thurloe, esq.* (7 vols., London, 1742), vol. 4, p. 316. Hereafter *Thurloe State Papers.*
2 Richard Gwinnett, *The country squire* (London, 1732); Edward Jerningham, *The Welch heiress* (London, 1795).
3 D. Underdown, *Pride's Purge* (OUP, 1971), p. 13.
4 *Local government and the work of Quarter Sessions* (GRO, 1955), p. 12 for such a remark in 1842.
5 C. Hill, 'Puritans and the dark corners of the land', in C. Hill, *Change and continuity in seventeenth-century England* (London, 1974); O. W. Jones, 'The Welsh church in the eighteenth century', in D. Walker (ed.), *History of the Church in Wales* (Cowbridge, Church in Wales, 1976), p. 104.
6 B. Manning, *The English people and the English revolution* (London, 1976), pp. 184, 260.
7 Howell, *Land and people.*
8 Dodd, *Studies*; P. D. G. Thomas, 'Society, government and politics', in Moore (ed.), *Wales in the eighteenth century*, pp. 15–16.

4 Law and order

1 Dodd, *Studies*, pp. 49–76; P. Williams, *The Council of the Marches in Wales under Elizabeth I* (Cardiff, 1959). For gentry opposition to the Council, see *Arguments proving the jurisdiction used by the president and the Council... to be illegal...* (London, 1641). NLW Add. MS 339F.

2 Abolition was little opposed, but see *Cal. Treas. Books 1694*, vol. 2, p. 416. NLW, KT, Romsey to Sir Charles Kemys, 20 January 1690; Edmund Matthews to Sir Charles, 24 January 1689.

3 BM Add. MS 35604, fo. 8.

4 M. Elsas, *Iron in the making* (Cardiff, 1960), pp. 207–9.

5 J. S. Cockburn, *History of English Assizes 1558–1714* (CUP, 1972); W. R. Williams, *The Welsh judges* (Brecon, 1899), Introduction.

6 CCL MS 2.716.

7 P&M L1500.

8 See below, Chapter 6.

9 P. Jenkins, 'Welsh anglicans and the Interregnum', *Journal of the historical society of the Church in Wales* (forthcoming, 1981); and P. Jenkins, 'Mary Wharton'.

10 See below, Chapter 6, Section 7.

11 J. R. Western, *The English militia in the eighteenth century* (London, 1965).

12 NLW KT, Robotham to Sir Charles Kemys, 3 January 1679; Thomas Mansell to Sir Charles, 8 September 1687.

13 Western, *Militia*, Chapters 2–3.

14 Bodl. MS Tanner 21, fo. 103. The names of militia officers under Charles II have been gathered from numerous passing references in gentry correspondence.

15 P&M 3467.

16 For names of deputy-lieutenants: PRO SP 29/88, fo. 95; *CSPD 1673–5*, pp. 115–16; PRO SP Entry Book 164, fo. 189; NLW Add. MS 17071E; *Calendar of Home Office Papers 1760–5*, p. 232.

17 Western, *Militia*.

18 Ibid.; L. V. Evans, 'The Royal Glamorgan Militia' in S. Williams (ed.), *Glamorgan historian* (1971), vol. 7, pp. 146–66; NLW MS 5189C. DWT, 3 August 1763.

19 Western, *Militia*, p. 432; see below, Section 6.

20 CCL MS 2.716, vol. 2, fo. 45; Elsas, *Iron*, pp. 207–9.

21 E. Moir, *The justice of the peace* (London, 1969), pp. 54–102; J. R. S. Phillips, *The justices of the peace in Wales and Monmouthshire* (Cardiff, University of Wales, 1975); K. Williams-Jones, *Calendar of the Merionethshire Quarter-Sessions Rolls* (Dolgellau, Merionethshire County Council, 1965). For a thorough discussion of the work of Welsh JPs see L. Glassey, *Politics and the commission of the peace 1675–1720* (OUP, 1979).

22 See, for example, W. E. Allin, 'Poor Law administration in Glamorgan before the Poor Law Amendment Act' (MA thesis, University of Wales, 1936), p. 299 for the use of removals.

23 *CSPD 1678*, p. 26.

24 For example, Hudson, *Patriotism*, p. 17.

25 Names of JPs are from Phillips, *Justices*; from NLW Gaol Files (Great Sessions) 600.1-620.2 (1691–1764), where lists of JPs can be found on the wrappers. PRO C 234/85; C 202/103–188; C 193/43–5; C 220/9/8.

26 Glassey, *Politics*, p. 15.

27 Williams-Jones, *Calendar*, p. lvii; see below, Chapter 6.

28 J. H. Matthews, *Cardiff records* (6 vols., Cardiff, 1898–1911), vol. 2, pp. 180–1.

29 Glassey, *Politics*.

30 PRO C 234/85; Glassey, *Politics*, pp. 223, 232.

31 *HMC Stuart MMS 56*, vol. 2, pp. 311, 317; vol. 3, pp. 202, 409, 516–18; compare P&M 1156, L840, L979, L1075.

32 PRO SP 35/54, fo. 84; 35/8, fo. 30.

33 Glassey, *Politics*, p. 243.

34 Davies, 'Bute estate', p. 50.

35 P&M L1244–5, L1395, L1401.

36 Phillips, *Justices*.

37 Commissioners under Land Tax Act of 1735 (8 Geo II, pp. 513–14).

38 CCL MS 2.716, vol. 1, fo. 18.

39 D. J. V. Jones, *Before Rebecca* (London, 1973), pp. 27–30.

40 Glassey, *Politics*, pp. 267–8.

41 PRO 193/43–5; NLW Add. MS 17071E.

42 S. and B. Webb, *English local government from the Restoration to the Municipal Reform Act* (London, 1924), vol. 1, *The parish and the county*, pt. 3, p. 384. For 'Laudian' claims in the 1720s, see Clement, *SPCK Correspondence*, p. 144.

43 Mingay, *Gentry*, pp 127–8; Webbs, *Government*, vol. 1, pt. 3, pp. 350–60.

44 BM Add. MS 35604, fo. 98.

45 Notably in the 1780s.

46 Jenkins, 'Two poems', p. 175.

47 *CSPD 1678*, p. 26.

48 E. Bagshaw, *Life and death of Mr. Vavasor Powell* (London, 1671), p. 140; DWT, 13 September 1762, 25 May 1763.

49 P&M L507; T. Edwards, *An address to the justices of the county of Glamorgan* (Cowbridge, 1782).

50 Giles Jacob, *The compleat sportsman* (London, 1718), and his *Country gentleman's vademecum* (London, 1717). GRO D/DQSM/ vol. 2, January 1759, for the purchase of Richard Burn's *Justice of the peace* (London, 1755).

51 Bodl. MS Tanner 146, fo. 138 for JPs defending dissenters about 1672.

52 P&M 2485: Jocelyn Sydney was the husband.

53 NLW Add. MS 1214D, discussed in *Gower*, 23 (1972), 51.

54 T. B. Macaulay, *History of England from the accession of James II* (6 vols., London, Albany ed., c. 1925), vol. 1, p. 336.

55 For example, CCL MS 1.535, written by Anthony Maddocks about 1740, and still in Hopkin Llewellyn's hands c. 1790.

56 Mingay, *Gentry*, p. 128. G. Williams, *High sheriffs of the county of Glamorgan* (Cheltenham, 1966). For a contract dividing duties between sheriff and under-sheriff, see CCL, BRA Deeds catalogue, 28 January 1709.

57 For elections, see below, Chapter 6; for the process of appointment, see the extensive Hardwicke correspondence: BM Add. MS 35602, fos. 236, 244; and MS 35603, fos. 11, 15; BM Stowe MS 246, fo. 175 r; GRO D/DN/231/11.

58 GRO D/DQSR/1733; compare Bodl. MS Rawl C.390, fo. 5.
59 GRO D/DQSMB/DWT, 15 July 1762, 1 May 1764; Jones, *Before Rebecca*, p. 175. Matthews, *Cardiff Records*, vol. 2, p. 211 for the 1759 riot.
60 R. Denning, 'The devil had a share', in S. Williams (ed.), *Glamorgan historian* (1968), vol. 5, pp. 110–20.
61 W. S. K. Thomas, 'History of Swansea 1485–1662' (Ph.D thesis, University of Wales, 1958). A. Oliver (ed.), *Journal of Samuel Curwen, loyalist* (Harvard University Press, 1972), p. 385.
62 CCL Bute MSS, bundles 23–5; CCL MS 4.829 for a borough feud between whig and tory in 1730s.
63 DWT, fos. 828, 833 5 October 1762; GRO D/DQSM, vol. 1, 1729, p. 309; P&M L731.
64 Jenkins, 'Gibbs family'; PRO C5/486/64; Bodl. MS Willis 36, fo. 107; GRO D/DQSM, vol. 1 (1927), fo. 311.
65 DWT, 5 August 1764; for warrants of reliability, see, for instance, NLW KT, B. Thomas to Sir Charles, 19 May 1736.
66 ULS Mackworth MSS, Box P, Clement Watkins to Herbert Mackworth, 11 August 1753.
67 D. Hay, 'Property, authority and the criminal law' in Hay *et al.*, *Albion's fatal tree*, p. 62.
68 P&M L392.
69 In Hay *et al.*, *Albion's fatal tree*, p. 327 (see also p. 298, note 2).
70 Jenkins, 'New source', p. 47; NLW Gaol Files 606/6; Clement, *SPCK Correspondence*, p. 239.
71 For the 'Corry men', DWT, 7 February 1765.
72 GRO D/DQSM 1/1733.
73 For a criticism of this interpretation of social protest – based on *Albion's fatal tree* – see T. L. Chapman, 'Crime in eighteenth-century England', *Criminal Justice History*, 1 (1980), 139–55.
74 GRO D/DQSM 1/37 (1719); NLW Donald C. Jones MS, bundle 1, letter to Richard Thomas, 1724.
75 Nathan Rogers, *Secret memoirs of Monmouthshire* (London, 1708); NLW Badminton MSS 2323, 11049–54; NLW Ashburnham MSS 259–84.
76 F. Jones, 'The affair of Cefn Arthen', *Brycheiniog*, 15 (1971), 23–37; Martin, 'Mineral property disputes'; Morgan, 'Glais boundary dispute', pp. 203–10.
77 Jenkins, 'New source,' p. 47; G. Roberts, *Aspects of Welsh history* (Cardiff, 1969), pp. 62–70; O. Beynon, 'Leadmining at Esgair y Mwyn in the time of Lewis Morris', *Transactions of the Cardiganshire Antiquarian Society*, 2 (1936), 30–9.
78 CCL MS 2.716, vol. 2, fo. 8.
79 DWT, 15 December 1763, 28 May 1765.
80 DWT 7–8 October 1766, 8 April 1767. Hay *et al.*, *Albion's fatal tree*, p. 327. GRO D/DOSM for some rioting at Tythegston in 1766.
81 For hatred of tithes, see the many comments in DWT – for example, 30 August 1762; Matthews, *Cardiff records*, vol. 3, pp. 194–7. For changing social relationships in England, see J. Money, *Experience and identity* (Manchester University Press, 1977), pp. 246–75.

82 A. L. Evans, 'Some eighteenth-century wrecks', *Transactions of the Port Tal-bot Historical Society*, 3 (1967), 90–4; Matthews, *Cardiff records*, vol. 2, pp. 205–7.

83 Frequent references in DWT – 27 February 1770, fo. 838, 17 July 1770, 8 October 1771 and others.

84 Evans, 'Wrecks', pp. 90–4.

85 DWT, 27 February 1770, 9 February 1775; GRO D/DC/F4 (John Carne's diary). J. G. Rule, 'Wrecking and coastal plunder' in Hay *et al.*, *Albion's fatal tree*, pp. 166–88, especially 175–7, 182.

86 Rule, 'Wrecking'.

87 GRO D/DC/F4; DWT, 9 February 1775; Rule, 'Wrecking', pp. 176–7, 182.

88 GRO D/DN/236/3; Matthews, *Cardiff Records*, vol. 2, p. 387–90; 'Smugglers of Glamorgan', in NLW Donald C. Jones MSS, bundle 27.

89 GRO D/DKT/1/86.

90 DWT, 1762–3, *passim*.

91 GRO D/DN/236/3.

92 Jones, *Before Rebecca*, pp. 251–63.

5 Political history 1640–1688

1 For the Civil Wars, see *GCH*, pp. 257–89. A. H. Dodd, 'Pattern of politics in Stuart Wales', *TCS* (1948), 8–91. For plots, *Discovery of a horrid and bloody treason and conspiracy* (London, 1641); *Great discovery of a damnable plot at Raglan Castle in Monmouthshire* (London, 1641). H. Durant, *The Somer-set sequence* (London, 1951), pp. 64–81. The catholic scholars at Raglan about 1640 included Tobie Matthew, Henry Turbervill, Augustine Baker and John Vaughan.

2 NLW Badminton MSS 11718–19.

3 *HMC Beaufort MSS*, pp. 3–4.

4 Aubrey, *Brief lives*, pp. 333–4.

5 K. Lindley, 'The part played by catholics in the Civil War' (Ph.D thesis, University of Manchester, 1968).

6 NLW Brogyntyn MS (Clenennau letters) 1019.

7 Dodd, *Studies* and 'Pattern'; V. A. Rowe, 'The influence of the Earl of Pembroke on parliamentary elections 1625–41', *EHR*, 1 (1935), 242–7.

8 *GCH*, pp. 221–3; G. T. Clark, *Cartae et alia munimenta quae ad dominium de Glamorgania pertinent* (Cardiff, 1886), vol. 6, pp. 2220–1.

9 E. B. Underhill (ed.), *Records of a church of Christ meeting in Broadmead, Bristol* (London, Hanserd Knollys Society, 1847), pp. 7–9; R. G. Gruffudd, *In that gentile country* (Cardiff, 1976).

10 G. F. Nuttall, *The Welsh saints 1640–60* (Cardiff, 1957).

11 Bodl. MS Tanner 147, fo. 121; Gwent RO John Capel Hanbury MSS 1955A.

12 NLW Sir John Williams Add. MS 128C, fos. 65–79, especially 78 v.

13 R. Prichard, *The Welshman's candle* (Carmarthen, 1771), p. 358.

14 A. M. Johnson, 'Wales during the Commonwealth and Protectorate', in D. Pennington and K. Thomas (eds.), *Puritans and revolutionaries* (OUP, 1978), p. 232; Hill, 'Dark corners'.

15 A. M. Johnson, 'Bussy Mansell (1623–99), political survivalist', *Morgannwg*, 20 (1976).

16 *GCH*, pp. 257–89, especially 266. J. R. Phillips, *Memoirs of the Civil War in Wales and the Marches* (2 vols., London, 1874), vol. 2, p. 23 for early violence against royalist forces.

17 Bodl. MS Wood F 30, fos. 14–16.

18 *CSPD 1645–7*, 96–7, 136, 455; Dodd, *Studies*, pp. 97–9.

19 Richard Parr, *Life of the Most reverend father in God, James Ussher, late Lord Archbishop of Armagh* (London, 1686), pp. 58–62.

20 Pembroke's role is stressed in David Williams, *History of Monmouthshire* (London, 1796), p. 311. *CSPD 1645–7*, pp. 120, 223; *1648–9*, pp. 328–9.

21 *A letter from the Marquess of Worcester to the committee of parliament sitting in the county of Monmouth* (London, 1646); T. Bayly, *Apothegmes of the Marquis of Worcester* (London, 1650).

22 *Heads of the present grievances of the county of Glamorgan* (London, 1647).

23 NLW Add. MS 6515B (14 June 1647); J. S. Morrill, *The revolt of the provinces* (London, 1976); Bodl. MS Tanner 58, fos. 173, 218, 228–30; *HMC Portland MSS I*, pp. 346–52.

24 Underdown, *Pride's Purge*, p. 180; Bodl. MS Wood F 30, fo. 17.

25 Veysey, 'Philip Jones', p. 8; GRO D/DF/L7. For Oldisworth, see below, Appendix 5.

26 D. Underdown, 'Settlement in the counties 1653–8' in G. E. Aylmer (ed.), *The Interregnum* (London, 1972), pp. 167–73, 177, 181.

27 A. H. Dodd, 'New England influences on early Welsh puritanism', *BBCS*, 16 (1954), 30–8.

28 C. Hill, 'Propagating the Gospel', in H. E. Bell and R. L. Ollard (eds.), *Historical essays 1600–1750* (London, 1963).

29 P&M L220, L347; W. Wynne, *The life of Sir Leoline Jenkins* (London, 1723), vol. 1, pp. iii-v.

30 *Cal. Comp.*, p. 1770; Bodl. MS Walker C4, fos. 63–72; pamphlet by Bassett Jones in Mackworth MSS, Box Q, no. 7 (1654); GRO D/DF/14, L27.

31 Bodl. MS Walker C4, fos. 63–72.

32 W. Williams, *The mystery of iniquity, or a remarkable relation of a Carmarthenshire cause* (London, 1656). NLW Llanstephan MSS 120, 145.

33 E. Bowen, *Bowen's Court* (London, 1942); Dodd, *Studies*, pp. 95–108.

34 *Thurloe State Papers*, vol. 2, p. 256.

35 Ibid., vol. 5, p. 242.

36 *CSPD 1651–2*, pp. 170, 445–7; *1655*, p. 92; *1656–7*, p. 55.

37 CCL Deeds 256; NLW Penllergaer MSS, parcel 16, no. 1 (1658).

38 Hill, 'Propagating the Gospel', pp. 39, 45.

39 Dodd, 'New England influences'.

40 Hill, 'Dark corners'.

41 Bodl. MS Walker C13, fos. 4–17; *Thurloe State Papers*, vol. 2, p. 129.

42 *Indictment, arraignment, trial and judgment of twenty-nine regicides* (London, 1713), pp. xvii-xviii; NLW Add. MSS 11437–40.

43 Bodl. MS Walker C4, fo. 69 r.

44 A. H. Dodd, 'A remonstrance from Wales 1655', *BBCS*, 17 (1958), 279–92.
45 *The second narrative of the late parliament (so-called) printed in the fifth year of England's slavery under its new monarchy* (London, 1658). See below, Appendix 5 for Thomas of Wenvoe.
46 E. Calamy, *The nonconformists' memorial* (London, 1713), vol. 2, especially entries for 'Glyncorrwg' and 'Llanmadoc'. John Walker, *Attempts towards recovering an account of the... sufferings of the clergy* (London, 1714), vol. 2, p. 97.
47 NLW Church in Wales MSS LL/QA/1; H. Owen (ed.), 'Additional letters of the Morrises of Anglesey', *Y Cymmrodor*, 49 (1949), 688–9.
48 BM Thomason Tracts E1832 (2), p. 2.
49 Discussed in G. E. Aylmer, 'Unbelief in seventeenth century England', in Pennington and Thomas (eds.), *Puritans and revolutionaries*, pp. 40–1. For his sister, F. Gawler, *Records of some persecutions inflicted upon some of the servants of the Lord in South Wales* (London, 1659), p. 27.
50 T. Edwards, *Gangraena* (3 vols., London, 1646), vol. 1, p. 77; C. Hill, *The world turned upside down* (London, 1975), pp. 73–85.
51 C. Hill, *Antichrist in seventeenth century England* (OUP, 1971), pp. 128–30.
52 Nuttall, *Welsh saints*, pp. 55–76, 88–90; BM Thomason Tracts, E868 (1), pp. 17, 20; E896 (2). J. Naylor, *Antichrist in Man, Christ's enemy* (London, 1656).
53 Gawler, *Record*, pp. 7, 17–18, 25.
54 Bodl. MS Walker C4.
55 B. Reay, 'Quaker opposition to tithes 1652–60', *Past and Present*, 86 (1980).
56 Jenkins, 'Welsh anglicans'.
57 Wynne, *Life of Jenkins*, vol. 2, pp. 144–5.
58 Bodl. MS Walker C4, fo. 72.
59 P. Jenkins, 'The origins of antipopery on the Welsh Marches in the seventeenth century', *Historical Journal*, 23 (1980), 275–93.
60 *Thurloe State Papers*, vol. 2, p. 256.
61 PRO SP 29/398, fos. 257–8; GRO D/DF/V 128, and L10–11.
62 J. Berry and S. Lee, *A Cromwellian major-general* (OUP, 1938), pp. 157–8; Bayly, *Apothegmes*.
63 Leading opponents of the quakers were the presbyterians Benjamin Flower and Joshua Miller. J. Miller, *Antichrist in man the quakers' idol* (London, 1655).
64 P&M L76, L78; Dodd, *Studies*, pp. 161–76; A. M. Dodd, 'Tuning the Welsh Bench 1680', *NLWJ*, 6 (1949–50), 254–60.
65 *CSPD 1659–60*, pp. 13, 24, 206, 223.
66 *CSP Ireland 1647–60*, p. 718.
67 G. R. Cragg, 'The collapse of militant puritanism' in G. V. Bennett and J. D. Walsh (eds.), *Essays in modern Church history* (London, 1966), pp. 77–102; A. H. Woolrych, 'The Good Old Cause and the fall of the Protectorate', *Cambridge Historical Journal* 13 (1958), 133–61.
68 Nuttall, *Welsh saints*, Chapter 4.
69 G. F. Nuttall, 'Early quaker letters from the Swarthmore MSS' (Friends' House, London, 1952), no. 511; Gawler, *Records*, pp. 7, 13.

70 A. Cole, 'The quakers and the English revolution' in T. Aston (ed.), *Crisis in Europe 1560–1660* (New York, 1967), pp. 358–76.
71 P. Jenkins, 'Old leaven'.
72 GRO D/DSF/313/3; PRO SP 29/97, fo. 47; T. Richards, *Wales under the penal code* (London, 1925), pp. 64, 70; *GCH*, pp. 468–73.
73 BM Thomason Tracts E1832 (2).
74 Bagshaw, *Vavasor Powell*, pp. 133–4.
75 C. Owen, *Some account of the life and writings of the late, pious and learned Mr. James Owen* (London, 1709), p. 9.
76 *CSPD 1672*, pp. 414–16.
77 P&M 3199–214, L148–52; NLW Edwinsford MS 1325; for the idea of Mansell as the son of a royalist martyr, Bodl. MS Tanner 146, fo. 133.
78 Bodl. MS Carte 130, fos. 272–82.
79 Jenkins, 'Welsh anglicans'.
80 Banks, *Antient usage of arms*, pp. 171–2. Patronage is an incessant theme of the *CSPD* in these years; see, for example: *1660–1*, pp. 49, 67, 240, 348, 380–1, 406, 433, 438; or *1661–2*, pp. 382–3.
81 *CSPD 1660–1*, p. 348; *1661–2*, pp. 213, 438.
82 Sir N. Harris Nicholas (ed.), *Flagellum parliamentarium* (London, 1827), pp. 29–30 for an attack on Welsh courtiers.
83 C. Dalton, *English army lists and commission registers* (London, 1960), vol. 1, pp. 220, 236; vol. 2, pp. 32, 193.
84 *CSPD 1677–8*, p. 421; A. Browning, *Thomas Osborne, Earl of Danby* (3 vols., Glasgow, 1944–51), vol. 3, pp. 60, 76, 96, 117. P&M 1128, 9049.
85 NLW KT, Robotham to Sir Charles, 14 December 1679.
86 *CSPD 1680–1*, p. 31; *1683–4*, p. 164.
87 PRO SP 29/97, fo. 47
88 Calamy, *Memorial*, vol. 2, pp. 721–9.
89 Bodl. MS Tanner 146, fo. 138; *DWB*; G. J. Williams; 'Stephen Hughes a' i gyfnod', *Y Cofiadur*, 4 (1926), 9; R. T. Jones, 'Relation between anglicans and dissenters' in D. Walker (ed.), *History of the Church in Wales* (Cowbridge, 1976), pp. 79–102.
90 Calamy, *Memorial*, vol. 2, pp. 624–8; *DWB*.
91 The diary was printed in *Transactions of the Neath Antiquarian Society*, 1 (1930–1).
92 Bagshaw, *Vavasor Powell*, pp. 132–42, 177–82.
93 Ibid., p. 195.
94 P&M 5642, 1002.
95 Jenkins, 'Old leaven'; for Sheldon's eclipse, see R. A. Beddard, 'The Restoration Church', in J.R. Jones (ed.), *The restored monarchy* (London, 1979), pp. 167–71.
96 *CSPD 1673–5*, p. 149; *1675–6*, p. 315; K. H. Haley, *The first Earl of Shaftesbury* (OUP, 1968), pp. 361–3.
97 Jenkins, 'Antipopery' and 'The Gibbs family'.
98 Bagshaw, *Vavasor Powell*.
99 Beddard, 'Restoration Church' in Jones (ed.), *Restored monarchy*, p. 169.

100 M. G. Jones, 'Two accounts of the Welsh Trust', *BBCS*, 9 (1939), pp. 71–6; Jenkins, 'Mary Wharton'; see Appendix 5 below.
101 Rogers, *Secret memoirs*, pp. 87–119.
102 *GCH*, pp. 385–9; P&M 3685, 9018/4. *CSPD 1678*, p. 25; *1679–80*, p. 74.
103 PRO SP 29/398, fos. 257–8; for the Strodes, see D. R. Lacey, *Dissent and parliamentary politics 1661–89* (Rutgers University Press, New Brunswick, NJ, 1969), pp. 442–3.
104 *CSPD 1678*, pp. 25–6.
105 Jenkins, 'Two poems', pp. 176–8.
106 J. P. Kenyon, *The popish plot* (London, 1972), pp. 122, 244–7; Jenkins, 'Anti-popery'; Dodd, *Studies*, pp. 219–34.
107 K. H. D. Haley, 'Shaftesbury's worthy men', *BIHR*, 43 (1970), 86–105.
108 Dodd, 'Tuning'.
109 Anthony Matthews and Michael Richards – *CSPD 1682*, p. 77; P&M 1137.
110 The quaker was Charles Evans: see NLW Add. MSS 1115–16D.
111 Rogers, *Secret memoirs; advice to the men of Monmouth concerning the present times* (London, 1681).
112 NLW KT, Robotham to Sir Charles, 14 April 1678, 5 September 1679, 28 February 1680.
113 *CSPD 1682*, p. 77; *HMC Ormonde MSS*, vol. 6, p. 148.
114 P&M L165, L170–1.
115 NLW Add. MS 11019E.
116 *CSPD 1682*, p. 318; *1683 (June–December)*, p. 262.
117 *CSPD 1680–1*, p. 247; *1682*, p. 476; *1684–5*, pp. 94, 239; *1685*, no. 832; Dillwyn, *Swansea*, pp. 12–13; P&M 5530.
118 Dineley, *Progress*, pp. 234–5.
119 T. Sprat, *True account and declaration of the horrid conspiracy...* 2nd edn (London, 1685), pp. 22–3.
120 P&M 1137.
121 Dodd, *Studies*, p. 217.
122 PRO SP 29/398, fos. 257–8. DWT, fo. 387; Bodl. MS Willis 36, fo. 107.
123 *GCH*, pp. 391–2; NLW KT, bundle 21, Mary to Sir Charles, 26 February 1688; Jenkins, 'Two poems', p. 174.
124 Duckett, *Penal laws*.
125 Jenkins, 'Old leaven'.
126 Jenkins, 'Two poems', pp. 176–8.
127 For riots, NLW Badminton MS 2323; *HMC Beaufort MSS*, p. 92; Dodd, *Studies*, pp. 227–34. P&M L203–5.
128 P&M L1403.

6 Political history 1688–1790

1 Plumb, *Growth*, p. 38.
2 Holmes, *British politics*, p. 171.
3 *Collection of white and black lists*, 2nd edn (London, 1715); H. Horwitz, *Parliament, policy and politics in the region of William III* (Manchester University Press, 1977), pp.191–2.

4 P&M L604.
5 ULS Mackworth MS BJ 506.
6 Macaulay, *History,* vol. 6, p. 138. Plumb, *Growth,* p. 99; BM MS 28883, fo. 145; BM Stowe MS 222, fos. 21. 225, 445.
7 Burton *et al.,* 'Political parties in the reigns of William and Anne', *BIHR* (1968), special supplement, p. 7.
8 Jenkins, 'Mary Wharton'.
9 Jenkins, 'Gibbs family'.
10 P&M A149; ULC Cholmondeley-Houghton MS 745 and lists 80/9.
11 Jenkins, 'Antipopery', pp. 289–90.
12 Matthews, *Cardiff records,* vol. 2, pp. 178–9.
13 K. Feiling, *History of the tory party 1640–1714* (OUP, 1970), pp. 496–8.
14 Ibid., pp. 126–7, 194–6. T. Richards, *Piwritaniaeth a pholitics 1689–1719* (Wrexham, 1927), pp. 17–21; P&M L215.
15 *HMC Portland MSS,* vol. 4, pp. 176–7. J. P. Jenkins, 'Francis Gwyn and the birth of the tory party', *WHR* (forthcoming, 1983).
16 MacInnes, *Harley,* pp. 26–59; *HMC Portland MSS,* vol. 3, p. 615; BM Loan MS 29/93, Gwyn to Edward Harley, 27 May 1724.
17 C. E. and R. C. Wright (eds.), *Diary of Humphrey Wanley* (London, 1966), vol. 1, p. 98.
18 Compare MacInnes, *Harley,* pp. 116–17.
19 Ibid., p. 35; Horwitz, *Parliament,* pp. 10, 179, 337–57.
20 See above, Chapter 3.
21 W. R. Ward, *The English land tax in the eighteenth century* (OUP, 1953), pp. 11, 49.
22 BM Add. MS 22851, fo. 110.
23 H. Horwitz (ed.), *Parliamentary diary of Narcissus Luttrell* (OUP, 1972), pp. 171–3, 265, 314, 445.
24 W.J. Smith (ed.), *Herbert correspondence* (Cardiff, 1963, Board of Celtic Studies), p. 56.
25 P&M L215, L345, L552; Horwitz, *Parliament,* pp. 337–57.
26 P&M L316–19; Horwitz, *Parliament,* p. 326.
27 P&M L1403.
28 P&M L347, L359; T. Richards, 'The Glamorgan loyalists of 1696', *BBCS* 2 (1923), 140–9.
29 P&M L427, L469; BM Add. MS 22851, fo. 110; BM Egerton MS 2540, fo. 140.
30 *Memoirs of the secret service of John Macky esq.* (London, Roxburghe Club, 1895), pp. 83–4.
31 P&M LS68.
32 P&M L365.
33 GRO D/DF/F/1/190.
34 T. Hancorne, *The right way to honour and happiness* (Bristol, 1710).
35 Clement, *SPCK correspondence,* p. ix.
36 Ibid., pp. 3, 26, 44, 97.
37 Bodl. MS Walker C4, fos. 63–72.

38 P&M L640.
39 J. P. Kenyon, *Revolution principles* (CUP, 1977), pp. 61–101; J. Withers, *The whigs vindicated* (London, 1715), pp. 19–30.
40 P&M L1431–2.
41 *Collection of white and black lists.*
42 NLW Add. MS 11447C, fo. 25; Phillips, *Vale of Neath,* p. 608.
43 R. Price, *Gloria Cambriae* (London, 1702); NLW KT, R. Price to Sir Charles Kemys, 31 May 1698; Bodl. MS Carte 130, fos. 325–407.
44 For jacobite propaganda, see, for example, P&M A136, 9022. M. Ransome, 'Parliamentary career of Sir Humphrey Mackworth', *University of Birmingham Historical Journal*, 1 (1948), 232–55.
45 NLW Nanteos MS 15; BM Loan MS 29/300, Mackworth to R. Harley, 17 October 1701; NLW Donald C. Jones MSS, bundle 1, letters of attorney of William Powell.
46 P&M L1385; ULS Mackworth MS BJ 508, D. Thomas to P. Williams, 26 November 1714; G. Powell to L. Howell, 9 November 1714.
47 Bodl. MS Rawl. D 722, fo. 72; compare BM Loan MS 29/147, E. Howorth to R. Harley, 29 November 1695.
48 P&M L298.
49 NLW KT, R. Gunter to Sir Charles Kemys, 26 April 1685; Perkins to Sir Charles Kemys, 26 April 1685; Perkins to Sir Charles, 1 November 1695; C. Price to Sir Charles, 5 March 1700; Perkins to Sir Charles, 9 March 1700.
50 P&M L228 (bishopric).
51 P&M L1357 (appeal to Pembroke). For the bridge dispute P&M L368–417, L1349–57; NLW KT, Sir Charles to 'Cousin Button', September 1700.
52 *HMC Portland MSS*, vol. 4, p. 329; *GCH*, pp. 397–405.
53 Thomas, 'Politics in Glamorgan', pp. 52–78.
54 Holmes, *British politics*, p. 315, based on P&M L678. For the parties, see, for example, P&M L558, L582, L591, L598, L1455, 5092.
55 P&M L284–8.
56 P&M L496–500.
57 P&M L522, A103. For the Neath dispute, see P&M 3249, and above, Chapter 3.
58 P&M 3249, 5092; ULS Mackworth MS BJ 508, letter of 12 October 1710.
59 P&M L543, L1443.
60 P&M 9018, appeal by Mansell and Beaufort; P&M L585–7, L1142–3. For Mansell's wide connections, see below, Appendix 4.
61 *HMC Portland MSS*, vol. 4, pp. 489–90, 533. P&M L570, L630, L718, L1009.
62 P&M L623–4.
63 P&M L495–7.
64 P&M L729 30, L553.
65 NLW Donald C. Jones MSS, bundle 1, letter of T. Mackworth to Sir Humphrey, 12 January 1707; P&M L458, L729.
66 P&M L970.
67 Hancorne, *Right way.*

68 P&M L718.
69 Bodl. MS Walker C4, fos. 63–70; BM Loan MS 29/102/4, 29/157 (letters between Harley and Mansell).
70 P&M L729.
71 P&M L604, L785, L847, L974, 9018. *HMC Egmont Diary*, vol. 2, p. 509 for Cadogan as a whig extremist.
72 See above, Chapter 4; Glassey, *Politics*, pp. 223–32; ULC Cholmondeley–Houghton MSS 745 and lists 80/9, 'Case of George Howell, esq.'.
73 P&M L634, L1441; Williams, *Welsh judges*, pp. 111–13.
74 P&M L763.
75 P&M L660, L757.
76 L.J. Colley, 'The Board of Loyal Brotherhood', *Historical Journal*, 20 (1977), 77–96. BM Add. MS 22, 221, fo. 154; MS 22, 222, fos. 6–15. 425–31. For south-west Wales, P&M L695.
77 Holmes, *British politics*, p. 301.
78 BM Add. MS 32686, fo. 106; PRO SP 35/12, fos 178–9. P. D. G. Thomas, 'Jacobitism in Wales'. *WHR*, 1 (1962); Jenkins, 'Jacobites and freemasons'.
79 PRO SP 35/8, fo. 30; 35/12, fos. 178–9; 35/54, fo. 84.
80 PRO SP 35/32, fo. 148.
81 Jenkins, 'Jacobites and freemasons'.
82 P. C. Yorke (ed.), *Life and correspondence of Philip Yorke, Lord Chancellor Hardwicke* (3 vols., CUP, 1913), vol. 1. pp. 26–7; for jacobite optimism in 1718, NLW Wynnstay MSS C 81–3.
83 Matthews, *Cardiff records*, vol. 2. pp. 187–92.
84 P&M L612, L634, L749, L1539; 2171, A106.
85 P&M 1029; BM Loan MS 29/151, Mansell to R. Harley, 23 October 1718. 20 September 1722.
86 *HMC Stuart MSS 56*, vol. 2, pp. 311, 317; vol. 3, pp. 202, 409, 516–18.
87 P&M L979, L1075.
88 Windsor Castle MSS, Stuart Archives, 65/16 (consulted on microfilm); Grant-Francis, *Smelting of copper*, pp. 97–8; ULS Morris MSS 'History of the copper concern'.
89 ULS Mackworth MSS 154, 971.
90 ULS Mackworth MS 156; Clement, *SPCK correspondence*, p. 143 for the Mackworths' loyalism in 1728.
91 Richards, *Piwritaniaeth*; Clement, *SPCK correspondence*, note 6; Dodd, *Studies*, p. 232; NLW Church in Wales MSS, SD/MISC 1164.
92 W. Rees, *Cardiff: a history of the city*, 2nd edn (Cardiff, 1969), p. 175; CCL MS 4.829.
93 NLW KT, N. Wells to Sir Charles Kemys, 17 October 1726.
94 J. A. Bradney, *A history of Monmouthshire* (4 vols., London, 1904–32), vol. 2, section 1, p. 166.
95 See above, Chapter 3, Section 4.
96 L. Stone (ed.), *The university in society* (2 vols., Princeton University Press, 1975), vol. 1, p. 55.
97 See below, Chapter 8; J. Trapp, *The Aeneis of Virgil* (London, 1718); sub-

scription list; J. Klingender, *Art and the Industrial Revolution* (London, 1972), pp. 16–18 for Yalden.

98 NLW Tredegar MS 53/120; GRO D/DKT/1/12; PRO SP 35/58, fo. 34; 36/21, fo. 162.

99 PRO SP 35/58, fo. 34; Chatsworth MSS, 1st series, nos. 167.0, 167.1; box 17, no. 1.

100 PRO SP 36/28, fo. 100; ULC Cholmondeley-Houghton MS 1739; NLW KT, letter to Edward Kemys, 15 November 1722.

101 NLW Tredegar MSS 53/112, 66/112.

102 PRO SP 35/32, fo. 91; NLW Badminton MS 14854.

103 ULC Cholmondeley-Houghton MS 745, lists 80/9.

104 Sir Thomas Jones, *Rise and progress of the most honourable and loyal society of ancient Britons* (London, 1717).

105 ULC Cholmondeley-Houghton MS 746.

106 GRO D/DN/230/24. E. P. Thompson, *Whigs and hunters* (London, 1975), pp. 100–11.

107 R. Sedgwick (ed.), *Lord Hervey's memoirs* (London, 1963), p. 115; ULC Cholmondeley-Houghton MS 2195; *HMC Egmont Diary*, vol. 2, pp. 148–51; C. J. Abbey, *The English Church and its bishops 1700–1800* (2 vols., London, 1887), vol. 1, pp. 157–8.

108 GRO D/DN/236/1; NLW Edwinsford MS 2945.

109 P&M L869, L955.

110 *GCH*, pp. 408, 486–7.

111 P. D. G. Thomas, 'Parliamentary elections in Breconshire 1689–1832', *Brycheiniog*, 6(1980), 106.

112 CCL MS 4.829; ULS Mackworth MS, Box P, letter of D. Rees, 22 September 1740.

113 ULC Add. MS 6851, fo. 3; GRO D/DKT/1/1–3, 22–3, 39, 41, 51, 75.

114 GRO D/DKT/1/8; CCL MS 4.829.

115 See above, Chapter 2, Section 4.

116 For voter pressure, NLW Badminton MSS 2120, 2123; for expenses, P&M L1200, GRO D/DKT/1/5, 7, 13, 14, 67, 74.

117 P. Langford, *The excise crisis* (OUP, 1975), p. 75.

118 NLW Tredegar MSS 66/1–2.

119 L. J. Colley, 'The tory party 1727–60' (Ph.D thesis, University of Cambridge, 1976), pp. 308–12.

120 GRO D/DKT/1/78.

121 Bodl. MS Willis 37, fos. 35–8.

122 J. P. Jenkins, 'From Edward Lhuyd to Iolo Morgannwg', *Morgannwg*, 23 (1979), 36–7.

123 Hancorne, 'Right way'; F. Jones, 'The society of Sea Serjeants', *TCS* (1967), part 1, pp. 57–92.

124 GRO D/DOSR1/1727.

125 E. Thomas, 'Short view of the conduct of the English clergy', in R. Barron (ed.), *The pillars of priestcraft and orthodoxy shaken*, 2nd edn (4 vols., London, 1768), vol. 2, pp. 1–106.

126 J. Besse, *Abstract of the sufferings of the people called quakers* (3 vols., London 1733–8); his Glamorgan sources were Gawler, *Record*, and GRO D/DSF/313/3).

127 ULS Mackworth MSS, Box P, Juliana to Herbert, unsorted and undated letter.

128 NLW Wynnstay MS C 95.

129 NLW Edwinsford MS 2919 for a copy of this paper in Brecon in 1737.

130 The 'federal' idea is based heavily on Colley, 'Tory party'; RISW, 'Swansea and Glamorgan calendar', vol. 1, p. 51.

131 ULS Morris MSS, 'History of the copper concern', fo. 153.

132 Jones, 'Sea Serjeants', pp. 57–92; Roberts, *Aspects*, pp. 59–80 for the Sea Serjeants and Carmarthen politics.

133 Jones, 'Sea Serjeants'.

134 NLW Add. MS 5458E; NLW Picton Castle MS 591; NLW Badminton MS 2396.

135 ULS Mackworth MS 1342.

136 GRO D/DKT/1/19, 31; ULS Mackworth MS 653, BJ 257.

137 GRO D/DKT/1/55.

138 N. Rogers, 'Aristocratic clientage, trade and independency; popular politics in pre-radical Westminster', *Past and Present*, 61 (1973), 70–106; for Edwin as a whig, see Kent RO V 1500 C 26/1 (a reference I owe to Dr Linda Colley). For the Electors' jacobitism, NLW Picton Castle MS 1492.

139 NLW MS 1352B, fo. 8; S. Ayling, *The elder Pitt* (London, 1976), pp. 48–9.

140 P&M L1258; for Coke and Hartington, P&M L1189, L1209, L1218, L1247–8.

141 The Earl of Ilchester, *Lord Hervey and his friends* (London, 1950), p. 75.

142 Wyndham, *Family history*, pp. 68–9, 85–7, 111–77.

143 Jenkins, 'Jacobites and freemasons', p. 401.

144 NLW KT, Edward Kemys to Sir Charles, 8 January 1731; and many other letters.

145 ULS Mackworth MSS – for example, 279, 313, 355, 421, 521, 667, 786, 852, 971 – but most of the letters from the 1730s mention these connections.

146 Clement, *SPCK correspondence*, p. 232; H. Erskine-Hill, *The social milieu of Alexander Pope* (Yale University Press, 1975), pp. 162–3.

147 *HMC Egmont Diary*, vol. 1, pp. 279, 337, 344; vol. 2, pp. 143, 348, 370, 376; vol. 3, pp. 142, 164, 168, 192–4, 219, 233–4, 279.

148 ULS Mackworth MSS, Box P, letters of P. Courteen to Herbert, 15 and 19 February 1737; Aubrey, Morgan and Edmund Thomas to Herbert, 17 February 1737.

149 ULS Mackworth MSS, Box P, Herbert to Aubrey, Thomas and Morgan, 19 February 1737; Herbert to Matthews, 29 December 1738.

150 NLW Add. MS 17068E; NLW Add. MS 1352B, fos. 46, 80, 103.

151 ULS Mackworth MS BJ 229.

152 Ibid.

153 GRO D/DKT/1/58.

154 GRO D/DKT/1/5–85 for the electoral correspondence on the tory side.

155 Cruickshanks, *Untouchables*, pp. 115–23.
156 NLW Add. MS 1098B.
157 PRO SP 36/80, fo. 391.
158 ULS Mackworth MS 1332.
159 Bodl. MS Rawl. D 848, fos. 96–8; see below, Appendix 5 for Morgan.
160 Jenkins, 'Jacobites and freemasons', p. 394.
161 NLW Add. MS 5471E.
162 PRO SP 36/76, fo. 440.
163 Jenkins, 'Jacobites and freemasons', p. 395.
164 Colley, 'Tory party'.
165 ULS Mackworth MS 667 B; compare NLW Abergavenny MS 801, letters 1,6,7.
166 NLW Add. MS 12427E, fo. 22.
167 NLW Brogyntyn MS 1112.
168 NLW Philipps of Picton MSS 571–3.
169 ULS Mackworth 1342.
170 Roberts, *Aspects,* pp. 63–8; Lewis, *Lead mining,* pp. 100–5; GRO D/DN/ 231/18; NLW Tredegar MS 72/55.
171 NLW Badminton MS 2215.
172 Martin, 'Mineral property disputes'; ULS Mackworth MS 1337; NLW Badminton MSS 2358, 2398.
173 NLW Badminton MS 2195, 2402.
174 GRO D/DKT/1/79; ULS Collins MS, Beaufort to Collins, 5 June 1754.
175 ULS Mackworth MS 1352; Davies, *Certaine schoole,* pp. 57–9; NLW Badminton MS 2335.
176 ULS Mackworth MS 1392, A. H. Newman, 'Leicester House politics 1750– 60', *Camden Miscellany* (London, Royal Historical Society, 1969), pp. 85– 229.
177 ULS Mackworth MS 791; J. Brewer, *Party ideology and popular politics at the accession of George III* (CUP, 1976), pp. 96–112.
178 DWT, 17 July 1768; GRO D/DN/266/1; Jenkins, 'Jacobites', p. 403.
179 H. Harris, *Brief account of the life of Howell Harris, esq.* (Trevecka, 1791), p. 84; P. Jenkins, 'A Welsh Lancashire: Monmouthshire catholics in the eighteenth Century', *Recusant History* (1980), 176–88.
180 Matthews, *Cardiff records,* vol. 2, p. 387.
181 Plumb, *Growth,* pp. 180–4.
182 *GCH,* pp. 468–86.
183 BM Add. MS 35602, fos. 242–4.
184 CCL MS 1.175; GRO D/DN/266/1.
185 See, for example, DWT, 9 April 1770, 28 January 1773, 9 June 1783, fo. 1132 – and numerous comments throughout the diary.
186 NLW Badminton MS 14827; John Telford (ed.), *Wesley's veterans* (5 vols., London, c. 1910), vol. 1, pp. 218–21; Harris, *Life,* pp. 45–7.
187 Watts, *Dissenters,* pp. 397–409.
188 Williams, *Wesley in Wales*; GRO D/DF/F 51–5 for gentry methodism. For the conservatism of the 1770s – NLW Add. MS 6869A, GRO D/DSY/16/74.
189 BM Add. MSS 32913, fo. 418; 32725, fo. 435; 35602, fo. 264.

190 BM Add. MSS 32703, fos. 376, 388; 32711, fo. 469.
191 BM Add. MS 32715.
192 GRO D/DN/232/12.
193 P&M 9074, letters of D. Rees to T. Matthews, March 1757.
194 Newman, 'Leicester House', pp. 146, 163–5, 169. BM Add. MSS 32723, fo. 281; 32913, fo. 60; 32867, fo. 423; 32869, fo. 130; 35604, fo. 6.
195 L. Namier, *The structure of politics at the accession of George III*, new edn (London, 1973), pp. 200, 427, 430.
196 P&M 9074, D. Rees to T. Matthews, 13 March 1757.
197 *HMC 11th report*, Appendix part 4, p. 321. BM Add. MS 6861, fos. 296–9.
198 J. C. D. Clark, 'The decline of party 1740–60', *EHR*, 93 (1978).
199 BM Add. MS 38201, fo. 1763.
200 NLW Aberpergwm MSS, 1475–7; DWT, 22 October 1773.
201 ULS Mackworth MSS 860, 1426.
202 ULS Mackworth MS 858.
203 BM Stowe MS 261, fo. 40; NLW Badminton MS 2396; GRO D/DKT/1/84–7. Jenkins, 'Roads', p. 100.
204 DWT, 17 June 1767, 20 July 1767; *GCH*, pp. 417–22.
205 DWT, 16 August 1762, 30 April 1763, 17 June 1767.
206 NLW Add. MSS 13077B and 10583E; CCL MS 2.76; J. Norris, *Shelburne and reform* (London, 1963), pp. 84–7, 105–6.
207 Jenkins, 'Jacobites and freemasons', pp. 391–406; Margaret Jacob, *The Radical Enlightenment* (London, 1981).
208 J. Stoughton, *Religion in England under Queen Anne and the Georges* (2 vols., London, 1878), vol. 2, p. 21; *DWB*.
209 DWT, 28 July 1766; Bagshaw, *Vavasor Powell* was reprinted in Welsh in 1772, NLW Add. MS 398B.
210 W. Morgan, *Memoirs of the life of the Rev. Richard Price* (London, 1815).
211 G. Rudé, *Wilkes and liberty* (OUP, 1972), pp. 117, 131, 178–9; Jenkins, 'Jacobites and freemasons', p. 400.
212 DWT, fos. 1166, 1171.
213 NLW Add. MSS 13145–6; 13150A, fo. 128; 13153A, fos. 337–341.
214 Bodl. MS Eng. misc. c. 132; Norris, *Shelburne*, pp. 84–7, 105–6.
215 O. Hufton, *Privilege and protest: Europe 1730–89* (London, 1980), p. 133.
216 Not only in Welsh counties: Money, *Experience and identity*, pp. 158–219; NLW Tredegar MSS 72/74, 72/81. D. A. Wager, 'Welsh politics and parliamentary reform 1780–1835' (MA thesis, University of Wales, 1972). T. H. B. Oldfield, *Entire and complete history...of the boroughs of Great Britain* (London, 1792), vol. 3, pp. 40–7.
217 P&M 9125; Ll. B. John, 'Parliamentary representation of Glamorgan 1536–1832' (MA thesis, University of Wales, 1934), pp. 103–10, 228–32.
218 NLW Tredegar MS 72/74–83; Oldfield, *Boroughs,* vol. 3, pp. 29–33.
219 Williams, *Merthyr rising*.
220 D. Davies, *The influence of the French Revolution on Welsh life and literature* (Carmarthen, 1926).

7 The idea of a gentleman

1 Dillwyn, *Contribution*, p. 20.
2 P&M 4946.
3 O. Goldsmith, *Life of Richard Nash esq., extracted principally from his original papers* (London, 1762), p. 24.
4 Byng, *Torrington diaries*, vol. 1. p. 288 for Peter Birt of Wenvoe.
5 P&M L163.
6 J. B. Hilling, *Cardiff and the valleys* (London, 1973), pp. 31–2. Royal Commission on Historical Monuments, *Glamorgan*, vol. 4, *Domestic architecture from the Reformation to the Industrial Revolution (The greater houses)* (London, 1981).
7 P. Moore, 'Penrice and Margam: building by a landowning family in Glamorgan' in Moore (ed.), *Wales in the eighteenth century*, pp. 73–88.
8 NLW Tredegar MSS 175, 102/80–90. P&M 2549, 2387; GRO D/DF, vol. 6; NLW Add. MS 6580E.
9 CCL MS 1.175.
10 NLW KT, Mary to Sir Charles Kemys, '6 March'.
11 For example, P&M L486, 5961–3; NLW Bute MS 7470.
12 P&M 1194; Bucks RP D/AF/273.
13 P&M 3161, 6004, 9081.
14 Matthews, *Cardiff records*, vol. 2, pp. 289–90.
15 J. E. Ross, *Radical adventurer* (Swansea, 1971).
16 NLW Tredegar MSS 53/107, 66/101; GRO D/DKT 1/43, 50.
17 P&M L399, L524.
18 P&M 6006.
19 P&M 9049; L495.
20 NLW KT, O. Robotham to Sir Charles, 14 April 1678.
21 Ibid.; *CSPD 1679–80*, p. 59; *DWB*, pp. 980, 1127. P&M L498.
22 Matthews, *Cardiff records*, vol. 2, p. 224.
23 P&M 4946.
24 E. Green, Sheridan and Matthews at Bath (London, 1912), pp. 23–7.
25 *CSPD 1679–80*, p. 59.
26 R. Halsband (ed.), *Complete letters of Lady Mary Wortley Montagu* (3 vols., OUP, 1965–7), vol. 2, pp. 457–8.
27 R. Sedgwick, *Lord Hervey's memoirs* (London, 1963), p. 19.
28 CCL MS 2.716, vol. 1, fo. 19; vol. 2, fo. 2, and many other references.
29 P&M A1–15, A52–3, A85–7; PRO 30/13; BM Har. MS 6831, fo. 393; CCL MS 4.87; Merthyr Mawr House MS F 123; GRO D/DE 439–440.
30 GRO D/DF genealogy rolls.
31 P&M L945, L958.
32 J. Steegman, *Portraits in Welsh houses* (2 vols., Cardiff, National Museum of Wales, 1962), vol. 2, 'South Wales'. Some of the best series of portraits are at the National Museum of Wales, Cardiff; at Penrice, Fonmon and St Fagan's; and at Chilton (Bucks.), the Aubrey-Fletcher seat.
33 NLW Dunraven MS 12; Matthews, *Cardiff records*, vol. 2, p. 21.

34 See below, Chapter 8.

35 G. R. Orrin, *The Gower churches* (Swansea, 1977).

36 P&M L330, L345, L623.

37 NLW KT, Worcester to Sir Charles, 11 December 1688; ULS Mackworth MS 68.

38 P. Jenkins, 'South Wales and Munster'.

39 P&M L437, L863; see also below, Appendix 4.

40 J. B. Davies, 'The Matthews family' in R. Denning (ed.), *Glamorgan historian* (1976), vol. 11, pp. 171–87.

41 GRO/DDF/F56.

42 P&M L430; *HMC Egmont Diary*, vol. 2, p. 143.

43 Bodl. MS Tanner 41, fo. 71.

44 G. Stradling, *Sermons and discourses* (London, 1692), biographical introduction; E. Ludlow, *Memoirs of Edmund Ludlow esq.* (3 vols. 'Vivay', Switzerland, 1698), vol. 3, p. 29. See below Appendix 5.

45 A. Macfarlane, *Origins of English individualism* (OUP, 1978).

46 NLW Bute MS 8215; Matthews, *Cardiff records*, vol. 2, pp. 178–9; G.J. Williams, *Traddodiad Llenyddol Morgannwg* (Cardiff, University of Wales, 1948), pp. 98–108; Johnes, *Essay*, p.9.

47 *GCH*, pp. 559–60; P&M 5937, 6369, 6593–5, 6625.

48 P&M A93, A102, A158.

49 Aylmer, 'Unbelief', pp. 40–1; NLW Add. MS 11447C, fo. 25.

50 Bayly, *Apothegmes*, p. 81.

51 P&M L1224.

52 *GCH*, p. 26 for Thomas Matthews of Castell-y-Mynach.

53 A recurrent theme in Glamorgan's history in the Civil War.

54 P&M L469, L863.

55 P&M 2753, 5543, 9083; ULS Mackworth MSS 128, 1282–4.

56 W. W., *Lamentable news out of Monmouthshire* (1608).

57 P&M L74, L237, L857; NLW Briton Ferry MS 124.

58 See, for example, P&M 5959, GRO D/DLL/E 118(1); GRO D/DOSM, vol. 9, July 1778; NLW Badminton MS 2249.

59 DWT, 1 January 1764.

60 G. J. Williams, 'Wil Hopcyn and the maid of Cefn Ydfa', in S. Williams (ed.), *Glamorgan historian* (1969), vol. 6, pp. 228–49.

61 Jenkins, 'Two poems'.

62 PRO SP 29/398, fos. 257–8.

63 NLW Add. MSS 6515–18E; DWT, fos. 544–6; NLW Bute MS 7437 for the repair of 'county' public buildings.

64 See, for example, P&M L452–3, 44456; GRO D/DKT/1/10, 17; NLW Badminton MS 2399; NLW Tredegar MS 66/1–2.

65 NLW Badminton MS 2235.

66 *CSPD 1676–7*, p. 513; *HMC Portland MSS*, vol. 3, p. 556; P&M L182, L779; GRO D/DN/239/4.

67 Bodl. MS Willis 38, fos. 377–8.

68 Williams, *Mystery*, p. 7; Dodd, 'Pattern of politics', pp. 88–90; P&M L492.

69 H. Durant, *Henry, first Duke of Beaufort and his Duchess, Mary* (Pontypool, 1973); BM Loan MS 29/233.
70 Jenkins, 'Jacobites and freemasons', p. 401.
71 Parr, *Life of Ussher*, p. 59; compare T. Godwyn, *Phanatical tenderness* (London, 1684), pp. 24–5.
72 CCL MS 4.87; J. E. Stephens, *Aubrey on education* (London, 1972), pp. 71–87.
73 Godwyn, *Phanatical tenderness*.
74 Thompson, 'Anonymity', p. 298.
75 For example, *CSPD 1667*, p. 217; P.&M L548; BM Loan MS 29/313, letter to Harley 1704.
76 Bodl. MS Wood F30, fos. 14–15.
77 ULS Mackworth MS 786; *HMC 11th Report*, Appendix, part 4 , p. 321.
78 E. P. Thompson, *Whigs and hunters* (London, 1977), p. 263.
79 E. Wynne, *Gweledigaethau y bardd cwsc,* translated by T. G. Jones (Gregynog Press, 1940), pp. 21–5, 133–5, 153–9.
80 Clement, *SPCK correspondence*, pp. 143–4.
81 Ibid., p. 248.
82 Owen (ed.), *Morris additional letters*, p. 611; J. Boswell, *Life of Dr. Johnson,* ed. R. W. Chapman (OUP, 1970), p. 1228.
83 Goldsmith, *Life of Nash*, pp. 27, 182, 209.
84 For example, the tomb of Mary Kemys (d. 1753) at Penmark.
85 P&M L1189, L1213, L1246; NLW MS 11464B; National Museum of Wales, portrait of Sir Charles Kemys-Tynte.
86 DWT, 22 March 1763. Only in 1730, witchcraft had been regarded as a grave accusation – Matthews, *Cardiff records*, vol. 3, p. 203.
87 *St. Peters' Magazine* (Cardiff, 1922), pp. i–iv.
88 J. Walters, *Dissertation on the Welsh language* (Cowbridge, 1771), pp. ii–iv.
89 Martin, 'Mineral property dispute'.
90 P. Burke, *Popular culture in early modern Europe* (London, 1979); I. F. Grant, *The Macleods* (London, 1959), pp. 329–30. G. H. Jenkins, *Literature and religion in Wales 1660–1730* (Cardiff, Board of Celtic Studies, 1978). For Brittany, Dodd, 'Pattern of politics', pp. 88–90.
91 See the remarks on this change by Yeats: W. B. Yeats, *Selected Prose,* ed. A. N. Jeffares (London, 1964), p. 215.
92 Hechter, *Internal colonialism*, pp. 101, 109–21; G. Williams, *Religion, language and nationality in Wales* (Cardiff, 1979), pp. 148–70.
93 Jenkins, 'Demographic decline'.
94 ULS Mackworth MS 799; John, 'Parliamentary representation', p. 106.
95 DWT, 4 November 1769, 1 February 1770; NLW Add. MS 6519.
96 CCL MS 2.716, vol. 1, fo. 6.
97 Jones, *Before Rebecca*, p. 63; P. Morgan, 'Hunt for the Welsh past', paper at *Past and Present* conference, 4 July 1977.
98 Walters, *Dissertation*, pp. ii–iv.
99 *Cambrian journal* 1854–5, p. 125. G. Eaton, 'The Williams family of Aberpergwm', *Transactions of the Neath Antiquarian Society* (1979), 19–37.
100 H. M. Vaughan, *The Welsh squires* (London, 1913); K. O. Morgan, *Wales in*

British politics (Cardiff, 1970), pp.1–27; Howell, *Land and people*, pp. 142–50, 85–92.

8. Education and culture

1 Stone, *University*, vol. 1, pp. 3–110; J. Lawson and H. Silver, *Social history of education in England* (London, 1973), pp. 177–80; Mingay, *English landed society*, pp. 131–8.
2 W. A. L. Vincent, *The grammar schools: their continuing tradition 1660–1714* (London, 1969); Davies, *Certaine schoole*, pp. 21–8.
3 Jenkins, 'Welsh anglicans'.
4 G. Grant-Francis, *The free school, Swansea* (Swansea, 1849); U. William, 'Education in Glamorgan 1650–1800' (MA thesis, University of Wales, 1956).
5 GRO D/DC1/1–(letterbooks); Baker, *Picturesque guide*, p. 104; Davies, *Certaine schoole*, pp. 37–8.
6 P&M L1007; N. Carlisle, *Complete description of the endowed grammar schools in England and Wales* (2 vols., London, 1818), vol. 2, pp. 952–62; Grant–Francis, *Free school*, pp. 13–14.
7 NLW KT, Edward Kemys to Sir Charles, 6 March 1694.
8 Davies, *Certaine schoole*, pp. 33–7.
9 Compare Vincent, *Grammar school*, p. 65.
10 P&M L74.
11 GRO D/DC1/1/5, 31 July 1740.
12 Davies, *Certaine schoole*, p. 34.
13 L. E. Tanner, *Westminster school*, 2nd edn (London, 1951); G. E. Russell Barker and A. H. Stenning, *Records of old Westminsters* (London, 1928).
14 For the cult of the old school, see J. H. Plumb, 'The new world of children in the eighteenth century', *Past and Present*, 67 (1975), 79.
15 Lawson and Silver, *Social history*, p. 179.
16 GRO D/DAu/66 (1772).
17 Lord Chesterfield, *The letters of Lord Chesterfield to his son*, ed C. Stachey, 3rd edn (London, 1932), p. xl. For Herbert, NLW Tredegar MS 32/19; and NLW Add. MS 2852E.
18 P&M L821; Lawson and Silver, *Social history*, p. 172.
19 ULS Mackworth MSS 657, 665. See above, Table 19(b), for these connections.
20 *Letters of Mrs. Elizabeth Gwynn of Swansea* (London, 1878), p. 20.
21 See, for example, Jerningham, *Welch heiress*.
22 *Aubrey, Brief lives*, pp. 121–3; Stephens, *Aubrey on education*, pp. 4, 26–7.
23 See, for example, Durant, *Duke of Beaufort*, p. 70; PRO SO 35/58, fo. 53.
24 P&M L715, L737.
25 NLW Sir John Williams Add. MS 128C; Clark, *Cartae*, vol. 6, pp. 2220–1.
26 J. Foster, *Alumni Oxonienses 500–1714* (Oxford, 1891), and *Alumni Oxonienses 1714–1886*.
27 Lloyd, *Gentry*, p. 216.

28 Jenkins, 'Welsh anglicans'.
29 Stone, *University*, vol. 7, pp. 58–102.
30 Based on Foster.
31 Chesterfield, *Letters*, letter 477.
32 P&M L897.
33 For the accumulation of debts at university, see, for example, P&M L850, L855, L905, L1003.
34 *Album studiosorum academiae Lugduno Batavae 1575–1873* (The Hague, 1875).
35 BM Add. MS 27606.
36 D. Seaborne Davies, 'Cardiganshire and the Inns of Court', *Cambrian Law Review* (1976).
37 J. R. Guy, 'The Gamage family', *Morgannwg*, 14 (1970).
38 ULS Mackworth MS 797.
39 'Dairy of Erasmus Philipps', *Notes and Queries*, 2nd ser., 10 (1860), 365–6, 443–5.
40 CCL MS 2.322; C. E. Williams, *A Welsh family from the beginning of the 18th century* (London, 1893).
41 P&M L840, L848, L1003, L1189–90. P. Jenkins, 'John Clephane', *NLWJ* (forthcoming).
42 Clark, *Cartae*, vol. 6, p. 2263; GRO D/DF F49–50.
43 DWT, 26 April 1771.
44 Jenkins, 'Mary Wharton'.
45 Jenkins, 'Clephane'.
46 P&M 9049.
47 NLW Harpton Court MSS C2–9.
48 Stradling, *Sermons*, introductions.
49 G. Scott Thomson, *Life in a noble house* (London, 1940), pp. 95–110.
50 Chesterfield, *Letters*, letters 139, 182.
51 P&M L1230.
52 P&M L1230 and many others.
53 Durant, *Somerset sequence*, pp. 156–7.
54 BM Add. MS 27606.
55 GRO D/DF/F48
56 Jenkins, 'Welsh anglicans'.
57 See above, Chapter 5.
58 DWT, 28 June 1767, 9 September 1781, and many other references to nonconformists as teachers.
59 *Trial of Regicides*, p. xxvii.
60 For a long political feud in the Monmouth free school, see Bodl. MS Rawl. A351, fo. 1045; *CSPD 1682*, pp. 275–6; *1689*, p. 170.
61 For a patronage contest in which Lord Mansell failed to win a client a teaching post at Charterhouse, P&M L816.
62 Many examples in GRO D/DCl/1–6. RISW, 'Swansea and Glamorgan calendar', vol. 3, p. 91.

63 GRO D/DKT/1/7, 79. D. W. Rennie, *Oriel College* (London, 1900), pp. 149–51.
64 Margam catalogues can be found in P&M 3802 (1700), 2206 (1740s), 3164 and GRO D/DP/885 (1750s). The Penllergaer list is in a commonplace book catalogued with P&M. Jenkins, *Literature and religion* for a general discussion of Welsh libraries. Mingay, *English landed society*, pp. 143–4.
65 NLW Cilybebill MS 234.
66 GRO D/DP/885.
67 For Chirk, Mostyn or Picton: NLW Chirk MS A32; NLW Add. MS 21244C; NLW Philipps of Picton MS 1740.
68 *Cal. Comp.*, p. 1855.
69 Evidence from many MS collections – NLWE P&M and Badminton, GRO Nicholl and Fonmon.
70 For Jones's collection, NLW Add. MS 11022. A. Dodd, *Studies*, p. 6.
71 G. H. Jenkins, 'Welsh books and religion 1660–1730' (Ph.D thesis, University of Wales, 1974), vol. 2, pp. 711–21.
72 Ibid.
73 NLW Add. MS 6518E.
74 For example, Stradling, *Sermons;* Hancorne, *Right Way;* Bodl. MS Carte 265; GRO D/DE 680–2; ULS Mackworth MSS, Box P, letter from Archbishop of York to Sir Humphrey, 10 May 1704.
75 P&M A1–A150.
76 GRO D/CL/1/4 (4 March 1738); 1/5; 1/9, fos. 403, 649.
77 H. Prideaux, *Life and writings of Humphrey Prideaux DD, Dean of Norwich* (London, 1748), pp. 267–80.
78 Aubrey, *Brief lives*, p. 464; A. Rudrum (ed.), *Complete poems of Henry Vaughan* (London, 1976), pp. 317–25, 644–5; Bodl. MS Aubrey 13, fos. 237–9.
79 Extensive correspondence in NLW KT during 1690; see also Jenkins, 'Mary Wharton'.
80 Jenkins, 'Mary Wharton'.
81 P&M 2719; see also NLW Cilybebill MSS 1833–1835, NLW Add. MSS 6514–15; Jenkins, 'Two poems'.
82 P&M 2206, and evidence in all the booklists.
83 NLW Add. MS 5457A.
84 NLW Add. MS 6517E for the book society.
85 NLW Add. MS 13077B, 10582E, CCL MS 2.76.
86 Ross, *Radical adventurer*, pp. 128–9; GRO D/DF, vol. 81; NLW Philipps of Picton MS 356.
87 The five were Ussher's *Primordia,* Camden's *Britannia* (1695 edn), Stillingfleet's *Orgines* (1685), Horsley's *Britannia Romana* (1732) and Rowlands' *Mona Antiqua* (1732); Jenkins, 'Edward Lhuyd to Iolo Morgannwg' for antiquarianism. See also S. Piggott, *William Stewkeley* (OUP, 1950) and his *Ruins in a landscape* (Edinburgh, 1976); D. C. Douglas, *English scholars 1660–1760* (OUP, 1939).

88 Bodl. MS Tanner 22, fo. 64; Aubrey, *Brief lives,* pp. 74, 146; Williams, *Traddodiad,* pp. 226–7; Bodl. MS Aubrey 12, fos. 6, 9.
89 BM Add. MS 15667; Gwyn was friendly with Hearne, Wanley and Hickes.
90 M. I. Williams, 'Edward Lhuyd and Glamorgan' in S. Williams (ed.), *Glamorgan historian* (1969), vol. 6, pp. 95–102; Lhuyd, 'Parochialia', pp. 1–160.
91 F. V. Emery, 'Edward Lhuyd and some of his Glamorgan correspondents', *TCS* (1965), 67–71.
92 GRO D/DC/F44, i–iii.
93 Emery, 'Correspondents', p. 72.
94 GRO D/DC/F44, i–iii for this approach to Margam's boundaries.
95 Emery, 'Correspondents', p. 64.
96 Ibid., pp. 67–71; R. Porter, *The making of geology* (CUP, 1977), pp. 33–40, 47–60.
97 Bodl. MS Aubrey 12, fos. 9, 247.
98 L. Alcock, *Dinas Powis* (Cardiff, 1963), Introduction.
99 J. Evans, *History of the society of antiquaries* (OUP, 1956), p. 93.
100 Jenkins, 'Edward Lhuyd to Iolo Morgannwg'.
101 For Williams, see above, Chapter 6.

9. The spread of metropolitan standards

1 For the social background, see C. Hill, *Reformation to Industrial Revolution* (London, 1971), pp. 171, 196–8, 206, 249; and his *Puritanism and revolution* (London, 1969); C. Wilson, *England's apprenticeship* (London, 1971); G. Rudé, *Hanoverian London* (London, 1971), pp. 65–8, 79–80; G. A. Cranfield, *Development of the provincial newspaper* (OUP, 1962).
2 Matthews, *Cardiff records,* vol. 3, pp. 108–9.
3 *CSPD 1657–8,* pp. 369, 552–3.
4 For rent bills, see P&M 1931; NLW KT, Wiseman to Sir Charles Kemys, 26 December 1700.
5 Rudé, *London,* pp. 38–47; GRO D/DKT/1/9, 19, 74; ULS Mackworth MS 228; GRO D/DF/F190; P&M 5092, L1207; NLW Bute MS 7470.
6 *HMC Egmont diary,* vol. 1, pp. 279, 307; vol. 2, pp. 164, 168; vol. 3, p. 194.
7 GRO D/DF/F, vol. 81; NLW Philipps of Picton MSS, Box 5A.
8 GRO D/DF/F, vol. 81; ULS Mackworth MS 812, BJ 257; Bucks RO D/AF/273.
9 See, for example, P&M L1255, L1087, L1340; ULS Mackworth MS 292, and many others.
10 NLW MS 1352B, fo. 54; P&M L364.
11 NLW KT, John Romsey to Sir Charles, 21 January 1689.
12 Goldsmith, *Life of Nash,* p. 21; GRO D/DKT/1/24.
13 GRO D/DKT/1/9.
14 DWT, 19 January 1769; NLW Penllergaer MS 773.
15 P&M L1255, Jacob, *Compleat sportsman,* dedication.
16 GRO D/DF/F49B–C.

17 P&M L468.
18 P&M L1173–4, 9032, 9049, 9053, 9089; GRO D/DC/F4; GRO D/DN/265/ 24.
19 Cranfield, *Provincial newspaper,* p. 201.
20 HMC *Delisle and Dudley MSS,* pp. 305–7; NLW KT, T. Catchmayd to Sir Charles Kemys, 13 July 1697.
21 J. Evelyn, *Diary,* 27 June 1654.
22 Goldsmith, *Life of Nash,* pp. 20–4.
23 See, for example, HMC *Portland MSS,* vol. 4, p. 329.
24 NLW Add. MSS 6869–70A; GRO D/DST/16/72–97.
25 Green, *Sheridan and Matthews.*
26 C. Price, *The English theatre in Wales* (Cardiff, 1948).
27 Jenkins, 'Mary Wharton'; see below, Appendix 5.
28 Denning, 'Devil had a share'.
29 M. R. Spencer, *Annals of south Glamorgan* (Carmarthen, 1913), pp. 225–6.
30 Williams, *Wesley in Wales,* p. 59.
31 NLW Bute MS 7437; GRO D/DF/F, vol. 81. For the improvement of Cardiff, see John Davies, *Cardiff and the Marquesses of Bute* (Cardiff, University of Wales, 1981).
32 Williams, *Welsh family,* pp. 40–1; ULS Mackworth MSS 790, 802; GRO D/ DF/F, vol. 81.
33 NLW MS 6517E; Davies, *Certaine schoole,* p. 375.
34 Young was equally enthusiastic: *Six weeks tour,* p. 169.
35 K. Kissack, *Monmouth* (London, 1975), pp. 241–61.
36 Davies, *Certaine schoole,* pp. 43, 60; GRO D/DN/236/10; Bucks RO D/AF/ 273.
37 CCL MS 2.716, vol. 2; *DNB* for 'Thomas Coke' and 'Walter Churchey'; *DWB,* 'Hugh Bold'.
38 R. Haslam, *Powys* (London, 1979).
39 Daunton, 'Towns and economic growth', pp. 266–9.
40 Price, *English theatre,* pp. 47–50; W. Minchinton, 'Visitors to Gower in the eighteenth century', *Gower,* 2 (1949), 24–6. Haslam, *Powys,* pp. 52–8 for the new spa at Llandrindod Wells.
41 R. C. Hoare (ed.), *Itinerary of Bishop Baldwin in Wales* (London, 1806), Introduction; W. Gilpin, *Observations on the river Wye and several parts of South Wales etc.* (London, 1782); Byng, *Torrington diaries.*
42 Klingender, *Art,* pp. 16–17.
43 See, for example, NLW Add. MSS 687B, 1084A, 9104C, 16989; Bucks RO D/DR/8/13/3.
44 Hibbert, *American,* p. 67.
45 Baker, *Picturesque guide,* p. 108; Boswell, *Life of Johnson,* p. 567.
46 Mingay, *Gentry,* p. 150.
47 CSPD 1677–8, p. 421.
48 R. Bayne-Powell, *Housekeeping in the seventeenth century* (London, 1956), pp. 27–62. For the old houses, see the inventories of Nash (GRO D/DC/ 1192), Ewenni (P&M 1867), or Fonmon (GRO D/DF/F178).

49 Jenkins, 'Mary Wharton'.
50 P&M 3164, 6559; ULS Mackworth MSS 403, 457.
51 M. Apted, 'Social conditions at Tredegar house', *Monmouthshire Antiquary*, 3 (1972–3), 125–55.
52 P&M 3164, 6559; NLW Bute MS 7470.
53 NLW Dunraven MS 248.
54 Apart from inventories already cited, see NLW Cilybebill MS 733; NLW Penllergaer MS 487.
55 M. I. Williams, 'General view of Glamorgan houses and their interiors', in S. Williams (ed.), *Glamorgan historian* (1974), vol. 10, pp. 157–76; and his 'Cardiff, its people and its trade' *Morgannwg*, 7 (1964), 74–97.
56 P&M L918; Williams, 'View'; ULS Mackworth MSS 456, BJ 243, 257.
57 G. N. Evans, *Social life in mid-eighteenth-century Anglesey* (Cardiff, 1938), p. 22.
58 NLW Brogyntyn MS 1158; P&M L89–L90.
59 Dineley, *Progress*, p. 249.
60 Owen (ed.), *Morris additional letters*, p. 531; Bodl. MS Willis 37, fo. 38.
61 I. G. Jones, *Aberystwyth 1277–1977* (Aberystwyth, 1977).
62 P&M 9054; ULS Mackworth MS 765; NLW Bute MS 7470.
63 NLW KT, 1699 Ruperra inventory.
64 J. H. Plumb, *The commercialisation of leisure* (University of Reading, 1974) and *The pursuit of happiness* (Yale Center for British Art, 1977), pp. 3–28.
65 PRO SP 36/21, fos. 58–9.
66 Williams, *Welsh family*, p. 40.
67 NLW Donald C. Jones MSS, bundle 1, letter of October 1784.
68 ULS Mackworth MSS 137, 154.
69 Davies, *Bute estate*, pp. 26–9.
70 DWT, 1 November 1770.
71 NLW Donald C. Jones MSS, bundle 20, 17 August 1929 newspaper account of CCL.
72 Dineley, *Progress;* NLW Tredegar MS 102/83; P&M L280; Malkin, *Scenery*, p. 74.
73 Williams, 'View of Glamorgan houses'.
74 NLW Add. MS 6516A; J. Thomas, 'Harps and harpers of Gwent and Morgannwg', *Cambrian Journal* (1855), p. 191.
75 P&M A56.
76 L. Stone, *The family, sex and marriage in England 1500–1800* (London, 1977), pp. 325–405.
77 R. Charles, 'Some Penrice pictures', in S. Williams (ed.), *Glamorgan historian* (1972), vol. 8. For a different view, see Ellen G. d'Oench, *The conversation piece* (Yale Center for British Art, 1980), pp. 1–34.
78 D. B. Hague, *Old Beaupre castle* (HMSO, London, 1965), p. 6.
79 P&M L182.
80 Macaulay, *History of England*, vol. 1, p. 336.
81 DWT, 31 March 1765.
82 Jenkins, 'Mary Wharton'; Mingay, *English landed society*, pp. 224–6.

83 Jenkins, 'Two poems', p. 172.
84 P&M L286–8.
85 Stone, *Family*, pp. 325–34.
86 Jenkins, 'Mary Wharton'.
87 Thomas, 'Family history', p. 36.
88 ULS Mackworth MS 130.
89 P&M 2485; *HMC Egmont Diary*, vol. 2, p. 437.
90 Women also tended to maintain their piety; see Goldsmith, *Life of Nash*, p. 156, and *Transactions of the Neath Antiquarian Society*, 7 (1936–7), 95–7.
91 See above, Chapter 8 for booklists.
92 ULS Mackworth MS BJ 254, and many unsorted MSS; Mingay, *English landed society*, pp. 146–7.
93 NLW Penllergaer MS, parcel 2, no. 20; GRO D/DE/680–2; D/DCL/1/10.
94 DWT, 17 January 1763, 7 March 1765, 4 November 1769, and fo. 565; Matthews, *Cardiff records*, vol. 3, p. 182.
95 CCL MS 2.76, P&M A84–8, NLW Cilybebill MSS 1833–5; NLW Philipps of Picton MS 1627; P&M L1239 for a bawdy painting. For Wilkinson, CCL MS 2.355.
96 Ross, *Radical adventurer*.
97 DWT, 20 September 1767; for the Edwin circle, Yorke, *Life of Hardwicke* vol. 3, pp. 258, 1252.
98 P&M L267, BM Loan MS 29/102.
99 P&M L1224.
100 Lindley, 'Part played by catholics', pp. 184–5.
101 D. Williams, *The vanity of childhood and youth*, 5th edn (London, 1758); E. Saunders, *A domestic charge* (Oxford, 1701).
102 Aubrey, *Brief lives*, pp. 48, 239.
103 P&M L959.
104 P&M 286–8, L347, L364, L354.
105 Jenkins, 'Two poems', p. 170.
106 Jenkins, 'Antipopery', p. 290.
107 E. Shorter, *The making of the modern family* (London, 1976); L. de Mause, *History of childhood* (New York, 1974). Compare Stone, *Family*.
108 Jenkins, 'Mary Wharton'.
109 ULS Mackworth MS BJ 146.
110 ULS Mackworth MS 284; NLW Bute MSS, letterbook 70, Mackworth to Lady Windsor, 16 August 1765.
111 For the life of children: GRO D/DN/231/15–16; Bucks RO D/AF/273; NLW Add. MS 6516A. For the danger of marrying servants: P&M L1486; BM Add. MS 24120, fos. 29–30. J. Methuen-Campbell, 'The children at Penrice', *Gower*, 26 (1975), 38–43.
112 Jenkins, 'Two poems'; Macaulay, *History of England*, vol. 1, pp. 239–41; Mingay, *English landed society*, pp. 145–54.
113 NLW KT, J. Romsey to Sir Charles Kemys, 26 June 1688; and other letters.

114 NLW KT, T. Morgan to Sir Charles Kemys, 27 April 1694.
115 L. Namier and J. Brooke, *The House of Commons 1754–90* (London, History of Parliament Trust, 1963).
116 See, for example, P&M 6593, A105, NLW Add. MS 12505D, fo. 1. *The pride of possession* (Welsh Arts Council, Cardiff, 1975).
117 Jacob, *Sportsman*, dedication; P&M L1218, L1247.
118 R. Longrigg, *History of foxhunting* (London, 1975).
119 GRO D/DC/F1; D/DF/F, vol. 81; D/DN/236/1; NLW Badminton MS 2185; P&M 2485.
120 Numerous references in NLW KT and other collections; BM Add. MS 32703, fo. 376.
121 F. M. L. Thompson, *English landed society in the nineteenth century* (London, 1971), p. 150. N. Cox, *The gentleman's recreation* (London, 1677), p. 3; Chesterfield, *Letters,* letters 180, 173, Matthews, *Cardiff records,* vol. 2, pp. 289–90.
122 G. J. Williams, *Iolo Morgannwg* (Cardiff, University of Wales, 1956), p. 26 note.
123 NLW Add. MS 1214D.
124 G. Borrow, *Wild Wales* (n.d., c. 1940), p. 535.
125 E. Moir, *The justice of the peace* (London, 1969), p. 82.
126 L. Stone, *Social change and revolution in England 1540–1640* (London, 1965), p. 33, note 11.
127 P&M 755; see below, Appendix 4.
128 See, for example, P&M L1033, ULS Mackworth MS 130; R. Longrigg, *History of horseracing* (London, 1972).
129 Kissack, *Monmouth.*
130 Price, *English theatre,* p. 8; NLW Philipps of Picton MS 589.
131 Rees, *Cardiff,* p. 188–90; DWT, 4 January 1764, 22 June 1767. For horse-breeding, P&M 6028, 5620, L680, L1085.
132 Price, *English theatre,* p. 8; DWT, 28 September 1765.
133 *CSPD 1657–8,* p. 369.
134 Rees, *Cardiff,* p. 187; GRO D/DN/269/31; CCL MS 4.27, fo. 2; NLW Aberpergwm MSS 1475–7.
135 P&M 9018; *HMC Beaufort MSS,* p. 90; GRO D/DF/F, vol. 81; Matthews, *Cardiff records,* vol. 2, pp. 288-9. For Neath, P&M A98.
136 Rees, *Cardiff,* p. 187. For wizards, see P&M A99–100; DWT, 19 February 1772, 12 January 1763.
137 Apted, 'Social conditions', p. 129; DWT, 14 October 1773; Yorke, *Life of Hardwicke,* vol. 3, p. 258.
138 Byng, *Torrington diaries,* vol. 1, pp. 17–30; Aubrey, *Brief lives,* p. 462; DWT, *passim.*
139 C. Owen, *Life of the late reverend and pious Mr. James Owen* (London, 1709), p. 15. R. W. Malcolmson, *Popular recreations in English society 1700–1850* (CUP, 1973), pp. 68–72, 158–71.
140 DWT, 1 October 1764; see also 1 June 1763, 22 October 1771, fos. 500–1.
141 P&M 755; see below, Appendix 4.
142 Harris, *Life,* pp. 38–45.
143 Ibid.

Conclusion to Part III: 'Conspicuous antiquity'

1 Jenkins, 'Ancient gentry'.

Aftermath: towards the Victorian world

1 B. Ll. James, 'Great landowners of Wales in 1873', *NLWJ*, 14 (1965–6), 301–20; G. C. Brodrick, *English land and English landlords* (London 1881); J. Davies, 'The end of the great estates', *WHR*, 8 (1974), 186–213. Nicholas, *Annals;* Howell, *Land and people;* Jenkins, 'Ancient gentry'.
2 R. Grant, *Parliamentary history of Glamorgan* (Swansea, 1978).
3 *Parl. Papers 1852–3*, vol. 89, pp. 121–2; Williams, *Merthyr rising.*
4 Jones, *Before Rebecca.*

Conclusion: from Civil War to Industrial Revolution

1 G. Parker, *Europe in crisis 1598–1648* (London, 1979), pp. 17–28.
2 Anthony F. C. Wallace, *Rockdale* (New York, 1978), pp. 482–3.
3 Burke, *Popular culture.*
4 De Tocqueville, *Regime*, pp. 72–80, 120–37.
5 D. Richet, 'Economic growth and its setbacks' in Ferro (ed.), *Social historians*, pp. 205–6.
6 J. M. Roberts, *Mythology of the secret societies* (London, 1974), pp. 36–8; Jacob, *Radical enlightenment.*
7 Crouzet 'England and France in the eighteenth century' in Ferro (ed.), *Social historians*, p. 79.
8 See above, Chapter 3; Macfarlane, *English individualism.*
9 S. W. Baskerville, 'The management of the tory interest in Lancashire and Cheshire 1714–47' (D. Phil. thesis, University of Oxford, 1976), pp. 13–25; Jenkins, 'Anti-popery'.
10 Money, *Experience and identity*, pp. 136–41.
11 See Wrigley, 'Modernisation'. For an example of the excellent regional studies of the role of French towns, see T.J.A. Le Goff, *Vannes and its region* (OUP, 1980).
12 Recent scholarship on colonial America also provides many instructive parallels. See, for example, Rhys Isaac, *The transformation of Virginia 1740–1790* (University of North Carolina, Chapel Hill, NC, 1982); Daniel B. Smith, *Inside the Great House* (Cornell University Press, 1980); Thad W. Tate and David L. Ammerman, *The Chesapeake in the seventeenth century* (New York, 1979).

Index

Aberafan, 28, 49, 160
Aberavon, *see* Aberafan
Abercrave, xvi
Aberdare, 16
Abergavenny, xvi, 226, 231
Abergavenny, Lord, 20
Aberpergwm, 201, 222, 254, 269
Aberthaw, 10, 11, 14, 53
Aberystwyth (Cards.), 253
Adams, John, 21
Addison, Joseph, 266
Africa, 67, 69, 232, 233
agricultural societies, 62–3
agriculture, improvement of, 6, 51–7,
    62–3
Albemarle, William Anne Keppel, 2nd Earl
    of, 159
Albion's fatal tree, 95
Alleine, Joseph, 126
America, xxv, 67, 184, 186, 334 n. 12; *see
    also* Georgia Society; Pennsylvania
American Revolution, 180, 184, 186–7
Amsterdam, 195
Angers, 227
Anglesey, 175
anglicans, *see* Church of England; clergy,
    anglican; high church party
Anguillara (Italy), 51
Anne, Queen of England, 137, 152, 163,
    179
anticlericalism, 97–8, 137, 163–4
anti-popery, 104, 124–133, 178; *see also*
    catholics
antiquarianism, *see* history and historical
    study
Apter, Professor M., 64–5
Archaeologia Britannia (Lhuyd), 235–6
archaeology, 6, 9, 234–8; *see also* history
    and historical study; William Stukely
arianism, *see* unitarianism
Aries, Professor P., 261

aristocracy: ecclesiastical patronage
    and, 13; income of, 48; land sales by,
    49–50, 123–4; new peers in, 41, 182,
    201; traditional families of, 20–1;
    weakness of, in Glamorgan, 76
Arlington, Henry Bennet, 1st Earl of, 126
army, 118, 120
Arnold family, of Monms., 69
Arnold, John, 125, 127–9, 137–8, 140,
    200
arson, 96–7, 266
art, *see* building activity; Gothic style;
    portraits
Ashburnham, John, 1st Baron, 242
assemblies, 243, 247–8
Association, the (1696), 142
Atterbury, Francis, 154, 156, 159
attorneys, *see* lawyers
Aubrey family, of Llantrithyd: as absentees,
    56; in Buckinghamshire, 89, 215; in
    duels, 200; income of, 48; kinship and,
    203, 208; portraits of, 262; as royalists,
    114, 120; as whigs, 159
Aubrey, John (antiquary), 210, 222, 235,
    260
Aubrey, Sir John (d. 1679) (1st Bt), 118,
    119–20, 123, 210, 222, 235, 242
Aubrey, Sir John (d. 1700) (2nd Bt), 138,
    269
Aubrey, Sir John (d. 1743) (3rd Bt), 148,
    229, 260, 263
Aubrey, Sir John (d. 1767) (4th Bt), 260
Aubrey, Sir John (d. 1826) (5th Bt), 184,
    186, 201
Aubrey, Colonel Richard Gough, 82
Aubrey, Colonel Sir Thomas, 51, 243
Austen, Jane, 274

Badminton (Glos.), 195, 244
Bagot, Sir Walter, 165
Baker, Augustine, 18, 311 n. 1

335

banks, 62
baptists, 17, 109–12, 117, 121, 132
bards, 205–7
Barebone's Parliament, 112
Barnstaple, 10
Barry, 99
Bassett family, of Aberthaw, 180
Basett family, of Beaupre, xv, 12, 37, 48,
    56, 68, 104, 109, 114, 119, 199, 203,
    205, 208
Bassett family, of Miskin, 37, 259
Bassett family, of Bonvilston, 93
Bassett, Christopher, 64, 66, 178
Bassett, Henry, 119–20
Bassett, Sir Richard, 118, 119, 123
Bassett, William of Miskin, 161, 215, 230
Bassett, Dr William, 119, 123
Bassett, Sir William, 119
bastardy, 259–60
Bates, Richard, 36, 213
Bath, 41, 88, 153, 200, 213, 245–6
Bath, Earl of, *see* Pulteney, Sir William
Baxter, Richard, 126
Beaufort, Dukes of: electoral power of,
    165, 170, 188; feuds with gentry of,
    16–17; as jacobite leaders, 153–5, 197;
    minority in family and, 160; power in
    Glamorgan of, 20, 77; sport and, 268–9;
    Welsh loyalties of, 210; *see also*
    Worcester, Marquises of
Beaufort, Charles Noel Somerset, 4th Duke
    of (d. 1756): fellowship at Oriel and,
    229; feud with western gentry of, 16–17,
    32, 61, 175, 214; house in London of,
    242; as jacobite leader, 173–6, 228;
    rejoices at victories in 1750s, 67;
    supports whig MP, 182, 209
Beaufort, Henry Somerset, 1st Duke of (d.
    1700): catholic steward of, 56;
    educational experiment of, 222; enclos-
    ure of commons and, xxii; opposes
    Association, 142; Popish Plot and,
    125–32, 202; as President of Council, 79,
    152, 254; retirement after 1688, 134;
    strength in west Glamorgan of, 137–8
Beaufort, Henry Somerset, 2nd Duke of (d.
    1714), 146, 148–9, 152–3
Beaufort, Henry Somerset, 3rd Duke of
    (d. 1745): 'country' sports and, 268–70;
    friendship with Mackworths and, 53; as
    jacobite leader, 157, 162–73, 228;
    marriage breaks up, 259; methodism
    and, 179, 270; minority of, 55
Beaufort, Henry Somerset, 5th Duke of,
    160, 185, 187, 229

Beaupre, xv, 35, 38, 56, 256
Beckett, Dr J. V., xvii
Bedfordshire, 22
Bedloe, William, 128
Benson, Martin, 159
Berkeley, James Berkeley, 3rd Earl of, 151
Berkshire, 158, 208
Bertie family, 165
Bevan family, 241
Bible, 149, 177, 180, 193, 212, 216, 231,
    256
Bideford, 11
Bird family, of Cardiff, 247
Bird, John, 54–5, 80, 253, 279
Birt, Peter, 198
bishops, *see* Llandaff, bishops and
    diocese of; St David's, bishops and
    diocese of
blackmail, 96
Blackstone, Sir William, 226
Blaenau (upland zone), 5, 11, 13, 15–19,
    27, 32, 105; local government in, 86–8
Blome, Richard, 21–2, 27, 30, 196
'bluewater' policy, xxv, 65–7, 141, 171,
    176
'Board of Loyal Brotherhood', 152, 166
Boarstall (Bucks.), 41, 138
Bohemia, 214
Bolingbroke, Earls of, 68
Bolingbroke, Henry St John, 1st Viscount,
    85, 143, 146, 154, 156
Bolton, Dukes of, 136
Bolton, Charles Paulet, 3rd Duke of (8th
    Marquis of Winchester), 79, 89, 157,
    167, 259
Bonfield, Dr L., 38
books, *see* libraries
Booth family, of Cheshire, 133
Booth's Rising (1659), 116
Bordeaux, xx, 9, 60, 285
boroughs, *see* towns
Borrow, George, 266
Boswell, James, 213
Boverton, 29, 90
Bowen family, of Kittle (Gower), 58, 219
Bowen family, of Methyr Mawr, 253, 259
Bowen, Professor E. G., 11
Bowen, Colonel Henry, 111, 113
Brackley (Bucks.), 138
Bradford, John, 186, 215, 238
Brecon, 3, 10, 12, 76, 129, 153, 161, 167,
    182
Brecon Old Bank, 62
Breconshire, 63, 129, 146, 151, 160, 175
Brewer, Professor J., 176

Bridgend, 14, 97, 138, 180, 185, 247, 253
Bridgewater, 10, 60
Brie, 51
Bristol: capital from, 60–1, 69; in Civil War, 107–8; families of, 36–7, 41; jacobites in, 153; metropolitan area of, xx–xxi, 3, 10–14, 231, 244–5, 252, 285; nonconformity in, 105, 113, 118; plots of 1680s and, 130–1; replaced by Swansea as 'metropolis', 248; trade with, 99, 277; war and, 66, 171
Bristol Channel, 10–12, 53, 65–6, 98–9, 151
Briton Ferry, 27–8, 35, 41, 50–51, 57–8, 68, 122
Brittany and Bretons, 10–11, 60, 99, 325 n. 90
Bro, see Glamorgan, Vale of
'Broad-bottom', 135, 166–73
Brooke, Lord, 20
Brown, Lancelot ('Capability'), 198
Bruce family, 275
Bruce, Rev. Thomas, 90
Brynllywarch, 226
Buckinghamshire, 41, 63, 68, 89, 138, 186, 215
building activity, 41–2, 197–8, 272–3, 302 n. 34
Bulkeley, James, 6th Viscount, 173
Bulkeley, Richard, 4th Viscount (d. 1724), 153
Burford (Oxon.), 268
Burke, P., 214
Busby, Richard, 221
Bute, Earls and Marquises of, 188
Bute, John Stuart, 3rd Earl of, 183
Bute, John Stuart, 1st Marquis of, 41, 50, 54, 80, 198
Bute, John Stuart, 2nd Marquis of, 275
Bute, John Patrick Crichton Stuart, 3rd Marquis of, 274
Button family, of Cottrell, 262
Button family, of Dyffryn, 127, 163, 226
Button, Martin, 52, 124, 127
Button, Miles, 119, 123
Button, Thomas, 148

Cadogan, William Cadogan, 1st Earl, 151, 318 n. 71
Cadogan, William, 111
Cadoxton-juxta-Neath, 61, 202
Caerleon, 104
Caernarvonshire, 44
Caerphilly, 7, 14, 28, 58, 81, 186, 237, 249
Caerwent, 15

Calamy, Edmund, 112
Calvinism, 173
Cambrian, The, 248
Cambridge, University of, 223
Cambridgeshire, 22
Camden, William, 234–5, 237
Campbell, Colen, 198
Canaletto, 244
Candleston, 6
Caradoc Vreichvras, 202
Carbery, Earls of, 136
Carbery, John Vaughan, 3rd Earl of, 137, 151
Carbery, Richard Vaughan, 2nd Earl of: army patronage and, 120; dominates Carmarthenshire, 21; as 'moderate' in Civil War, 108, 110; as President of Council, 79, 118; Welsh sympathies of, 210
Cardiff: bank of, 62; Bute estate and, 54–5; decline of (1670s), 49; gentry in, 20, 42, 201, 202; 'improvement of', 247–9, 252–4; merchants of, 35–7, 67; nonconformity in, 105–6, 113, 115, 122, 129; nonjurors in, 156, 185; port of, 65, 93; southwestern links and, 9–12, 14; tories in, 97, 149, 154, 160–1; whigs in, 85, 129, 156
Cardiff bridge dispute, 95, 147
Cardiff Castle, 29, 198
Cardigan, 76, 161, 253
Cardiganshire, 48, 59, 157, 165, 171, 175, 250, 252–3
Carlisle, 119
Carmarthen, 3, 12, 76, 97, 153, 248; dissenting academy, 226
Carmarthenshire: aristocratic domination of, 20–2, 136, 157; constituencies in, 76, 146; Glamorgan links of, 30; industry in, 61; Mansell power in, 151; population of, 12; whigs in, 148, 167, 182
Carne family, of Ewenni, 12, 28–9, 69, 114, 132, 154, 203, 208–9
Carne family, of Nash, 114, 132, 150
Carne, Eleanor, 256
Carne, Rev. John, 51, 90, 98
Carne, Sir John, of Ewenni, 118, 120, 123, 131
Carne, Richard, 38, 256–7
Carter, Richard (Judge), 80, 158–9, 181
Castell-y-Mynach, 41, 50
castles, 244; constables of, 37, 55, 59; garrisons in, 82, 117, 119, 125; ruins of, 9, 234, 237; use of, against invasion, 65–6

catholics, 10; Chapter 5, *passim*; in Civil
   War, 104; decline of, 173–4, 178; in
   Interregnum, 114–5; loyalties of, 211;
   pilgrimages of, xvi; strength of, 125; *see
   also* anti-popery; Popish Plot
Cefn Mabli, 27, 30, 32, 38, 50, 91, 130,
   251, 254
Celtic Christianity, xvi, 129
Chambers, Profesor J. D., xvii
Chancery, 147 *see also* Lords Chancellor
Channel Islands, 9, 60
chaplains, domestic, 159, 222, 235, 263
charities, political role of, 170; *see also*
   Georgia Society; Society for the Propa-
   gation of Christian Knowledge; Welsh
   Trust
Charles I, King of England, 106–7, 210
chartism, 19
Chepstow, 9, 109, 119, 125, 265
Cheshire, xvii
Chester, 11, 119
Chesterfield, Philip Dormer Stanhope, 4th
   Earl of, 221, 224, 228
childbirth, 258
children, 260–3
Chillingworth, William, 232
Chilton (Bucks.), 262
China, 232
Chippenham, 76
chinoiserie, 244
Chippendale furniture, 244
Chippenham (Wilts.), 171
Church of England: as focus of loyalties,
   211–12; in Interregnum, 114–15; indus-
   trialisation and, 18, 275; *see also* Church
   courts; clergy, anglican; Llandaff,
   bishops and diocese of; St David's,
   bishops and diocese of; high church
   party; nonjurors
Church courts, 14, 93–4
cider, 53
Cider Act, the, 183
Cilybebill, 32, 38, 57
Civil War: economic consequences of, 68,
   276–80; effects of, 28–30; events of,
   107–9, 206–7; memories of, 95, 110,
   144–5; parties in, 104-7, 210
Clarendon, Edward Hyde, 1st Earl of, 124
Clarges, Sir Thomas, 140
Clark, Dr J. C. D., 182
Clarke, Samuel, 159, 163
classical scholarship, 212, 219, 264
Clay, Dr C., xvii
Clayton, Sir Robert, 69
Clemenston, 32

Clephane, John, 227–8
clergy, anglican, 37, 180, 204; incomes of,
   49, 197, 253; as justices, 89–91, 98,
   143–4, 151, 171; as teachers, 222–3; *see
   also* high church party
clerk of the peace, 91
Cliffe, Dr J. T., xvii
clocks, 251
clothes, 199
clothing industry, 11, 14, 69
clover, 52–3
clubmen, 108–9, 210
clubs: in London, 242–3; *see also* 'Cycle
   Club'; freemasonry; Sea Serjeants,
   Society of
Clyne Castle, 273
coaches and carriages, 198
coal: mining of, 16–17, 57–9, 61; trade in,
   58–60, 65
coastal trade, 10, 14
cockfighting, 207, 268–70
Cocoa Tree, 152, 165–7, 186
Coity, 20
Coke, Edward, 167, 265
Cole, Dr A., 117
Cole, William, 250
Coles, William, 61
Colley, Dr L., 174
Collingbourne (Wilts.), 175
Collins family, 165
Colston, Edward, 69, 156
Comenian theories of education, 210, 222
'commercialisation of leisure', 253–6
Commission for the Propagation of the
   Gospel in Wales, 112–16
commons, disputes over, 15–17, 32, 60–1;
   see also enclosures
compounding, 68
Coningsby, Thomas, Earl, 157
constables (parish), 93
Conway, Earls, 140
copper industry, 59–62, 66, 155
Cork, xx, 9
Corneille, 210, 233
Cornwall, xx, 9–12, 59–60, 65, 99, 152,
   164, 277
coroner, 185
corporations, *see* towns
'Corry men', 96
Cotes, Charles, 170
cottages, 15, 83
Cottrell, estate, 41, 52, 61
Council in Wales and the Marches, 79–81,
   118, 125–6
'country' ideology, 264–6, 268–71

county loyalties, 208–9
Courtenay family, 28
Cowbridge: agriculture in, 53, 63; elite of, 35, 58, 154; as gentry centre, 208, 262; government of, 94, 130; improvement of, 247–9; population of, 12; races in, 266–8; roads in, 7; trade of, 14
Cowbridge book society, 232–4
Cowbridge grammar school, 185, 217–20, 222
Coychurch, 14
Cradock, Walter, 106, 111, 122
Craftsman, the, 164, 233, 320 n. 129
Cragge, John, 115
Craven, William Earl of, 131
Crawshay family, 88, 198, 273–4
Crawshay, Richard, 63, 88
crime, xxvi, 10, 96–9, 177
Cromwell, Oliver, 110, 112, 114–16, 118, 122, 143
Cromwell, Richard, 117
Cruickshanks, Dr E., xxv, 173–4
Cudworth, Ralph, 233
Curre family, of Clemenstone, 184
Curwen family, 62
custos rotulorum, office of, 80, 151, 158
'Cycle Club', the, 153, 165
Cyfarthfa, xxvi, 273–4

Dafydd, Edward, 215
dairy industry, 14
Danby, Thomas Osborne, 1st Earl of (Duke of Leeds), 125, 146
'dark corners of the land' (theory of), 71, 107
Daunton, Dr M. J., 67, 248
David, Richard, 202
Davies, Francis, 110
Davies, Thomas, 143–4, 237
Dawkins family, of Kilvrough, 219
Dawkins, Rowland, 110–13, 127
dearths, 18, 63, 96–7
death, attitudes to, 260, 262; *see* funerals; tombs
debt and credit, 20, 67–70, 250
Declaration of Indulgence (1672), 126
Deere family, 32, 93, 112, 184
Deere, John, 37, 69
Deere, Matthew, 36
Defoe, Daniel, 234
deism, xxv, 145, 163, 185–6, *see also* freemasons
de Mause, Professor L., 261
demographic crisis, xxi, 3–4, 38–41, 45, 50, 90, 160, 214, 277, 279–80, 284–5

Denbighshire, 171
depressions, agricultural, 49–50, 53–4, 278
deputy-lieutenants, 42, 81–3
Derby, 173
Derbyshire, 41, 214
Devis, Arthur, 255
Devonshire, xvi, 7, 10–11, 14, 53, 107, 269
Devonshire, William Cavendish, 1st Duke of, 138
Devonshire, William Cavendish, 2nd Duke of, 157
Devonshire, William Cavendish, 4th Duke of (Marquis of Hartington), 167, 267
Digby, Lords, 157, 170
Digby, Edward, 6th Lord, 170
Digby, Juliana, 164, 254, 258, 262
Digby, Robert, 155
Digby, William, 5th Lord, 155
dilettanti, 194
Dillwyn family, 275
Dillwyn, Lewis Weston, 273
Dinas Powis, 90, 95, 237
disinheritance, 260–1
dissenters, *see* nonconformists
dissenting academies, 142, 150–1, 226
doctors, 35–6
Dodd, Profesor A. H., 72, 102
Dorset, 22, 41, 58, 140, 170, 245
Dowlais, xxvi, 37, 61, 274
drama, 248, 254; *see also* theatres
drinking, 91, 204, 264, 269
druids, 237–8, 272
duels, 193, 199–201, 212–13
Dugdale, Sir William, 234
Dunraven, 27, 38, 40
Dunraven, Earls of, 274
Durel, Daniel, 219–20, 222, 229, 232–3
Durham, bishops and diocese of, 159
Dutch influences, *see* Holland
Dyffryn, 38, 274
Dyffryn Aberdare, 90
Dyffryn Clydach, 231, 269
Dynevor, Earls of, 182

Eaglesbush, 60
East Indies, 69
East India Company, 150
Edinburgh, 178
Edmondes family, 56, 184, 244, 247, 267
Edmondes, Thomas, 35, 51, 63, 221
education, 210; Chapter 8 *passim*, 262; *see also* dissenting academies; Oxford, University of; schools
Edwards family, of Llandaff, 36, 91

Edwards, Thomas, 35–6, 55, 91, 176, 207
Edwards, William, 248
Edwin family, of Llanmihangel, 160, 176, 178, 180, 183, 208, 265, 269
Edwin, Ann, 40
Edwin, Charles (d. 1756): in election of 1745, 161; house in London of, 242, 251; inheritance of, 40, 188; methodism of family, 180; as opposition MP, 166–72, 175, 259–60, 320 n. 138
Edwin, Charles (1731–1801), 184, 188
Edwin, Lady Charlotte, 180, 245
Edwin, Sir Humphrey, 30, 57, 138, 148, 166, 208
Egmont, John Perceval, 1st Earl of, 170, 181, 242–3
eisteddfod, 215
election petitions, 161, 171
elections, parliamentary, 146; elections of: 1708, 147–9; 1734, 161–2; 1737, 161; 1745, 171–2; 1780, 183–4; 1789, 187; costs of, 160–2, 179; electoral structure of county, 20; attempts to alter, 160–1
Elizabeth I, Queen of England, 99
Ely, Isle of, 22
enclosures, 16–17, 53, 97, 187; *see also* commons
Energlyn, 254
Epsom, 267
Erbery, Dorcas, 113
Erbery, William, 105–6, 112–13, 129, 212
Essex, Robert Devereux, 3rd Earl of, 108
estates: administration of, 54–7; comparison with Europe, 51; land values of, 53; size of, 44–5; wealth of, *see also* feudal dues; incomes, gentry
Eton, school, 221, 263
Evans family, of Eaglesbush, 58, 235
Evans, Charles, 129, 315 n. 110
Evans, David, 49, 115, 127
Evans, Sir Herbert, 95, 123
Evans, Thomas, 132
Everitt, Professor A., xxiii
evictions, 49, 54, 206
Ewenni, 28–9, 32, 256
excise and excisemen, 96, 111, 158, 164

fairs and markets, 14, 49, 63
Falkland, Lords, 221
family structure, 255–63
Fazakerley, Nicolas, 165
fertilisers, 52–3; *see also* lime
feudal dues, 16, 54–5, 57, 60–1, 187
Feiling, Sir Keith, 140
Fielding, Henry, 234

'Fifth Monarchy men', *see* Powell, Vavasor
Firmin, Thomas, 126
Fitzherbert, Maria Anne, 250
Fleetwood, Charles, 111
Flintshire, 161
floods, 6, 207
Florence, 227
Foley, Paul, 141
food, tastes in, 252
Fonmon, 29, 55, 57, 67, 198
food-riots *see* dearths; riots
Forde Abbey, 41
Forest, 54, 269
Forster, Professor R., 51
Fowler, Richard, 44
Fox family, 170, 221
Fox, Charles, 142
Fox, Charles James, 183–4
Fox, George, 117
Fox, Henry, 170
France, xviii, 9-10, 65, 142, 211, 281–3, 285
Franklen family, 32, 244, 247, 258, 275
Franklen, John, 63
Franklen, Richard, 221
Franklen, William, 199
Franklin, Benjamin, 186
Frederick the Great, King of Prussia, 211
Frederick, Prince of Wales, 77, 167, 176, 181
freemasonry, xxv, 63-64, 135, 153, 167, 175, 177–8, 184–6, 280–1, 285
'French prophets', 179, 280
French Revolution, 18–19, 180, 187–8
Friars, 38
Fritz, Professor P. xxv
funerals, 215
furniture, 250–3

Gainsborough, Earls of, 168
Gamage family, 37, 114, 205, 225
gambling, 67
Game Laws, 93, 187, 230, 266
games and pastimes, 253–5
gardens, 198, 272
Gawler, Francis, 118
Gawler, Major John, 113, 117–18
Gelligaer, 9, 17, 87, 132
genealogy and heraldry, 201, 215, 236, 250
Gentleman's Magazine, the, 233
gentry: changing ideology of, Chapter 7, *passim*; decline of traditional families of, 38–42; definition of, 15–16, 21, 196–7; elite families and, 28–30; geographical distribution of, 27–8, 30–5; income of,

see incomes, gentry; lesser families of, 30–5; new families of, 42, 56; numbers of, 15–16, 22, Tables 1–2, 27–8; 'urban', 42
geographical context, xxi, Chapter 1, *passim*
George II, King of England, 162, 177
George III, King of England, 35, 156, 176, 182
Georgia Society, the, 170
Germany, 59, 137
Gibbins family, 62
Gibbon, Matthew, 113, 117
Gibbons, Grinling, 244
Gibbs family, of Neath, 35–6
Gibbs, David, 35–6
Gibbs, Marmaduke, 36, 95, 125, 137–8, 285
Gibson, Edmund, 234
Gildon, Charles, 145
Gileston, 52
Gilpin, William, 249
Glamorgan, Earl of, *see* Worcester, Edward; Somerset, 2nd Marquis of
Glamorgan, lordship of, 5
Glamorgan, topography of, 5–9
Glamorgan, Vale of: crime and disorder in, 95–8, 189; description of, 5-8; estates in, 50–2; gentrification of, 22, 27–9; justices in, 87; nonconformity in, 113, 180; society of, 11–15
Glassey, Dr L. K. J., 84–5
'Glorious Revolution' (1688), xxiii, 16, 131–4
Gloucester, 107, 246
Gloucester, Vale of, 5
Gloucestershire, xvii, 41, 53, 152, 210, 245
Gnoll, 27, 30, 35, 52, 56, 58, 66, 251
Godfrey, Sir Edmund Berry, 122
godparents, 202
Golden Grove (Carms.), 76, 79, 114
'Good Old Cause', the, 116
Gore, Hugh, 219
Gothic style, 272–3
Gower, 7, 10, 14, 52, 102, 236; dialect of, 7
Gower, John Leveson-Gower, 1st Earl of, 164–5
Gower, lordship of, 5, 16, 109
Grand Tour, 227–8
Gray, Thomas, 234
Great Tew, 114
Guest family, 273–5
Guest, Lady Charlotte, 273
Gwinnett family, of Cottrell, 259

Gwinnett, Richard, 71
Gwyn family, of Llansannor, 29, 160, 171, 198, 209
Gwyn, Francis: at Cowbridge, 130; in Dorset, 41; historical studies of, 140, 210, 231–2, 235–7; industry and, 58–9; as jacobite, 154; as justice, 85; Rochester and, 202; as Secretary of State, 76, 80, 119–21, 269; tory party and, xxiv–xxv, 134, 139–41, 145–8, 151
Gwyn, Francis, the younger, 157, 202
Gwynne family, of Llanelwedd (Radnorshire), 118
Gwynne family, of Taliaris, 163
Gwynne, George, 116, 119
Gwynne, Marmaduke, 182
Gwynne, Sir Rowland, 69, 128–30, 132, 137, 158, 161, 177

Habakkuk, Professor Sir John, xvii, 44
Halifax, George Savile, 1st Marquis of, 129, 140
Halifax, William Savile, 2nd Marquis of (Lord Elland), 129
Hall family, 273
Hampshire, 41, 76, 152, 158
Hanbury, Capel, 266, 269
Hanbury family, 62, 181
Hanbury, John, 59
Hancorne family, 37, 163, 165
Hancorne, Thomas, 143, 145, 150
Harcourt, Simon Harcourt, 1st Viscount, 146
Hardwicke, Philip Yorke, 1st Earl of, 85
Harley family, of Herefordshire, 48, 106, 115, 140; *see also* Oxford, Earls of
Harley, Sir Edward, 127
Harley, Robert, *see* Oxford, Robert Harley, 1st Earl of
harps and harpists, 254, 272
Harrington, James, 185, 232
Harris, Howell, 178–9, 270
Harris, Rev. James, 143–4, 164, 237
Harrison, Thomas (Major-General), 111–12, 122, 132
Hartington, Marquis of, *see* Devonshire, William Cavendish, 4th Duke of
Haslam, Mr Richard, 248
Haverfordwest (Pembs.), 12, 112, 153, 267
hawking, 265
Hay, Professor D., 95, 212
Hearne, Thomas, 140
hearth-tax, 12, 21–22, 198
Heathcote, Sir William, 170

Hechter, Professor Michael, 214
Hellfire Club, the, 184, 259–60
Hensol, 27, 38, 41, 50, 159, 266, 273
Herbert family, of Cherbury, 118, 133
Herbert family, of Friars, 21, 29, 41, 79, 81, 198, 201, 202, 205
Herbert family, of Roath, 35, 105–6, 109
Herbert, Henry Arthur, *see* Powis, Henry. Arthur Herbert, 4th Earl of
Herbert, John, 105, 113
Herbert, Richard, 57, 230
Herbert, Thomas, of Friars, 221
Herbert, William, of Friars, 90, 123
Hereford, 246
Hereford, Price Devereux, 9th Viscount (d. 1740), 179
Herefordshire, 22, 48, 53, 157
Hervey, John, Baron, 167, 200
Hessian soldiers, 158, 164
Hickes, George, 140
high church party, 138, 142–6, 150–7, 185; *see also* Beaufort, Dukes of
Highlight, 50
Hill, Christopher, 72, 107, 276
Hirwaun, 61
history and historical study, 202, 209, 234–8, 272–3; *see also* Celtic Christianity; genealogy and heraldry; Roman remains
History of Myddle, The (by Richard Gough), xix
Hoare, Richard Colt, 249
Hoby family, of Neath Abbey, 121, 128, 137
Hoby, Philip, 91, 122, 128
Hogarth, William, 201, 255
Holland, 10, 102, 117, 126, 130, 138, 187, 225, 246, 285
Holland, Henry, 198
Holles, Denzil, 1st Baron, 80
Hollingsworth, Professor T. H., 38
Holmes, Professor G. S., xxiv, 136, 148
Homfray, Jeremiah, 88
Hopkin, Lewis, 215
Horsley, John, 237
horses and horseracing, 156, 165, 266–8, 270
Hotwell (Bristol), 244–5
Howe, John, 143
Howell, Dr D., 72
Howell, Sir George, 35, 139, 141, 148, 151,158
Howell, George, 158, 208
Hoyle, Edmund, 253
Hughes, Professor E., 54

Hughes, Stephen, 121
Humphrey Clinker (Smollett), 249
hunting, 264–6, 268–71; opposition to, 266
Huntingdon, 118
Huntingdon, Selina Hastings, Countess of, 180, 245
Hurst family, of Gabalfa, 42, 259

Iestyn ap Gwrgan, King of Morgannwg, 235
Ilchester (Som.), 182
Ilston (Gower), 17, 113
impeachments, of 1701, 142, 148; of the Earl of Oxford, 156
incomes, gentry, Tables 1 and 7; pp. 45, 48–51, 275
Independent Electors of Westminster, 166–7, 172–3, 186
Independent Whig, the, 233
India, 232
Industrial Revolution, 57–65, 276–86
industry, 57–62, 65–7, 277; jacobite links and, 155; political importance of, 135, 186; *see also* coal industry; copper industry; iron industry; tinplate industry
inns, 249; Bear (Cowbridge), 83, 249; Mackworth Arms (Swansea), 249; Ship (Newport), 156; Ship and Castle (Neath), 249; Wyndham (Bridgend), 249
Inns of Court, 36, 225–6
insurance, 65–6
interior decoration, 250–3, 255–6
Interregnum, the, 109–17, 242; and spread of puritan ideas, 17
invasion threats, 65–6, 82, 153
Iolo Morgannwg, 186–7, 215, 238, 266
Ireland and Irish: in civil wars, 111-12; decline of perceived threat of, 134, 178; education in, 225; fear of, 132; as political issue (1780s), 184–6; relationships with, 28, 214; road to, 7; trade with, xxi, xxv, 9–11, 60, 69; whiggery of, 103, 143
Ireton, Henry, 143
Irish massacre (1641), 144
iron industry, 37, 58–61

Jacob, Giles, 91
jacobites: at Bath, 245; economic development and, xxii, 279; growth of, in 1690s, 141–4; growth of, after 1710, 151–7; Hanoverians and, 162–75; importance of, xxv; as justices, 85–7; martyrs of 1746, 136; in Revolution of 1688, 132;

survival of, 184–5; *see also* 'Cycle Club';
   Sea Serjeants, Society of
James II, King of England, 84, 101, 120,
   126, 128, 131–2, 144, 154
James, Mr B. L., 51
Jeffreys, George (Judge), 131
Jenkins family, of Hensol, 29, 114, 159,
   205
Jenkins, Judge David (d. 1664), 71, 76,
   104–5, 107, 109, 136, 231
Jenkins, David, of Hensol (d. 1696), 120,
   123
Jenkins, Elias, 36
Jenkins, Sir Leoline, 76, 80, 114, 120, 218,
   220, 229, 232
Jenkins, Richard, of Hensol, 138, 147–9,
   214, 254
Jenner family, of Wenvoe, 42
Jephson family, of Mallow (Ireland), 38,
   203
Jerningham, Edward, 71
Jersey, William Villiers, 2nd Earl of, 154
Jockey Club, the, 267
Johnes family, of Cardiganshire, 188
Johnson, Dr A. M., 107
Johnson, Dr Samuel, 250, 258
Jones family, of Fonmon, 69, 103, 154–5,
   160, 178, 201–4, 242, 267–8
Jones, Dr G. E., xvii
Jones, John (Cromwellian lord), 112
Jones, Mary, 244
Jones, Philip, 29, 56, 76, 109–13, 115–16,
   118, 124, 152, 201
Jones, Philip, of Carmarthenshire, (fl.
   1755), 204
Jones, Robert (d. 1715), 143, 154
Jones, Robert (d. 1742), 85, 155, 180,
   227–8, 242, 244–5
Jones, Robert (d. 1793), xxvi, 51, 67, 82,
   95, 98, 183–4, 243, 269
Jones, Samuel, 121, 126, 129, 222, 231
Jones, Sir Thomas, 35, 138, 158
judges, 80, 88, 151, 158–9, 181, 188
'Jumpers', 179
Junto, 138
justice, administration of, xxvi; Chapter 4,
   passim
justices of the peace, 83–92, 131, 171, 232

Kemys family, of Cefn Mabli, 30, 52, 68,
   81, 89, 103–5, 114, 203–5, 209, 211,
   264
Kemys, Sir Charles (d. 1658), 242
Kemys, Sir Charles (d. 1702): as
   antiquary, 235; and Beaufort's family,

145, 202; coach of, 198; family and, 30;
   feud with Mansells of, 146–7, 200;
   industry and, 58; in parliament, 69, 264;
   reading of, 232–3; as royalist, 120, 123,
   129–31, 278; Welsh loyalties of, 210; as
   whig (1690s), 138
Kemys, Sir Charles (d. 1735): debts of, 67;
   extinction of family of, 285; as jacobite
   leader, 135, 146, 154–6, 162, 165–7;
   portrait of, 262; sickness of, 243–4;
   Wharton links of, 138
Kemys, Edward, 162, 219
Kemys, Mary, *see* Wharton, Mary
Kemys, Sir Nicholas, 77, 104, 108–9, 119
Kemys-Tynte family, of Cefn Mabli, 215
Kemys-Tynte, Sir Charles, 50, 163, 166,
   171–2, 175–6, 182–3, 198, 229, 242
Ken, Thomas, 232
Kenfig, 6
Kent, 44, 215
Kenyon, Professor J. P., 144–5
Kilvrough, 274
King, Peter, 1st Baron, 137, 151, 157
'King's Evil', 210
kinship, 28–30, 201–5; and politics, xxiv;
   see also family
Klingender, Professor J., 249
Knight family, of Tythegston, 244
Knight, 'Captain' (smuggler), 99
Knight, Henry, of Tythegston, 183, 200–1
Knight, Richard, 64, 178

Lambarde, William, 234
Lambert, John, 116
'Lampoon on the Glamorganshire Gentle-
   men' (Philip Williams), 264, 269
Lancashire, 9, 165, 284
Lancaster, 82
Landor, Walter Savage, 250
Landore, 60
Languedoc, 214
Lansdowne, George Granville, Baron, 154
Laud, William, 101, 107, 133
Laudians, 89, 102
law enforcement, *see* justice, administration
   of
laws of Hywel D da, 215
Lawson, J., and Silver, H., 221
lawyers, 17, 35–8, 207, 209
lead industry, 61–2, 175
leases, 54
Lee, Nathaniel, 254
Leeds, Duke of, *see* Danby, Thomas
   Osborne, 1st Earl of
Leicester, Earls of, 48, 50

Leicester, Philip Sidney, 3rd Earl of, 76
Leicester, Robert Sidney, 2nd Earl of, 108, 120, 222
Leicester House, *see* Frederick, Prince of Wales
Lely, Peter, 201
Lethieullier, Smart, 237
Lewes, Sir Watkin, 63, 184–6
Lewis family, of Van, 41, 48, 58, 106, 141, 143, 163, 198, 205, 220, 229, 235
Lewis, Sir Edward, 106
Lewis, Erasmus, 151
Lewis, Evan, 56, 109–10
Lewis, Nicholas, 106
Lewis, Richard, 139, 146
Lewis, Thomas, 144, 148, 155, 160
Lewis, Sir Thomas, 106, 123
Lewis, William, 106, 109, 222
Lewis, Sir William, 106
Leyden, University of, 225
Lhuyd, Edward, 225, 234–8
libraries, 230–4
Lichfield (Staffs.), 165, 268
lime, 6, 52
Lindley, Dr K., 104
Lisburne, Lords, 137; *see also* Vaughans of Crosswood
Lisburne, John Vaughan, 1st Viscount, 137
Lisburne, John Vaughan, 2nd Viscount, 157
Liverpool, 245
Llanblethian, 204
Llanbradach, 87
Llancaeach, 87, 109
Llancarfan, 11, 15, 106
Llandaff, 14, 20, 28, 36, 143, 198, 267, 273
Llandaff, bishops and diocese of, 13, 20–1, 147, 163, 177–8, 202, 209, 237
Llandaff, Lords and Earls of, 95
Llandaff, Francis Mathew, 1st Earl of, 41
Llandyfodwg, 87
Llanelli, 18
Llanfaches, 105
Llangibby (Monms.), 265
Llangiwg, 16
Llangyfelach, 7–9, 15–16, 19, 32, 52, 105, 199
Llanharan, 54, 90, 94, 202, 231
Llanmihangel, 27, 30, 38, 40, 57, 70
Llanofer, 254
Llanover, Augusta Waddington, Baroness, 273
Llansamlet, 16, 18

Llansannor, 27, 142, 277
Llantrisant, 12, 94, 143, 247
Llantrithyd, 27, 114, 198
Llantwit Major, 12, 14, 112
Llewellyn family, of Coedarhydyglyn, 56, 247
Llewellyn family, of Cwrt Colman, 16
Llewellyn family, of Ynysgerwn, 15, 32, 175
Llewellyn, Henry, 91
Llewellyn, Hopkin, 36, 55, 98, 207, 221
Llewellyn, John, of Penllergaer, 82
Llewellyn, John, of Ynysgerwn, 61
Lloyd family, 56
Lloyd, Dr H. A., xvii
Llwyd, Morgan, 185, 212
Lockwood and Morris (copper co.), 60, 155
London, 18, 37, 40, 89, 136, 156, 165–6, 187, 194, 231, 241–4; and Chapter 9, *passim*
London, areas of: Bloomsbury, 194, 242, 250; Essex St Chapel, 186; Leicester House, 176; Mayfair, 242–3; Newgate, 151; Soho, 194, 242; Vauxhall, 243
London, schools in and near, 221; *see also* Westminster School
Lords Chancellor, 79, 85, 92, 159
lords-lieutenant, 79–80
Lougher family, of Tythegston, 81
Lougher, Richard, 115, 123
Loughor, 12
Love, Christopher, 77, 115
Lowther family, 62, 138
Lucas family, 227
Lucas, William (army officer), 151
Lucas, William (constable), 93
Ludlow, 11, 119
Ludlow, Edmund, 112, 122, 204–5, 232, 257
Lundy Island, 99

Mabinogion, 273
Macaulay, Thomas Babington, xvii, 91, 230, 241, 256, 263–4
Macclesfield, Charles Gerard, 1st Earl of, 79
Mackworth family, of Gnoll, 30, 81, 97, 157, 160–2, 164, 171, 183, 201, 211
Mackworth, Herbert (d. 1765): as agricultural improver, 53, 63; as antiquary, 237; coal-trade and, 65–6; debts of, 67; estate of, 56; family of, 257, 262; in London, 243, 252; as MP, 69; as tory, 155, 164–7, 171–6, 183

Mackworth, Sir Herbert (d. 1791), 56, 62–3, 82, 178, 221, 226, 253, 262
Mackworth, Sir Humphrey: family of, 262; feud with Mansells of, 148–9; house of, 251, 253; industrial career of, 59–60, 249, 277, 283–4; reading of, 232; SPCK and, 212; as tory, 143, 146, 152, 155
Mackworth, Juliana, *see* Digby, Juliana
Maddocks, Anthony, 35–6, 162, 166, 207–8
'Maid of Cefn Ydfa' (legend), 207
Malcolmson, Dr R. W., 269, 283
Malkin, Benjamin H., 53
Manchester, Charles Montagu, 1st Duke of, 142
Manchester, Edward Montagu, 2nd Earl of, 80, 116, 119, 122, 124
Manning, Dr B., 71
manorial rights, *see* feudal dues
Mansell family, of Briton Ferry, 27–8, 59, 121, 126–30, 205, 219, 242
Mansell family, of Margam, 21, 28–30, 48, 51, 59–61, 66, 81; Chapters 5 and 6 *passim;* 201, 203, 205, 211, 215, 219, 224, 232, 235, 242, 263
Mansell, Anthony, 203
Mansell, Bussy, of Briton Ferry (d. 1699), 109, 116, 122, 124, 127, 129–30, 137, 207, 214, 264, 278
Mansell, Bussy, 4th Lord (d. 1750): debts of, 68; duels of, 200–1; family of, 204, 257; house of, 242; jacobite links of, 154, 157; as tory leader, 160, 162, 164, 167, 171, 229; whig friendships of, 181
Mansell, Christopher, 3rd Lord, 68
Mansell, Edward of Swansea, 110, 144, 150–1
Mansell, Sir Edward (d. 1706): as antiquary, 231-2, 242; beliefs of, xvi, xxvi, 96, 199, 206–9; family of, 203–4, 257, 260–1; gentry community and, 48, 52, 91, 95, 264; Interregnum and, 116; as opposition leader, 126–32, 200; at Restoration, 118–24; whiggery of, 141–2, 147, 149, 160
Mansell, Sir Edward, of Trimsaran, 203
Mansell, Francis, 107, 114, 210, 228
Mansell, Sir Lewis, xv, 106, 109, 121
Mansell, Sir Richard, 199, 203
Mansell, Robert, 85, 154–5, 160, 228, 260–1
Mansell, Thomas, 1st Lord: beliefs of, 203–4, 207; dissenting education and, 121; family of, 227, 257, 260–1; ecclesiastical patronage and, 27; histori-

cal study and, 201, 235; as MP, 69; opposes James II, 132; as tory leader, 77, 80, 135, 139–42, 145–54, 156–60; Welsh loyalties of, 210
Mansell, Thomas, 2nd Lord, 39, 50, 85, 167, 170, 200, 204, 206, 227–8, 242–3, 251, 265
Mansell, Thomas, of Briton Ferry (MP), 129, 140
Mansell, Thomas, of Briton Ferry (d. 1706), 149
Mansell, Sir William, 200, 203
Mansell-Talbot family, of Margam, 175, 230
Mansell-Talbot, Christopher Rice, 273–5
Mansell-Talbot, Thomas, 63, 82, 215, 265, 272
Manton, Thomas, 122, 260
mapsants, 93, 270
Mar, John Erskine, 6th Earl of, 154
Macross, 38, 50
Margam, xvi, 27–9, 32, 38, 41, 48, 51–3, 57, 59, 66, 68, 90, 94, 98, 121, 130, 142, 145, 198, 202, 215, 230–1, 254, 267, 272–3, 277
Marlborough, John Churchill, 1st Duke of, 82
marriages: aristocrats, 28; gentry, 257; merchants, 37; out-county, 40
Martin, Dr J. O., 38, 44, 50, 54
Mathew, *see also* Matthews
Mathew, Tobie, 311 n. 1
Mathews, *see* Matthews
Matthews family, of Aberaman, 28–9
Matthews family, of Castell-y-Mynach, 28–9
Matthews family, of Llandaff, 28, 41, 64, 159, 163, 172, 203, 266–7
Matthews family, of Radyr, 28, 202
Matthews, David, 123, 127
Matthews, Edward, 70, 77, 130–1, 143, 278
Matthews, Humphrey, 231
Matthews, Marmaduke, 121, 128
Matthews, Admiral Thomas, 64, 159–60, 171–2
Matthews, Thomas, of Castell-y-Mynach, 123
Matthews, Thomas, of Llandaff, 41, 201, 246
Matthews, Thomas William (MP), 175–8, 182–5, 209, 225, 227, 246
Medmenham (Bucks.), 184, 259
memorial inscriptions, 202
merchants, 35–8

Merionethshire, 44
Merrett, Robert, 233
Merrick, Rice, 234
Merthyr Mawr, 52, 253
Merthyr Tydfil: as centre of communications, 7–9; clergy in, 143, 151; gentry in, 87; industrialisation of, 18, 53, 88, 187, 248; population of, 12, 66; puritanism in, 17–19, 113, 275; radical plots in, 118,122, 129, 132; Welsh culture in, 254
methodism: anticlericalism and, 98; Bath and, 245; calvinist, 179, 189; country sports and, 270–1; education, 226; improvers, 63; origins of, 179–80, 229; Wesleyan, 11, 180
Meyrick family, of Pembs., 143
'middle class', 35–8; Chapter 9, *passim*
Midlands, 97, 155
militia, xxvi, 81–3, 99, 183
Milton, John, 258
Mine Adventurers, Company of, 59, 149
Minehead, 10–11, 14, 60, 76, 154
Mingay, Professor G. E., xvii, 44, 48, 50, 52, 54, 62, 89, 240, 250
minorities, 55, 160
Miskin, 35, 230
Mitchell, Andrew, 182
'moderates', 103; Chapter 5 *passim*
modernisation, theories of, xviii, xxii, 45, 62–5
Moir, Dr E., xvii
Moll Goch, 97
monasteries, dissolution of the, 28–9
Money, Dr J., 97, 284
Monknash, 161
Monmouth, 104, 111, 184, 231, 247, 267–8, 270, 327 n. 60
Monmouth, James Scott, 1st Duke of, 130
Monmouth rebellion, xvi, 49, 130–1
Monmouthshire: Beaufort's power in, 20; catholics in, 102, 104, 126–30; depression in, 50; links with Glamorgan of, 10–11, 32, 53; militia in, 82, 89; Morgans in, 146, 158, 162; protest and crime in, 96–7, 266, 269; tories in, 155, 172, 175; whigs in, 136–7
Montgomeryshire, 153, 155
Montpellier, 227
Moravians, 180
Morgan family, of Coedygoras, 120
Morgan family, of Ruperra, 105
Morgan family, of Tredegar (Monms.), 48, 56, 80, 92, 125–7, 130, 137, 157–9,

162, 181, 198, 203, 208, 215, 268
Morgan, Anna, 246
Morgan, David, 77, 136, 143, 166, 173, 175
Morgan, Howell, 268
Morgan, John, 215
Morgan, Thomas, of Tredegar (d. 1700), 197
Morgan, Thomas, of Tredegar (d. 1769), 160
Morgan, Thomas, of Machen, 116
Morgan, Thomas, of Ruperra, 181
Morgan, Thomas (of Swansea), 233
Morgan, William, of Tredegar (d. 1680), 120, 126
Morgan, Sir William, 157–8
Morrill, Dr J. S., xvii, 108
Morris family, of Clasemont, 198, 267, 281
Morris, Lewis, 213
Morris, Robert, 178, 184–5, 200–1, 234, 259–60
Morriston, 18, 66
Moulton, 106, 113
Mountstuart, Lord, *see* Bute, John Stuart, 1st Marquis of
Musgrave family, 139
Musgrave, Sir Christopher, 141–2, 146, 154
music, 242–3, 253–4; *see also* harps
Myddelton family, 162

names, Christian, 216; *see also* patronymics, use of
Namier, Sir Lewis, xxiv, 172, 182
Nanteos (Cards.), 252–3
Nantes, 285
Nash, 52, 90, 213; *see also* Monknash
Nash, 'Beau' Richard, 213, 245
Nash, John, 248
navy, 37, 64, 66
Naylor, James, 113
Neath: cockfights in, 268–9; development of town, 247–9; elite of, 35–6, 42; government in, 130, 149, 199; industry in, 53, 57–9, 61; nonconformity in, 18; population of, 12; tories in, 155; trade of, 9–10
Neath Abbey, 55, 249, 254
Neath, river, 27, 32, 61
Needham, John Turberville, 227
Netheravon (Wilts.), 175
Netherlands, *see* Holland
neutralism, xxiii, 107–9

New England, 110
Newborough, Lord, 253
Newburgh, Lords, *see* Newborough, Lord
Newcastle-upon-Tyne, 66
Newcastle, Thomas Pelham-Holles, 1st Duke of, 181, 183
Newfoundland Company, 69
Newick (Sussex), 68
Newmarket, 267
Newport, 7, 9, 49, 104, 156, 231, 248
newspapers, 244–5, 248
Newton, Isaac, 233
Newton Nottage, 10, 14
Nicholas, Edward, 140, 142, 146
Nicholl family, 32, 42, 262, 267, 275
Nicholl, David, 204
Nicholl, Rev. John, 177
Nicholl, Jonathan, 204
Nicholl, Sir John, of Merthyr Mawr, 188, 221
Nicholson, William, 234
Nicolas, Dafydd, 222
Noble, George, 165
nonconformists: decline of, 178–9; electoral strength of, 159; growth during Interregnum, 113; jacobites and, 173; James II and, 132; mystical element and, 18; numbers of, 17, 87; occasional conformity of, 145–9; origins of, 17–18, 105–7, 229; persecutions of, 117–9; toleration of, 121–4; unitarian trends and, 18; *see also* methodists; quakers
nonjurors, 139, 155–7, 173, 222, 284
Norfolk, 40, 44, 53
Norman Yoke, theory of, 128–9, 145; *see also* Saxon Yoke
Normandy, 60
Northumberland, 284
Norway, 214
Nottingham, Daniel Finch, 2nd Earl of, 140
Nottinghamshire, xvii
Nowell, Thomas, 185, 229

Oates, Titus, 137
Ogmore, 138, 264, 266, 268
Ogwr, river, 63
old age, 261
Oldisworth, Michael, 110, 204
Orford, Edward Russell, 1st Earl of, 137
Ormonde, James Butler, 1st Duke of, 119, 124
Owen, Arthur, 115

Owen, James, 118
Oxford, Earls of, 165
Oxford, Edward Harley, 2nd Earl of, 165, 209
Oxford, Robert Harley, 1st Earl of, xxiv–xxv, 134,140, 142, 145, 152, 154, 156
Oxford, 3rd Earl of, 175
Oxford, University of, 156–7, 165, 223–35; colleges: All Souls', 229; Christ Church, 156–7, 167, 224; Jesus, 106, 224, 230–1; Magdalen, 157; Oriel, 175–6, 185, 229; debts at, 68, 224–5
Oxfordshire, 22
Oxwich, 249

'Mr Packer', 96
Padley family, of Swansea, 36
Paine, Thomas, 19
Pakington, Sir John, 163
Parc, 95
Paris, 227
parishes, areas of, 13; importance of, 93-4
parliament, families represented in, 27, 76, 275, Appendix 1
parties, political: origins of, xxiv, 146; *see also* tory party, whig party
Pascal, Blaise, 233
'pastoral-industrial' areas, 15–19, 72; *see also Blaenau*
paternalism, 78–9, 205–8
'patriots' (political label), 18, 148, 176, 187
patronage: colonies and; customs office and, 150, 161; ecclesiastical, 13, 119–20, 159; educational, 229; Hanoverians and, 157–9; importance of, 149–51, 157; Newcastle and, 181–3; Restoration and, 118–21; *see also* army, navy
patronymics, use of, 15–16, 93
Paul, St, and Pauline ideas, 122, 180, 193, 212
peers, *see* aristocracy
Pelham family, 181–2
Pembroke, 249
Pembroke, Earls of, xxiii–xxiv, 5, 20, 29, 48, 56, 77, 102, 105–6, 123–4, 126, 130, 211; *see also* moderates
Pembroke, siege of (1648), 109
Pembroke, Henry Herbert, 10th Earl of, 221
Pembroke, Philip Herbert, 4th Earl of, 105, 108, 110, 209–10

Pembroke, Philip Herbert, 5th Earl of, 118, 120
Pembroke, Philip Herbert, 7th Earl of, 129
Pembroke, Thomas Herbert, 8th Earl of, 79, 147
Pembroke, William Herbert, 6th Earl of, 118, 222
Pembrokeshire, 10–11, 21–2, 50, 155, 173, 180
Penclawdd, 67
Penllergaer, 60, 230–1, 274
Penlline, 37
Penmaen, 202
Penmark, 50, 202
Pennsylvania, 130
Penrice, 82, 198, 273
Penrice family, of Gower, 275
Pepys, Samuel, 125
Percy, Thomas, 234
Peter, Hugh, 111
Philipps family, of Picton (Pembs.), 130, 143, 170, 180, 188
Philipps, Erasmus, 226
Philipps, Sir John, of Picton, 165–6, 171, 173–5, 182, 212, 234, 267
Philipps, William, 148–9
'picturesque', 249
Piercefield (Monms.), 198
piracy, 65
Pitt, William (Earl of Chatham), 176
Pitt, William (the younger), 184
Plot, Robert, 234, 236
Plumb, Professor J. H., xxiv, xxv, 136, 178, 241, 253
Plymouth, 9, 61, 66, 245
Plymouth, Other Lewis Windsor, 4th Earl of, 41, 80, 82, 268
poaching, 91, 97
poetry, 232–3
Pontypridd, 249
Poor Law, 83
Popham family, 11
'Popish Plot', 103, 122, 128–31
Popkins family, of Forest, 32, 59, 89, 165, 180, 184
Popkins, Robert, 61
Popkins, Thomas, 148
population, 12, 18, 66
Port Talbot, xv
Portland, William Bentinck, 1st Earl of, 138, 145
portraits, 20, 255, 262
Portrey family, 37
pottery industry, 61
Powell family, of Energlyn, 89

Powell family, of Llanharan, 42, 202, 247, 258
Powell family, of Nanteos (Cards.), 80
Powell family, of Swansea, 55, 207, 219
Powell, Gabriel (1676–1736), 56, 155, 165
Powell, Gabriel (1710-88), 62, 82, 176
Powell, Gervase, 88, 246
Powell, Rhys, 232
Powell, Roger, 144, 151, 199
Powell, Vavasor, 91, 111–12, 117, 122, 125, 129, 132, 179, 185
Powell, William, 146, 153
Powis, Marquises and Earls of, 133, 211
Powis, Henry Arthur Herbert, 4th Earl of, 157, 183
Powis, William Herbert, 1st Marquis of, 131–2, 134
Powis, William Herbert, 2nd Marquis of, 173
Poyer, John, 119
presbyterians, 94, 115–16, 121–4, 260
'Presidents', *see* Council in Wales and the Marches
Pretender, Old, *see* Stuart, James Edward
Pretender, Young, *see* Stuart, Charles Edward
Price family, of Briton Ferry, 105
Price family, of Gellihir, 110
Price family, of Penllergaer, 15, 32, 89, 215, 244
Price family, of Tynton, 226
Price, Charles, 56
Price, Richard, 18, 185–7, 210
Price, Robert, 145, 165
Price, Rev. Thomas, 87, 143–4, 151
Price, Thomas, of Watford, 61, 63
Price, Thomas, of Penllergaer, 230
Prichard family, of Llancaeach, 109
Prichard, Mary, of Llancaeach, 220
Prichard, Rhys ('The Vicar'), 106, 121
Prideaux, Humphrey, 232
Priest family, of Cardiff, 36, 67
printing, 247–8
prisons, xxvi, 20
privateers, 65–7
Probyn, Sir Edward, 181
professions, 35–8
'Propagation', *see* Commission for the Propagation of the Gospel in Wales
Pryce, Thomas, 98
Pryse, John Pugh, 176, 184
Pryse, Lewis, 146, 152–7, 165
Pulteney, Sir William (Earl of Bath), 167
Purcell family, of Cardiff, 36, 154, 156
puritans, *see* nonconformists

Pwllywrach, 201
Pyle, 81
Pytt, Rowland, 281

quakers: origins of, 113–14; persecution
of, 10, 118, 164; plots of 1680s and,
129–30; Restoration and, 117; tories
and, 143, 164; whigs and, 137
Quarter Sessions, *see* justices of the peace

Radnorshire, 44, 129, 250
Radyr, 28
Raglan (Monms.), 104, 210, 250, 260, 311
n. 1
Raglan Castle, siege of (1646), 108, 206–7
Ramsay, Allan, 201, 255
ranters, 113
Reay, Dr B., 114
regicides, 122
religion, *see* catholics; Church of England;
deism; nonconformists
rentals, *see* incomes, gentry
Restoration, 117–24
Reynolds, Sir Joshua, 201
Rhondda, 16, 57
Rhymney, river, 28
Rice, George, 182, 183; *see also* Dynevor,
Earls of
Richards family, of Cardiff, 36, 91
Richards, Michael (d. 1729), 139, 149
Richards, Michael (clerk of peace), 91
Richards, Michael (exclusionist), 315 n.
109
Richards, Michael (JP), 90
Richards, Thomas, 231
Richards, William, 85
Richardson, Samuel (of Hensol), 62
Richardson, Samuel, 234
Richet, Professor D., 282
Richmond, Charles Lennox, 2nd Duke of,
221
riots, 97–100, 153; in 1790s, 18–19
roads and tracks, 7–9, 63
Roath, 105–6, 129, 139, 149
Robbins, Dr M., xvii
Rochester, Lawrence Hyde, 1st Earl of,
138, 140, 142, 146, 202
Rochford, William Henry Zuylestein, 1st
Earl of, 137
Roebuck, Dr P., xvii, 44, 55
Roman remains, 5–7, 9, 234, 237, 298 n.
12
Rome, 227
Romsey family, of Monmouthshire, 80
Romsey, Colonel John, 130

Roses, Wars of the, 29
Royal Oak, Knights of the, 119, 123–4
royalists, Chapter 5, *passim*
Rudé, Professor G., 185
Rugby, school, 221
Rule, Professor J. B., 98–9
Rundle, Thomas, 159, 163
Ruperra, 30
Russia, 232–3
Rye House plot, 130

Sacheverell, Henry, 143, 150, 185
St Andrew's, 270
St Athan, 15
St Aubyn, Sir John, 164
St Bride's Major, 202
St David's (Pembs.), 7
St David's, bishops and diocese of, 163
St David's Day, 210
St Donat's, 38, 41, 50–1, 54, 114, 143,
161, 230, 277
St Fagan's, 41, 262, 270
St Fagan's, battle of (1648), 109
St James's Magazine, the, 234
St John family, of Highlight, *see*
Bolingbroke, Earls of
'St Nicholas Club', 148
St Nicholas 'mutineers', 95
Sancroft, William, 232
Saunders, Erasmus, 260
Savage, Richard, 233, 250
Savile family, *see* Halifax, Marquises of
Savours family, 37
Savours, William, 157
Sawtry (Hunts.), 118
Saxon Yoke, theory of, 186, 236
Schism Act, 150
schools, 217–22
Scilly Islands, the, xxi, 37
Scotland, 71, 103, 143, 145, 174, 214, 225,
272
Sea Serjeants, Society of, 153, 165, 184,
258
seabathing, 248–9
sea trade and communications, 9–12; *see
also* coastal trade; ships and shipping
Secker, Thomas, 159
Secretaries of State, *see* Gwyn, Francis;
Jenkins, Sir Leoline; Williamson, Sir
Joseph
Sedgemoor, battle of (1685), 130
'Seekers', 113
seignorial rights, *see* feudal dues
servants, 198, 255, 263
Seven Years War, the, xxv, 183, 211

sex and sexuality, 259–60, 263
Seymour family, of Somerset, 28
Seymour, Sir Edward, 140, 146
Seys family, of Boverton, 29, 235, 258
Seys, Evan, 29, 111–12, 116, 124, 231, 235, 261
Seys, Richard (c. 1611-80), 83, 90, 114, 123, 128
Seys, Richard (1639–1714), 137, 250
Seys, Roger, 261
Shaftesbury, Anthony Ashley-Cooper, 1st Earl of, 125–6, 128
sheep, 53
Shelburne, William Petty, 1st Marquis of, 186
Sheldon, Gilbert, Archbishop of Canterbury, 80, 114, 119, 124, 228
Shelvocke, George, 263
sheriffs, 92–3, 161, 179
Shewen family, of Swansea, 36
Shiers family, of Cardiff, 36
ships and shipping, 57, 98; *see also* sea trade
Shorter, Professor E., 261
Shovell, Sir Clowdisley, 37
Shrewsbury, 11, 226
Shrewsbury, school, 220
Shrewsbury, Earls of, 182
Shropshire, 22, 30, 56, 67, 143, 157
Singleton Abbey, 273
Sker, 6, 98
Skirrid (Monms.), xvi
slaves and slave trade, 67, 187, 255
smallholdings, concentration of, 13, 15
Smollett, Tobias, 234, 248
smuggling, 99
Society for the Propagation of Christian Knowledge, 143–4, 170, 212
Society of Ancient Britons, 158
Society of Antiquaries, the, 237
Society of Supporters of the Bill of Rights, 186
Solimena, 255
Somerset, 10–11, 14, 50, 118, 210, 215, 245
Somerset family, *see* Beaufort, Dukes of; Worcester, Marquises of
Somerset, Charles Noel, *see* Beaufort, Charles Noel Somerset, 4th Duke of
South Sea Company, 69
Southampton, 76
Southey, Robert, 250
Spain, 211
Spectator, the, 194, 233, 239, 258
speech, standards of, 258

'Squire Western', 241
Stafford, William Howard, 1st Viscount, 211
Staffordshire, 22, 164–5
Stalling Down, 267
Stamford, Thomas Grey, 2nd Earl of, 137
Stanhope, James, 1st Earl of, 137
steam engines, xvi, 60, 280
Stepney, Sir John, 264
stewards and agents, 37, 54–7, 64, 96, 176
Stewkeley, William, *see* Stukely, William
Stillingfleet, Edward, 126, 232
stockbreeding, 52–3
Stone, Dr J. F., 22
Stone, Professor L., 22, 217, 223, 257
Stowe (Bucks.), 166
Stradling family, of St Donat's: at Cowbridge, 219–20; as jacobites, 154–6, 160–1; library of, 230, 235; prestige of, 21, 81, 198; royalism of, 104, 109, 119, 123; as tory leaders, 143; at university, 224; wealth of, 48; whig links of, 204–5
Stradling family, of Roath, 35, 109
Stradling, Sir Edward (d. 1660) (3rd Bt), 242
Stradling, Sir Edward (d. 1685) (4th Bt), 68, 120, 123, 129
Stradling, Sir Edward (d. 1735) (5th Bt), 85, 142, 147–9, 155, 161
Stradling, Edward (d. 1726), 157, 214, 227
Stradling, George, 204–5, 227–8, 232, 235
Stradling, Lamorack, 123
Stradling, Colonel Thomas, 118, 120, 132, 210
Stradling, Sir Thomas (d. 1738) (6th Bt), 200, 225, 227, 229, 243
Strafford, Thomas Wentworth, 1st Earl of, 104
Strickland, Walter, 112
Strickland, William, 112
strikes, 18–19
Strode, Colonel William, 127
Stuart, Charles Edward (Young Pretender), 173–4, 176
Stuart, James Edward (Old Pretender), 143
Stukely, William, 234, 236
Suffolk, 22
Sunderland, Charles Spencer, 3rd Earl of, 157
superstitions and popular beliefs, xvi, 206
surnames, *see* patronymics, use of
Surrey, 22
Sussex, 58, 181

Swansea: Beaufort's power in, 20, 94, 144, 165, 176, 187, 284; elite of, 35–7, 42, 196–7, 207; gentry in, 30, 197, 273; industry in, 53, 58, 61, 155; jacobites in, 151, 155; as 'metropolitan' centre, 247–50; nonconformity in, 16–18, 105, 118, 132, 156, 173, 179; population of, 12; port of, 65–6; tories in, 176; trade of, xx, 9–12, 67, 252
Swansea Castle, 20
Swansea grammar school, 219
Sydney, Algernon, 106
Sydney, Jocelyn, 20, 151, 167, 257, 259
Symonds, Richard, 48

Talbot, Lords and Earls of, 159, 163, 177
Talbot family, of Margam, *see* Mansell-Talbot family, of Margam
Talbot, Charles, 1st Baron, 96, 159, 163
Talbot, Christopher, 200–1
Talbot, John (MP), 181, 290
Talbot, John Ivery, 204
Talbot, Rev. Thomas, 90, 165, 175, 179
Talbot, William, Bishop of Durham, 159
Talbot, William, 1st Earl, 41, 50, 160, 166–83 *passim*, 201, 243, 259, 266
Tamworth (Staffs.), 170
tanning, 14
Tatler, the, 233
Taunton, 126
Tawe, river, 5, 7, 15, 61, 109, 298 n. 1
taxation, 141; *see also* excise; hearth-tax
Taylor, Jeremy, 114
Taynton family, 36, 162, 166
Taynton, Nathaniel, 36, 166, 285
teachers, 229
Tenby (Pembs.), 249
Test and Penal Acts, 131
Tewkesbury, 226
theatres, 249; *see also* drama
Thirsk, Professor J., 72
Thomas family, of Llanmihangel, 30, 69, 209
Thomas family, of Swansea, 58
Thomas family, of Wenvoe, 122, 159, 172
Thomas, Edmund (d. 1677), 29–30, 111–12, 116, 122, 194
Thomas, Edmund (d. 1723), 2nd Bt, 143, 148
Thomas, Sir Edmund (d. 1767), 3rd Bt: anticlericalism of, 163; debts of, 67, 70; as JP, 90, 94; London society and, 242–4; militia and, 82, 99; as opposition whig, 77, 159, 170–1, 176–7, 181–3, 211; Welsh loyalties of, 194, 210

Thomas, Sir Edward, 68, 109, 122, 261
Thomas, Elizabeth, 257
Thomas, Frederick, 200–1, 213
Thomas, Sir Noah, 35
Thomas, Professor P. D. G., 72, 136, 147
Thomas, Robert, 138
Thomas, Sir Robert, 30, 68, 70, 124–30, 261, 278
Thomas, William, the diarist, xix, xxvi, 50, 90, 99, 222
Thomas, William, 127
Thomason, George, 231
Thompson, Professor E. P., 96, 158, 212
threshing machines, 63
Tillotson, John, 126
timbers, 45, 60, 66
tinplate industry, 61–2
tithes, 45, 98, 114, 164
Tocqueville, Alexis de, xviii, xxvi, 281
Toland, John, 145, 232
tombs, xv, 202, 213
Torrington, John Byng, Viscount, 272
tory party: 'country' and, 266–71; methodism and, 179–80, 270–1; new toryism of 1790s, 187; origins of, 139–42; survival after 1720, 162–6; *see also* high church party; jacobites
Toulouse, diocese of, 51, 282
tourism and tourists, 6–9, 249–50, 263
towns: charters of, 111; development of, after 1740, 246–50; elites of, 35–8; gentry control of, 147–9, 160; government of, 94; populations of, 12; purges of (1680s), 130–1; as radical centres, 117
Townsend, Chauncy, 61
Townsend, James, 184
Townshend, George, 1st Marquis, 182
Traherne family, 56, 247
Trapp, Joseph, 157
treasurer, county, 91
Tredegar, 57, 198, 254
Trefecca (Brecs.), 179, 226
Tregroes, 253
Trevor family, of Denbighshire, 143
Trotter, Alexander, 148, 151
Troy (Monms.), 244
Turberville family, of Ewenni, 172
Turberville family, of Penlline, 37, 104, 259
Turberville family, of Sker, 12, 104
Turberville, Edward, of Sker, 70, 125, 128, 278
Turberville, Edward, of Ewenni, 38
Turberville, Henry, 311 n.1

Turberville, Richard, 53, 183, 215
Turkey, 232
turnips, 52
Tynte family, *see* Kemys-Tynte family, of Cefn Mabli
Tynton, 269
Tyrrell, James, 122
Tythegston, 41

under-sheriffs, 92
Underdown, Professor D., 110
'ultras', 103–4
unitarianism, 113, 159, 163, 177, 179, 185, 238
Ussher, James, Archbishop of Armagh, 235

Van, 32, 38, 41, 199, 222
Van family, of Coldra (Monms.), 127
Van family, of Marcross, 68
Vansittart family, 184
Vaughan family, of Carmarthenshire, *see* Carbery, Earls of
Vaughan family, of Courtfield, 173
Vaughan family, of Crosswood (Cards.), 48, 80; *see also* Lisburne, Lords
Vaughan, Henry, 216, 232
Vaughan, John, 311 n.1
Vaughan, Colonel William Gwyn, 160
Venice, 227
venison, gifts of, 265
Verney family, of Bucks., 68, 250
Vernon, Barons, 172
Vernon, George Venables Vernon, 1st Baron, 41
Vernon, George Venables Vernon, 2nd Baron, 183, 214, 229
'Victorian' ideas, 274
Vivian family, 275
Voltaire, 19, 234

Wales: contempt for, 71, 214; as focus of loyalty, 208, 210; lack of unity of, 11; legendary poverty of, 44–5, 71–2; nationalist ideas in, 189, 210, 215–16, 238; vogue for, 272–3
Wallace, Professor A., 280
Waller, Sir William, 129
wallpaper, 251
Walpole, Sir Robert, 160, 164, 166–7, 170–1
Walters family, of Llandough, 254
Walters, Daniel, 263
Walters, John, 215, 222

Wanley, Humphrey, 140
war: conscription for, 59, 65; economic importance of, 13, 65–7, 186; politics and, 141; *see also* 'bluewater' policy
Warwickshire, 22, 170
Watkins, John, 208
Watson, Richard, Bishop of Llandaff, 178
weaving, 14
Wedlock, Timothy, 113
Wells (Som.), 76
Wells family, of Cardiff, 36, 156
Wells, Cradock, 144
Wells, Rev. Nathaniel, 90, 95
Welsh language, 14–15, 99, 194, 205–6, 209–10, 213–16, 218, 220, 222–3, 263
'Welsh Trust', 126, 143
Wentwood Chase (Monms.), 97
Wenvoe, 38, 55, 67, 69
Wesley, John, 178, 180
Western, Professor J. R., 81
West Indies, 36, 67, 69, 171, 186, 268
Westminster, 76, 92, 166, 170; *see also* Independent Electors of Westminster
Westminster School, 220–1
Weymouth, 249, 274
Wharton, Lords, Marquises and Dukes, 227
Wharton, Mary, 227, 233, 251, 257, 261–3, 278
Wharton, Philip, 4th Lord, 52, 80, 124, 126, 137–8
Wharton, Thomas, 1st Marquis of, 138, 267
whig party: in George I's reign, 157–9; in opposition, 166–72, 181; origins of, xxiv, 136–9
Whitelock, Sir William, 143
White Rock, 60, 67
Wick, 161
Wilkes, John, and Wilkites, xxvi, 184–6
Wilkins family, of Llanblethian, 62, 188, 235
Wilkins, John, 63
Wilkinson, John, 167, 259
William III, King of England, 69, 137, 246
Williams family, of Aberpergwm, 32, 215
Williams family, of Dyffryn Clydach, 89, 165, 259
Williams, Charles, 137, 151
Williams, Daniel, 260, 261
Williams, David, of Caerphilly, 186–7, 238
Williams, Professor D., 72
Williams, Edward, *see* Iolo Morgannwg
Williams, Professor G., xvii

Williams, Henry, 132
Williams, John, 222, 232, 235–6, 238
Williams, Morgan, 91
Williams, Philip, 44, 128, 132, 137, 202, 231–3, 236–7, 254, 264, 269
Williams, Sir Trevor, 108, 115–16, 120, 126–9, 137–8
Williams, Sir William, 131
Williams-Wynn family, 188
Williams-Wynn, Sir Watkin, 153, 155, 164–5, 171, 173–4, 176, 179, 268
Williamson, Sir Joseph, 120, 127, 250
Willis, Browne, 237
Wilton, 29
Wiltshire, 11, 41, 53, 146, 220, 235, 245
Winchester, Marquis of, *see* Bolton, Dukes of
Windsor, 41, 263
Windsor, Viscounts, 20, 51, 56, 176, 197, 274
Windsor, Herbert, Viscount, 171–2, 176, 242
Windsor, Thomas, Viscount (d. 1738), 20, 27, 50, 149, 152, 154–5, 165
Winnington, Thomas, 167
Winstanley, Gerrard, 18, 185
Wissing, William, 201
witchcraft, 213, 325 n. 86
women, role of, 221–2, 256–8
Wootton, John, 244
Worcester, Earls and Marquises of, xxiii–xxiv, 5, 16, 48, 102–4, 119, 201, 211, 235, 284; *see also* Beaufort, Dukes of
Worcester, Charles Somerset, 4th Marquis of, 132, 139, 202, 233

Worcester, Edward Somerset, 2nd Marquis of ('Earl of Glamorgan'), xxii, 108, 118–20, 280
Worcester, Henry Somerset, 1st Marquis of, 104–5, 108, 115, 206–7, 210
Worcester, Henry Somerset, 3rd Marquis of, *see* Beaufort, Henry Somerset, 1st Duke of
Wotton, William, 237
wrecking and coastal plunder, 98–9
Wrigley, Dr E. A., 64
Wroth, William, 106, 207, 222
Wyndham family, of Dunraven, 29, 127, 172, 202, 208; *see also* Dunraven, Earls of
Wyndham, Humphrey, 112, 116, 123
Wyndham, John (d. 1697), 49, 124, 126–7
Wyndham, John (d. 1725), 40
Wyndham, Thomas (d. 1752), 40, 53–4, 167
Wyndham, Thomas (d. 1814), 188, 215
Wyndham, Sir William, 154
Wynn family, of Wynnstay, 139
Wynne, Ellis, 212

Yalden, Thomas, 157, 249
Yarranton, Andrew, 52
Yeats, William Butler, 325 n. 91
Ynyscedwyn, 90, 269
Ynysgerwn, 59
York, James, Duke of, *see* James II, King of England
Yorkshire, xvii, 18, 44, 55, 267; *see also* Roebuck, Dr P.
Young, Arthur, 52, 249